Analyzing Race Talk

Multidisciplinary Perspectives on the Research Interview

The interview is one of the most important sources of social scientific data yet there has been relatively little exploration of the way interviews are conducted and interpreted. By asking internationally respected scholars from a range of traditions in discourse studies including conversation analysis, discursive psychology, and sociolinguistics to respond to the same material, this exciting new book sheds light on some key differences in methodology and theoretical perspective. Key topics are addressed such as the forms of knowledge produced in interviews, the interview as social interaction and the foundations for the study of talk and texts in qualitative research. The use of interviews exploring issues of race and racism further broadens the scope of the book, enabling the contributors to explore sensitive questions around the construction and interpretation of interviews on controversial topics.

HARRY VAN DEN BERG is an Associate Professor at the Vrije Universiteit, Amsterdam. He is the author or editor of fifteen books on different topics and has published numerous articles and book chapters. He is a member of the Committee of Quality Inspection of the MOA (The Dutch Market Research Association).

MARGARET S. WETHERELL was appointed to a Personal Chair at the Open University in 2000. She is the author or editor of twelve books and has published over sixty articles and book chapters. She is one of the most widely cited psychologists in the UK with over 1,000 citations of her single and joint authored research as measured by the SSCI. Currently she is co-editor of the *British Journal of Social Psychology*.

HANNEKE HOUTKOOP-STEENSTRA was an Associate Professor at the University of Utrecht. She authored or edited five books and published numerous articles and book chapters. She played an outstanding role in the development and application of methods of conversation analysis especially in the field of interview discourse. She died in December, 2002 just after the completion of this book at the age of fifty-two.

Analyzing Race Talk

Multidisciplinary Perspectives on the Research Interview

Harry van den Berg
Vrije Universiteit Amsterdam

Margaret Wetherell
The Open University

Hanneke Houtkoop-Steenstra

CAMBRIDGE
UNIVERSITY PRESS

PUBLISHED BY THE PRESS SYNDICATE OF THE UNIVERSITY OF CAMBRIDGE
The Pitt Building, Trumpington Street, Cambridge, United Kingdom

CAMBRIDGE UNIVERSITY PRESS
The Edinburgh Building, Cambridge, CB2 2RU, UK
40 West 20th Street, New York, NY 10011–4211, USA
477 Williamstown Road, Port Melbourne, VIC 3207, Australia
Ruiz de Alarcón 13, 28014 Madrid, Spain
Dock House, The Waterfront, Cape Town 8001, South Africa

http://www.cambridge.org

First published 2003

Printed in the United Kingdom at the University Press, Cambridge

Typeface Plantin 10/12 pt.   *System* LʰTₑX 2ₑ   [TB]

A catalogue record for this book is available from the British Library

Library of Congress Cataloguing in Publication data
Analyzing race talk / Harry van den Berg, Margaret Wetherell, Hanneke
  Houtkoop-Steenstra, editors.
    p.   cm.
Includes bibliographical references and index.
  ISBN 0 521 82118 5 – ISBN 0 521 52802 X (pb.)
  1. Interviewing in sociology.   2. Interviewing in sociolinguistics.
  3. Racism in language.   I. Berg, Harry van den.   II. Wetherell, Margaret.
    III. Houtkoop-Steenstra, Hanneke.
  HM526.A53 2003
  300′.7′23–dc21   2003046129

ISBN 0 521 82118 5 hardback
ISBN 0 521 52802 X paperback

Dedicated to the memory of
Hanneke Houtkoop-Steenstra

Contents

     MAYKEL VERKUYTEN

9   The frame analysis of research interviews: social
     categorization and footing in interview discourse   156
     TITUS ENSINK

10   Affiliation and detachment in interviewer answer
     receipts   178
     TOM KOOLE

11   Interviewer laughter as an unspecified request for
     clarification   200
     TONY HAK

12   Perspectives and frameworks in interviewers' queries   215
     ANITA POMERANTZ AND ALAN ZEMEL

     Appendix: Interview transcripts   232
     Index   309

Contributors

CHARLES ANTAKI, Ph.D., is Reader in Language and Social Psychology at the Loughborough University, England. He is a member of the Discourse and Rhetoric Group in the Department of Social Sciences, an active circle of academics and students who study spoken and written discourse from a variety of perspectives. His research interests are in conversation analysis.

RICHARD BUTTNY, Ph.D., is Professor of Speech Communication at Syracuse University. His publications include *Talking Problems: Studies in Discursive Construction* (2003) and *Social Accountability in Communication* (1993). His scholarly interests pertain to accounts and social accountability, reported speech, talk in institutional settings, discursive constructions of race matters, and environmental communication.

DEREK EDWARDS, Ph.D., is Professor of Psychology in the Department of Social Sciences, Loughborough University. His interests are in the analysis of language and social interaction in everyday and institutional settings. His books include *Common Knowledge* with Neil Mercer (1987), *Ideological Dilemmas* with Michael Billig and others (1988), *Discursive Psychology* with Jonathan Potter (1992), and *Discourse and Cognition* (1997).

TITUS ENSINK, Ph.D., is Associate Professor of Discourse Studies and Rhetoric in the Faculty of Arts at the Groningen University, the Netherlands. His research interests include political rhetoric in relation to commemorations and the frame analysis of texts and media messages.

TONY HAK, Ph.D., is Senior Lecturer in Research Methodology at the Faculteit Bedrijfskunde/Rotterdam School of Management, Erasmus University, Rotterdam, the Netherlands. He has published on discourse analysis, ethnomethodology, doctor–patient communication, and the social research interview. In 2002 he received an ASA/NSF fellowship for research within the US Census Bureau on the response process in business surveys.

HANNEKE HOUTKOOP-STEENSTRA, Ph.D., was Associate Professor at the Utrecht Institute of Linguistics (UIL-OTS) and the Institute for Dutch Language and Culture at Utrecht University. Her research focused on the development and application of methods of conversation analysis, especially in the field of interview discourse. Her books include *Interaction and the Standardized Survey Interview: the Living Questionnaire* (2000).

TOM KOOLE, Ph.D., is Researcher at the Utrecht Institute of Linguistics (UIL-OTS) and Lecturer at the Institute for Dutch Language and Culture at Utrecht University. His research has focused on interactions in intercultural and interethnic contexts, and his present concern is with student participation in multi-ethnic and multi-lingual classrooms.

DAVID LEE, Ph.D., is Associate Professor in Linguistics in the School of English at the University of Queensland. He teaches and researches in cognitive linguistics and discourse analysis. He has written numerous articles and books, including *Competing Discourses* (1992) and *Cognitive Linguistics: an Introduction* (2001).

ANITA POMERANTZ, Ph.D., is Associate Professor in the Communication Department at the University at Albany, SUNY. She has published articles on strategies of seeking information, methods of negotiating responsibility, practices for giving feedback, and interaction in medical settings. She serves on the editorial boards of *Communication Monographs*, *Research on Language and Social Interaction*, *Language in Society*, and *Discourse Studies*.

SRIKANT SARANGI, Ph.D., is Professor and Director of the Health Communication Research Centre at Cardiff University. His research interests are in discourse analysis and applied linguistics, language and identity in public life, and institutional/professional discourse. His recent book-length publications include *Discourse and Social Life* with Malcolm Coulthard (2000) and *Sociolinguistics and Social Theory* with Nik Coupland and Chris Candlin (2001).

HARRY VAN DEN BERG, Ph.D., is Associate Professor in the Department of Social Research Methodology at the Vrije Universiteit. His current research focuses on the quality of public opinion research and on a variety of methodological issues concerning research interviews, including questionnaire design, the social interaction between interviewer and interviewee, and discourse analysis of qualitative interviews. His books include *Opinie-maken of Opinie-meten: De rol van Stellingvragen in Markt- en Opinieonderzoek* [Opinion Making or Opinion Measuring:

The Role of Assertions in Public Opinion Research] with Hanneke Houtkoop-Steenstra and others (2002).

MAYKEL VERKUYTEN, Ph.D., is Associate Professor in the Faculty of Social Science at Utrecht University. He is also Senior Researcher at the European Research Center on Migration and Ethnic Relations (ERCOMER) at the same university. His research interests include ethnic identity and inter-ethnic relations. With Jessica ter Wal, he edited the collection *Comparative Perspectives on Racism* (2000).

MARGARET WETHERELL, Ph.D., is Professor of Social Psychology at the Open University, UK, and co-editor of the British Journal of Social Psychology. Her books include *Discourse and Social Psychology* with Jonathan Potter (1987) and *Discourse Theory and Practice* and *Discourse as Data*, both with Stephanie Taylor and Simeon Yates (2001). Her empirical research on discourse includes work on racism, masculinities, and the governance and forms of identity.

ALAN ZEMEL is a Post-Doctoral Fellow at Southern Illinois University School of Medicine. He received his Ph.D. from Temple University in 2002, and he is trained as a conversation analyst. His research focuses on medical education.

Preface

During the very last phase of our work on this book, we received the devastating news that our co-editor, Hanneke Houtkoop-Steenstra had died. We knew that she was severely ill but her sudden death was unexpected. We mourn her passing and miss her greatly.

Hanneke studied linguistics at the University of Amsterdam. After finishing her Ph.D. thesis in 1987 on the analysis of proposal-acceptance sequences, she was appointed to a position at the Utrecht Institute of Linguistics (UIL-OTS) and the Institute for Dutch Language and Culture at Utrecht University. She was a dynamic and wholehearted researcher fascinated by the structure and organization of ordinary conversation and conversation within an institutional context. Hanneke's contributions are numerous. She had a particular interest in the interaction between interviewer and interviewee in research interviews and is, of course, well known for this work. Hanneke liked to transgress conventional disciplinary and institutional borders, and she demonstrated, for example, the relevance of conversation analysis for critical reflection on traditional survey methodology. She played a crucial role in the design and editing of this book and was inspirational in pushing forward our scheme of encouraging researchers from many different perspectives to analyze the same data set. Her comments on all our work were marked by a delightful combination of professional rigor, straightforwardness and disarming humour. We only wish that she could have been here to share our pleasure in its publication.

To honor her contribution to the field of conversation analysis as well as to the field of the methodology of research interviews, we dedicate this book to her memory.

HARRY VAN DEN BERG AND MARGARET WETHERELL

Acknowledgments

We want to thank all those who contributed to this book and pay tribute to their willingness to play the game proposed to them. It is not easy to work on shared data to analyze texts produced in very unfamiliar contexts. The result, however, has proven well worth the effort.

We gratefully acknowledge the continuing support for this project by the editor at Cambridge University Press, Sarah Caro.

We are grateful to the Faculty of Social Sciences of the Vrije Universiteit Amsterdam for offering the opportunity to organize and pursue the project by a grant.

We would like to thank Barbara Fehr and Marjon Vos van der Born for the very precise and careful retranscription of the audiotapes of the interviews.

Last but not least we would like to thank Kate Henning for her major contribution to the administration and management of the editing process.

Transcriptions symbols

I = interviewer
R = respondent
D = respondent's daughter (in Interview 44)

[xxx] [yyy]	overlapping talk
word= =Word	latched utterances; no interval
(1.0)	timed silence in seconds
(.)	micropause (less than 0.3 sec)
word.	falling intonation
word,	continuing intonation
word?	rising or questioning intonation
word!	exclamation like prosody
wor-	abrupt cutoff
↑word	higher pitch
↓word	lower pitch
wor:d	stretched sound
word	emphasis
WORD	louder talk
°word°	quieter talk
>word<	faster talk
<word>	slower talk
wo(h)rd	laughingly spoken
.hhh	inbreath
hhh	outbreath
((note))	transcriptionist's note and comment
(word)	transcriptionist's uncertain understanding
[. . .]	lines omitted

Introduction

Harry van den Berg, Margaret Wetherell, and
Hanneke Houtkoop-Steenstra

Discourse analysis is a rapidly expanding field of research and theorizing. The growing interest in this field of research reflects a threefold linguistic turn in the social sciences. First, there has been a developing appreciation among social scientists of the central role of discursive practices in social life. The conception of language as a mere technical means of communication has been superseded. Language has been re-conceptualized as social activity. As a consequence, the traditional boundaries between linguistics and the social sciences have become blurred. To fully understand contemporary social life, researchers have had to turn their attention to a diverse range of new phenomena. These include, for instance, the large-scale discursive practices that make up postmodern reflexive culture and the small-scale organization of talk in the call centers of the new service economies, the formulation of social policy and the detail of social interaction. The study of discourse is inseparable from the study of society.

Second and more generally, the concept of discourse has produced new and fruitful angles on the old themes of the social sciences such as the nature of power and the construction of social identities. Many recent theoretical debates and controversies within the social sciences are concerned with the way the notion of discourse is used, and its potentialities and limits. Third, there has been a growing recognition that social research is itself a discursive practice. Scientists' discourse emerged as a research topic for discourse analysts at the beginning of the 1980s. Nigel Gilbert and Michael Mulkay (1984), for example, in one of the first studies of this kind, explored the variability of the accounts biochemists used in different situations for their research practice. Along with these studies of the accounting devices used in scientists' discourse, it has become apparent that even the so-called "hard facts" of social research are discursive in nature. The empirical data of social research are predominantly products of specific discursive practices.

All three of these moments of the linguistic turn (discourse as topic, as theory/epistemology, and as reflexive exploration) are illustrated in this book. The book itself is the product of an unusual collaboration coordinated by Harry van den Berg and Hanneke Houtkoop-Steenstra. A group of discourse scholars from a range of different perspectives and geographical locations (North America, Australia, the United Kingdom, and the Netherlands) were brought together and asked to focus their attention on a common set of materials. All agreed to study three interviews independently and then to report their findings. The interviews (conducted by Margaret Wetherell) came from a large-scale project on racist discourse and were relatively informal and open-ended in nature. (They are reproduced for the reader in the appendix.)

The range of perspectives shared by the group included conversation analysis and ethnomethodology, cognitive linguistics, Goffman's frame analysis, critical sociolinguistics, discursive psychology, and Foucauldian-influenced styles of critical discourse analysis. In working with the interviews, our contributors became interested in a huge range of phenomena. These included reported voices, the formulation of the mind/world relationship in talk, absurdity and laughter, and the cultural resources comprising "common sense." Contributors looked at contradictions and their functions and effects, the development of categories and representations of agency, the interviewer's actions and the kinds of frames these created for those being interviewed, along with the subtle coordination of talk.

The chapters in this volume illustrate some of the key methods and approaches available in social science and linguistics for investigating discursive practices. The shared empirical ground allows the reader to compare different theoretical perspectives and methodological approaches and to evaluate the process of making inferences. It has been a fascinating exercise to see how each discourse scholar has dealt with these interviews. Research data are not neutral, and empirical data are always constructed within a specific research practice. Our contributors had to work with material that was not their own, but in each case they good humoredly set about locating it and defining it as the kind of object they could analyze. In the process they demonstrated their typical working assumptions, preferred research questions, and procedures for producing knowledge. The empirical material in this respect proved to be both negotiable and non-negotiable. It metamorphosed into a different kind of data with exposure to each new act of scrutiny, yet it also remained "relatively autonomous," and thus dialogue and communication became possible between different theoretical and methodological positions.

The contributors report a number of new empirical findings on the rhetorical organization of discourse about issues of race, and, more generally, on the organization of talk on "controversial issues" and interaction in interviews. They also discuss some current live theoretical debates.

Should, for instance, discourse be understood as social action and/or as a product or expression of the (individual or collective) mind? Should discourse analysis be "emic" or "etic" in approach? Should discourse analysts, in other words, restrict themselves to the categories used by the participants, or should analysts also use theoretical categories to understand the discourse in question? How relevant is the wider social and institutional context? Is it relevant at all? Where do discourses end and the rest of "the social" begin? Should discourse analysts take a critical stance? Should discourse analysis, for example, be primarily oriented to the production of knowledge, or should it take into account political goals, such as supporting groups in their struggle for liberation and social equality?

As it turned out, this collaborative exercise has perhaps revealed most about the third twist of the linguistic turn noted above – the application of discourse theory and method to understand the discursive practices of social science itself. What interested many of the contributors were not the topics but the organization of the interviews as a research activity. (Indeed, it is difficult to comment on content with such a small sample and where the context was unfamiliar.) This focus is valuable. It has been estimated that over 90% of social research is based on interview data (Brenner 1981). Social research, whatever discipline or approach taken, relies heavily on interviewing people about their experiences, opinions, hopes, fears, reactions, and expectations. The research interview is a discursive act. It is jointly produced by the participants, and the interviewer is as involved in this production as the interviewees. It is highly appropriate, therefore, that the methods and theories of discourse analysis are applied to this practice. In the remainder of this introduction, we want to comment more generally on this central theme before introducing the structure and organization of the book as a whole.

The research interview: instrument or topic?

Many social scientists treat the research interview as an instrument for developing the empirical foundations of social scientific knowledge. Opinion polls based on survey interviews are often presented as windows onto the world of what people believe and want. In the field of qualitative research, terms such as "in-depth interview" and "open interview" suggest that it is possible to go beyond the superficial style of standardized survey interviews to unravel a deeper or more essential reality. Indeed, a crucial assumption of much qualitative as well as quantitative research practice is that it is possible to make inferences from the information produced in interviews that go beyond the specific context of those interviews. This assumption is very often taken for granted.

As a consequence it is common to find that qualitative researchers, just like their quantitative colleagues, neglect the constructed nature of their data. Interviewees' answers are interpreted without taking into account their local construction or the ways in which they are produced by the joint effort of the interviewer and interviewee within a highly specific context. Although there is an awareness of the active role of the interviewer, often presented as the problem of "reactivity of measurement," in mainstream methodological texts on interviewing, the presupposition remains that the ultimate ideal for interviewing is to obtain answers that are not "disturbed" by the interviewer's behavior. The misleading metaphor of "data collection" is still dominant, in other words, in the way the interview process is framed.

The interviewee is approached as a vessel of pre-given data, and interviewing strategies or styles are conceptualized as ways to open the vessel to "collect" the data without transforming them (cf. Holstein and Gubrium 1995). This metaphor provides some common ground for mainstream qualitative and mainstream quantitative research, although these approaches differ substantially in their views on how to "open up" the interviewee. Standardizing the behavior of the interviewer, neutrality, and detachment are the central methodological guidelines for survey interviewing, while flexibility of interviewer-behavior, empathy, and openness are the central methodological guidelines for qualitative interviewing (cf. Rubin and Rubin 1995). Notwithstanding these differences, in both cases, the "logic in use" (Kaplan 1964) of interviewing promises an entrance to the "real" experiences, attitudes, opinions, and emotions of the interviewee.

This view of the interview as an instrument for empirical research is a contested one. Scholars working within related research traditions such as ethnomethodology, sociolinguistics, conversation analysis, and discursive psychology have demonstrated the constructed nature of interview data (for example: Cicourel 1964; Briggs 1986; Pomerantz 1988; Heritage and Greatbatch 1991; Houtkoop-Steenstra 1996, 1997, 2000; Baker 1997). From this approach comes the notion that a research interview has to be understood as a specific social context (defined and redefined during the interaction between interviewer and interviewee) within which answers are locally constructed. Answers should be analyzed as the product of a joint effort of interviewer and interviewee. Research interviews are thus viewed as an interesting research topic in their own right because they constitute a specific category of institutional talk that can be studied in itself.

This recognition of the discursive character of the empirical data produced in social research has far-reaching implications for the traditional "logic in use" found in survey research, as well as in qualitative social research. Both strands of social research neglect and underestimate the effect of context, for example. Interviewees typically articulate opinions that do not necessarily correspond with those articulated in other conversational situations, such as in conversations with friends or neighbors and conversations in the workplace. This variability, which is such a problem for the instrumental view of interviewing, is grist to the mill for those who study interviews as discursive acts.

The research community in which interviews are viewed and used as a more-or-less reliable and valid research instrument, and the research community in which interviews are regarded as a research topic have up until now formed two different cultures. There has been very little debate between these research communities. Very often their positions are presented as incompatible and opposing alternatives. Nevertheless, there are initiatives oriented toward bridging the gap. There have been attempts to use the knowledge produced by research on interviews as social events for social research based on interviews as a method of data collection. Hammersley and Atkinson (1995) have developed an ethnographic approach, for example, with reflexivity as a cornerstone, that doesn't fall into the trap of naturalism or positivism. This approach recognizes the ways in which the researcher is part of the social world he/she wants to investigate and the necessity of taking into account the role the researcher plays in producing the outcome of ethnographic research.

Reflections on the implications of the constructed character of interview data have produced profound insights into the interview as a social practice. In qualitative research, Holstein and Gubrium (1995) have advocated the concept of the "active interview" to underline their perspective on the research interview as a process in which both the interviewer and the interviewee play a creative role. Within the tradition of standardized survey interviews, authors like Schuman (1982) have argued for an approach in which reactivity is not viewed as a methodological problem but as an opportunity. It is not seen as something that needs to be solved in order to avoid a supposed "bias of measurement"; instead it is viewed as relevant information about the context dependency of an interviewee's behavior. The common denominator here is the methodological conviction that social research should avoid the trap of decontextualizing the interviewee's discourse, which is still characteristic of the "logic in use" of much mainstream qualitative and quantitative research. This methodological conviction stresses the importance of studying interview discourse as a social activity, thereby creating common ground to discuss the potential applications of discourse analysis to the interviewing practice of social research. One of the principal contributions of this book is to further open up this possibility. The contributors have extended the systematic study of the research interview in ways that can only be helpful for researchers collecting data through this method.

The materials for analysis

As noted earlier, an unusual and unique feature of the collaborative exercise underpinning this book is that every contributor was invited to analyze the same textual data. Every author received transcripts of three research interviews. These interviews had been re-transcribed in fine detail to make them suitable for as diverse a range of styles of analysis as possible. The interviews were part of a large-scale research project conducted by Margaret Wetherell in the mid-1980s on racism and race relations in New Zealand. (The project and the main findings are summarized in detail in Wetherell and Potter 1992.) Although racism and race relations was the main focus, the interviews covered other matters such as economic relations with Australia, and New Zealand's relation with Britain as the former colonial power still linked through the Commonwealth of Nations.

In line with the focus on racism and race relations, the interviews covered three main controversial issues in New Zealand in the 1980s. First, the events and protest around the South African (Springbok) rugby tours of New Zealand in the 1970s and early 1980s were targeted. These tours defined relations between New Zealand and the then apartheid government of South Africa and were a recent source of major social upheaval and civil disturbance. Second, the interviews focused on relations between the two main ethnic groups in New Zealand – the indigenous minority, the Maori people, and the majority group, white New Zealanders of European descent (frequently described as Pakeha New Zealanders). Specific themes here included the government's multicultural policy and emphasis on New Zealand as "one nation, one people," and recent Maori campaigns over land rights, language issues, and affirmative action policies. Finally, the interviews usually also focused on immigration issues, in relation particularly to migrants from the Polynesian Islands. From a corpus of over eighty interviews, three of the "most memorable" interviews were selected for our contributors to examine. More detail on the interviewing strategy and approach can be found in the chapter from Margaret Wetherell that follows this introduction.

The choice of interviews on race relations for the collaborative exercise was not accidental. Open-ended interviews on sensitive and controversial topics such as prejudice, ethnocentrism, ethnic categorization, and stereotyping are difficult to interpret. These interviews very often produce many ambiguous statements. Traditional (qualitative as well as quantitative) research on the fields of ethnicity, racism and nationalism, and gender and sexism has encountered severe difficulties in coping with the ambiguities and contradictions within interview discourse on these topics. The turn to discourse, in contrast, opens up ways of analyzing these ambiguities and contradictions in terms of the situational dependencies of discourse, giving full attention to the flexibility of accounting practices. For example, discourse analysis draws attention to the possibility that the interviewee may switch between different ways of framing the question topic, and may use different interpretative repertoires in answering questions about a topic considered to be controversial. Ambiguities may be due to changes in the way the interview situation, the relation between interviewer and interviewee, and the general research goal are framed during the course of the interview (Van den Berg 1996). The outcome of these framing activities can be crucial for the unfolding discourse between interviewer and interviewee and the strategies used by each. The analysis of such interviews is seldom straightforward in other words, and presented a considerable test or challenge to our contributors and their methodology.

The complete transcripts are included in the appendix. An important function of this appendix is to give readers the opportunity to "check" the interpretations developed by the authors and to facilitate the comparison of different approaches to discourse analysis. It is possible, for example, for the reader to reanalyze the fragments selected by the authors within the context of the transcribed interview as a whole and to compare the selected fragments with other parts of the interview. Note, however, that readers should seek permission (see details given in the appendix) before making any other use of the interview material.

The structure of the book

In the first chapter, Margaret Wetherell sketches the broader background to the research interviews used in this exercise. She describes the general research aims of her project and the discourse analytic procedures used in analyzing the interviews. Attention is especially focused on the general methodological/theoretical aspects of the relationship between discourse and context. Following the discussion a few years ago in *Discourse and Society*, Wetherell outlines her approach, perhaps best described as "critical discursive social psychology" (Wetherell 1998; Schegloff 1997, 1998, 1999a, 1999b; Billig 1999a, 1999b).

In chapters 2 and 3, two further general theoretical/methodological positions are presented and illustrated by exemplary analysis of the selected interviews. In chapter 2, a discursive psychological perspective strongly influenced by conversation analysis is outlined by Derek Edwards. Edwards takes a more fine-grained approach to discursive psychology and examines the ways in which the participants in the interviews constructed and used various versions of mind/world relationships. In chapter 3, David Lee presents a view from cognitive linguistics on how categorizations and agency are constructed in interview discourse. In chapter 4, the critical sociolinguist, Srikant Sarangi, approaches the interviews as a specific form of talk, which he characterizes as "hybrid." He demonstrates that, in addition to the institutional frames normally guiding interviewer- and interviewee-role identities, other frames are used, such as professional frames and life-world frames.

Chapters 5 and 6 primarily focus on some of the specific devices used by the interviewees in presenting their accounts of race relations and ethnicity. In chapter 5, Charles Antaki analyzes the function of absurdity in interviewees' discourse. Why did those interviewed produce such colorful descriptions at certain points of the interview? What functions does this "color" serve? In addition to the use of absurdity in expressing views, attention is also given to the use of caricature in descriptions of "others" and some of its possible effects. In chapter 6, Richard Buttny focuses on the use of "voice" in discourse on race. He examines the use of reported speech in constructing the (racialized) other as deficient and ascribing unreasonable political positions to this "other."

Chapters 7, 8, and 9 take up further substantive aspects of the discourse, focusing on the (ethnic/racial) categorization and stereotyping (co)produced in the course of the interview. In chapter 7, Harry van den Berg analyzes different types of contradictions in interviewee's discourse and looks at how these inconsistencies are constructed. In chapter 8, Maykel Verkuyten analyzes how the notion of happiness features in interviewees' discourse and the ideological functions these constructions fulfill. His emphasis, as in Chapter 1, is on the interpretative or cultural resources participants draw upon to construct their versions of events. In Chapter 9, Titus Ensink illustrates the value of concepts taken from Goffman's work. He explores the "footing" of the interview participants in particular and how they categorize themselves and the world they live in.

Following this emphasis on more substantive aspects, chapters 10, 11, and 12 turn back again to one of the main themes of this book: the characteristics of the interaction between interviewers and interviewees. These chapters focus on the role of the interviewer. In chapter 10, Tom Koole develops a fine-grained analysis of the tightrope walk interviewers take between conflicting interactional goals such as affiliation and detachment.

The analysis focuses on the different types of answer receipts used by the interviewer and their functions in relation to these broader goals. In chapter 11, Tony Hak focuses on interviewer laughter in the context of instances of racist talk produced by the interviewee. Why does the interviewer laugh at these points? What might it signify for the general process of interviewing? In the last chapter, Anita Pomerantz and Alan Zemel conclude the book through their examination of the ways in which perspectives and frameworks are constructed in interviewer's queries. They look at how adjustments are made when there are different perspectives between interviewer and interviewee and draw attention to the implications of their study for the practice of researchers who use the interview as an instrument or research tool.

Here then is a fascinating range of attempts to analyze the interview as a discursive practice. The chapters in this book showcase different styles of discourse analysis, and we believe that they offer considerable insight into the social situation of the interview.

References

Baker, C. 1997. Membership categorization and interview accounts. In *Qualitative research; Theory, method and practice*, edited by D. Silverman. London: Sage. 130–143.

Billig, M. 1999a. Whose terms? Whose ordinariness? Rhetoric and ideology in conversation analysis. *Discourse and Society* 10, 4: 543–547.

1999b. Conversation analysis and the claims of naivite. *Discourse and Society* 10, 4: 543–547.

Brenner, M. 1981. Patterns of social structure in the research interview. In *Social method and social life*, edited by M. Brenner. New York: Academic Press. 115–158.

Briggs, C. L. 1986. *Learning how to ask; a sociolinguistic appraisal of the role of the interview in social science research*. Cambridge: Cambridge University Press.

Cicourel, A. V. 1964. *Method and measurement in sociology*. New York: Free Press.

Gilbert, G. N. and Mulkey, M. 1984. *Opening Pandora's box: a sociological analysis of scientists' discourse*. Cambridge: Cambridge University Press.

Hammersley, M. and Atkinson, P. 1995. *Ethnography; principles in practice*. London: Routledge.

Heritage, J. and Greatbatch, D. 1991. On the institutional character of institutional talk: the case of news interviews. In *Talk and social structure*, edited by D. Boden and D. Zimmerman. Cambridge: Polity Press.

Holstein, J. A. and Gubrium, J. F. 1995. *The active interview*. London: Sage.

Houtkoop-Steenstra, H. 1996. Probing behavior of interviewers in the standardized semi-open research interview. *Quality and Quantity* 30: 205–230.

1997. Being friendly in survey interviews. *Journal of Pragmatics* 28: 591–623.

2000. Interaction and the standardized interview. The living questionnaire. Cambridge: Cambridge University Press.

Kaplan, A. 1964. *The conduct of inquiry*. Scranton, PA: Chandler Publishing Company.
Pomerantz, A. 1988. Offering a candidate answer: an information seeking strategy. *Communications Monographs* 55, December: 360–373.
Rubin, H. J. and Rubin, I. S. 1995. *Qualitative interviewing; the art of hearing data*. London: Sage.
Schegloff, E. A. 1997. Whose text? Whose context? *Discourse and Society* 8, 2: 165–188.
    1998. Reply to Wetherell. *Discourse and Society* 9, 3: 413–416.
    1999a. "Schefloff's texts" as "Billig's data": a critical reply. *Discourse and Society* 10, 4: 558–571.
    1999b. Naivite vs sophistication or discipline vs self-indulgence. *Discourse and Society* 10, 4: 577–582.
Schuman, H. 1982. Artifacts are in the mind of the beholder. *American Sociologist* 17, 1: 21–28.
Van den Berg, H. 1996. Frame analysis of open interviews on interethnic relations. *Bulletin de Methodologie Sociologique* 53: 5–32.
Wetherell, M. 1998. Positioning and interpretative repertoires: Conversation analysis and post-structuralism in dialogue. *Discourse and Society* 9, 3: 387–412.
Wetherell, M. and Potter, J. 1992. *Mapping the language of racism*. New York: Harvester Wheatsheaf.

1 Racism and the analysis of cultural resources in interviews

Margaret Wetherell

My goal in this chapter is to illustrate a style of discourse analysis focusing on the cultural resources constituting racist ideological practices. I am interested in the way people tell stories: how they organize their versions of events, and how they build identities for themselves and others as they speak. I am also interested in how powerful majority groups are constructed in discourse, how the members of those groups justify their position, and how they make sense of their history and current actions in relation to their constructions of disadvantaged minority groups. In more general terms, my focus is on what Rosie Braidotti has called "the traffic jam of meanings . . . which create that form of pollution known as common sense" (1994, 16). Meaning coagulates in a culture and becomes temporarily stuck or jammed. The study of ideological practices involves investigating what these sticking points look like and how they occur, along with the social and political consequences.

As noted in the Introduction, the chapters in this volume have a common focus: transcripts from three interviews that I conducted in the 1980s that form part of a larger corpus of over 80 interviews with white New Zealanders (Wetherell and Potter 1992). As I conducted these interviews, I have a different relationship to the data than the other contributors to this volume, who have come to the re-transcribed interviews fresh. I will return to the advantages and pitfalls of this "insider" knowledge in the last section of the chapter, but one difference is that in illustrating my approach to the analysis of discourse I can draw on the history of the project and the data corpus as a whole.

My approach to the analysis of interview transcripts and other textual material falls within the general rubric of discursive psychology (Billig 1987; Edwards 1997; Edwards and Potter 1992; Harré and Gillett 1994; Potter and Wetherell 1987; Wetherell and Potter 1992). Discursive psychology is a broad church, however (see Wetherell 2001a for a description). It encompasses work on psychological topics and issues influenced by conversation analysis and ethnomethodology, by the Bakhtin/Volosinov writings, by Wittgenstein's language philosophy, and by Foucault's notions of discourse, power and subjectivity, among other sources. Other chapters in this volume from discursive psychologists (see Edwards and Antaki) develop a finer-grained mode of analysis that is more attentive to the methodological prescriptions of conversation analysis. But just how attentive the analyst should be to these prescriptions is a matter of debate in the field (see Billig 1999a; Schegloff 1997, 1999a; Wetherell 1998). Like the approaches of Edwards and Antaki, my approach aims to focus on people's situated activities in talk, but I also try to locate the forms of making sense evident in talk within more global accounts of their place in the broader social and cultural context. To illustrate this approach, I will first describe in more detail the analytic assumptions and procedures behind this work. I will then outline a specimen analysis and go on to discuss some of the methodological and theoretical issues involved in combining in this way the study of "small discourse" (conversations in interviews) with conclusions about "big discourses."

Analytic assumptions

What can be said about racism in a society like New Zealand from the analysis of interviews with members of the majority group white (Pakeha) New Zealanders? Conventionally, one might answer that such interviews can tell us about the cognitive states and the patterns of thought of those with racist attitudes. Such interviews might also provide us with descriptions about how things were in this society when the interviews were conducted. The political climate in New Zealand has shifted considerably since the 1980s, but perhaps the interviews might be informative nonetheless about the way things used to be, as people tell us about policy developments and discuss problem areas and points of dispute between the two main ethnic groups. These are reasonable expectations. Discourse analysis, however, explodes these comfortable assumptions of the social scientist, and particularly the social psychologist.

If they share little else, discourse analysts share their skepticism about simple reference or correspondence models of language: the notion that language neutrally describes a world of entities, whether those be external (policy developments, the state of play between groups) or internal (thoughts, attitudes, and mental states). It is argued that the state of play, policies, groups, identities, and subjectivities are instead constituted as they are formulated in discourse. The criteria for truth (what counts as correct description) are negotiated as humans make meaning within language games and epistemic regimes and, often, locally and indexically in interaction, rather than guaranteed by access to the independent properties of a single external reality.

Following this logic, racism is not first a state of mind and then a mode of description of others. It is a psychology (internal monologue/dialogues and modes of representing) that emerges in relation to public discourse and widely shared cultural resources. Similarly, inequality is not first a fact of nature and then a topic of talk. Discourse is intimately involved in the construction and maintenance of inequality. Inequality is constructed and maintained when enough discursive resources can be mobilized to make colonial practices of land acquisition, for instance, legal, natural, normal, and "the way we do things." Or, to give another example, when affirmative action policies are successfully opposed through the merito-cratic reasoning that "everybody should be treated the same." Less easily for the analyst, the definition of racism becomes a discursive practice also. To say that a mode of representing is racist is to engage in an argument. It is to make an interpretation. These I think are useful arguments for social scientists to get involved in, but they are discursive acts nonetheless.

So in terms of these new formulations, characteristic of social scientific research after the "discursive turn," what can interviews tell us? I think they can tell us crucial things about a segment of a society's conversations with itself, about the ways in which the world is typically legitimated, or-ganized, and justified. These are often efficacious forms of making sense, if simply because any policy is formed in relation to and has to take ac-count of public opinion. Interviews tell us about the cultural resources people have available for telling their patch of the world. This is partic-ularly so when the corpus of interviews is relatively large, there is a lot of homogeneity, and repetition and clear patterns emerge. Indeed, in the corpus of interviews from which the three studied in this volume were selected, the same kind of constructions were very frequently repeated. In this sense the social (the collective voices of culture) was not outside, but rather permeated the individual voices of the interview. The inter-view is a highly specific social production, but it also draws on routine and highly consensual (cultural/normative) resources that carry beyond the immediate local context, connecting local talk with discursive his-tory. The speaker weaves the available threads and voices differently on different occasions. They are worked up as an appropriate and effective turn in a conversation according to what is going on, but speakers do not invent these resources each time. The argumentative fabric of society is continually shaping and transforming, but for recognizable periods it is the same kind of cloth. Such resources are both independent of local talk in a limited sense and need to be continually instantiated through that talk.

In effect, analysis proceeds through two related movements. One is the identification and analysis of pattern (cultural resources), while the other is theorizing and explaining this pattern. And, in developing an explanation of the broader social organization of discourse, the analyst can draw on some familiar social scientific debates and concepts. Indeed, this kind of study of discursive practices was previously subsumed under studies of ideology and the history of ideas. The definition of ideology I have used, however, for my work is a particular one (see Wetherell and Potter 1992, chapter 3). It is a view of ideology as practical discursive action linked to power. This is a non-cognitive account (Billig et al. 1988). Ideology is not seen as defined through specific ideas or specific contents or through the categories or logic of thought. It is defined through a reading of the practical effects of the mobilization of discourse. This is also a view of ideology that does not contrast false beliefs with, for instance, scientific truth. Following Foucault (although he preferred not to use the term ideology), the interest is in how the effect of truth is created in discourse and in how certain discursive mobilizations become powerful – so powerful that they are the orthodoxy, almost entirely persuasive, beyond which we can barely think. To describe a piece of discourse as ideological, therefore, is an interpretative act; it is a claim about the power of talk and its effects. Not every piece of talk needs to be interpreted in this way.

Accounts of social influence

I will try now to make this approach to analysis more concrete by introducing one example taken from the broader project. In the various analyses we conducted of our corpus of interviews, including the three that provide a common focus for this book (Potter and Wetherell 1988, 1989; Wetherell and Potter 1989, 1992), one theme was the ways in which our participants formulated various social processes. I am interested in how participants *talk about* society, rather than the veracity or validity of these accounts of society. Just as people often act as lay psychologists, they also often act as lay sociologists, and as lay social theorists. Here I am taking constructions of social life and social relations in the interviews as topics rather than as resources, following standard ethnomethodological procedure. How did people construct accounts of social processes, and why were these accounts organized in the ways they were? A particular interest was in formulations of *social influence* and *social conflict*. How did the Pakeha people interviewed make sense of Maori protest? How did they formulate the influence process? What interpretative resources did they use to present and package Maori protest movements? And then, from a broader ideological standpoint, how do those resources function to protect Pakeha interests and reflect the playing out of colonial history?

My units of analysis were patterns across the whole corpus of eighty or so interviews, rather than one interview or one section of an interview.

The general procedure was to extract material that I saw as relevant to a particular topic such as, for example, accounts or descriptions of protests and protestors. With a data file of this kind (say around sixty instances, each consisting of several turns of talk before a topic change would occur) I would then look for common and shared ways of making sense across those instances – the interpretative resources. Given the research aims, commonality or pervasiveness was an important criterion for validity. I was looking for not the novel or idiosyncratic, but the routine arguments and standard rhetoric.

To try and illustrate the analytic procedures in more detail, I want to focus now on three extracts, one from each of the three interviews used in this book. These extracts were all part of the same large original data file.

Extract 1 (Appendix: New Zealand Interview 2: 257/258)

```
 1.  R:  E:hm (0.2) I think this:-  an' that's the biggest division (1.0) a:nd (0.4)
 2.      a lot of the (.) racial (0.[4) prejudice I-
 3.  I:                            [(Uh huh)
 4.  R:  I think is brought on you know by the Eva Rickards that a
 5.  I:  Yes (0.4) [mm mhm
 6.  R:            [that stand up=I::'ve been out (.) time after time and played
 7.      golf at- at [[place name]
 8.  I:              [[place name]
 9.  I:  Yes yeah
10.  R:  And (0.2) eh playing on the golf course there I've played with Maori
11.  I:  Mm mhm
12.  R:  people and they said "Oh ya'know this the- this is the old burial- burial
13.      ground,=Hi'ya Roger" ya'know an'
14.  I:  Yes
15.  R:  and'a ya'know "nobody minds you playing golf?" an' I'll say "No no no
16.      (.) It's fi[ne"
17.  I:             [Yes
18.  R:  And it takes Eva Rickard to [c(h)ome down from somewhere else
19.  I:                              [((laugh))
20.  I:  Yeah
21.  R:  to ah to [stir the whole bloomin pot (1.0) [and ehm ya'know
22.  I:           [( )                              [Mm mhm
23.  R:  then the government gets in and'a
24.  I:  Yeah
25.  R:  buys the land (o:r well I don't know) they- they sorted it all
26.      [out an given the- given them all a brand new ehm golf
27.  I:  [Yes
28.  R:  course there an' [I haven't been down an' tried the new one
29.  I:                   [((laughs)) yeah
30.      (1.0)
31.  I:  Yes
32.      (0.2)
```

Extract 2 (Appendix: New Zealand Interview 44: 297/298)

1. I: >One of the-< The other thing that (.) I'm interested is the (0.4)
2.   multiculturalism and (0.6) what people think about sort of race
3.   relations (0.4) scene. >Sort of< There's been quite a change in that
4.   over the six years I've been away, There's a much greater emphasis now
5.   on ehm Maori culture and the use of the Maori language (1.0) an' so on.
6.   (0.6) Do you think in general that's been (0.4) uh constructive or (1.4)
7.   what do you feel about the way things are going (0.2) on that front?
8.   (2.0)
9. R: I think they'll end up having Maori w:ars if they carry on
10.   the way [they have I mean no it'll be a Pakeha war
11. I: [((laugh))
12. I: Yes
13. R: U::hm (1.6) they're ma:king New Zealand a racist cu- country uhm but
14.   ya'know you usually feel (.) think that racism is uhm (1.4) putting th-
15.   putting ([.) the darker people down
16. I: [Yes
17. R: [but really they're doing it (.) the other way around
18. I: [( )
19. I: A sort [of reverse [racism
20. R: [I feel   [yes
21. I: Yeah
22. R: U:hm (1.4) everything (0.6) seems to be to help (0.2) the Maori people,
23.   (1.0) a::nd ya'know (0.4) I think (1.4) at the moment sort of (0.6) the
24.   Europeans are sort of (0.4) They're just sort of watching [and putting
25. I: [Yeah
26. R: up with it
27. I: Yeah
28. R: But (.) they'll only go so fa:r
29. I: Right yeah
30. R: U:hm (1.0) tsk (1.0) ya'know we- we've got (.) Maori friends out he:re
31.   uhm who we have into the house so yu- ya'know they're friends
32.   (0.6)
33. R: U::hm (2.0) but when things happen an' they- they suddenly say "Oh
34.   they're going to make (.) M- Maori language compulsory"
35. I: Yeah (.) yeah
36. R: U:hm (0.4) but that is an- antagonizing
37. I: Yeah
38. R: And- (1.4) the Maori friends that we::'ve got (1.0) they don't agree with it
39. I: Yes (.) yeah
40. R: U::hm (0.2) okay yu- you've got extremists th[ere too
41. I: [Mm mhm
42. R: the ones who feel that ya'know that everyone should learn it but u:hm
43.   (2.0) I think the average Maori sort of perhaps is worried ↑too
44. I: Yeah So there's a sort of split in the Maori com[munity
45. R: [Yes
46.   (0.6)
47. I: between the: yeah (.) yeah

48.   (2.0)
49. I: Yes
50.   (1.0)

Extract 3 (Appendix: New Zealand Interview 16: 278/279)

1. I: Yea:h it's a difficult problem isn't it? .hh ehm ↑ (.) Finally (.) the last
2.   section of questions (1.0) is about'em (0.6) New Zealand as a
3.   multicultural society (.) Do you think there's still differences between
4.   Maori and Pakeha people in terms of temperament and interests (0.6)
5.   or are we really (.) o:ne- (0.4) one nation, one people
6.   (2.2)
7. R: There is a lot of difference (1.0) uhm New Zealand is basically a whi:te
8.   (1.0)
9. I: °Mm mhm°
10. R: a white society a::nd (1.0) some of the Maoris fit in
11. I: °Mm mhm°
12.   (1.6)
13. R: And the ones- some of the ones in the cities fit in the ones in the
14.   country (1.6) are quite happy where they ↑are
15. I: °Mm mhm°
16. R: U::hm (2.6) so probly- (they don't/it may not) really bother them I
17.   don't really know.
18. I: Yeah
19. R: But then you've got the misfits that don't fit in.
20. I: Yeah
21. R: A::nd (0.6) and you've got- (1.4) Like (0.4) with this u:hm (2.0) Treaty
22.   of Waitangi thing
23. I: Mm mhm
24. R: You've got a minority.
25. I: Yes
26. R: that expect the- expect more
27. I: Mm mhm
28.   (0.6)
29. R: A:::nd if you see that going to its full extent it will eventually go to an
30.   underground terrorist organisation.
31. I: Mm mhm
32. R: That- because they don't get the:ir way >although probly with the
33.   Labour Party they will get their ↑way<
34. I: Mm mhm
35. R: A::nd (1.4) they will eventually start striking back an' blowin' things up
36. I: Yeah
37.   (0.6)
38. R: We've got Joe- (   )- (we've/with) Joe Hawke at Bastion Point
39. I: °Mm mhm°
40. R: When le:aders of the tribe
41. I: °Mm mhm°
42. R: turned round an accepted the government's
43. I: Yeah

44.   (0.2)
45. R: thing. >They accepted the <u>land</u> the government gave them an'
46.   two hundred thousand dollars compensation.<
47. I: °Mm mhm°
48. R: Then Joe Hawke said "No we don't agree" He's not even recognized by
49.   the elders of the tribe.
50. I: Yeah
51. R: Yet he's meeting with the- (0.4) with the Labour Party's lan- Lands
52.   Minister
53. I: °Mm [mhm°
54. R: [And they're gonna work something out
55. I: Yeah
56.   (0.4)
57. R: Yeah sure they'll work something out it's just (his) pressure group
58. I: Yes (0.2) mm mhm
59. R: And <u>that's</u> (0.4) whe:re a lot of Labour Party votes come from
60. I: Mm mhm
61. R: is from the Maoris and the Islanders
62. I: Yeah
63.   (0.8)
64. R: Because that's probly what they're told to vote so they vote it
65. I: Yes
66. R: They probly don't under↑stand
67. I: Ye:s
68.   (1.4)

In the case of extracts 2 and 3, this is part of the interviewees' response to my first question about Maori/Pakeha relations. In extract 2, the respondent has been asked what she thinks about the greater emphasis now on Maori culture, while the respondent in extract 3 has been asked whether there are still differences between Maori and Pakeha or whether they could now be described as one nation or one people. Extract 1, taken from interview 2, comes at a different point in the interview, some way in on the set of questions on race relations. This is part of the respondent's reply to a question about whether there is racial prejudice in New Zealand, and he develops a narrative about a particular land dispute at Raglan (a small New Zealand town) over the ownership of a golf course built on a Maori burial ground. In this case an action group led by Eva Rickard successfully campaigned for the return of the land. The respondent, in a very common move, displaces the accusation of prejudice and projects it outwards. Here prejudice is not so much a property of Pakeha. It is something that is caused by Maori activists.

The feature that holds these extracts together and makes them part of the same data file (although they do other things too, and would also have been included in other topic files) is that each contains a formulation or account of Maori people as protestors or activists. These extracts all include accounts or versions of Maori demands for change. In common with the other instances in the same file, they contain an attempt to *discredit* movements for change and Maori people's attempts to obtain redress for land confiscation, for instance, or to introduce Maori language and culture in schools.

One of the things that interested me, then, was how the discrediting was done and the shared interpretative resources this discrediting seems to assume. What is taken for granted here? What counts as a good enough argument, as a telling point, as having done enough to establish or make one's claim? What kinds of appeals will do this? What is it sufficient to say to bring off a discrediting, and what assumptions organize the interpretative resources people draw on? What seems to be at stake in each of these extracts is the construction of an impression of illegitimacy. There were a number of highly routine ways for doing this. I want to discuss here just two methods and some of their implications.

First, to develop their discrediting, the respondents in extracts 1–3 construct, in a condensed fashion, a social landscape populated with characters and social actors. In particular, a distinction is made between two kinds of Maori people. On the one hand there are what tend to be constructed as "average," "normal," "representative," or "majority" Maori, and on the other hand there are "extremist," "minority," and "stirring" Maori. (The term "stirring" has a number of connotations. In the New Zealand language community it became synonymous with "protesting." The very commonly repeated trope was protestors are people who "stir for the sake of it.") The respondent in extract 1, for instance, makes a distinction between activists such as Eva Rickards who stand up, and the Maori people he plays golf with, who are presumably local, and thus ratified in comparison with Eva Rickards who comes from "somewhere else." The respondent in extract 2 talks about "average Maori," who like her are worried at the actions of extremists, while the respondent in extract 3 makes a distinction between Maori who form a "pressure group" and the "elders of the tribe."

Through the construction of these two categories, those Maori campaigning for change are presented as non-organic and as unrepresentative. They become represented as an oddity or extrusion from the main body of Maori and thus as hearably illegitimate. The speakers in extracts 1 and 2 could also be read as doing a bit of credentialling here. In other words, they are reinforcing their expertise as people who know about these things because they are in touch with majority Maori opinion. The respondent in extract 1 constructs some reported speech from Maori he knows and plays golf with to validate his perspective, while the respondent in extract 2 constructs average Maori as also friends, people you have into the house.

Dualisms and binaries such as the average versus the extremist, the minority versus the majority, the moderate, normal, and local versus the deviant agitator from outside, set up or depend upon a shared lay theory of what counts as proper and improper social influence. Proper influence is reasonable, rational, majority-based, asocial, unmotivated, factual, normal, moderate, and practical, while improper influence is emotional, not authentic as a consequence, motivated, immoderate, and minority-based.

The identification of moderation is particularly interesting. As Michael Billig (1982) has pointed out, one peculiarity of moderate political positions is that their moderation can only be defined and identified through contrasts with extreme positions. Moderation is not simply there to be discovered. It has to be constructed through the binary. Why does moderation, however, acquire this rhetorical value? I have argued elsewhere (Wetherell and Potter 1992, chapter 6) that answering this question involves exploring the broader recognizable discourses that constitute liberalism and capitalism, modernity and Enlightenment politics. I also argue that these very same resources can be shown to be at work in nearly every professional academic social psychology of social influence. But that is a story for another day.

The second common move I want to note is related to this construction of proper and improper influence processes and influence agents. One other preferred way for the sample as a whole to establish illegitimacy was to construct a sense of suddenness, an "out of the blue"-ness, a sense of coming from nowhere. The respondent in extract 2, for instance, talks about an undifferentiated "they" who "suddenly" say they are going to make Maori language compulsory, while the male respondent in extract 1 stresses the normality and everydayness of playing golf at Raglan: he says he has been out on the golf course time after time. In extract 3, Joe Hawke's actions at Bastion Point are presented without context as an unexpected and inexplicable intervention.

What I find significant in accounts like these is who is seen as active and as powerful and the way in which the post-colonial activities and power of Pakeha people are made obscure. These extracts depend on what you could call a "consensus," rather than "conflict," construction of society. What is being taken for granted here is the solidity of the status quo. Let me say a bit more about what I am getting at. Typically, across the sample, the majority were presented directly or by implication as placid and passive, going about their everyday business, being normal, peaceful, quiescent, and largely invisible; not social actors, but reacting. In contrast

Maori people and others seeking change became highly visible, the active irritants on the social body. It is they who initiated friction, division, and disruption and who thus disturbed what is constructed as the harmonious resting state of New Zealand society. The notion of "stirring," or "stirring the whole blooming pot" in extract 1, also conveys the flavor of this sense of disturbance from outside on a quiet mass.

As a consequence, the "ordinary majority" being constructed here can seem rather weightless and powerless. All the power and energy appears to be elsewhere. Weight comes, however, from the ascriptions of norma-tiveness, continuity, stability, cohesion, and orderliness. Maori groups thus become like the bee that stings the elephant. The elephant may be slow to rouse and not unduly bothered, but remains full of latent power that is not applied or exerted. The respondent in extract 2 constructs, for example, Pakeha people as watching and putting up with it, but only being prepared to go so far. This is a wonderfully efficient rhetoric in terms of obscuring power relations. Pakeha New Zealanders become in-active, doing nothing out of the ordinary, legitimate, and invisible, while Maori groups become visible, active, and simultaneously deviant and il-legitimate. Their behaviour becomes uncaused and anomalous. The dis-cursive effect is similar to the one Reicher (1987) notes for theories of crowds. The social context surrounding such action (Maori protest) is magically stripped away. The other social groups involved and the his-tory of conflict disappear, while the actions of those one disagrees with become meaningless, frenzied, and inexplicable.

Some objections

With this brief example, I have tried to indicate how a discourse analysis of the cultural and ideological resources people have available for mak-ing sense of a charged political situation might proceed. My interest has been in the transcripts as examples of racist discourse, that is, in how the discourse of the white New Zealanders interviewed sustains and legiti-mates social inequalities and the injustices originating from colonialism. I assumed that to properly understand any one extract, it must be placed within the broader discursive context. I also assumed that part of the an-alyst's task is to develop theories and concepts for explaining that broader context, and the notion of ideology has been one such theory.

Few other chapters in this volume, however, share this focus or these aims (although see Buttny and Verkuyten). Most are concerned with the interviews in themselves and with "internal" features of the talk, rather than with the wider discursive pattern. This is for good reasons. It is difficult to provide an analysis that goes beyond the immediate data if you are unfamiliar with the broader social and historical context of New Zealand/Aotearoa, or unless you are have a good working knowledge (either explicitly or more tacitly) of the representational patterns found in similar discursive contexts where race is the topic. But there is also another, less contingent, reason why some discourse analysts stick as closely as possible to the text. For many analysts, this is a core epistemological and methodological principle. These principles have been extensively discussed in recent years (Billig 1999a and b; Schegloff 1998, 1999a and b; Weatherall 2000; Wetherell 1998. See Wetherell 2001b for an overview), and in this section of the chapter I want to take up this debate. I want to review the kind of objections that have been made to the mode of discourse analysis I am advocating.

The conversation analyst Emmanuel Schegloff (1991, 1992, 1997) has argued that analysis should only be concerned with the activities found in the stretch of talk in the interviews in front of analysts, and with the participant orientations these activities reveal. In his view this is the only analytic focus that can be justified, and this would be the first main objection. Schegloff suggests that analysts should not impose their own interpretations or their own frame of reference on the data. The participants have already interpreted the events of consequence for them, and the analyst's task is simply to show how this has been done as part of the study of the regular ways in which people organize their talk. At the most extreme, these principles would suggest that contextual factors are only relevant and should only be mentioned by the analyst when they are demonstrably relevant to the participants. Analysts, for example, should bracket or put to one side their knowledge that in an interaction one speaker is a child and the other speaker is an adult, unless in some visible way this knowledge is relevant to the speakers themselves. Speakers might make it relevant through direct reference, or it might be made relevant because the sequencing and organization of the turn taking and other conversational features confirm that one or both of the participants are orienting to this knowledge when designing their responses. Without those signs of relevance, in Schegloff's view, these participant statuses must be outside the frame for the analyst and cannot be used as an explanatory resource.

From this general perspective, my form of analysis, or any analysis that studies "racist discourse," risks three basic mistakes. First, analyses that work across large samples and reach general conclusions about the patterning of racist discourse in a community are in danger of ignoring the specificity of the local and immediate discursive contexts. These analyses involve working at quite a high level of abstractness and generality. Prevalent constructions and versions are summarized with some attention to how they are typically organized in rhetorical activities such as "discrediting," but they are not studied in terms of the specific conversational activities evident on each occasion of use.

Second, such analyses seem to risk making a "category error." I noted earlier that discourse analysts share in common their skepticism about correspondence theories of meaning. Discourse is not analyzed referentially (as an accurate or inaccurate description of the world) but as a form of social action. Interviews, for instance, are analyzed as joint productions or constructions of a meaningful social world. The discourse analyst is interested in the process of production or construction and not in verifying whether any specific description or account the participants offer is true or false. This stance assumes a particular theory of language and action, and it also offers a consistent and coherent epistemological procedure. Critical analysis seems to depart from this consistent procedure, however. When we describe discourse as racist and talk about colonization, for instance, or "powerful majority groups" and "disadvantaged minority groups" are we drawing upon social phenomena outside discourse? Is this a category error in the sense that we have shifted by stealth from a constructionist to a realist or referential theory of meaning? Can discourse analysts only be consistent with their constructionist meta-theory if they stick with just what is demonstrably relevant to participants?

Finally, the form of analysis I am advocating seems to risk "knowing better than the participants." Indeed, ideological analysis (as defined earlier), or any form of "critical" discursive analysis, involves an *evaluation* of discourse. It puts that discourse in a broader context. This ideological critique is not intended to be "ad hominem." It is directed at the broader political climate, the organization of society, and the discursive resources available to its members, not at the individual speaker. It is a political rather than a psychological critique. For Schegloff, however, this violates the notion that the role of the analyst is simply to study how the world has already been interpreted. He suggests that to offer a critique is to engage in "analytic imperialism." It is to privilege the interpretations of the analyst above those of the participants, and who is to say that analysts know best, especially if their interpretations are no longer grounded in the actual back and forth of the data?

Some responses

I have described these various objections at length since they are so central to the conduct of discourse analysis and explain a great deal about the topics, foci, and organization of many of the subsequent chapters in this volume. In response I want to argue that these prescriptions about what analysts can say about interview data rely on a misleading conception of context and discourse (see Wetherell 1998, for a more elaborated account). My approach, like those of many other discourse analysts (particularly those influenced by post-structuralism), sees productive and constructive discursive processes as extending way beyond the bounds of the activities in the immediate conversation. The constructive process emerges historically. Past and current collective negotiations organize the spaces (physical, institutional, and symbolic) in which conversations take place, for example, as well as the ways in which people and events can be represented within them. As Michael Shapiro notes:

Intelligible exchanges are always situated . . . the context-meaning relation subsumes a complex history of struggle in which one or more ways of establishing contexts and their related utterances has vanquished other competing possibilities. (1992, 38)

Indeed, the complete *absence* of certain possible constructions of Maori/ Pakeha relations in our corpus of discourse is as revealing as the constructions that dominate and are most taken for granted.

The insistence found in Schegloff's work, in conversation analysis, and in some ethnomethodological research, on focusing only on the activities evident in the talk under investigation rests in part, I believe, on a mistaken theory of discourse and context and an unsustainable distinction between "talk" and "society beyond the talk." It suggests that the discursive can be easily distinguished from the extra-discursive and, broadly, that these are marked by the boundaries artificially created by the analyst around an extract isolated for study. Thus some context is relevant and some distal contexts outside the talk are beyond discourse. As a sociology, this assumes a constructed world of conversations, interviews, and talk of all kinds, where meanings are jointly produced and a world outside conversation of real objects (roles, groups, physical environments) with a different kind of status. An important consequence of Foucault's work, however, has been to explode any simple categorization of the real and the constructed. Foucault's work draws attention to how every social practice (even the most obviously "material") is also a discursive practice. He suggests a much broader definition of discourse as a consequence, as the making of meanings in general. Adopting this reasoning, Laclau and Mouffe (1987), for example, argue for a conceptualization of all social practices as comprising a vast, interlinked, argumentative cloth. And, indeed, when we locate particular bits of discourse from white New Zealanders in the context of colonization, for example, we can see how threads woven through colonial history are worked afresh. At its most extensive, we are linking the present instance to a continuous and historically changing constructive process that has involved huge movements of people and radical changes to landscapes.

I am suggesting therefore that, if we make the kinds of connections that are central to the type of analysis I proposed earlier, no epistemological shift is required. There is no appeal here "beyond discourse." I am also suggesting that if we take this broader perspective we can see how interview talk can be generalized beyond its immediate occasioned activities. When over a large corpus of data the same kinds of constructions are repeated, it becomes apparent, as noted earlier, how the social (collective) practices are not outside, but infuse, the individual voices of the interview. Interview talk is in no sense self-contained. The interview is a highly specific discursive genre, but it also often rehearses routine, repetitive, and highly consensual (cultural/normative) resources that carry beyond the immediate local context, connecting talk with discursive history. Speakers do not invent these resources each time. The argumentative fabric of society is continually shaping and transforming, but for recognizable periods it is the same kind of cloth. Such resources are both independent of local talk in a limited sense and need to be continually instantiated through that talk.

Part of what is attractive about the conversation analytic stance is that it offers a clear approach to validating discourse analyses (through pointing to where things happen in the transcript). If we take a broader approach and locate specific instances in the wider social discursive context, methods of justification and validation become more varied. Developing an analysis, in my view, always involves making an argument. Often that argument is grounded by demonstration (by pointing to some pattern in the data) and, given the authority of empiricism, that can be pretty persuasive. There is more to the knowledge game of scholarship than argument by demonstration, however. When an interpretation is developed of the more global patterns in discourse and then of their effects and consequences for power relations, different resources are usually marshalled such as historical arguments, reference to other lines of research, accumulation of examples from different contexts, and so on. I disagree, therefore, with Schegloff. He implies that, when an analyst goes beyond the participants' interpretations, nothing of value can be added. It is a strong claim to maintain that an analyst might know "better" than the participants, and I am suggesting simply that analysts know different things. In the past these forms of knowing derived from scholarship have been useful and powerful. And I believe scholarly critique and investigations of ideological practices will continue to be so.

Insider knowledge and constructing the object of study

Against some contemporary strands of thinking in conversation analysis, I have argued that it is valid for the discourse analyst to go beyond the immediate data. Indeed, I have suggested that a complete analysis of extracts such as those from our racism project *needs* the analyst to do so, because participants draw on cultural resources that have a history, and the repetition of these resources has important social consequences that we need to study. Analysis in this sense depends on external knowledge outside the immediate talk. But what about the other kinds of knowledge an interviewer might possess? What about the "insider" knowledge that comes from being an actual participant in the interview?

Social science data are not often shared. The norms of the scientific community include openness, transparency, and accountability, but due to publishing conventions, and for a range of often good, and sometimes not so good, practical reasons, data tend to remain private. It is usually left to the researcher to control what enters the public domain. Sharing three interviews from our project in New Zealand for the purposes of this book has thus been a new and challenging process. One of the most intriguing things is having one's own discourse analyzed. As my colleagues came to focus (rightly and appropriately) as much on my discourse as the interviewees', I have often wanted to say, "Oh, but what I was really doing there was . . . ," and "That laugh there, that didn't mean that I was . . . ," and so on, and so on. But my utterances have mostly trailed off, because what would be the point in saying these things?

Why have I censored myself in this way? Why is this type of knowledge or contribution different from drawing on social analysis and critique to understand the cultural resources evident in the talk? I think the difference is that when I say "What I was really doing there was . . . ," I have stopped analyzing the discursive context and begun making experiential or factual claims. I would be making the kind of category error discussed earlier. I would no longer be in the business of making interpretations about the patterning of discursive resources (whether at a global or local level). I would be in the business of arbitrating truth and deciding on what actually happened. I don't believe, however, that accounts of experience have this privileged status. I don't accept, in other words, that by asking people about their intentions and beliefs we can close things off with the conclusion "Now we know what that was really all about." There is no "horse's mouth," just more discourse.

Interviewers may not be able to close off further analysis and offer a definitive account, but we do co-construct the object of study through our actions, and we are accountable to the wider scientific community for that construction. One of the distinguishing features of science, as opposed to other forms of knowledge making, is self-conscious reflection on method. And so in the last section of this chapter, I want to discuss in a bit more detail the particular organization of these interviews. If the research aim is to identify cultural resources, what is the best way of conducting interviews to that end?

When considering this in advance of the project, we decided that we wanted to produce a situation that would encourage those interviewed to rehearse as extensively as possible all their typical and usual ways of making sense of the issues at stake. In line with the social psychological theories of racism and discourse we were developing, we wanted to focus on the collective common sense of the ordinary middle-class members of the white community (and the sample was selected for their "typicality" in this respect). We thought that explanations of racism focused on psychological pathology had not been very productive, and instead we wanted to look at the ways in which racism was linked to everyday, unexceptional discourse. The aim, therefore, in the interview was to facilitate, in the most ordinary of ways, the emergence of the everyday common sense of our participants. We hoped that they might say the kinds of things that they would regularly say in other contexts, such as around their own dining tables with friends.

Other decisions followed from these preliminary views. The ideal interview should be a series of monologues in response to questions rather than a dialogue. Questions about race and protest over the Springbok tours (the main foci) should be embedded in a longer series of questions about recent politics in New Zealand and some of the current salient "burning issues." I felt my role as the interviewer should be self-effacing. My own views were irrelevant, and to expound upon them would be self-indulgent. My task instead was to be a "good listener," to be attentive and supportive. I should give the (correct) impression that what they said was important to me, while bracketing the content for consideration later. This felt appropriate given that my aim was not to develop a critique of them as people but to develop a critique through the analysis of the discursive resources their culture offered them. Further, where interviewees (such as the participant in interview 44) were nervous, hesitant, and doubtful whether they had anything interesting to say, my task was to reassure them that their voice was important and enable them to speak.

These procedures were effective by and large in allowing us to identify the available stock of tropes, arguments, commonplaces, versions, and repertoires in the community we were studying. But all procedures have advantages and disadvantages. The interviews were conducted in the mid-1980s, at a time when debate was beginning about the impact of discourse theory on method. Social scientists were beginning to explore the notion that the interviewer's discourse was as relevant as the respondent's, that there are no neutral questions, and that the interviewer was active and not an objective measuring instrument (see Potter and Mulkay 1985, for an early exploration of these ideas). Subsequent work has made it very clear that the interviewer's orientation is unavoidably a factor in the unfolding interaction (e.g. Antaki et al. 2000; Houtkoop-Steenstra 2000; Houtkoop-Steenstra and Antaki 1998; Rapley and Antaki 1998). Some of the specific effects of "friendly interviewing" have also become apparent (Houtkoop-Steenstra 1997), and, in line with the general epistemological shifts, interviewers have become freed up to depart radically from conventional notions of interviewing.

There is no reason why an interviewer should remain faceless, for instance. It might be highly productive for interviewers to express "strong views" themselves, rehearse their own opinions in depth, challenge and argue with their participants. This might be particularly important when interviewees are expressing racist views that the researcher finds offensive. It could be that, with these styles of interviewing, research would proceed in a more honest fashion (see Hak this volume) and be less complicit with those perspectives identified as racist. Whether this is a more ethical procedure than "friendly interviewing" and producing the most caring and constructive response to those who have agreed to help you with your research is a matter of debate. It would make the position of the interviewer more comfortable certainly, but it violates the implicit contract and expectations of those about to be interviewed. It is also problematic when interviews take place in people's homes and are seen as an act of hospitality. Complicity, invisibility, and lack of authenticity might be the price one pays for the privileges of the ethnographer. There needs to be much more discussion, however, among discourse researchers about creative ways of doing research, and, indeed, watching skilled interviewers at work, it is evident that there are ways of expressing disagreement that might be registered and be productive without being heard as "arguing back."

A researcher does not just construct the object of study through choices about interviewing styles. Choices about the level and style of transcription are also important. One of the benefits of sharing data for this volume is that there were resources to re-transcribe the three interviews selected for discussion to the fine-grained level required for conversation analytic studies. The new analyses enabled as a consequence have been rich and insightful. The re-transcription of the interviews has been a reminder of the ways in which transcription is a theory of the data. Transcription constructs what the data is. For pragmatic (financial) reasons, our original transcription of the sample of eighty interviews could not be so fine-grained. The focus for that transcription was on content with some relatively minimal attention to features of the interaction. The validity of the level of transcription chosen of course depends on the research questions. I believe our original transcription was valid for the questions we asked of the data. Re-transcription has not altered any of our substantive conclusions. What is exciting, however, is to see what other researchers and readers make of the interviews. Although the contributors to this volume have to work with the object of study I constructed through my activities as the interviewer, their different emphases, backgrounds, and interests have also created new objects of study. The subsequent chapters report their discoveries.

References

Antaki, C., Houtkoop-Steenstra, H., and Rapley, M. 2000. "Brilliant. Next question . . .": high-grade assessment sequences in the completion of interactional units. *Research on Language and Social Interaction* 33: 235–262.

Billig, M. 1982. *Ideology and social psychology*. Oxford: Blackwell.

  1987. *Arguing and thinking: a rhetorical approach to social psychology*. Cambridge: Cambridge University Press.

  1999a. Whose terms? Whose ordinariness? Rhetoric and ideology in conversation analysis. *Discourse and Society* 10, 4: 543–547.

  1999b. Conversation analysis and the claims of naivete. *Discourse and Society* 10, 4: 543–547.

Billig, M., Condor, S., Edwards, D., Gane, M., Middleton, D., and Radley, A. 1988. *Ideological dilemmas*. London: Sage.

Braidotti, M. 1994. *Nomadic subjects: embodiment and sexual difference in contemporary feminist theory*. New York: Columbia University Press.

Edwards, D. 1997. *Discourse and cognition*. London: Sage.

Edwards, D. and Potter, J. 1992. *Discursive psychology*. London: Sage.

Harré, R. and Gillett, G. 1994. *The discursive mind*. London: Sage.

Houtkoop-Steenstra, H. 1997. Being friendly in survey interviews. *Journal of Pragmatics* 28: 591–623.

  2000. *Interaction and the standardized interview. The living questionnaire*. Cambridge: Cambridge University Press.

Houtkoop-Steenstra, H. and Antaki, C. 1998. Creating happy people by asking yes/no questions. *Research on Language and Social Interaction* 30: 285–313.

Laclau, E. and Mouffe, C. 1987. Post-Marxism without apologies. *New Left Review* 166: 79–106.

Potter, J. and Mulkay, M. 1985. Scientists' interview talk: interviews as a technique for revealing participants' interpretative practices. In *The research interview: uses and approaches*, edited by M. Brenner, J., Brown, and D. Canter. London: Academic Press.

Potter, J. and Wetherell, M. 1987. *Discourse and social psychology: beyond attitudes and behaviour*. London: Sage.

1988. Accomplishing attitudes: fact and evaluation in racist discourse. *Text* 8: 51–68.

1989. Fragmented ideologies: accounts of educational failure and positive discrimination. *Text* 9: 175–190.

Rapley, M. and Antaki, C. 1998. "What do you think about . . .": generating views in an interview. *Text* 18: 582–608.

Reicher, S. 1987. Crowd behavior as social action. In *Rediscovering the social group: a self-categorisation theory*, edited by J. Turner, M. Hogg, P. Oakes, S. Reicher, and M. Wetherell. Oxford: Blackwell.

Schegloff, E. A. 1991. Reflections on talk and social structure. In *Talk and social structure*, edited by D. Boden and D. Zimmerman. Cambridge: Polity.

1992. In another context. In *Rethinking context*, edited by A. Duranti and C. Goodwin. Cambridge: Cambridge University Press.

1997. Whose text? Whose context? *Discourse and Society* 8, 2: 165–188.

1998. Reply to Wetherell. *Discourse and Society* 9, 3: 413–416.

1999a. "Schegloff's texts" as "Billig's data": a critical reply. *Discourse and Society* 10, 4: 558–571.

1999b. Naiveté vs sophistication or discipline vs self-indulgence. *Discourse and Society* 10, 4: 577–582.

Shapiro, M. 1992. *Reading the postmodern polity*. Minneapolis: University of Minnesota Press.

Weatherall, A. 2000. Gender relevance in talk-in-interaction and discourse. *Discourse and Society* 11: 286–288.

Wetherell, M. 1998. Positioning and interpretative repertoires: conversation analysis and post-structuralism in dialogue. *Discourse and Society* 9, 3: 387–412.

2001a. Editor's introduction: minds, selves and sense making. In *Discourse theory and practice: a Reader*, edited by M. Wetherell, S. Taylor, and S. J. Yates. London: Sage and Open University.

2001b. Debates in discourse research. In *Discourse theory and practice: a Reader*, edited by M. Wetherell, S. Taylor, and S. J. Yates. London: Sage and Open University.

Wetherell, M. and Potter, J. 1989. Narrative characters and accounting for violence. In *Texts of identity*, edited by J. Shotter and K. Gergen. London: Sage.

1992. *Mapping the language of racism*. London: Harvester Wheatsheaf.

2 Analyzing racial discourse: the discursive psychology of mind–world relationships

Derek Edwards

Introductory remarks

The aim of this chapter is to illustrate discursive psychology and its methodology by examining some extracts from the interview materials. "Discursive psychology" studies the relationships between mind and world, as psychology generally does, but as a discourse topic, that is, as a participants' concern, a matter of talk's business, talk's categories, talk's rhetoric, and talk's current interactional concerns. This contrasts with most other psychological approaches, in which talk is treated as the expression and communication of thoughts and communicative intentions. Among various inspirational sources for the discursive approach taken here, I would list Harvey Sacks' (1992) lectures on conversation, Melvyn Pollner (1987) on reality disjunctures, Dorothy Smith (1990) on factual discourse, Jeff Coulter (1990) on language and mind, Michael Billig (1987) on rhetoric, and Potter and Wetherell (1987) on the relevance of discourse studies to social psychology (see also Harré and Gillett 1994; Smith, Harré, and Langenhove 1995). Examples of my own work include various books and articles (Edwards 1991, 1995, 1997; Edwards and Potter 1992, 1993) that investigate how common-sense conceptions of mind and world are deployed in everyday talk and text.

One basic theme in all of this work is the way that mind and world are generally played against each other, in a conceptual and rhetorical trade-off between the world "out there" and the mental world "within," including whatever characteristics or "dispositions" may be claimed by, or assigned to, people. In fact, this feature pertains in standard psychology too, but there it figures as the psychologists' own explanation of how mind and behavior actually work (attribution theory, schema theory, cognitive models, social identity theory, social cognition, etc.). In contrast, discursive psychology approaches the mind–world relationship as a participant's common-sense *basis for talking*. And that produces a number of fundamental differences and tensions between discursive and standard psychology, somewhat akin to those between ethnomethodology and the rest of sociology, between conceptual analysis and the rest of philosophy, and (glossing rather extravagantly) between sociology of scientific knowledge and the prior history of science studies.

Methodological approach

The various contributors to this volume were invited to consider the following three points:

1. Interviews on controversial topics such as prejudice, ethnocentrism, ethnic categorization, and stereotyping are difficult to interpret.
2. These kinds of interviews often entail contradictory and ambiguous statements.
3. Meanings depend on the interview as an interaction.

Item (1) directly involves what may be called mind–world topics, relationships between what happens in the world, and what people make of it. What people "make" of it need not be approached mentalistically. Rather, talking about minds, thoughts, wishes, preferences, and so on, is among the ways that participants conduct their lives, and that is something we can study empirically. Items (2) and (3) are also grist to the discourse analytic mill, rather than being "difficulties" for discursive psychology. This situation can be explained in terms of three methodological stances.

First, the discursive psychological approach does not try to apply a litmus test, to see if people really are prejudiced, whether openly or behind the camouflage of their talk. Prejudice, or any other mental state or interpersonal disposition, is approached analytically as something that may be attended to in various ways in talk itself. Many of the "problems" that various qualitative analysts have with talk are engendered by their approach to it, as something they are trying to see through, or see past, to some other reality behind or beneath, in particular, the realities of mind and world – the world the talk reports on, and the mind of the speaker. In contrast, discursive psychologists aim to avoid coming to conclusions that analysis can reveal people's true beliefs and attitudes. We avoid coming to such conclusions not because it is wrong to do so, but as a matter of methodological principle. Furthermore, we avoid this practice in relation to every topic, not just on sensitive topics such as racial prejudice, but on the most mundane things, such as what a person remembers, or wants, or intends – in other words, "mind" in general, and "world" in general, are approached as talk's business, not analysts' business (cf. Wieder 1988). Yet once this methodological move is made, it turns out to be not so much an avoidance of the real issues, of dealing with "actual" prejudice, attitudes, memories, causal explanations, and so on. Rather, it becomes a re-definition of what prejudice, etc., is. That is why we call it discursive psychology, rather than just a way of avoiding doing psychology at all.

The second methodological point relates to contradictions, inconsistencies, and ambiguities. If these arise, then they are likely to be important and interesting, rather than a kind of nuisance that analysts might wish were absent. They are only a nuisance if we start by expecting and hoping for their opposites – for consistency, clarity of thought, and a singular, "mapping" relationship between versions (descriptions, formulations, etc.) and a coherent mind or world beyond them. They are a nuisance only if we approach talk as a kind of veil to be penetrated, behind which lies what we are really after – mind and world. But if we start from an interest in how talk works, as an arena of activity, as *managing* these kinds of concerns about mind and world rather than expressing them, then what at first looks like an analytic nuisance becomes precisely what is most interesting.

However, it is only a first and partial move to make, analytically, to point to contradictions and inconsistencies, or variability (Potter and Wetherell, 1987), between what a person says on one occasion compared to another. It is not something to hold onto and explain, as a phenomenon, because it may have a dubious status as a phenomenon. For example, it may be something that analysts note by comparing one bit of talk with another, rather than something that participants themselves pick up and deal with. Rather, variability is a *way into* examining what talk does, on occasions, sequentially and in context, and rhetorically. Once we are focused on those things, then in a sense we are no longer dealing with contradictions. They were contradictions only on the normative assumptions of mind-mapping and world-mapping, where a statement about X in one context ought logically, or morally, to be the same as a statement about X in another. If we examine talk for the situated actions it performs, then inconsistencies and contradictions are best used as potential paths into those actions for analysts, rather than as the basic phenomena themselves, or analytic conclusions about those phenomena.

The third point, regarding methodological/theoretical orientation, is that mind–world issues are at stake, topicalized, managed, and so on, as part of talk's routine business, pervasively and generally, in talk of all kinds, and not just on sensitive social issues. So I do not approach these materials as anyone especially interested in race and ethnicity, nor in the problems of analyzing interviews. But mind–world talk is obviously very relevant to these matters. The notion that talk expresses minds and reflects worlds is not totally gotten rid of, but features as part of talk's performative business, as a participants' basis for talking, a possible participants' orientation to the status of what they are saying.

Discursive psychology, as a general field, already includes a variety of theoretical and methodological perspectives that approach psychological topics through the study of discourse concepts and practices. The relations and differences between these perspectives reflect their different aims and origins, and there are significant tensions between them; they do not all add up to a unified, comprehensive approach. Most practitioners take a perverse, argumentative pleasure in that. For example Billig (1987) focuses on rhetoric and ideology, seeking the ways in which ideological and political themes are embedded and put to use in discourse. In contrast Coulter (1990) analyzes the logical properties of concepts-in-use, taking inspiration from Wittgenstein, Sacks, and ethnomethodology, and focusing on the social nature of psychological concepts. Harré (1983; Harré and Gillett 1994) also draws on Wittgenstein, but develops his discursive psychology out of cross-cultural and historical studies of language, together with an extension of the "ethogenic" study of everyday accounts, tied to a social psychological theory of agentive, meaningful, social action. The analysis offered in this chapter demonstrates a form of discursive psychology derived most directly from conversation analysis, conceptual analysis, and the kind of "discourse analysis" first developed in social studies of science (Gilbert and Mulkay 1984; Potter and Wetherell 1987), hence its focus on the conversational deployment of concepts of mind and reality. For extended applications of this perspective to topics such as mental states, emotions, causal explanations, narrative accounts, event descriptions, acts of remembering, and a variety of other discursive-psychological themes, see Edwards (1997), Edwards and Potter (1992), and Potter (1996). For an illustrative study *not* focusing on racial discourse, see Edwards (1995).

Analysis

The discourse of mind–world relations includes offering one's thoughts, opinions, policies, and ideas as constrained by the nature of the world. Examples include offering beliefs as based on personal experiences, on shared experiences, on consistent experiences, on consensus, on rational inferences from the facts, and so on. Three examples of this kind of common sense discourse are selected for analysis: (1) links between mental states, events, and rational inferences; (2) scripts and dispositions; (3) reluctance to come to a view, along with coming to a view "unlooked for," serendipitously, or by accident, which is to offer a certain view or version as not having been worked up artfully for an argument. Participants sometimes offer a point of view, an observation, or a conclusion, as a kind of casual noticing, as something that they have not really thought

much about. One thing that such an offering can do is to counter the idea
that what the offerers are saying is in any way prepared, or pre-established
in their minds, let alone any kind of axe they are grinding. So, offering
a report of something on the basis that it was not really in one's mind
to start with, but was accidentally observed, can counter the category of
being, in a general sense, prejudiced.

Mental states and epistemic inferences

In extract 1 (below) the interviewee offers a generalized gloss on racial
problems in schools (lines 1–2), and unpacks (or instantiates) it in the
form of a specific narrative of a Maori woman's thoughts and experiences.

Extract 1 (Appendix: New Zealand Interview 44: 298/299)

```
1.  R:  An' I- I know that uhm (2.0) you know there is a- a problem
2.      in the schools here (.) the- the blacks and whites sort of thing
3.      a::nd (1.0) there's a Maori lady down the corner down here (1.4)
4.      an' she's got two boys (1.0) well she was thrilled that her boy
5.      was going to a class with a lot Europeans
6.  I:  ((lau[gh)) yes
7.  R:         [Because she was worried [uhm that he would get into a class
8.  I:                                  [(     )
9.  R:  with quite a few Maoris and therefore they'd form a gang
10. I:  Yes [(.) and he'd stop worki[ng yeah
11. R:      [And                     [and once they're a gang [then
12. I:                                                        [Yeah
13. R:  they- they (loll it not seem to apply) themselves
14. I:  Yes
15. R:  If they (.) ya'know are not interested- got more interested
16.     agitating in the classroom than
17. I:  than working
18. R:  Mmm
19. I:  Yeah (.) right (.) I know
20. R:  But I- I don't- It makes you wonder sort of the people that make
21.     (2.4) these laws and rules Do they know what's really going on
22. I:  ((l[augh))
23. R:     [in the- in the
24. I:  yeah
25. R:  you know the average school and
26. I:  Yeah
27. R:  an' home and everything
28. I:  Probably not
```

There are a number of psychological descriptions (if I may use the
notion of "psychological" loosely) in extract 1, including the notions

thrilled, worried, interested, wonder, and various expressions to do with knowing. The latter are mostly casual-looking tokens, such as the pervasive "you know" (lines 1, 15, and 25). There are also a couple of uses of "I know" (lines 1 and 19). I take it that there is a face-value relevance, in any study of attitudinal or race-prejudice-relevant talk, of how people invoke psychological reactions to, or assessments of, racially categorized events. Extract 1, and the talk that precedes it, deals with a question posed by the interviewer of what R thinks of the recent increased emphasis on Maori culture and language in the schools. R has suggested that not only Pakeha people, but Maoris themselves, including some who are R's friends, are worried about the compulsory introduction of Maori language. Of course, whatever the factual merits of that information, that R has Maori friends and that they share her worries are also ways of countering any implication that R's judgments stem from any kind of anti-Maori prejudice.

Consider now some details from extract 1, concerning "knowing." In lines 1–2, the section "I- I know that uhm (2.0) you know" frames the "problem in the schools," and its categorial status as involving "blacks and whites," as something that not only R knows about personally, and might need to provide evidence of, but something knowable by the interviewer, and potentially anybody else, too ("you know"). I am not suggesting that "you know" has to be an explicit, literal invocation of what somebody else knows; rather, I am suggesting that its use is associated with appeals to intersubjectivity, to not having to spell things out. The expression "sort of thing" (line 2) adds to this status of racial problems as something generally knowable, and vaguely formulatable, such that R need not explicate what she means in any detail; it is not something she treats here as new or controversial information. Introducing the nature of the world as common knowledge, or framing descriptions as uncontroversial, are ways of talking, and, as such, can be ways of packaging potentially controversial matters as nothing of the sort. I shall return to this possible rhetorical trajectory later.

Note similarly, in line 20, "it makes you wonder." This is another avowal of a mental state as jointly available ("you"). The expression is a cliché, of course, but, like any cliché, it has a particular content that is relevant to its selection and its occasions of use. The term "wonder" is used to question a state of affairs without having to offer a confident description or critique of it. The component "it makes you" suggests that the questioning, the potential criticism, is objectively, rather than subjectively, derived – a function of the object or event itself rather than the speaker's attitude or disposition. The critical intent of "it makes you wonder" is later endorsed by the interviewer (line 28, "probably not"), following another appeal by R to what is intersubjectively available (line 27, "and everything"), completing a three-part list that includes the "average" school and home, introduced by another "you know" (line 25). So we can start to analyze mental state expressions (think, know, wonder), even when they occur within idiomatic expressions, as performative, interaction-oriented tokens in talk, and to pick out what their interactional import might be.

The notion of a racial problem in schools (lines 1–2) is developed, not via R's own experiential narrative, but by way of another person's story, that of "a Maori lady down the corner here" (line 3). Although personal, eye-witness accounts generally have a rhetorical force all their own, in this instance the story is second-hand. One relevant consideration may be that a claim made by a white, Pakeha observer about problems between "blacks and whites" courts the danger of being taken as possibly a "white" claim, indexical of the speaker herself, of her potentially relevant racial identity, attitudes, or prejudices. Another possibility is that her conclusion about racial problems is otherwise somewhat distant from whatever events in schools she is able to cite as a basis for it. But whatever the second-hand narrative might be doing here, there are again traces in R's talk of an orientation to the epistemic grounds of what she is saying. The "Maori lady" serves as a vicarious eye witness and experiencer (being variously "thrilled" and "worried," lines 4 and 7), being close enough to serve as a known witness ("down the corner here," line 3), but also Maori enough that her worries are not identifiable merely as R's, or Pakeha worries. So R's racial concerns, voiced in lines 1–2, emerge as rationally founded, carefully arrived at, and as shared (not hers alone), particularly by those (Maori) against whom she might otherwise be taken as positioned.

Note how a nice contrast case is provided for R's well-informed and carefully drawn rational inferences by the lawmakers (lines 20–28). *These* are the people who, in contrast to R, are ignorant of what is "really going on" in schools (and this extends to the "home and everything") and, therefore, are presumptive of (prejudiced about) racial problems in "the average school." So R's rationally based, knowledgeable inferences stand in rhetorical contrast to the uninformed, distant viewpoints of policy makers.

I must display a bit of inferential circumspection myself here; I am at least as concerned to display the rational basis of my own remarks as R is. In assigning to R the categories "white" and "Pakeha," I am somewhat presuming their relevance to what she is saying in extract 1. That kind of indexical relevance for the speaker is, in fact, oriented-to throughout the interviews we were given to analyze, where it crops up in varying degrees of explicitness. Indeed being white, Pakeha, and talking about ethnic issues were understood bases on which the interviewees were selected and the interviews conducted. Nevertheless, the important things about extract 1 are what it contains rather than what might lie behind it. Among its contents are R's own uses of the categories "black and white" as the "problem"-definitive categories for persons involved, and "Maori lady" as the relevant category of person whose perspective R provides as an example (cf. Jayyusi 1984). These categories tie in to the various play-offs between external events (in schools), psychological states (thrilled, worried, wonder, interested, know), and R's own bases for rational inferences. For example, note how the Maori lady's being "thrilled" (line 4) about her son's joining a mainly "European" class is linked to her "worry" about what would happen if he were placed with other Maoris (lines 7–18). It is the notion of an *emblematic* narrative, such as an appeal to what projectably "would" happen, that I shall focus on next.

Scripts and dispositions

R's version of racial problems in schools (extract 1) hinges on a "scripted" story of what *generally* happens when Maori children are separated in schools, put into groups, form gangs, lose interest in school work, start agitating, and so on (lines 7–18). This part of the account is framed not as a specific, witnessed episode, but as a known and predictable pattern – what I have called a "script formulation" (Edwards 1994, 1995, 1997). The scripting is done by various grammatical activity-generalizing devices. In extract 1 there is the iterative present tense ("they'd form a gang"), the use of the modal "would" (lines 7, 9) to provide a sense of predictable *types* of event sequences, and the use of conjunctions and adverbs such as "therefore" (line 9), "once," and "then" (line 11) in conveying a kind of predictable sequential logic of activities. The sequential logic of activities in the world is conflated with the speaker's rational inferences about them (see also the discussion of narrative and logical "then" in Edwards 1997).

One way that scripted versions of events work is that formulating events as regular makes them both factually robust and also somewhat knowable in advance without having to wait and see for any specific instance. Script formulations are presented as if based on lots of instances, and perhaps lots of people's repeated (consensual) experiences of instances. So a narrated sequence of events can be offered as an expectable sequence. There are two features here with regard to mind–world relations. First, events are offered as falling into a regular pattern, and therefore an empirically

robust one, so despite the pattern in extract 1 being offered as hypothetical, a "worry," it is also formulated as what is "really going on"
(line 21) in "the average school." Second, being a regular pattern, it is
therefore indicative of *dispositional tendencies* that can be attributed to the
actors (cf. Smith 1978). These are very general and pervasive features of
script-and-disposition talk, and we find them in lots of discourse settings.
Person-characterizing formulations, such as racial characteristics or the
speaker's own balanced point of view, can be descriptively built as script
and disposition formulations.

There are many further examples of script and disposition formulations
in these materials. Consider extract 2, in which R suggests that various
newspaper reports were biased against the police.

Extract 2 (Appendix: New Zealand Interview 16: 275)
1.   R: Yeah you [don't hear what the clo:wns did to the police
2.   I: [Yeah
3.   I: Mm mhm
4.   R: Ya'know I mean as far as they're concerned all they wanted
5.   to do was walking down the street
6.   I: Yes
7.   R: And they suddenly got set upon. Rub[bish.
8.   I: [Mm mhm mm mhm
9.   R: The police I know wouldn't- ya'know they- they don't do that
10. I: Yes [yeah
11. R: [Not in New Zealand anyway
12.   (1.0)
13. I: Mmm [It must have been a very- Sorry
14.   [(   )-
15. R: There will have been a motive for the police to [do something about it
16. I: [Yeah
17. I: Yeah
18.   (1.2)
19. R: There will have been a motive=okay they may have used excessive force
20. I: Mm mhm
21.   (0.4)
22. R: But I think the police got frustrated
23. I: Ye:s well that was the third t[est wasn't it yeah
24. R: [Ya'know they- they were caught in the
25.   middle
26. I: Yeah

The practical reasoning here works as follows: Knowing what the police
are like dispositionally (line 9) permits the inference of an emblematic
narrative, a scripted version of what "must have" or "will have" happened
(lines 13–15) on an occasion when they resorted to violence, even though

the speaker did not witness that event. It is because the police "don't" do that kind of thing (line 9) that, on some occasion when they did, it had to be exceptional. Being exceptional, rather than dispositional, is to say that it was out of character. And to say it was out of character is to say that its cause was external rather than internal (Edwards and Potter 1992, cf. Jones and Davis 1965), that the police must have been provoked into acting that way (lines 15–22). Police violence, being abnormal, requires a "motive" account (lines 15, 19).

What we have here is a bit of common-sense narrative–normative reasoning, reminiscent of Sacks' (1992) "A3N," the "Account Apparently Appropriate Negativer." In Sacks' example, an apparently accountable action (being in possession of a gun) is characterized as normal ("everybody does it"), such that no special account (motives, reasons, etc.) need be given. In contrast, R constructs the action (excessive police violence) as *ab*normal, as out of character, and therefore as requiring a special explanation ("motive"), rather than altering a basically favorable view of the police as typically restrained and not generally prone to doing that kind of thing. The narrative itself works via a contrast structure (Smith 1978), using an alternative scripted sequence. In contrast to a scenario where a group of people are walking down the street, supposedly harmlessly (as reported in the press), and are suddenly set upon by unprovoked police violence (lines 1–7), knowledge of the police's dispositionally restrained character permits us to infer the occurrence of excessive or sustained provocation (without having to witness it), followed by something like a threshold of tolerance being breached (lines 19–25). So police violence is given the common-sense status of the exception that proves the rule.

I would assume that this kind of inferential play-off between scripted action sequences and actors' general dispositions and specific mental states is a strong feature of everyday reasoning with regard to the management of reality and mind, as well as speakers' avoidance of categories that might be implied about themselves, such as being prejudiced or irrational. Again, it is not just that, for such a speaker, racial or ethnic prejudice is a socially vilified thing these days, and therefore a characterization to be avoided. It is that *any* kind of prejudice is tantamount to irrationality, to an undermining of the factual grounds for judgments and beliefs, for accountable mappings between reality and mind, in that a concern for common-sense rational accountability is pervasive in discourse of all kinds (Garfinkel 1967; Pollner 1987). In sustaining a negative view of a group of people, while guarding against a disarming accusation of prejudice, the thing to do is to bring off that view as rationally (and, as we shall see, even reluctantly or accidentally) arrived at.

Extract 3 (Appendix: New Zealand Interview 16: 283)

```
1.   R:  It's normally that- Okay that argument gets put in that Maoris never get
2.       the jobs okay but you look. hh when they turn up for an interview
3.   I:  Yes
4.   R:  What's he wearing how's he sitting
5.   I:  Yeah
6.   R:  How's he talking >ya'know what I mean< an' there's no
7.       point in having a receptionist that picks up a phone "Yeah
8.       g'day 'ow are ya" ((strong New Zealand accent))
9.   I:  Ye:s (0.4) [mm mhm
10.  R:             [I mean they want someone that is- (0.4) that is
11.      gonna put their clients at ea:se
12.  I:  Right (.) [Mm mhm
13.  R:            [You don't wanna shop a- a shop assistant who's smelly
14.  I:  [Yes
15.  R:  [who's got un-dirty unkempt hair [an' tattoos all over your
16.  I:                                   [Mm mhm
17.  R:  arms [an' fingers all that sort of thing
18.  I:       [Yeah
19.  I:  Mm mhm
20.  R:  Because people are not gonna feel- (0.2) they're not gonna- wanna buy
21.      things from people like that
22.  I:  Right (.) mm mhm
23.      (1.2)
24.  I:  So sometimes the bias is justified really (0.4) yeah
25.  R:  Mhm.
```

Note again briefly in extract 3, in the first three lines, the *rhetorical* context, just like in extracts 1 and 2. As Michael Billig (1985) pointed out, talk about social categories tends to be argumentative, not just an expression of views, but a denial of counter views. In these cases, the speaker R sets up an argument, or presumption, that "Maoris" (i.e., *as* Maoris) "never get the jobs," and counters it via a series of script and disposition formulations. Again, these take the form of iterated activities, of "what happens when," a routine wherein Maoris *accountably* fail to get the jobs they go for. And it is all done dispositionally, as due to various emblematic Maori characteristics, presented as if recognizably characteristic of the category "Maori."

Note the detail in line 2, "you look .hh when they turn up for an interview." This appeals not only to scriptedness ("when they turn up for an interview"), but also to an event's experiential basis ("you look"), and an indefinitely repeated experiential basis at that ("Maoris never," "when they turn up"). It formulates what anyone ("you," not just the speaker personally) can look to see, and repeatedly see, about Maoris per se, as a category. Again, "when they turn up" deploys the generalized, iterative present tense (see Edwards 1995: 345 for a further list of grammatical scripting devices), rather than offering this description as a specific episode where somebody turned up once. It is not a specific narrative event about a particular person on a particular day. The whole sequence is scripted and generalized this way. Note again the generalizing expression "all that sort of thing" (line 17), and the insertion ">ya'know what I mean<" (line 6), with their implications of common knowledge and experience, of not having to elaborate further specifics.

Consider also lines 10–21: "they want," "you don't want," etc. As with the Maori woman quoted as being worried about her kids in extract 1, the account here is an externalized one, cast in terms of what other people (employers, customers) want and see, rather than the current speaker personally. And it is cast in terms of generalized and normative concerns rather than personal ones, such as the requirement for a shop business to sell its goods to its customers (lines 10–11, 20). Again, psychological dispositions ("you don't wanna," "they're not gonna wanna") are provided for, as rationally tied to the way the world is, which is to say, how Maoris generally behave and look. The contrast case to "rational" is implicit here; that characteristics assigned to Maoris, and job opportunities refused to Maoris, might otherwise be ungrounded and prejudicial. But if prejudice *were* the issue (line 24), then script and disposition formulations are ways in which whatever one is saying about the world is presented as fixed in that world, and rationally inferred from it, rather than residing in the speaker's ways of seeing.

Beliefs reluctantly arrived at, and knowledge unlooked for

The rhetoric of reality and mind involves grounding knowledge states as reflections of the world (Edwards 1997), which may involve working them up as based on repeated experiences, or as regular and recognizable event sequences, as in script formulations. Another way of grounding factual claims is to offer them as reluctantly arrived at, or even precisely counter to, not only what others may think, but also one's own presumptions and biases (Potter 1996) or, in gestalt jargon, counter to "mental set." This is another very powerful way of attending to the rhetorically dangerous notion that you believe what it suits you to believe, what you believed before you looked, or that your beliefs are a function of mental predisposition rather than external reality; that is, of attending to a possible accusation of pre-judgment or prejudice. But note again how general this is. It is a basic feature of factual accounting, of the mind–world play-off, not just something located in the arena of sensitive social issues such as racism. For

example, it is commonly used in advertising (Edwards 1997). Extract 4
is an example from the interview materials.

Extract 4 (Appendix: New Zealand Interview 2: 245)

```
1. R:  Uhm (1.2) I would li:ke to see apartheid done away with (1.0) but can
2.      anybody come up with a-[      a (.) positive way of saying
3. I:                          [Mm mhm
4. R:  "This is how it can be done"
5. I:  Mm mhm
6. R:  It's all very well to turn round and say "Give 'em a vote"
7. I:  Yes
8. R:  I mean the majority of them (1.0) don't know what a vote is
9. I:  Mm mhm
```

The interviewee manages to make a case for retaining apartheid as
something that is forced by the realities of no alternative, a move reminiscent of one of Margaret Thatcher's famous arguments for her controversial economic policies in the 1980s. The notion that the speaker might
be saying this out of some kind of preference or liking for apartheid, that
is, because of mental disposition rather than world, prejudice rather than
reality, is further countered by locating his preferences as precisely the
opposite. He would *like* it done away with (line 1), if only that were real-
istically possible. Again, although this counter-dispositional construction
is a recognizable feature of talk about sensitive and controversial issues,
it draws on a very general device in factual discourse, which is making a
version factually robust by playing off mind against world, by formulating
a conclusion as reluctantly arrived at.

Extract 5 (Appendix: New Zealand Interview 2: 260)

```
1. I:  (. . .) d'you think there should be res- (.) restrictions on immigration?
2.      (.)
3. I:  How do you [feel about
4. R:             [Oh yes.= There's got to be.
5. I:  Ye[:h
6. R:    [Unfortunately,
7. I:  my[e:h
8. R:    [I would love to see the whole wor:ld y'know, jus where you: (.) go
9.      where you like,
```

Similarly in extract 5, R appeals to necessity (line 4), rather than
personal preference or desire (line 6), a disposition bolstered by a rather
extreme ("would love," "whole wor:ld," line 8) counter-preference for a
world *sans frontières* (lines 8–9). One use of "extreme case formulations"
(Pomerantz 1986) of this kind is to display, via the extremity of
a formulation and its potential for being non-literal or exaggerated,
the speaker's investment in, or attitude towards, what is being said

(Edwards 2000). In this case, R displays reluctance in supporting anti-immigration policies. Note that analyzing how talk works in this way entails no commitment to the reality of reluctance, preference, or any other mental state that might be conceptualized, managed by, or at issue in, such talk. These are ways of talking.

R's talk in extract 6 continues soon after extract 4. I include this final extract in order to point out some quite subtle features of this kind of discourse, and particularly of "knowledge unlooked for." Once again, we are concerned with participants' common sense, offered bases for knowing things and offering judgments.

Extract 6 (Appendix: New Zealand Interview 2: 245/246)

```
 1.  R:   E:hm (0.6) but- (1.0) I mean what African country
 2.  I:   °Mm mhm°
 3.  R:   that u:sed to have European ru:le
 4.  I:   °Mm mhm°
 5.  R:   that is now ruled (0.6) totally by the blacks
 6.  I:   Mm mhm
 7.       (1.0)
 8.  R:   What (.) one can you hold up as an example and say "We would like
 9.       South Africa to follow that (one)?"
10.  I:   Mm mhm
11.       (1.0)
12.  I:   [°Yes°
13.  R:   [Nigeria? Ghana? (1.0) Sierra Leone?
14.  I:   °Y(h)es°
15.  R:   °a:ny of them°
16.  I:   °Yeah°
17.  R:   Zem- m Zimbabwe or- >an' I don't know the names of half
18.       of them< it's [a long time since I was the[re
19.  I:                 [yes                        [yes
20.  R:   Any of them I mean [they are absolute (0.6) diabolic places
21.  I:                      [yes
22.       (0.6)
23.  I:   Well it's a very complex [problem isn't it that whole [thing
24.  R:                            [(ghh.)                      [I mean
25.       there are- [what is it I was readin (.) (somewhere there)
26.  D:              [yeah
27.  R:   nineteen of the (.) countries that [were colonized
28.  I:                                      [yeah
29.       (0.6)
30.  I:   °M[mm°
31.  R:     [there (0.4) are no:w (0.4) dictatorships. One party states
```

Consider lines 15–20. The expressions "any of them" (in both 15 and 20), and "I don't know," occur around a point where the speaker appears to be having trouble with producing further examples of ex-colonial African countries. As we saw with the item "you know" in extract 1, speakers' appeals to what is known, or intersubjectively available, are a pervasive feature of talk that can serve a variety of activities. "Any of them" serves here as a kind of "et cetera" clause (Garfinkel 1967), invoking a longer list of countries that might be enumerated, given time. It appeals to the notion that whatever the speaker is getting at is founded in solid fact, such that he would be in a position to fill in further details, to sep-arate Zambia from Zimbabwe (for instance), or to come up with further examples, if this information were only fresher in his mind (lines 17–18). Further, "any of them" directly bolsters, in a way that "you know" would not, R's block categorization of black-ruled ex-colonial countries as equiv-alent, having the same characteristics, and sharing the same awful fate. So the speaker's difficulty in naming and enumerating these countries is put to rhetorical advantage: they are all the same, QED. The important thing to note here is that appeals to shared knowledge, to what is known, or available to be known, or temporarily unavailable to consciousness, are categories that are locally and interactionally produced in this way, irrespective of what a speaker may "actually think" is known (Edwards 1997).

Ignorance claims, or claims about forgetting, are as interactionally po-tent as knowledge claims (cf. Beach and Metzger 1997; Coulter 1985; Edwards 1995; Lynch and Bogen 1996; Potter 1997). As I have noted, the "I don't know" formulation in line 17 flirts with the rhetorical danger, in this instance, of R's not knowing what he is talking about, of not hav-ing a sufficient factual or experiential basis for the contentious claims he is making. R has presented himself (prior to extract 6) as someone who has visited Africa, as a basis for knowing what he is talking about when recommending what Africans and Aotearoans should do with their lives. But what we get here ("It's a long time since I was there," line 18) are formulations of not knowing. We might ask, what are these "not know-ing" formulations doing here, in a stretch of argumentative talk where "knowing" might be thought more persuasive?

Formulations of ignorance can be exploited as a way of saying that one has not worked up one's position artfully, as any kind of prepared, re-hearsed, prior position on things. One is offering a series of observations, with no axe being ground. Consider line 25, "what is it I was reading somewhere." This does a number of things. It attends to R's knowledge claims as based not merely on out-of-date personal experience (line 18), but as also externally provided for, based on "reading." The items "what is it" and "somewhere" contribute something too, which is the sense of all this as something not seriously attended to, not information specifically prepared, researched, diligently noted, and so on, but casually obtained, from somewhere or other. And that helps to play down any notion, should it arise, that R is coming to these conclusions from any kind of concerted campaign against African emancipation. It is a formulation that might be useful if the place he forgot he read about it happened to be in the memoirs of ex-President Botha, or some pamphlet put out by the New Zealand National party. Of course, I have no basis for any such supposition, and I do not suggest it. But for a useful perspective on how claims of ignorance and of forgetting function in sensitive domains involving factual accuracy and speakers' accountability, see Lynch and Bogen's (1996) study of Oliver North's testimony to the Iran-Contra hearings.

Last words

The analytic comments I have made range from the very specific to the speculative, being an effort at demonstrating an analytic approach and what it rests on, rather than producing a fully substantiated analysis. More data and analysis would certainly be needed in order to pursue some of the lines of investigation that I have touched on. If the project were my own, I would also want to obtain more spontaneous talk in preference to interviews, difficult though that obviously is. The interviews are certainly very analyzable as they stand for the kind of work I do, as I hope I have shown. Indeed, I have tried to locate the analysis in the details of the transcripts as provided, and in the participants' own interactional orientations.

My aim has been to show how various features of "discursive psychology" are pertinent to the analysis of social issues such as prejudice and racism, and to social interactions such as interview talk. One basic point is that the resources for doing this analysis are also the resources used when approaching discourse of *any* kind. To the extent that "attitudinal" talk involves a play-off between mind and world, it shares that with mundane and institutional talk of all kinds, not just in recognized sites of prejudicial discourse, and it involves the same kinds of devices and rhetoric found virtually anywhere else we may look. One thing that the approach I have taken does *not* do is offer a historical or cultural analysis of where such participants' resources (devices, categories, positionings, rhetorical moves, etc.) might come from (see Wetherell and Potter 1992). But I recommend that any such investigation be grounded in examining what those resources are, in terms of how they are used (cf. Schegloff 1997). One additional upshot of locating them as very pervasive kinds of discourse devices is that it reduces, without removing, the explanatory burden faced by theories of race relations in accounting for the linguistic features of racial discourse (indeed, locating them thus provides a platform for such accounting).

References

Beach, W. A. and Metzger, T. R. 1997. Claiming insufficient knowledge. *Human Communication Research* 23, 4: 562–588.

Billig, M. 1985. Prejudice, categorization, and particularization: from a perceptual to a rhetorical approach. *European Journal of Social Psychology* 15: 79–103.

1987. *Arguing and thinking: a rhetorical approach to social psychology*. Cambridge: Cambridge University Press.

Coulter, J. 1985. Two concepts of the mental. In *The social construction of the person*, edited by K. J. Gergen and K. E. Davis. New York: Springer-Verlag.

1990. *Mind in action*. Oxford: Polity.

Edwards, D. 1991. Categories are for talking: on the cognitive and discursive bases of categorization. *Theory and Psychology* 1, 4: 515–542.

1994. Script formulations: a study of event descriptions in conversation. *Journal of Language and Social Psychology* 13, 3: 211–247.

1995. Two to tango: Script formulations, dispositions, and rhetorical symmetry in relationship troubles talk. *Research on Language and Social Interaction* 28, 4: 319–350.

1997. *Discourse and cognition*. London: Sage.

2000. Extreme case formulations: softeners, investment, and doing nonliteral. *Research on Language and Social Interaction* 33, 4: 347–373.

Edwards, D. and Potter, J. 1992. *Discursive psychology*. London: Sage.

1993. Language and causation: a discursive action model of description and attribution. *Psychological Review* 100, 1: 23–41.

Garfinkel, H. 1967. *Studies in ethnomethodology*. Englewood Cliffs, NJ: Prentice-Hall.

Gilbert, G. N. and Mulkay, M. 1984. *Opening Pandora's box: a sociological analysis of scientists' discourse*. Cambridge: Cambridge University Press.

Harré, R. 1983. *Personal being: a theory for individual psychology*. Oxford: Blackwell.

Harré, R. and Gillett, G. 1994. *The discursive mind*. London: Sage.

Jayyusi, L. 1984. *Categories and the moral order*. London: Routledge.

Jones, E. E. and Davis, K. E. 1965. From acts to dispositions: the attributional process in person perception. In *Advances in experimental social psychology*, vol. 2., edited by L. Berkowitz. New York: Academic Press.

Lynch, M. and Bogen, D. 1996. *The spectacle of history: speech, text, and memory at the Iran-Contra hearings*. Durham, NC: Duke University Press.

Pollner, M. 1987. *Mundane reason: reality in everyday and sociological discourse*. Cambridge University Press.

Pomerantz, A. 1986. Extreme case formulations: a way of legitimizing claims. *Human Studies* 9: 219–229.

Potter, J. 1996. *Representing reality: discourse, rhetoric, and social construction*. London: Sage.

1997. Discourse analysis as a way of analyzing naturally occurring talk. In *Qualitative research: theory, method and practice*, edited by D. Silverman. London: Sage.

Potter, J. and Wetherell, M. 1987. *Discourse and social psychology: beyond attitudes and behavior*. London: Sage.

Sacks, H. 1992. *Lectures on conversation*, vols. 1 and 2, edited by G. Jefferson. Oxford: Basil Blackwell.

Schegloff, E. A. 1997. Whose text? Whose context? *Discourse and Society* 8, 2: 165–187.

Smith, D. 1978. K is mentally ill: the anatomy of a factual account. *Sociology* 12: 23–53.

1990. *Texts, facts and femininity*. London: Routledge.

Smith, J. A., Harré, R., and Langenhove, van L., editors. 1995. *Rethinking psychology*. London: Sage.

Wetherell, M. and Potter, J. 1992. *Mapping the language of racism: discourse and the legitimation of exploitation*. Brighton: Harvester.

Wieder, D. L. 1988. From resource to topic: some aims of conversation analysis. In *Communication yearbook II*, edited by J. Anderson. London: Sage. 444–454.

3 Constructivist processes in discourse: a cognitive linguistics perspective

David A. Lee

Introduction

In this paper I attempt to apply the general framework of cognitive linguistics (Fillmore 1982; Lakoff 1982, 1987; Langacker 1987, 1988, 1990, 1991) to the analysis of a particular set of discursive processes in the texts that are the focus of the papers in this volume.[1] The processes in question are (a) categorization, (b) the construction of agency, and (c) conversationalization. By categorization, I mean the process whereby speakers adopt or construct conceptual categories of events and situations as part of the process of explaining and justifying the views they express. By the construction of agency, I mean the process whereby speakers identify what they see as the causative factors responsible for given situations (in this case the disadvantaged position of many Maoris in New Zealand society). By conversationalization, I mean the process whereby speakers mark the assimilation of "counterdiscourses" (i.e. the expression of other points of view) into their turns by such conversational features as *oh, sure, OK, yeah, alright*, and so on. Before developing these points, however, I should explain why I have chosen cognitive linguistics (CL) as the framework of reference.

One of the most salient ways in which CL differs from other theories of language is the central role of the notion of "construal." Whereas linguistic theories such as generative grammar tend to assume a level of autonomous semantic structure (represented in early models by the notion of "deep structure," and in more recent models by that of "logical form"), CL claims that the role of language is not to map some independently structured level of meaning onto linguistic form but to impose a particular "imaging" on a situation (Langacker 1990: 5–15). It is my contention that this feature of CL has the potential to make it a fruitful tool for discourse analysis. Underlying this claim is the view that discursive interactions are concerned in large part with the alignment of construal processes across participants.

The notion of construal involves a number of different dimensions. Of particular relevance here is the concept of "frame" (in the specific sense in which it is used in CL). This concept is invoked in CL to capture the fact that the meanings of words and utterances are inevitably located within, and understood with respect to, some larger conceptual framework. For example, a word like *wicket* (and, *a fortiori*, the kind of expressions in which *wicket* occurs, such as *take a wicket, lose a wicket, keep wicket*, etc.) would make little sense to anyone who did not know anything about the game of cricket, even if they were supplied with a dictionary definition, like that found in the Oxford English Dictionary (1989): "a set of three sticks called *stumps*, fixed upright in the ground, and surmounted by two small pieces of wood called *bails*, forming the structure (27 × 8 in) at which the bowler aims the ball, and at which (in front and a little to one side of it) the batsman stands to defend it with the bat."

There is, however, one respect in which the CL concept of frame is too restricted for discourse analysis. CL has inherited from other linguistic approaches the practice of focusing on decontextualized sentences, a practice that has led practitioners of CL to apply the concept of frame principally to words (cf. discussions of words such as *breakfast, orphan, blame, accuse, criticise, buy, sell, spend, cost, charge* [Fillmore 1982], *bachelor* [Lakoff 1982: 164], *lie* [Coleman and Kay 1981; Sweetser 1987], *mother* [Lakoff 1987: 74–84], *island, peninsula* [Langacker 1990: 7] and many others). One problem with this practice is that it tends to suggest that all the members of a particular speech community interpret words and expressions in "the same way" based on common frames of understanding. But this is clearly not so in many cases. The knowledge base of the individual plays a major role in determining the nature of the interpretation applied to utterances. As a small example of this point (discussed in greater detail in Lee 1990), consider a situation in which a garage mechanic tells a motorist that her car is not running well because of "a distributor problem." Clearly, the richness of the interpretation that the hearer assigns to this utterance is a function of the extent of his or her knowledge about the workings of car engines. Interpretive differences of this kind are best explored by the study of language in use. (For another example of the application of CL to discourse, see Lee 1997.)

Not only do we need to build into the notion of "frame" what might be called differential "cognitive" knowledge (e.g. different degrees of understanding about the internal workings of car engines), but also different discursive histories of individual speakers. For example, Frazer and Cameron (1989: 32–3) note that their respondents (teenage girls) do not have a unitary and consistent attitude to the topics they discuss (lesbianism, cot death, baby battering). They argue that the "contradictions" that characterize these discussions derive from the fact that the girls are exposed to a variety of "ways of talking," such as "the populist authoritarianism of the tabloids," as well as "the discourse of liberalism with its emphasis on the freedom of the individual, privacy in sexual matters, rationality, etc." In other words, such "contradictions" arise from the "plurality of concrete practices in any society." Clearly this kind of discursive heterogeneity is possible only if individuals have been exposed to (and participated in) a range of discursive practices, and if such discourses have become integrated into their knowledge bases. It seems plausible to suggest that the degree to which individuals typically adopt one type of discourse as opposed to another is a function of their personal discursive history, including the degree of exposure and the circumstances in which such exposure took place.

Another important dimension of construal in CL involves what Langacker (1990: 5) calls "profiling." Different codings of "the same situation" are the result of differences with respect to foregrounding and backgrounding. For example *John bought the car from Mary* "profiles" (or foregrounds) John's role in the process, whereas *Mary sold the car to John* profiles Mary's role. One reflex of this difference shows up in the way in which the phrase *for a good price* is interpreted in each case. In *John bought the car from Mary for a good price*, we would normally assume that the price was relatively low, but we would tend to make the opposite inference in *Mary sold the car to John for a good price*.

The concept of profiling is closely related to that of "frame," and indeed to categorization in general. Consider, for example, the opposition between the terms *European settlement* and *European invasion* as contrasting ways of referring to the colonialization of Australia. *Settlement* locates the event in a demographic frame, whereas *invasion* invokes a military frame. These contrastive framings produce different profilings. The military frame profiles or highlights those aspects of the process that relate it to prototypical invasions (e.g. the German invasion of Poland in 1939). *Settlement*, on the other hand, profiles quite different aspects of the process: those having to do with the notion of people coming to inhabit a place that is thought of as being previously "unsettled" in the sense of "unoccupied" (and perhaps also in the sense of "not at peace"). I return to this example below.

The constructivist nature of categorization

CL assumes a prototype model of categorization (Lakoff 1982; Rosch 1978), such that certain phenomena constitute central members of the category and others peripheral members (to a greater or lesser degree). The gradient nature of categorization, and the flexibility of the motivating factors involved in assigning a particular phenomenon to a particular category, make it a constructivist process. Since a given phenomenon can be assimilated to a number of different categories on the basis of perceived similarities with target category members, the process can become a site of negotiation and contestation.

In an earlier study (Lee 1992: 14–17), I considered an example of the constructivist nature of categorization that proves to be highly relevant to the transcripts that are the focus of this volume. The text in question is an extract from a book by the Australian historian Geoffrey Blainey. Blainey is the author of several significant studies of Aboriginal history, and therefore speaks from a position of some authority within the Australian establishment. In recent years, he has moved into the arena of public political debate with a number of controversial statements on issues related to immigration and multiculturalism. He has argued in particular that tighter controls should be imposed on what he calls "Asian immigration."

Blainey's text indirectly addresses the moral issues associated with the European presence in Australia, placing these issues in the context of Aboriginal history. It reads as follows:

> In central Australia . . . the Pitjnantjajara were driven by drought to expand into the territory of a neighbour. Several of these invasions might be partly explained by a domino theory: the coastal invasion of the whites initially pushing over one black domino which in turn pushed down other dominoes. But it would be sensible to believe that dominoes were also rising and falling occasionally during the centuries of black history. We should be wary of whitewashing the white invasion. We should also be wary of the idea that Australia knew no black invasions. (Blainey 1980: 88–89)

Here Blainey incorporates into the category of "invasions" the incursions of Aboriginal peoples into the territories of their neighbours in precolonial times. The point of this, of course, is to suggest that the moral judgments that apply to the European "invasion" also apply to "black invasions," thereby undermining the moral challenge that *invasion* poses to the term *settlement*.

The prototype model of categorization helps to avoid what would otherwise be a problem in explaining this dialectic. If categories conformed to what Lakoff (1987: 157) calls the "objectivist paradigm," it would in fact be difficult to explain the rhetorical effects observed here. Suppose, for example, that all members of a given category had equal status by virtue of possessing a given set of sufficient and necessary properties that define the category. Now if the defining criteria for members of the category "invasion" simply involved territorial violation, there would be no explanation for the fact that moral judgments relating to this category seem to derive their power from the connotations of the military frame, since military invasions (and all that they imply) would occupy no special status within the category as a whole. There would be no more reason to condemn "black invasions" than to condemn "tourist invasions," for example. On the other hand, if the defining criteria for the category "invasion" involved territorial violation by military force (in some Western sense of that term), then Blainey's attempt to assimilate aboriginal incursions to the category would be implausible, and therefore rhetorically ineffective. Arguably this is also true of the rhetorical move to which Blainey is responding here, i.e. the application of *invasion* to the European incursion into Australia (though this is clearly a more controversial issue). The problem then is how to explain the fact that "European invasion" and "black invasions" have the potential to attract the same degree of moral opprobrium, given that there are major differences between these phenomena. In other words, how are we to account for the fact that all members of the category seem to be equal in some respects (e.g. in the potential to attract similar moral judgements) but unequal in others (e.g. in terms of their constitutive properties)?

This problem does not arise in the prototype view of categorization. Here the privileged position of the central members of a category means that they have special salience, so that the connotations associated with them are potentially applicable to all members of the category. Conversely, the fact that categories also have a peripheral region means that the outer boundaries are permeable, allowing the assimilation of non-prototypical phenomena. It also explains the fact that some rhetorical moves might be judged to be more legitimate than others, and therefore to have different degrees of rhetorical impact.

Blainey's text finds a striking echo in one of the transcripts:

Extract 1 (Appendix: New Zealand Interview 44: 299/300)

```
1.  R:  And the Maori likes to forget that they came and (.) ate the Moriori.
2.  I:  Y(h)eah
3.  R:  They- they  [put that into the back of their minds.=They seem
4.  I:             [Yeah
5.  R:  to think that they were the fi:rst here
6.  I:  Yes
7.  R:  But really (1.2) I wonder if perhaps when we came here we should have
8.      done what any other (0.6) uhm invading country would do and that's
9.      WIPE OUT
10. I:  Yes
11. R:  the lot!
12. I:  Yes
13.     (1.0)
14. R:  Which is what they did
```

Like the Blainey extract, this text constructs a single category connecting (alleged) events in aboriginal history to the arrival of the Europeans. In both texts the motivation for this move is clear: it subverts interpretations of the colonial invasion as a unique historical event, to which special moral censure can be applied.

There are certain features that distinguish the above interview extract from the Blainey text. Here the process of category construction is enacted not through lexicalization (*invasion*) but through topic structure. The speaker introduces the eating of the Moriori in the general context of the discussion of the European incursion. This mode of category construction is less overt than the process of nomination used by Blainey. Nevertheless, there are significant similarities between the two processes. By discursively linking the Maori's treatment of the Moriori to the European presence in New Zealand, and by identifying the former episode as something that "the Maori like to forget," this respondent reifies the constructed categorical relationship. The effect of this process is to position the reader as someone who shares this construction, just as Blainey's term "black invasions" positions the reader as one for whom such a category is unproblematic.

A further feature of the New Zealand text involves the characterization of genocide as a *natural* component of the invasion process: it is "what any other invading country would do." This point takes up Wetherell and Potter's (1989: 214) observation concerning accounts of police violence. One general mode of mitigation of violence involves the construal of violent behaviour as a natural human response to certain circumstances. Again the concept of "frame" is relevant here. The speaker constructs a frame of conceptualization, whereby genocide is construed as the natural companion of invasion, thereby removing it from moral censure.

There is in fact an apparent paradox here. Although the speaker's view seems to be that genocide would not have been morally censurable in these circumstances, there is nevertheless a suggestion that the fact that it did not (quite) happen is to the moral credit of the invaders. This paradox can be explained in terms of there being two distinct discursive frames in play here. One involves naturalization of the invasion–genocide connection, the other involves conventional discourses on genocide. This observation connects with Frazer and Cameron's (1989: 32–33) claim (noted above) that it is a mistake to think of speakers as ideologically coherent. Individuals appropriate into their own discursive practices discursive tensions in the local social context.

The construction of agency

In cognitive linguistics the construction of causation is part of the process of construal. Most events in the real world are the result of the interplay

of many causal factors, so that agency becomes a prime site for interpretation and contestation. Langacker (1990: 214) makes the point in
the following terms, linking the construction of agency to the fact that
selectivity is one of the central features of the linguistic production of
meaning:

Linguistic coding is highly selective. Typically, a conceived event comprises an
intricate web of interactions involving numerous entities with the potential to be
construed as participants, yet only a few of these interactions and participants are
made explicit, and fewer still are rendered prominent. An example that should
make this graphically apparent is the following, not at all implausible scenario:
Floyd's little sister, Andrea, has been teasing him mercilessly all morning. An-
gry and desirous for revenge, Floyd picks up a hammer, swings it, and shatters
Andrea's favourite drinking glass. The shards fly in all directions; one of them
hits Andrea on the arm and cuts it, drawing blood. Hearing the commotion,
their mother comes in and asks what happened. In response, Andrea utters these
immortal words: *Floyd broke the glass.*

In an earlier work (Lee 1992: 17–20) I illustrated this point with reference to an incident in E. M. Forester's novel *A Passage to India.* When
Ronny arrives at Fielding's school, he is shocked to find his fiancée Adela
alone in the company of two Indians, Professor Godbole and Dr. Aziz.
The three of them had decided to rest and chat, while Fielding and
Mrs. Moore visited the school grounds. On Fielding's return, Ronny
rebukes him in the following terms: *I say old man do excuse me but I think
perhaps you oughtn't to have left Miss Quested alone.* Thus, through the
proposition "You left Miss Quested alone," Ronny assigns to Fielding
sole agency for a situation that was in fact collaboratively constructed by
all members of the group.

This tendency to explain complex situations in terms of individual
human agency shows up in the New Zealand texts in the way respondents
deal with the causes of social disadvantage experienced by Maori people.
Almost without exception these respondents identify the attributes of
individual human actors as the sole causative factor involved in both social
disadvantage and social success within a general discourse of equality of
opportunity.

Extract 2 (Appendix: New Zealand Interview 44: 301)

1. R: . . . u:hm (1.2) ya'know I think they do have a lot of opportunities that-
2.   that- that we haven't got and if they [can't make the most of them
3. I: [( )
4.   (0.6)
5. I: It's really their problem [I spose
6. R: [Yes

Extract 3 (Appendix: New Zealand Interview 44: 300/301)

1. R: But the ones who- who- who want to get on <u>do</u>! Tha- that's
2. I: Mm mhm
3. R: wh- (0.4) I mean there's some- some (0.4) terrific statesmen an' and
4.   (1.0) Maoris who've done ya'know great jobs

Extract 4 (Appendix: New Zealand Interview 16: 282/283)

1. R: and there are some- these two guys that <u>I</u> know, they- one's a Samoan
2.   an' one's a Maori, an' they're re::ally nice guys
3. I: Yeah (0.4) [mm mhm
4. R: [Ya'know he's- whenever they are out they're always clean,
5.   they're tidy
6. I: Mm mhm
7. R: well-presented [well-dressed, they- ya'know, they've got
8. I: [Mm mhm
9. R: ↑<u>bra:ins</u>
10. I: Mm mhm (0.4)
11. R: If the:y can do ↑it (.) so can the others
12. I: Yeah (0.6)
13. R: It's just that they want to

Extract 5 (Appendix: New Zealand Interview 2: 243)

1. R: But there's- If you've got a real <u>clever</u> (0.4)
2. I: Mm mhm
3. R: person I think (every) born in the back end of Otara
4. I: Y(h)eah!
5. R: the a [ya'know (0.4) they could (0.4) still finish up
6. I: [Yes
7. I: yeah
8. R: eh you know a Rhodes scholar or any[thing
9. I: [°Mm mhm°
10.   (1.0)
11. R: b[ecause ther- there's oppor<u>tun</u>ity there
12. I: [Yes
13. I: Mm mhm
14. R: for them.

Extract 6 (Appendix: New Zealand Interview 16: 278)

1. R: But then you've got the misfits that <u>don't</u> fit in.

Extract 7 (Appendix: New Zealand Interview 16: 282)

1. I: So do you thi- do you think there's any racial prejudice in
2.   New Zealand? (0.6)
3. R: Yes a lot. (0.2) But I think- (0.2) I think you- (0.2) they ask for it

Extract 8 (Appendix: New Zealand Interview 2: 242)

1. R: a:nd (1.0) <u>here</u> (0.6) eh you make your own (0.4) class

Extract 9 (Appendix: New Zealand Interview 44: 300)

1. R: The Maoris who wa::nt to get on and <u>do::</u> things <u>do</u> it
2. I: Yeah (1.4)
3. R: They <u>a:re</u> a lazy ra:ce most of them

Extract 10 (Appendix: New Zealand Interview 44: 302)

1. R: But if you're going to try and keep to em (0.4) an integrated
2. I: Yeah
3. R: society (0.4) they shouldn't have Maori ↑seats
4. I: Right [yes
5. R: [When someone like Ben Couch can go ahead and become an MP
6.   in his own right

There is a striking similarity here with Labov's (1972) observations that the relative lack of success of black children in the American educational system is often attributed to the personal deficiencies of the children themselves (and hence of their race) rather than to structural factors, even by "experts" in the field (e.g. educational psychologists):

If Operation Headstart fails, the interpretations which we will receive will be from the same educationalists who designed this program. The fault will be found not in the data, the theory, nor in the methods used, but rather in the children who have failed to respond to the opportunities offered to them. (Labov 1972: 208–209)

This tendency to identify the prime cause of complex social situations as the individual human agent (as opposed to social structures and social processes) is so pervasive that it requires some explanation. Part of this explanation must have to do with the obvious salience of personal agency in human cognition. Linguistic reflexes of this fact are (a) the universality across human languages of the notion of "agent" in the form of morphological or syntactic marking, and (b) the grammatical salience of the relevant markers. In English, for example, this manifests itself in the fact that almost every sentence requires a grammatical subject. In other languages the relevant grammatical marker may not be quite as salient as this (particularly if it is a morphological marker), but it would always rank as one of the most frequent formatives and (more significantly) one of the earliest acquired by children.

Crucially, however, the concept of agent is not only salient, but it is also subject to prototypicality effects. The prototypical agentive situation involves an individual human agent applying some kind of force to a typically inanimate object, as Langacker (1990: 210) notes:

> The archetypical "agent" role is that of a person who volitionally carries out physical activity which results in contact with some external object and transmission of energy to that object.

In other words, I suggest that several interrelated factors have a powerful influence on human interpretive strategies in the area of causation. These are (a) the inherent cognitive salience of the notion of agency, (b) the fact that the prototypical agent is an individual human actor, and (c) the salience of the corresponding grammatical markers in discourse. This is not to adopt an extreme Whorfian position; it would clearly be absurd to claim that language does not allow us to deal with complex causalities. What I am suggesting, though, is that these factors lead language users to look in the first instance to the individual human actor as the primary causative force.

It might be argued that the nature of local discursive practices offers a better explanation for these data than the cognitive explanation advanced here. These two forms of explanation, however, are not incompatible. The widespread distribution and persistence of explanatory strategies of disadvantage based on individual human agency itself requires explanation, and it is at this level that the cognitive factors I have indicated here have potential explanatory relevance.

Conversationalization

The third constructive process I consider here relates directly to local discursive practices. I am concerned with the process whereby respondents incorporate opposing views into their discourses. An interesting feature of this process is that, in a significant number of cases, respondents introduce these moves with discourse markers such as *oh, sure, OK, yeah,* and so on. I refer to this process as "conversationalization." The basic function of such discourse markers is to mark the speaker's response to a previous move by a conversational partner. In these transcripts, however, they have a different character, since they are not responses to moves by the interviewer. Rather they are responses to hypothetical moves by a constructed conversational partner. This practice enables speakers to elaborate their views, to pre-empt objections, and to suggest that they have formed their opinion after taking into account opposing viewpoints (Antaki, this volume).

An example of this process of "conversationalization" occurs in the following extract, involving the discourse marker *oh.*

Extract 11 (Appendix: New Zealand Interview 44: 288)

```
1.  I:   ↑Uhm (0.8) what are the things that you: value about living in
2.       New Zealand (0.6) things that (0.8) really appeal to you about life here
3.       or (1.0) that you see as the most positive aspects
4.  R:   Well we're not poo:r, none of us are
5.  I:   Yes
6.  R:   A[:nd
7.  I:    [Mm mhm
8.       (0.6)
9.  R:   You might think "O:h that's okay for her she's on a farm" but we're not
10.      I mean we're only employed
11. I:   Mm mhm
12. R:   Ya'know (0.2)u:hm (0.4) but there's no nee:d for anyone in
13.      New Zealand (0.6) to be ↑poo:↓r
14. I:   Mm mhm
15.      (0.8)
16. R:   A::nd (0.4) there's still plenty of ro:om (0.4) in New Zealand ya'know
17.      (0.2) and (.) if you want to live in the country you ca:n (0.4) even if
18.      that means going and renting a place you can do it.
```

The basic function of *oh* is to mark a change-of-state reaction to an immediately preceding "informing" by a conversational partner (Heritage 1984: 300). Here, however, it is clearly not a response to a previous utterance; rather, it marks a transition to another voice. The utterance *Oh that's OK for her she's on a farm* is the voice of a hypothetical interlocutor challenging the respondent's right to make the claim that there is no poverty in New Zealand. In other words, underlying this response is something like the following conversational extract, in which speaker A is the respondent herself and speaker B a hypothetical conversational partner, producing an *oh*-prefaced response to A's expression of opinion.

```
A:  We're not poor, none of us are
B:  Oh, that's OK for you, you're on a farm
A:  But we're not . . . I mean we're only employed you know[2]
```

Other examples of conversationalization are:

Extract 12 (Appendix: New Zealand Interview 16: 271)

```
1. R:  Ya'know it says- it says- in the Bible that'em (.) you're to honour the
2.      government because [the government's
3. I:                     [Yeah
4. R:  been put there by God
5. I:  Mm mhm
6. R:  And sure okay (1.6) what the government (1.0) may do may not be right
7.      but you have to honor what the government says
```

Extract 13 (Appendix: New Zealand Interview 16: 270)

1. R: A::nd (1.4) So I think (1.2) the majority of- >yeah=aw'right< the
2.   majority of the pro:-tour people
3. I: Mm mhm
4.   (0.6)
5. R: basically just wanted to go an' watch the rugby

In Extract 12, the phrase *sure OK* is clearly a response to an objection by a hypothetical voice to the respondent's claim that the government needs to be honored. In this case, then, the expression constructs a three-part conversational exchange of the following kind:

A: You need to honor the government
B: But the government isn't always right
A: Sure OK but you have to honor what the government says

In Extract 13 the phrase *yeah aw'right* seems to be a response to an objection to an utterance that the speaker had planned but had not completed, suggesting an underlying exchange along the following lines (with the planned completion in square brackets):

A: I think the majority [of New Zealanders just wanted to watch the rugby]
B: It wasn't the majority of New Zealanders who wanted to watch the rugby
A: Yeah, aw'right – the majority of the pro-tour people wanted to watch it

More schematically, then, we can say that these moves construct conversational exchanges that have the character of (a) respondent's statement of own point of view, (b) counterdiscourse from constructed other speaker, and (c) respondent's reaction to counterdiscourse. The process of conversationalization can apply either to (b) as in (11), or to (c) as in (12) and (13). These moves introduce into the discourse opposing voices that allow speakers to respond to potential objections, cf. (11) and (13), or to make concessions, cf. (12).

There are various ways in which we can interpret this process of conversationalization and the underlying interactions that it constructs. It may in part be a response to constraints on the role of the interviewer in this situation. Respondents must be well aware that the interviewer is unable to take on the role of a "normal" conversational partner, and in particular that it would be difficult for her to voice overt disagreement. At the same time, they probably know that the interviewer is indeed likely to disagree with some of their views. It is possible then that conversationalization functions in part as a way of compensating for these constraints, enabling respondents to engage the interviewer covertly in the discussion, but with the benefit that this engagement is subject to their control.

A further factor in the process may have to do with the idea that it is a mistake to regard the self as necessarily ideologically coherent. I have referred above to observations by Frazer and Cameron (1989: 32–33) to this effect. In a similar vein, Wetherell and Potter (1988: 171) note that "speakers give shifting, inconsistent and varied pictures of their social worlds" at different times, in part because of the fact that discourse is oriented to different functions. This view runs contrary to psychological trait theory (Eysenck 1953), for example, which views the self as a "solid, unfragmented, coherent character or 'personality'" (Wetherell and Potter 1989: 206). So, the possibility arises that the examples of conversationalization found here are the reflex of conflicts within the speaker's own discursive repertoire; conflicts that reflect discursive tensions in the host society and that are typically enacted in conversational interaction.

In making this suggestion, I am not arguing that there is a straightforward relationship between respondents' modes of expression and their previous discursive experiences. I am certainly not arguing, for example, that speakers simply repeat extracts of prior discourse *verbatim*. Work in cognitive linguistics is based on the idea that human experiences are subject to processes of abstraction and idealization as they are incorporated into human memory. Representations of structure and experience are schematic. In other words, I am suggesting that these discourses are derived from abstract schemata based on respondents' previous discursive experiences.

As evidence for this view, it is worth noting that the constructed conversational partner has a quite specific identity in some of these cases (and perhaps in all of them, as far as the speaker is concerned). For example, the challenge in (11) seems to come from an urban worker, one who would regard people who own and run a farm as members of a privileged elite. The speaker knows very well how her views would be received by such a person, and her response is tailored quite specifically to a challenge from such a source (*I mean, we're only employed, you know*).

The particular use of discourse markers illustrated here is another example of prototype category structure. In this case, however, the category involves functional, rather than representational, elements. The fact that the primary function of discourse markers is oriented to conversational interaction means that they can be used to invoke such hypothetical interactions as a means of achieving speakers' current rhetorical ends. Conversationalization is an enhanced discursive tool that helps not only to make presentations more lively. In constructing the presentation as a dialogic interaction, it has the very useful rhetorical effect of making sure that speakers have "the last word."

Conclusion

My aim in this paper has been to bring into interaction various elements of several approaches to linguistic analysis that have quite separate origins and quite disparate aims but that nevertheless share sufficient common ground to make the interaction potentially fruitful.

The recent emergence of cognitive linguistics has moved linguistic theory much closer to ethnographical and ethnomethodological approaches than was the case while the discipline was dominated by generative models. The centrality of the concept of construal within CL sits more easily with the view that language is the primary medium for the ongoing construction of social reality by social actors than does the view that language is a formal code for the mapping of an autonomous semantics. Concepts such as prototype category structure, motivation, frame, and profiling help to explain some of the ways in which respondents inscribe themselves in local discursive interactions and construct the conceptual bases for their moral judgments and explanations. This suggests that the paradigm shift (Kuhn 1970) represented by the advent of cognitive linguistics is an important development for discourse analysis. For the first time, a linguistic theory is emerging that has the potential to serve as a theoretical basis for an integrated approach to language, drawing on a wide spectrum of approaches to discourse.

NOTES

1. I am most grateful to an anonymous referee for insightful comments on an earlier draft.
2. There is one discrepancy between this constructed text and the speaker's actual discourse, namely the substitution of second person pronouns for the third-person pronouns that B actually uses. It would in fact have made perfect sense if B had said *You might think "Oh that's OK for you, you're on a farm,"* explicitly positioning the interviewer as an overt antagonist in the current conversation. The use of the third-person pronoun mitigates this effect, constructing the move either as a thought in the interviewer's head (to which she responds as if it were a conversational move) or as a remark addressed to some third party in some other (constructed) conversation outside the current interview situation.

References

Blainey, G. 1980. *A land half-won*. Melbourne: Macmillan.
Coleman, L. and Kay, P. 1981. Prototype semantics: The English verb *lie*. *Language* 57: 26–44.
Eysenck, H. J. 1953. *The structure of human personality*. New York: Wiley.

Fillmore, C. 1982. Frame semantics. In *Linguistics in the morning calm*, edited by Linguistic Society of Korea. Seoul: Hanshin. 111–137.

Frazer, E. and Cameron, D. 1989. Knowing what to say: the construction of gender in linguistic practice. In *Social anthropology and the politics of language*, edited by R. Grillo. Sociological Review Monograph 36. New York: Routledge.

Heritage, J. 1984. A change-of-state token and aspects of its sequential placement. In *Structures of social action*, edited by J. M. Atkinson and J. Heritage. Cambridge: Cambridge University Press. 299–345.

Kuhn, T. 1970. *The structure of scientific revolutions*. University of Chicago Press.

Labov, W. 1972. The logic of non-standard English. In *Language and social context*, edited by P. P. Giglioli. Harmondsworth: Penguin. 179–215.

Lakoff, G. 1982. Categories: an essay in cognitive linguistics. In *Linguistics in the morning calm*, edited by Linguistic Society of Korea. Seoul: Hanshin. 139–193.

1987. *Women, fire and dangerous things*. University of Chicago Press.

Langacker, R. W. 1987. *Foundations of cognitive grammar*, vol. 1. Stanford University Press.

1988. An overview of cognitive grammar. In *Topics in cognitive linguistics*, edited by B. Rudzka-Ostyn. Philadelphia, PA: John Benjamins. 3–47.

1990. *Concept, image and symbol: the cognitive basis of grammar*. New York: Mouton.

1991. *Foundations of cognitive grammar*, vol. 2. Stanford University Press.

Lee, D. A. 1990. Text, meaning and author intention. *Journal of Literary Semantics* 19: 166–186.

1992. *Competing discourses*. Harlow: Longman.

1997. Frame conflicts and competing construals in family argument. *Journal of Pragmatics* 27: 339–60.

Rosch, E. 1978. Principles of categorization. In *Cognition and categorization*, edited by E. Rosch and B. B. Lloyd. Hillsdale, NJ: Lawrence Erlbaum Associates. 27–48.

Simpson, J. A. and Weiner, E. S. C. 1989. *Oxford English Dictionary*, Vol. 20. Oxford: Clarendon Press.

Sweetser, E. E. 1987. The definition of *lie*: an examination of the folk models underlying a semantic category. In *Cultural models in language and thought*, edited by D. Holland and N. Quinn. Cambridge: Cambridge University Press. 43–66.

Wetherell, M. and Potter, J. 1988. Discourse analysis and the identification of interpretative repertoires. In *Analysing everyday explanation*, edited by C. Antaki. London: Sage. 168–183.

1989. Narrative characters and accounting for violence. In *Texts of identity*, edited by J. Shotter and K. J. Gergen. London: Sage. 206–219.

4 Institutional, professional, and lifeworld frames in interview talk[1]

Srikant Sarangi

Introduction

This chapter, like other contributions to this volume, is concerned with the interpretive procedures surrounding interview talk. In focusing on interpretive procedures, I have a two-fold focus: (1) how interviewers and interviewees as participants jointly accomplish the interview activity by taking on questioner and answerer identities, and (2) what inferencing resources are available to discourse analysts in order to make sense of the interaction order. In other words, my discussion will center around the accounting practices of participants vis-à-vis the sense-making practices of discourse analysts in their warranting and backing of claims. For analytic scrutiny, the interactional and interpretive framing of the interview activity (i.e., the how) is as important as the range of topics that is being talked about (i.e., the what). Equally, in the context of this volume, it is relevant to keep separate the participants' and analysts' interpretive procedures as far as practicable, while also acknowledging the fact that the researcher-interviewer who participated in the interview activity, unlike the discourse analyst(s) examining the transcripts, occupies the position of a participant-analyst.[2]

At first sight, it may appear that research interviews, by definition, are designed to access informants' lifeworld experiences in a structured manner. The participants, interviewer and interviewee, use the interactional resources available to them to seek/formulate opinions on specific topics (here racism, multiculturalism, etc.). The primacy of the question-answer format is indicative of the structural organization of the interview activity. Research interviewers will inevitably be influenced by their professional training in the conduct of this information-exchange activity. Interviewees, for their part, will relate differently both on the basis of their lived experiences and their assessment of the interview activity itself.

In what follows, I first draw attention to the topic–resource dichotomy, which continues to be debated across different sociological traditions of the research interview. I then go on to examine the research interview as an activity-type, with its attendant interpretive procedures. In foregrounding the institutionality of the interview activity, I suggest that the interviewer and the interviewee orient primarily to the task of information exchange, but they do so by attending to aspects of role-relations and facework, and by shifting between institutional, professional, and lifeworld frames in subtle, but different, ways (for a detailed discussion, see Sarangi and Roberts 1999).

Research interview as resource and as topic

As Silverman (1993) rightly points out, we now live in an "interview society." Opinion polls, market-survey research, job interviews, and political interviews are everywhere, and they fill our lives. Interviews, in this wider sense, are a means for gathering information, selecting a good candidate, establishing facts, displaying (dis)agreements, and so on. The dichotomy between treating the interview as a research instrument for collecting empirical data and treating it as a topic in itself meriting social scientific inquiry is a long-standing one. Often referred to as the resource/topic dilemma (Zimmerman and Pollner 1971), this tension generally applies to investigation of everyday life and the social order. However, in the context of research interviews, the resource/topic dilemma is embedded within a larger debate along the lines of positivism versus social constructionism. Let me briefly spell out these two traditions.

The first tradition, positivism, which stresses objectivity, assumes that research interviews (or other instruments such as questionnaires) are sites for generating raw data. These raw data, at the analytic stage, can be upgraded to count as observable evidence in order to (dis)prove specific hypotheses, and thus advance social theories. In addition to this simulated objectivity, which marks the essence of positivism, the informant is regarded as "the knowing subject" in the Foucauldian sense, as one who can provide access to social life, attitudes, opinions, etc. (see Prior 1997 for a discussion).[3] Generally speaking, individual informants are regarded as knowledegeable, and so, when prompted by researcher's questions, they can unproblematically access their deeper level mental processes and relate them accurately for objective scrutiny. Language is thus seen as a mode of representing external and mental realities in an unproblematic way.

A critique that is leveled against the positivistic approach concerns how the informant also simultaneously occupies the opposite of the "the knowing subject" position discussed above. As Holstein and Gubrium (1997: 116) put it, "in traditional approaches, subjects are basically conceived as passive vessels of answers for experiential questions put to respondents by interviewers."[4] Even here, language and interaction are viewed as transparent mechanisms. Interviewee responses are seen as offering facts beyond the interview situation, which can be categorized and evaluated to identify underlying patterns beyond the surface level of language and interaction. This process–product equation forms the epistemological basis of traditional sociological enquiry. To question the validity of the interview as an instrument would amount to questioning the epistemological and ontological status of empiricism.

The second tradition, social constructionism, focuses on intersubjectivity and the joint construction of reality in the local context. Among others, Briggs (1986), Cicourel (1964), Denzin (1970), Mishler (1986), and Silverman (1973) stress the jointly constructed, situated nature of interview talk, and thus question its factual, objective status. It seems though that the informant is still regarded as "the knowing subject" in this view, endowed with agency, in that his or her common-sense accounting practices are not dismissed as atheoretical. However, language is not seen as a transparent channel or conduit to reality outside the activity/text. In other words, it is not a pipeline for transmitting knowledge, attitudes, opinions, etc. World and words are not regarded as separate entities; rather, the world is the "worded entity" (Rose 1960). As Potter and Mulkay (1985: 269) suggest:

Although we have abandoned the traditional assumption that we can infer from interview talk what actually happens in the social realm under investigation, we nevertheless continue to assume that we can, in a more restricted sense, generalise from interviews to naturally occurring situations. For we are assuming that the interactional and interpretative work occurring in interviews resembles to some degree that which takes place outside the interviews.

This observation poses a set of interesting questions: can we rely on interview talk to make claims about social reality, in this case the scale and nature of racist practices in New Zealand? Or, is interview talk, strictly speaking, setting specific, and therefore without informational or communicative import beyond its occasioning? Is interview talk inherently different from naturally occurring talk? I have posed these questions in a way that pre-empts an either/or answer, although it is the case that interview talk is hybrid and multi-layered; it moves constantly between the social and the local; it is both naturalistic and simulated.

Among others, Miller and Glassner (1997) question the dualism between positivists (the view that a pure interview enacted in a sterilized context provides a mirror reflection of reality that exists out there) and social constructionists (the view that no knowledge about an outside reality can be obtained through an interview). The proposition that interview talk is meaningless beyond the context in which it occurs is too extreme. As we see in our data corpus, interviewees do fall back on "lived experience" to back up their denials of racist practices. But, given an opportunity of a follow-up feedback session, there is the possibility that informants would disclaim what they said in the interview as being setting specific. In its extreme form, then, interview talk becomes synonymous with playing the game, rather than committing oneself to the reported version of "real/lived experience."[5]

As Silverman (1993) points out, interviewees do not only construct narratives (i.e., setting-specific accounts in a responsive mode); they also recreate social worlds. This perspective aligns with the tradition of symbolic interactionism, which holds that knowledge about the social world beyond the interaction can be obtained:

The subject is more than can be contained in a text, and a text is only a reproduction of what the subject has told us. What the subject tells us is itself something that has been shaped by prior cultural understandings. Most important, language, which is our window in to the subject's world (and our world) plays tricks. It displaces the very thing it is supposed to represent, so that *what is always given is a trace of other things, not the thing – lived experience – itself.* (Denzin 1991: 68, emphasis added)

This pronouncement goes hand in hand with the current wisdom that language is more than a medium of representation. Within speech act theory, for instance, language is primarily regarded as action: we do things with words. Each occasion of accounting is an act of (re)production that bears traces of past histories while it (re)creates new meanings in order to accommodate different audiences. In the context of research interviews around the theme of racism, therefore, interviewees may be inclined to repackage their lived experiences so as to make them credible to the interviewer who is the co-present addressee and audience. Whether the interviewer is seen as a member of the ingroup or outgroup can easily influence what is said and how something is said.[6]

The topic/resource dilemma is particularly salient in the context of interview talk around sensitive issues, of which accounts of racism and discrimination are one example. In focusing on majority groups and their perceptions of racism and discrimination, as is the focus here and in the study of van Dijk (1984), the interview activity runs the risk of making the topic of racism salient and encouraging certain kinds of accounts, including denials of racism (Sarangi 1996). Indeed the interview activity itself can be used as a resource by interviewees, especially the dominant group, to deny racist practices with the use of a double strategy of positive self-presentation and negative other-presentation. Such strategies are abundantly present in the data corpus we have here. We can easily imagine how minority groups might likewise use an interview setting to affirm the racist practices of the dominant group, again using similar strategies (Essed 1991). In both instances, the interviewees display cooperativity in producing accounts based on "lived experiences," while also attending to the issue of self/other presentation in the local setting. The interview activity affords participants the opportunity to accomplish the interview agenda within the bounds of social-interactional resources available to them.

Research interview as an activity type

One particular analytic framework that is well suited to examining participants' interpretive procedures in research interviews is "activity type" (Levinson 1979).[7] Levinson (1979: 368) defines an "activity type" as:

a fuzzy category whose focal members are goal-defined, socially constituted, bounded, events with constraints on participants, setting and so on, but above all on the kinds of allowable contributions. Paradigm examples would be teaching, a job interview, a jural interrogation, a football game, a task in a workshop, a dinner party and so on.

We see here an analytical perspective that focuses on the ways in which "the structural properties of an activity constrain [especially the functions of] the verbal contributions that can be made towards it" (Levinson 1979: 370).[8] Levinson (1979: 370–371) also goes on to argue that "there is another important and related fact, in many ways the mirror image of the constraints on contributions: namely, the fact that to each and every clearly demarcated activity there is a corresponding set of inferential schemata." As far as participants are concerned, their interpretive procedures would display some kind of activity specificity. And this notion of inferential schemata also extends to how analysts should engage with their data.

Indeed we can see a parallel between activity-specific "inferential schemata" as outlined by Levinson above and the "documentary method of interpretation" suggested by Garfinkel (1967: 78):

The method consists of treating an actual appearance as "the document of," as "pointing to," as "standing on behalf of" a presupposed underlying pattern. Not only is the underlying pattern derived from its individual documentary evidences, but the individual documentary evidences, in their turn, are interpreted on the basis of "what is known" about the underlying pattern. Each is used to elaborate the other.

As an example of the documentary method of interpretation, Garfinkel (1967: 186–207) shows how medical records are treated as accounts that do not just report facts, but make available displays of justifiable medical work for later inquiries. In a similar vein, interview talk can be regarded as not being factual and objective as such, but as a display of a justifiable account. The focus in both Levinson's and Garfinkel's frameworks is on the indexical and context-bound character of talk/text.

There is of course some correlation between a given activity type and the talk/text it generates. Silverman (1973) points to what makes interview talk recognizable as such: "given that talk serves to display its setting (this is its reflexive character), talk becomes interview talk as members' managed accomplishment of a knowable context." According to him:

Such talk is never heard *in itself* but as representing or corresponding to some reality routinely available in the world (and of interest to the interviewer) in terms of which it must be decoded. This may be seen as a fact, a belief about what the facts are, feelings, standards of action, present or past behaviour, or unconscious reasons for beliefs, feelings, policies or behaviour . . . (1973: 33; his emphasis)

We can only make sense of what "interview talk" is by calling upon a body of knowledge of social structures "which provides ways of seeing what situated utterances really mean or signify." However, in this notion of "interview talk" we can also see the possibility of going beyond a one-to-one correspondence between physical setting and language form/function. When we turn our analytic gaze to interview talk as a topic of inquiry, we may discover that there are some stable features that are characteristic of interview talk (whether stylistic jargons or interactional features such as absence of receipt tokens, tolerance of pauses, etc. See below). In this sense, the recognizability of such talk as interview talk is no longer setting or context dependent. But what is equally significant is the level of fuzziness and hybridity that is characteristic of interview talk. In the spirit of indexicality and reflexivity, the occurrence of such talk will lead to (re)definitions of the situation participants find themselves in. We can stretch Silverman's (1993) view about the "interview society" to include the scenario that "interview talk" is everywhere.[9]

The term "activity type" does presuppose some kind of idealized total speech situation (in the Habermassian, Weberian sense), whereby nonconformity is likely to be regarded as a deviation from the norm, rather than a "(re)definition of situation." But we should bear in mind Levinson's point about fuzziness that makes boundary marking within and across activity types a difficult task not only for analysts but also for participants.[10] Note Levinson's stress on the identification of "focal members" of an activity type. He draws on the model of prototype as a way of moving away from the either/or model of truth–logic semantics. Also, Levinson's model does have an overtone that language users are consciously and rationally pursuing interactional goals. But if we set this form of individual rationality against the fuzziness of activity types, we can see how Levinson's framework is not as deterministic as it may seem at first sight.[11] It is this interplay between the interactional frames and the contents, as we have discussed above, which gives this framework a double-edged advantage to examine: (1) how participants orient to the activity on a moment-by-moment basis and (2) how discourse analysts have to position themselves in relation to their object of analysis. In Cicourel's (1964: 76) terms, this framework amounts to "how common-sense interpretations must be used as technical knowledge by the interviewer for deciding how the information obtained from the respondent is to be interpreted."

For our current purposes, it is encouraging that many discourse and conversation analytic researchers are beginning to treat interview talk as an object of analysis, although not in the activity-type-specific framework outlined above (Baker 1997; Hester and Francis 1994; Hutchby and Wooffitt 1998; Myers 1998; Rapley and Antaki 1998; Widdicombe and Wooffitt 1995). With regard to focus groups, for instance, Myers (1998) draws our attention to the tensions between moderator's constraints and participants' formulations of opinions, including (dis)agreements. One important insight that has emerged from such scrutiny is the fact that, like other interactional events, research interviews are sites for negotiating role identities, knowledge asymmetries, and so on, through a manipulation of discourse devices available to participants. Using the notion of activity type as an overall setting, we can draw on Goffman's (1974) ideas about frames and shifts in footing in order to account for the dynamics of participant structure as it unfolds in a given research interview activity.

The institutionality of interview talk

In talking about the institutional frame of the interview activity, I follow Drew and Heritage's (1992) lead that institutionality is primarily a matter of task orientation and inferential processes. The task orientation, broadly speaking, requires a conflation of different frames, but with the institutional frame retaining centrality.

Let us now consider the different realizations of institutionality, with specific examples from the data corpus. First and foremost, the institutional nature of the interview is manifest in the fact that such interviews are pre-arranged in terms of time and place, and that they are organized around a pre-set agenda, however tentative. In discursive terms, the institutionality is made visible by what we might call the "'definition of situation" (McHugh 1968), or, simply, the naming of the activity, which is primarily done by the interviewer. A clear illustration of this can be seen in the prefacing of questions:

Extract 1 (Appendix: New Zealand Interview 44: 287)

1. I: U:hm (0.4) The first set of questions are actually very (0.6) general ones
2.   (0.4) and people find them quite d(h)ifficult as a result I think. (0.6)
3.   U:hm (1.2) now first of all you're- (.) one of those people that (.) sort of
4.   feels a bo:nd (.) still with Britain . . .

Extract 2 (Appendix: New Zealand Interview 16: 278)

1. I: Finally (.) the last section of questions (1.0) is about 'em (0.6)
2.   New Zealand as a multicultural society (.) Do you think there's still
3.   differences between Maori and Pakeha people in terms of temperament
4.   and interests . . .

Extract 3 (Appendix: New Zealand Interview 2: 259)

1. I: Um this is a bit repetitive you've probably already answered it, but um
2.   that do you think um do you feel optimistic about race relations in
3.   this country, thinking particularly of the Maori/Pakeha, Polynesia/Pakeha?

Such formulations suggest that the interviewer is speaking from a script, thus making salient the structured agenda as far as topics are concerned. The metacomments (e.g., *the first set of questions are actually general; people find them difficult; this is a bit repetitive you've probably already answered it*) are targeted at defining the interview situation and, within it, the interviewer–interviewee identities. Mishler (1986) provides similar examples, but also shows how such prefacing can vary with different interviewers, and more importantly, produce different responses.

Definition of situation also includes framing of time, as interviewees are required to respond to questions such as the following from a specific context:

Extract 4 (Appendix: New Zealand Interview 44: 293)

1. I: I know it's a long time ago n(h)ow .hh can (0.2) is it something that you
2.   felt strongly about at the time=can you remember back to what you
3.   thought (0.6) during that period=did you think that'a (0.4) the
4.   teams should have come (0.4) o:r

This kind of framing, which has some resonance with psychoanalytic and therapeutic talk, suggests that interviewees have to offer an account of what they might have felt about an event in another time and place (i.e., their lifeworld experiences) in an institutional way.

While discussing the institutional framing of the research interview, we have to take into account the fact that both interviewer and interviewee are constrained by the frame. The following example in the medical oral examination setting concerns the interviewer's question regarding the candidate's suitability:

Extract 5 (Sarangi 2000: 8)

1. E: What are the features of your personality that you think that suits general
2.   practice?
3. C: It's very difficult for somebody to praise himself (. . .) but I'm in an exam
4.   and I have to give you a firm answer
5. E: Yes
6. C: And that's what I'm going to do
7. E: Good
8. C: I am a highly qualified person – I have postgraduate qualification apart
9.   from the medical degree [. . .]

The metacomment *I'm in an exam* defines the situation, and thus fore-grounds the institutional frame. This framing, which is acknowledged by the examiner (lines 5, 7), now makes it possible for a successful accomplishment of positive self-presentation. Much of the denial of racism and positive self-presentation on the part of interviewees in the data corpus, however, are accomplished implicitly without proffering a definition of situation.

From the participants' perspective, research interviews, like other interviews, are occasions where individual experiences and opinions are reframed to count as institutionally credible (cf. Gubrium and Holstein's [1995] notion of "deprivatisation," and Baker's [1997] discussion of "membership categorisation"). For example, interviewees do not only appeal to their lifeworld experiences; they also provide rational accounts to justify opinion. There is more than one subject behind the respondent: the "activated subject pieces experiences together, before, during and after assuming the respondent role" (Holstein and Gubrium 1997: 117). In paying particular attention to the metacommunicative aspects of interviewer and interviewee orientations to interview activity, we can see that interview talk is geared primarily toward "accounting" rather than "reporting."

Parallel with the institutional identities of interviewer and interviewee, both participants take on and demonstrate their questioner and answerer identities. Zimmerman (1998), in his study of helpline calls, suggests a distinction between discourse identity and situational identity: the former relates to taking up questioner and answerer identities on a moment-by-moment basis, whereas the latter refers to more stable forms of identities, for example, witness, complainant, etc. These two identities are however loosely linked, in the sense that participants may choose to retain one set of identities while flouting the others. As Zimmerman shows with the example of a prank call, the caller may refuse to provide the precise information sought by the call taker, and yet display that s/he is honoring the question–answer format.[12] What Sacks (1985) takes to be generic of conversation also applies here: the speaking right is usually retained by the questioner once a response is offered, and in this way topics can be controlled by the interviewer-questioner. This is done in the way s/he prefaces the questions (as in the examples above), and in how specific topics are sustained and/or terminated. In other words, both interviewers and interviewees have to sustain and monitor their discourse identities as questioner and answerer. However, the interviewer-questioner also has other (professional, social) identities that s/he may orient to, a point I will return to later. In fact, extending Zimmerman's example above, we can say that the institutionally sanctioned interviewer and interviewee identities make it possible for both participants to incorporate a range of available positions of speaking.

The occurrence and tolerance of long pauses can be taken as an indication of participants' orientation to the questioner-answerer identities. The following example is illustrative:

Extract 6 (Appendix: New Zealand Interview 2: 233)

1. I: What do you value most about living in New Zealand
2.   (1.4)
3. R: E::h hh. I don't know that's a difficult one .hh e:m (1.0) chm. I came
4.   here to make my fortune in the colonies (0.4)
5. I: [(((little out breath laugh))
6. R: [and'a (.) I'm still here
7. I: ((little out breath laugh))
8. R: a::nd (3.4) I just like the (2.4) way of life . . .

This question happens to be one of the general ones that is difficult to answer, and hence the prefacing in line 3 (cf. the earlier examples where the interviewer defines the questions as difficult). The interviewer posits a question to elicit a list of goodies about New Zealand life style (which finally follows, not shown above). This expectation of a list of goodies accounts for the tolerance for pauses, because the turn is regarded as a continuation of the interviewee's floor, and so interactional space is made available for the accomplishment of the list. The similar pattern of hesitation and pause can also be seen in the response to the question *do you see any disadvantages in living here* a little later on the interview. In fact, this pairing of questions (asking for advantages, followed by asking for disadvantages) shows that the questions are pre-planned and that they have an institutional character (it would be odd to follow such strict routines in ordinary conversation).

A further example would help to clarify this point:

Extract 7 (Appendix: New Zealand Interview 16: 263/264)

```
1.  I:  Mhmm. ↑So (1.0) if I asked you to pick out some New Zealanders that
2.      you admire (.) for their achievements what people (1.4) come to mind
3.      (1.2)
4.  R:  I don't know I've never really thought about it
5.      (1.0)
6.  I:  Well (.) I'll give [you a m(h)inute
7.  R:                     [U:hm what sort of politically [or
8.  I:                                                    [politically (0.4) e:hm
9.      culturally (1.0) people that you think have made sort of outstanding
10.     contributions (0.6) ya'know done- have done some- (0.6) the
11.     people that should be- (.) one should- you could almost use as a model
12.     for your own life (.) say
13.     (5.0)
14. R:  That's difficult I've never really thought about (.) that
15. I:  Yeah well don't worry if you can't
```

In line 4, R signals his unpreparedness for answering the question, and later goes on to ask for clarification (line 7). But what is interesting is I's comment in line 6, *I'll give you a m(h)inute*, which reinforces the institutional need for the maintenance of questioner-answerer roles, and, subsequently, for tolerance of long pauses (note the five seconds pause which follows the interviewer's attempt at reformulating the question after the elaboration offered in lines 8–11). Boden (1994) even claims that tolerance of long pauses is a characteristic feature of other institutional settings.

A further institutional aspect is realized at the interactional level through the interviewer primarily retaining a neutral stance, as is the case in news interviews (Clayman 1992; Heritage and Greatbatch 1991) or in business meetings (Boden 1994). For instance, in the data corpus there are not many receipt tokens such as "oh" (what Heritage [1984] calls "change-of-state tokens") from the interviewer, although the information provided by the interviewees from their position of the "knowing subject" must be newsworthy. Interviewers generally withhold personal opinions and evaluations of what the respondents say. Although withholding of opinion and assessment is commonplace in such settings, the interviewer in our corpus does occasionally provide "change-of-state-tokens," as can be seen in the following example:

Extract 8 (Appendix: New Zealand Interview 44: 302)

```
1. I:  Yes I- I'm going to interview [name of person] t- tomorrow morning
2.      a:nd [I'm going to ask him ([ )
3. R:       [Oh yes             [My dad taught him
4. I:  Really?
```

5. R: Mmm
6. I: ↑O::h
7. R: He's [father's name]
8. I: Yeah
9. R: And he taught him at [school name]
10. I: O::h yeah that's interesting

As I in line 1 announces her interview agenda beyond this local setting, R interrupts to volunteer information about the relationship between the person about to be interviewed and her father. This is no doubt newsworthy, as can be seen from repeated display of surprise in lines 4, 6, and 10. This example makes the point that change-of-state tokens are not usually present in institutional talk, and their very presence could potentially signal a change of frame, as is the case above. In other words, I and R jointly construct a side-sequence made possible within the institutional frame, as signaled by the receipt tokens. Therefore, a discourse analytic claim that absence of receipt tokens such as "oh," "really" is characteristic of institutional talk may hide the fact that such tokens are used as resources by participants to move between institutional and lifeworld frames.

The absence of "change-of-state tokens" corresponds with the prevalence of back-channelling cues, as is the case in many other institutional settings, such as medical interviews and news interviews. As Heath (1992) shows, when doctors deliver bad news, patients tend to use back-channelling rather than change-of-state tokens, despite the fact that the diagnosis is very likely to be newsworthy. In our data corpus, however, the interviewer uses back-channelling as a way of displaying listenership while remaining neutral, by not disclosing her own views and opinions. Natural conversation and interviews share "preference for agreement" (Heritage and Greatbatch 1991).

The institutional character of the interview is particularly noticeable at the transitions between topics, as interviewers tend to summarize the interviewees position. In a recent paper, Rapley and Antaki (1998) claim that the interviewer may skew information by generalizing what individual interviewees report with the use of a particularistic rhetoric. So, it is not just in the data analytic stage, but also in the interaction itself, that interviewers can introduce bias.

Interactional complexities and the multiple framing of research interviews

From what we have discussed so far, the interview activity appears to be hybrid and complex. As an activity type, it allows for shifts between different frames for both interviewers and interviewees. Within an interview,

I would suggest, participants initially position themselves in interviewer and interviewee role-identities, which are institutionally sanctioned, but they do not necessarily remain interviewers and interviewees for the rest of the encounter. The interviewer and interviewee identities are part of the institutional frame, but in occupying these positions participants are able to draw upon their lifeworld frames. Even the question–answer sequence, which is a definitional feature of research interviews, is open to variation.[13] Viewed from this perspective, activity type as an analytic framework allows for identifying these frames, but it also offers us a possibility of seeing how participants jointly (fail to) negotiate alignments across and within different frames. These frames are overlapping in a given interactional setting, but it is this interrelation which provides a useful basis for participants and analysts to make sense of interview talk, or, in Silverman's (1973) terms, "what makes it recognisable as interview talk."

The overlay of the institutional, professional, and lifeworld frames

From an analytic perspective, the distinction between institutional and lifeworld frames is perhaps less problematic. Mishler's (1984) characterization of medical discourse in terms of the "voice of medicine" versus the "voice of lifeworld" is a starting point, although his categorical attribution of one mode to doctors and another to patients is open to question. In the same way that both doctors and patients can speak from either position, interviewers and interviewees have at their disposal different frames to shift between.[14] Such shifts in frames, as we have seen, can be accomplished within the question–answer format. It is perhaps true to say that interviewers are more likely to orient to the institutional frame, as they rarely talk about their lived experiences. They tend to follow their own agendas as to what counts as an adequate response to a specific question. But there are occasions when the interviewer shifts to the professional and lifeworld modes, as can be seen in the following example:

Extract 9 (Appendix: New Zealand Interview 2: 259/260)

1. I: Yes, so you think um you think the best hope's going to come through
2.   assimilation really the sort of fusing of the best cultures together
3. R: Yes
4. I: Rather than what's called you know pluralism, or the separate
5.   development
6. R: Yes, I don't believe in apartheid ((laughs))
7. I: Yeah (hhhh) So there's no future really in the sort of importing Maori
8.   language into the schools or

```
 9.  R:  Not in my opinion no
10.  I:  Right um some people I've talked to actually think it was er I talked to
11.      someone from the New Zealand Party, um who said that he objected to
12.      er commissions for race relations and the Race Relation Conciliator and
13.      all the rest of it, because it prevented freedom of speech essentially,
14.      people become very self conscious about what they said or did as a
15.      result was was a sort of undemocratic loss of freedom
16.  R:  Well to me it gets it gets so ridiculous, you've been in New Zealand a
17.      few months, did you hear the commentary in the rugby match?
18.  I:  Oh yes the Maori side step
19.  R:  The Maori side step
20.  I:  Yes
```

Unusually, we see here the interviewer sidestepping the institutional role in various ways. First of all, she speaks in a professional mode, as someone who has expert knowledge about different forms of multiculturalism (definition of assimilation, gloss on pluralism and race relations). Note that the interviewee here is a merchant seaman, who can be spoken to at this level of sophistication. A further professional frame is realized when the interviewer makes salient her researcher identity (a form of social identity in Zimmerman's terms) when she foregrounds the interview agenda beyond the immediate setting (*some people I've talked to actually think*, *I'm going to talk to [name of person] tomorrow*). This episode ends with R drawing the interviewer's attention to her own lifeworld experience about the commentary in the rugby match.

Turning now to the interviewees, we would expect them to choose between different social identities that are available to them in light of the topic under discussion. It is also possible that interviewers may put the interviewees in certain positions of speaking. One social identity that may be available as a resource is the interviewee's professional identity. The merchant seaman, for instance, responds to the question *what's wrong with our economy* first with a preface, *I don't know unless I- unless I start- you start getting into politics*, followed by a back-up from his experience in his professional life:

Extract 10 (Appendix: New Zealand Interview 2: 236)

```
1.  R:  ehm (0.4) I mean we see it on the- (0.4) ships this a- I was complaining
2.      very bitterly just the other day
3.  I:  Mm mhm
4.  R:  We have an absolute useless drunk on the ship
5.  I:  Mm mhm
6.  R:  and he's a n:ice fellow but he's drunk [utterly totally
7.  I:                                          [Yeah
8.  I:  he needs [treatment
```

```
 9. R:              [incapable by [ten o'↑clock and all- >every morning<!
10. I:                          [Yeah
11. I:     ((ironic laugh)) Yes that's a bit off isn't it [.hh
12. R:                                                    [and ah he's getting paid
13.        twenty odd thousand dollars a year
14. I:     Ohh.
15. R:     and only from six months of the year to get it
16. I:     [Yeah
17. R:     [And he's never sober after ten o'↑clock
18.        (0.6)
19. I:     That's terrible isn't it
20. D:     Yeah
21. I:     So you can't get rid of him.
22. R:     No (I mean) the way the unions are a[t the moment
23. I:                                          [Mm mhm
24. I:     [Yes
25. R:     [I think- what you (want/ought) to do is a- a thesis into the a
26. I:     Mm mhm
27. R:     operation of maritime u:nions
28. I:     .hh (0.4) Yes (.) that would be in- Yeah thad be very interesting. It'd
29.        probably be difficult for me to get access to some of the (1.0) the
30.        materials
```

The topic of "trade union" partly prompts a shift to R's professional life, but, in choosing to talk about his drunken colleague, he manages to do two things at once. While offering us a slice of his professional life, he is able to demonstrate the helplessness of the trade union. However, this negative evaluation of the trade union is accomplished jointly, with I's two summary contributions *that's terrible isn't it* (line 19) and *so you can't get rid of him* (line 21) playing a significant part. To some extent, the very display of involvement on I's part may have contributed to R's suggestion about writing a *thesis into the operation of maritime unions*.

Although, as I have shown earlier, the interviewer usually refrains from displaying her own opinions and attitudes, we have several instances of evaluative comments coming from the interviewer. Such responses only illustrate how the interviewer slips away from the institutional frame and shares her professional or lifeworld experiences, however (albeit in a restrained way, as she does not volunteer to narrate her own experience). Notice, however, how the interviewer appeals to the lifeworld by prefacing some of the questions with, for example, *I have been away for six years*, as a way of signaling how the questions are a genuine attempt to seek information. At other times, evaluative comments showing agreement or disagreement, instead of institutional detachment, serve to foreground the lifeworld frame.

Conclusion

As Brenner (1978: 123) points out, the problems of the interview arise from its very nature: it is bound up with social interaction and the communication of meaning in language. This tension is even present in structured survey interviews (Suchman and Jordan 1990; Houtkoop-Steenstra 2000). Interviewees and interviewers are expected to attend to the rituals of social interaction while carrying out a predominantly information-exchange activity based on elaborate question–answer sequences. On the one hand, the nature of information exchange requires an asymmetrical role relationship (one as questioner and the other as answerer, the former seeking information, which the latter is assumed to have in possession). This is the institutional framing of the interview activity, as we have seen above, which both participants orient to. On the other hand, given that the activity takes place face to face and concerns a disclosure of lived experience, the participants also have to display conduct in a naturalistic way (Erickson and Shultz 1982).[15]

This tension between the institutional and the lifeworld is not only endemic to the interaction itself; it continues to haunt the analyst at the next stage of interpreting interview talk. Briggs (1986), among others, draws attention to the fundamental misapprehension about both the nature of the interview as a communicative event (in the social interactional sense), and the nature of the data that it produces. He points out that researchers as interviewers rarely examine the compatibility of interviews as a means of acquiring information with the ways in which their respondents typically convey information to one another. This has led him to convincingly argue that these oversights often blind interviewers to ensuing errors of interpretation (or to use his term, "communicative blunders"). According to him (1986: xiv): these blunders follow from the imposition of one set of communicative norms, those embedded in the interview situation, on a speech community that organized talk along opposing lines.

The general point here is that interview talk is not only a resource for social inquiry, but also an object of analysis in its own right. I have shown how metacommunicative acts not only define the interview as an institutional site, but also allow participants to manage the hybridity and ambiguity of the interview situation by shifting between institutional, professional, and lifeworld frames. In fact these shifts are crucial for managing the interview activity. This may suggest that a clear-cut methodological dichotomy between topic/resource is not very useful. It seems that the interview activity is both a resource and a topic for participants as well as analysts. As a resource, the interview occasions the possibility for participants to assess their views/opinions/attitudes as they slip between different modes. Thus, the Foucauldian notion of the knowing subject is partly valid, as it will continue to remain a tool for researchers to access peoples' lived experiences:

But the interview is still more than tool and object of study. It is the art of sociological sociability, the game which we play for the pleasure of savoring its subtleties. It is our flirtation with life, our eternal affair, played hard and to win, but played with that detachment and amusement which give us, win or lose, the spirit to rise up and interview again and again. (Benny and Hughes 1956: 138; cited in Denzin 1970: 122)

NOTES

1. A concise version of this paper was first presented at the Workshop on Methods in Discourse Analysis, 14–15 March 1997, Amsterdam.
2. The idea of examining the same data set from different analytic perspectives is a useful heuristic for scrutinizing the interpretive procedures that analysts bring to bear on data, including issues of proof and observability (Sacks 1985; see also Sarangi and Candlin 2001). For a parallel exercise in multiple interpretation of interactional data, see Dillon et al. (1989), where analysts of different persuasions (sociolinguistics, conversation analysis, discourse analysis, rhetoric, symbolic interactionism, etc.) debate the interpretive procedures they draw upon to account for their readings.
3. Indeed, Foucault distanced himself from this line of social inquiry as he developed his genealogical approach, which focused on "epoches," "epistemes," and "orders of discourse," rather than on individual accounts.
4. A strikingly opposite position is taken up by Pawson (1989). He argues in favor of a theory-driven interview format that calls for a rethinking of the role of the informant as data is constructed, rather than collected, around the theory in question.
5. At the time of writing, an interesting issue has emerged with relation to the Stephen Lawrence case in the UK. Following the murder of a black teenager, the media had covertly filmed the suspects' racist outbursts (including stabbing episodes) in a private, secluded place. The video clips, which are now in the public domain, can potentially be used as evidence against the suspects. But the mother of one of the suspects has claimed publicly that these clips are instances of "play acting" and "bravado." If we extend this tension to research interviews, there is apparently a risk that interview talk may simply be equated with simulated role-plays.
6. In several mainstream sociolinguistic studies, researchers take the precaution to match the ethnicity, gender, and so on, of interviewers and interviewees (see for instance the Linguistics Minority Project 1985). However, such a matching does not alleviate other difficulties at the relational and institutional levels between interviewers and interviewees.
7. Mishler (1986) calls the interview a speech event (after Hymes' [1964] notion of ethnography of speaking and Gumperz's [1968] notion of speech

community). It should be noted that these concepts are closely related, deriving from Wittgenstein's (1958) notion of language games.

8. Hymes (1964) was the first to suggest as many as eight variables (under the acronym SPEAKING) that can act as constraints in different activities in different societies: setting, participants, ends, acts, key, instrumentalities, norms, and genre. The main drawback with Hymes "taxonomic approach," however, as Levinson (1979) points out, is that it assigns equal significance and importance to all the eight variables.

9. Fairclough's (1989) notion of "discourse type" is useful here in order to capture how certain "talk-types" travel across and colonize different activity types (see Sarangi 2000 for a detailed discussion).

10. See Jefferson and Lee (1981) for an interesting account of how participants shift between troubles-telling and service-encounter activities. Similarly, Gaik (1992) provides a useful analysis of slippage between therapy and counseling activities.

11. See, for instance, Fairclough's (1995: 45) critique: "[this model] regards properties of a particular type of interaction as determined by the perceived social functions of that type of interaction (its 'goal'), thus representing the relationship between discourse and its determinants as transparent to those taking part."

12. In activity-specific terms, interviewers primarily ask questions based on an agenda, and this may explain why the question–answer sequences differ across institutional settings. While a research interview will allow for a lifeworld experience to be told in detail, as is the case in this corpus, in a police interview or a courtroom interrogation the questions will be framed in a way to minimize narrativity.

13. Several researchers, including Denzin (1970), even define interviews as one party asking questions and another party taking on the answerer role. This definition raises the question of what constitutes a "question," since respondents can use rhetorical questions in framing their answers, and is problematized by the fact that informants do ask questions of interviewers.

14. Focusing on interviews in the medical examination context, elsewhere (Roberts and Sarangi 1999) I have claimed that a major tension lies between managing the institutional and professional frames, both for participants and discourse analysts.

15. Labov (1972) refers to this as the "observer's paradox" (see also Wolfson 1976). For a general discussion of observer's paradox in relation to participant's paradox and analyst's paradox, see Sarangi (2002).

References

Baker, C. 1997. Membership categorization and interview accounts. In *Qualitative research: theory, method, and practice*, edited by D. Silverman. London: Sage. 130–143.

Brenner, M. 1978. Interviewing: the social phenomenology of a research instrument. In *The social contexts of method*, edited by M. Brenner, P. Marsh, and M. Brenner. London: Croom Helm. 122–139.

Boden, D. 1994. *The business of talk: organizations in action*. Cambridge: Polity Press.

Briggs, C. L. 1986. *Learning how to ask: a sociolinguistic appraisal of the role of the interview in social science research*. Cambridge: Cambridge University Press.

Cicourel, A. V. 1964. *Method and measurement in sociology*. New York: Free Press.

Clayman, S. 1992. Footing in the achievement of neutrality: the case of news interview discourse. In *Talk at work: interaction in institutional settings*, edited by P. Drew and J. Heritage. Cambridge: Cambridge University Press. 235–267.

Denzin, N. 1970. *The research act: a theoretical introduction to sociological methods*. Hawthorne, New York: Aldine.

  1991. Representing lived experiences in ethnographic texts. *Studies in Symbolic Interaction* 12: 59–70.

Dillon, G. L., Doyle, A., Eastman, C., Schiffman, H., Silberstein, S., Toolan, M., Kline, S., and Phillipsen, G. 1989. Analysing a speech event: the Bush–Rather exchange. A (not very) dramatic dialogue. *Cultural Anthropology* 4, 1: 73–94.

Drew, P. and Heritage, J., editors. 1992. *Talk at work: Interaction in institutional settings*. Cambridge: Cambridge University Press.

Erickson, F. and Shultz, J. 1982. *The counsellor as gatekeeper: social interaction in interviews*. New York: Academic Press.

Essed, P. 1991. *Understanding everyday racism: an interdisciplinary theory*. Newbury Park, CA: Sage.

Fairclough, N. 1989. *Language and power*. London: Longman.

  1995. *Critical discourse analysis: the critical study of language*. London: Longman.

Gaik, F. 1992. Radio talk-show therapy and the pragmatics of possible worlds. In *Rethinking context: language as an interactive phenomenon*, edited by A. Duranti and C. Goodwin. Cambridge: Cambridge University Press. 271–290.

Garfinkel, H. 1967. *Studies in ethnomethodology*. Engelwood Cliffs, NJ: Prentice Hall.

Goffman, E. 1974. *Frame analysis*. Harmondsworth: Penguin.

Gubrium, J. F. and Holstein, J. A. 1995. Life course malleability: biographical work and deprivatisation. *Sociological Inquiry* 65: 207–223.

Gumperz, J. 1968. The speech community. In *International encyclopaedia of the social sciences*. London: Macmillan. 381–386.

Heath, C. 1992. The delivery and reception of diagnosis in the general practice consultation. In *Talk at work: interaction in institutional settings*, edited by P. Drew and J. Heritage. Cambridge: Cambridge University Press. 235–267.

Heritage, J. 1984. *Garfinkel and ethnomethodology*. Cambridge: Cambridge University Press.

Heritage, J. and Greatbatch, D. 1991. On the institutional character of institutional talk: the case of news interviews. In *Talk and social structure: studies in ethnomethodology and conversation analysis*, edited by D. Boden and D. Zimmerman. Cambridge: Polity Press. 93–137.

Hester, S. and Francis, D. 1994. Doing data: the local organization of a sociological interview. *British Journal of Sociology* 45, 4: 675–695.

Holstein, J. A. and Gubrium, J. F. (1997) Active interviewing. In *Qualitative research: theory, method, and practice*, edited by D. Silverman. London: Sage. 113–129.

Houtkoop-Steenstra, H. 2000. *Interaction and the standardized survey interview: the living questionnaire*. Cambridge: Cambridge University Press.

Hutchby, I. and Wooffitt, R. 1998. *Conversation analysis: principles, practices, and applications*. Cambridge: Polity Press.

Labov, W. 1972. Some principles of linguistic methodology. *Language in Society* 1, 1: 97–120.

Hymes, D. 1964. Introduction: towards ethnographies of communication. *American Anthropologist* 66, 2: 12–25.

Jefferson, G. and Lee, J. R. E. 1981. The rejection of advice: managing the problematic convergence of a "troubles teller" and a "service encounter." *Journal of Pragmatics* 5: 399–422.

Levinson, S. 1979. Activity types and language. *Language* 17: 5–6, 365–399.

Linguistic Minorities Project (LMP) 1985. *The other languages of England*. London: Routledge and Kegan Paul.

McHugh, P. 1968. *Defining the situation: the organisation of meaning in social interaction*. Indianapolis: Bobbs-Merrill.

Miller, J. and Glassner, B. 1997. The "inside" and the "outside": finding realities in interviews. In *Qualitative research: theory, method and practice*, edited by D. Silverman. London: Sage. 99–112.

Mishler, E. G. 1984. *The discourse of medicine: dialectics of medical interviews*. Norwood, NJ: Ablex.

1986. *Research interviewing: context and narrative*. London: Harvard University Press.

Myers, G. 1998. Displaying opinions: topics and disagreement in focus groups. *Language in Society* 27: 85–111.

Pawson, R. 1989. Theorizing the interview. *British Journal of Sociology* 47, 2: 295–314.

Potter, J. and Mulkay, M. 1985. Scientists' interview talk: interviews as a technique for revealing participants' interpretative practices. In *The research interview: uses and approaches*, edited by M. Brenner, J. Brown, and D. Canter. London: Academic Press.

Prior, L. 1997. Following Foucault's footsteps. In *Qualitative research: theory, method, and practice*, edited by D. Silverman. London: Sage. 63–79.

Rapley, M. and Antaki, C. 1998. 'What do you think about . . . ?': generating views in an interview. *Text* 20: 3, 307–345.

Rose, E. (1960) The English record of a natural sociology. *American Sociological Review* 25 (April): 193–208.

Roberts, C. and Sarangi, S. 1999. Hybridity in gatekeeping discourse: issues of practical relevance for the researcher. In *Talk, work, and institutional order: discourse in medical, mediation, and management settings*, edited by S. Sarangi and C. Roberts. Berlin: Mouton de Gruyter. 473–503.

Sacks, H. 1985. The inference-making machine: notes on observability. In *Handbook of discourse analysis*, vol. 3, edited by T. van Dijk. London: Academic Press.

Sarangi, S. 1996. Conflation of institutional and cultural stereotyping in Asian migrants' discourse. *Discourse and Society* 7, 3: 359–387.

2000. Activity types, talk types, and interactional hybridity. In *Language and social life*, edited by S. Sarangi and M. Coulthard. London: Pearson. 1–27.

2002. Discourse practitioners as a community of interprofessional practice: some insights from health communication research. In *Research and practice in professional discourse*, edited by C. N. Candlin. Hong Kong: City University Press 95–135.

Sarangi, S. and Candlin, C. N. 2001. Motivational relevancies: some methodological reflections on social theoretical and sociolinguistic practice. In *Sociolinguistics and social theory*, edited by N. Coupland, S. Sarangi, and C. N. Candlin. London: Pearson. 350–388.

Sarangi, S. and Roberts, C. 1999. The dynamics of interactional and institutional orders in work-related settings. In *Talk, work, and institutional order: discourse in medical, mediation, and management settings*, edited by S. Sarangi and C. Roberts. Berlin: Mouton de Gruyter. 1–57.

Silverman, D. 1973. Interview talk: bringing off a research instrument. *Sociology* 7, 1: 32–48.

1993. *Interpreting qualitative data: Methods for interpreting talk, text, and interaction*. London: Sage.

Suchman, L. and Jordan, B. 1990. Interactional troubles in face-to-face survey interviews. *Journal of the American Statistical Association* 85: 232–253.

van Dijk, T. A. 1984. *Prejudice in discourse*. Amsterdam: Benjamins.

Widdicombe, S. and Wooffitt, R. 1995. *The language of youth subcultures*. Hemel Hampstead: Harvester Wheatsheaf.

Wittgenstein, L. 1958. *Philosophical investigations*. Oxford: Blackwell.

Wolfson, N. 1976. Speech events and natural speech: some implications for sociolinguistic methodology. *Language in Society* 5: 189–209.

Zimmerman, D. 1998. Identity, context, and interaction. In *Identities in talk*, edited by C. Antaki and S. Widdicombe. London: Sage. 87–106.

Zimmerman, D. and Pollner, M. 1971. The everyday world as a phenomenon. In *Understanding everyday life: toward the reconstruction of sociological knowledge*, edited by J. D. Douglas. London: Routledge and Kegan Paul. 80–103.

5   The uses of absurdity

Charles Antaki

This chapter is about how interviewees go about using absurdity in their expressions of their own views and their descriptions of others'. Expressing one's own views absurdly gets them registered, yet protected against the potential accusation that one "really meant it." It is a way of doing what the discursive psychologists Edwards and Potter call "attending to stake and interest" (Edwards and Potter 1992). Absurdity can also feature in descriptions of others' views. That is a riskier proposition, but it can be done if you cloak it in a certain kind of concessionary form (the "show concession," Antaki and Wetherell 1999). If you do, the absurdity damages the opposition's case while seeming fairmindedly to yield something to it.

Views and attitudes

Why approach these data with an interest in looking into speakers' expressed views at all, let alone "absurd" ones, and why look into them, as I shall be doing, by close examination of exactly how those views are delivered in talk?

The first question is easy. For one thing, it is hard to read the interviews, or listen to them, and not get a feeling that at least one thing the speakers are doing, at least sometimes, is expressing what we would say in short-hand are "deeply held" or "powerful" opinions; just the sort of thing that Michael Billig's pioneering work on arguing (1989, 1991) encouraged us to linger over as "strong views." Speakers time and again say things like "I think it's totally wrong . . ." and "I think it's disgusting . . . ," and so on. And they often put such things in ludicrous extremes: "I could shoot them all," "my politics are slightly to the right of Genghis Khan," and so on. So one thing that warrants our analysis is that this is a rather colorful feature of these data. The fact that they are colorful, when they need not be, prompts us to wonder just what it is they are doing.

But there is another reason besides. We will see that the speakers have these vivid views (or are led to have them) about Maoris, civil-rights protestors, and the police (to pick three things from the transcripts). As social scientists we are sensitized, rightly or wrongly, to see talk like that as telling us something about the traditional concerns of structural sociology: race, class, the State, and ideology in general.

At this point the quantitative researcher might raise a question. If what interests us are respondents' views about "societal issues," vivid or not, then why look at messy interview talk rather than cleaner questionnaire items? To express a view, surely, is just to express an attitude, and one could investigate such things quantitatively. We could maybe use the material in these transcripts as a pool from which, with appropriate pilot work, we could construct proper, well-grounded questionnaires and statistically hygienic variables for later work with a properly representative sample.

There is, of course, still a healthy trade in such work, as a glance at any social psychology journal will show. That trade might be interested in the sort of talk we see here, but only as a preliminary to the real work, which would go on elsewhere, with cleaner instruments offering greater control. We could make a contribution to the literature on attitudes toward social issues by digging up some raw clay from which proper pots could be turned.

But there has, since the 1980s at least, been a rival industry that uses the clay as found. It doesn't dispense with the notion of attitudes, just refrains from going the psychological step of insisting that they are mentally held, silent, and slow to move. Rather, since Potter and Wetherell's classic exposition of the argument in *Discourse and social psychology* (1987), the idea is to look at attitudes as shifting and partial devices by which social business is done in talk. The focus moves from the mental to the discursive, from the image of an attitude as something stored for preservation to something deployed for effect. Indeed, on the face of it, this seems to be better suited to the notion of attitudes in their everyday sense, and certainly when one remembers the vivid colors in which they can be expressed. It certainly seems appropriate to the sort of attitudes we see in these interview transcripts. Our speakers are not just locating themselves on some abstract questionnaire dimension, but actively conjuring up arguments volubly, in detail, and not impartially. And, of course, they have all the weapons of rhetoric to do it with, including hyperbole. You can say about yourself that you are somewhere to the right of Genghis Khan, but you are unlikely to put a tick over by the margin, beyond the last cell in the row on a printed questionnaire (and if you do, it will be ignored by the collator).

To return to Billig's analysis of "ideological" talk, his respondents are expressing "strong views" (Billig 1989) not merely as a matter of dusting down some well-preserved relics from the mental warehouse. They are conjuring them freshly. As the discursive psychologists Edwards and Potter put it, following Harvey Sacks' work on categorization (which I shall come to in more detail below), the expression of views is "organised rhetorically to work against widely available alternatives" (Edwards and Potter 1992: 165). If we follow this sort of account of "strong views," we have to move, as they do, away from traditional faith in stable attitudes, and toward a position that takes verbal expression more seriously. We want to spot novelty, indexicality, and argument. We want to see what it means to express views ludicrously, something you would never have the chance to do on a sober questionnaire.

Discursive psychology always wants to know what it is that the talk accomplishes, especially any talk that might deal in "psychological" terms, for example, attitudes, feelings and beliefs (Edwards and Potter 1992; Potter 1996; Edwards 1995, 1997). One of the most solid planks of its platform is that attitudes and so on are all working descriptions of states of affairs (the ethnomethodologists' "versions"; see, for example, Cuff 1994; Jayyusi 1984). Their expression promotes some end. Yet one is always on the watch that that end isn't too obvious or challengeable: one doesn't want what one says to be written off as merely partisan. So, as Edwards and Potter put it, one of the most pervasive features of descriptions is making them *not* look partisan. One designs one's talk, they say, so that one gives "accounts which attend to interests without being undermined *as* interested" (Edwards and Potter 1992: 158, emphasis added).

Views are displayed and received by participants (leave aside the watching psychologist) as being accountable, on or off record, jocular, deadly serious, and so on in a long list; it is up to the speaker and listener to dispose of them as they will. The discursive psychologist will follow the ethnomethodological line of looking to the participants to determine what has gone on; more specifically, he or she will follow the conversation analytic principle to see how the words play out in sequence, each turn following the other and getting its sense from what has gone before.

Responding and "expressing a view"

We might characterize at least some aspects of the data in these transcripts as conforming to the institutional pattern of an interview, in that the speakers work to a profound imbalance of rights and obligations to ask and answer questions. We see it in the design of turns, in the asymmetry in turn distribution, in speakers' choice of terminology, and in the overall structural shape of the interaction. All these features (which I take from Drew and Heritage's useful outline, Drew and Heritage 1992) communicate a sense of institutional goals being pursued. Given that the encounters are supposed to work as open-ended interviews, with the interviewer using such prompts as "what do you think about . . . ," "do you see any disadvantages in . . . ," "what kind of things . . . ," and so on, perhaps it is not surprising that much of the respondent's talk is going to be heard as expressing a view.

But how does the respondent ensure that his or her talk comes across as expressing a view, rather than reporting a fact, entering an objection, or any number of other possibilities? Let us leave aside the notion of how it might get registered as such in a sociological survey or a psychological assessment, and just concentrate on how it gets registered for the benefit of the speaker and hearer (in this, of course, I am following the ethnomethodological line on taking interviews as interactions first and foremost; see, respectively, Hester and Francis 1994; Hutchby and Wooffitt 1998; Silverman 1993). The first thing to do is to see how *else* a speaker's talk could be heard in this environment. One obvious alternative is answers to questions as factual inquiries. Perhaps because the tape or the transcription only starts once any "cover sheet" exchanges have passed, we don't see many of such exchanges in these data, but they are a standard gesture of any social science research interview where some record is to be kept of respondents' demographic characteristics. One of the few examples in the three transcripts we have for analysis is where the interviewer (I) asks the respondent (R), "U:hm (1.00) have you travelled at all or," and he answers, "I go to sea for a living." Presumably the interviewer's questions about age, profession, and so on, were treatable as affording "factual" answers.

It seems safe to take it that that sort of "expression of fact" is at least one sort of base contrast with expressing something as a "view," that is, something potentially arguable or controversial, and to be elaborated and backed up. The crucial issue would be that thread of disputability, the edge of anti-normativeness in the talk; otherwise, if what one said was blandly true or uncontroversially hedged, it wouldn't seem to qualify, at first sight, anyway, as a "view," let alone a strong one (it could, of course, be made to be so, if an interlocutor challenged it, or one went back and revisited it later, and so on, but we are talking now about how things are done on the first go).

That is a conceptual, armchair distinction that wants confirmation in how the speakers themselves treat the talk. If one looks for "disputable" versus "neutral" sorts of statement, perhaps the best illustration is in the contrast between the respondent's descriptions and those of the interviewer. For example, in this stretch, R is talking about the power of some organizations in determining who gets a job:

Extract 1 (Appendix: New Zealand Interview 2: 237)

1. R: If my son wanted to go to sea as an a-[as an <u>AB</u>
2. I: [Yes
3.   Yes
4.   (0.6)
5. R: The ↑first thing he would have to do would [be to get into
6. I: [Mm mhm
7. R: the [name of organization] (0.8) An' with me as his father he'd
8.   never stand a chance ((smile voice))
9. I: ((burst of laughter)) So there's a sort of patronage system

There are some obvious features of R's talk that make it come across as arguable, controversial, to-be-backed-up-if-necessary. The most prominent, perhaps, is his use of extreme case formulations (Pomerantz, 1986). The *first thing* his son would have to do is such and such, and he would *never stand a chance*. Contrast this with the interviewer's gloss of the situation as a neutral report of a fact of society: there's *a sort of patronage system*. No extreme-case formulations and, to make the description still more passive and unthreatening, no agent, and all mitigated by *sort of*. Or consider another example:

Extract 2 (Appendix: New Zealand Interview 2: 245/246)

1. R: Nigeria? Ghana? (1.0) Sierra Leone?
2. I: °(Y(h)es)°
3. R: °any of them°
4. I: °Yeah°
5. R: Zem- Zimbabwe or- > an' I don't know the names of half of
6.   them< it's [a long time since I was the[re
7. I: [Yes   [yes
8. R: <u>Any</u> of them I mean [they are a<u>bso</u>lute (0.6) dia<u>bol</u>ic places
9. I: [yes
10.   (0.6)
11. I: Well it's a very complex problem isn't it that whole thing

"I don't know the names of half of them," says R, and they are "<u>absolute</u> (0.6) dia<u>bol</u>ic places." Sweeping extremity. Like somebody *never standing a chance* (in example 1 above), Nigeria et al. being <u>*absolute*</u> *(0.6) diabolic places* is extreme and personally held. And like *there is a sort of a patronage system* in the earlier example, *it's a very complex problem* is mitigated, neutral, vague, and impersonal.

So there we have a simple exemplification of how one description can come across as "opinionated" by comparison with another (and it is hardly a coincidence that it is the interviewer's that is the less risky and more palliative of the two descriptions), and we have seen the glimmerings of extreme, highly colored descriptions. Later, in the second half of the chapter, I'll talk about how it is that the speaker can paint *others'* positions in outlandish colours. But for the moment let us concentrate on these extreme cases, and more absurd ones, in speaker's accounts of their own positions.

Extremity and absurdity

We have in mind, then, those times when speakers will use highly colored, extreme language in getting across their view of events. Those are the "strong views" we are puzzling over. But now let me introduce a distinction between two sorts of extremity. One is the sort we have seen already, and was identified analytically in Pomerantz's highly influential account of extreme case formulations. Pomerantz made the point that extreme case formulations (things like *burning hot*, *all day*, *never in my life*, and so on) were hearably different from "ordinary" descriptions; they cast the thing described as remarkable and rhetorically conclusive. We have seen how this is done here in the *first thing* my son had to do and *diabolic places*, and so on.

But Torode (1996) has argued that there is a grade of extremity higher than that. Certainly, he argues, locutions like *first thing*, *all the time*, *brand new*, and so on, are extreme, but they are all, nevertheless, conceivable. They are what Sacks calls "possible descriptions." On the other hand, Torode identifies a different class of descriptions that he calls "impossible." He argues that there seems to be a qualitative step between extremity and these other descriptions. A description of this latter sort, according to Torode, trumps a merely extreme description. A statement like "he wanted me *to be in two places at once*" or "she thinks I'm *made of money*" is not only a commonplace that helps to bring a topic to a close (Drew and Holt 1988). It is also a conventional impossibility that beats a merely extreme rival description like "he was *all over* the place" or "*thousands* of pounds"

Now I think that is right, and there is indeed a class of super-extreme (if we can call them that for the moment) descriptions that beat the extreme ones, but I am not sure I agree with Torode that their defining characteristic is that they are conventionally or conceptually impossible. Certainly the formulaic "impossible descriptions," like being in two places at once, and so on, clearly do work by virtue of their physical or conceptual impossibility, but other such extra-extreme cases don't. What I think is really the difference is how they are delivered and the context in which they come, aspects of which will make these sound *absurdly* extreme as opposed to *seriously* extreme.

An example of absurdity beating extremity

What I mean is perhaps best illustrated by looking at a stretch of data. Let us use Torode's own example, where he goes over some data from Pomerantz's collection to spot, first, a "normal" extreme-case formulation (the caller saying "everyone has a gun"). That is "normal" in the sense (for Torode) that it is conceivably possible that literally everyone *could* have a gun. He contrasts that with what he calls an "impossible" description (the call taker saying that he supposes that "you have a forty five and it's loaded and uh I suppose maybe everyone in Burnside Park has one"). This, Torode says, is literally impossible, and built to reject the merely possible extreme case that the caller is putting forward.

Extract 3 (Torode [1996], quoting Pomerantz [1986])

```
1.  CALLER:   Mm hm, It-u-Everyone doe:s, don't they?
2.            (1.7)
3.  DESK:     Yah ee- e-:ah::: ih You have a forty
4.            fi:ve and it's loaded
5.  CALLER:   Mm:mm
6.  DESK:     A:nd uh (0.4) I suppose maybe everyone
7.            in:hh evrywuh- in Burnside Park has
8.            one I don't kno:w
9.  CALLER:   Well no: but I mean- (0.2) a lot
10.           of people have guns
11. DESK:     Oh su: [re
12. CALLER:          [I mean it's not- (.) [unusual.
13. DESK:                                 [I s::
14.           I: see.
```

Torode's case is that the two descriptions are at odds with each other, and that the sequence plays out in such a way as to show that the call taker (Desk) is using his description to trump or beat what the caller is claiming. There is definitely something antagonistic going on between the two descriptions. Caller's claim defends her ownership of the gun, while Desk's description, pushing the case beyond conventional plausibility, queries it. That seems right; see how the caller backs down in line 9 (*well no but I mean.*) But I am not sure that this functional rivalry is brought about by one extreme description being literally impossible, while the other is not.

What I think is the difference between the two is that Desk's description, by loading more detail (*a forty five and it's loaded*) onto Caller's formulaic description, brings it crashing down as just ludicrous. It's the absurdity of this second description that makes the difference. Caller's claim that "everyone" has a gun is extreme, but not less impossible than

Desk's claim that maybe everyone in *this* place has *this* sort of gun in *this* condition, a "loaded forty five." What is different is the weight of detail that makes the latter state of affairs not just impossible but laughable.

So I am agreeing with Torode in seeing that there is a functional or consequential difference between two ways of using extremity, but I'm disagreeing with his claim as to the feature on which it hangs. One sort of extreme description helps a case be taken seriously, while another helps to undercut it. Where Torode sees the difference hanging on possibility versus impossibility, I think we should see it as hanging on something like "hearably serious" and "hearably absurd." I should stress that this defining characteristic of absurdity can only be absurdity-in-the-circumstances, because we are of course dealing with indexical descriptions that must take their coloring from the surrounding foliage.

Absurdity in describing one's own position

Now let us turn to see examples of absurd (or absurd in the circumstances) extremity in extracts from the transcripts. While all the descriptions in the examples below are certainly extreme case formulations, they go one step beyond that. Not to being physically or conceptually "impossible" descriptions, but to sounding ludicrous, laughable. In the first extract below, R is talking about what "things" are like (in the country, generally):

Extract 4 (Appendix: New Zealand Interview 44: 289)

```
1. R:  You can see things are wrong I mean every now and then you
2.     get stirred up enough to feel that ya' [know well I'd like
3. I:                                         [Yeah
4. R:  to go out an' shoot (Holmes)
5. I:  ((laughs)) yes
```

In this next extract R is asked about Waitangi Day, a national holiday in New Zealand to commemorate a treaty signed between Europeans and Maoris:

Extract 5 (Appendix: New Zealand Interview 44: 299)

```
1. I:  [. . .] Do you feel that we should ta keep on with Waitangi Day
2.     or that we should have some other day for a national holiday
3.     (3.2)
4. R:  Well each year there seems to be (1.0) quite a fuss over it
5.     and really uhm (0.2) I mean (3.2) it's just another day
6.     I mean (.) [ya'know you don't sort of think "Oh! the Treaty
7. I:            [Yes
8. R:  of Wai[tangi Day's today" ya'know
9. I:        [((laugh))
```

In both cases the laughable impossibility asks to be recognized as such, and the interviewer obliges with laughter. R designs her talk so that she cannot be taken "seriously" to mean that she will go out and shoot Holmes, nor that she "really" expects the interviewer to agree that one says to oneself, "Oh! the Treaty of Waitangi Day's today." Nobody would do either of those absurd things. So she can't personally be taken to be committed to them (far from it).

Compare those absurdities with "mere" extremity, where the description is not meant to be patently false, but just the opposite, that is, incontestably true:

Extract 6 (Appendix: New Zealand Interview 16: 283)

1. R: [. . .] there's no point in having a receptionist that picks up a phone
2.   "Yeah g'day 'ow are ya" ((strong New Zealand accent))
3. I: Ye:s (0.4) [mm mhm
4. R: [I mean they want someone that is- (0.4) that is
5.   gonna put their clients at ea:se
6. I: Right (.) [Mm mhm
7. R: [You don't wanna shop a- shop assistant who's smelly
8. I: [Yes
9. R: [Who's got un-dirty unkept hair [an' tatoos all over your
10. I: [mm mhm
11. R: arms [an' fingers all that sort of thing
12. I: [Yeah

There the arrowed, non-absurd, Pomerantz-type "ordinary," serious extreme cases make the claim undeniable; indeed, no one *would* want a receptionist who is all of those extreme things. The extreme descriptions help to make the speaker's case sound unarguably right. The speaker could happily defend it. Would *you* want such a receptionist, they could ask, "seriously." The absurd ones do just the opposite: they carry with them their own retraction.

What does absurdity do in such expressions of one's views?

Why should someone splash such mad color over his or her descriptions? To return to the Edwards and Potter argument that descriptions can be tailored to disguise one's own interests, it might be that clownish extremity is good camouflage. If there is something dangerous about an opinion cast neutrally, then casting it absurdly allows one to laugh it off. The upshot is that the talk gets said, but is eminently retractable. It was so absurd that it could not have been meant seriously. Indeed it invites laughter, not challenge, as we have seen above.

Let us finish off this section then by looking in a bit more detail at how the speaker uses absurdity to fend off a "serious" accusation, while at the same time getting his or her views heard and registered. Consider this example:

Extract 7 (Appendix: New Zealand Interview 2: 244)

1. R: They ↑want ↑separate de↑ve:lopment
2. I: Mm mhm
3. R: They want (0.6) a Minister of Ma- Maori A↑ffairs
4. I: Mm mhm
5.   (0.4)
6. R: ↑Where's the Minister of ↑Pakeha Affairs
7. I: Mm mhm
8. R: Can you give me his a↑ddress

This is an example of classical antithesis, or what Atkinson (1984), in his study of crowd-pleasing rhetoric, calls a "contrastive pair." It is an *X but Y* formula, with the *X* being a description of the Maori-rights case (*they want separate development, they want a Minister of Maori Affairs*), and the *but Y* antithesis being a *reductio ad absurdum*. There is no pretence of seeing the other side's point of view here; the argument is built deliberately as a visible destruction of the opposing case. The *X but Y* formula is used simply to parody the Maori case, without any claim that the speaker is showing himself to be "being fair" to *them*. If he's being "fair," he's being fair to his *own* side: where, he asks, in a (nearly) parallel formulation of what the Maoris want, is the Minister for *his* group? And, as a rhetorical *coup de grace*, what (absurdly!) is his address?

Using caricature in descriptions of others' positions

Absurdity in expressing one's own views, then, protects against them being "taken seriously," even as one gets them on record. Now let us see how one might do the same in describing the *other's* view or case. You could, in principle, simply describe someone's position *as* absurd: you could just say, "well, that is a ludicrous argument," and so on, but that might leave you open to simple rebuttal.[1] There is another way of doing the job, and one that is less challengeable. It involves, as we shall see below, setting up the talk so that what you seem to be doing is giving a fair account of the other party's position, as a *concession* to them.

The situation arises when the speaker is being "fairminded," that is, she or he is making plain the existence of rival, perhaps even opposite and disputatious, versions of what he or she is saying. This happens in an environment where speakers are making clear their appreciation of others' views. It was an early part of Harvey Sacks' work on categorical membership to show that speakers can turn such descriptions on and off in talk for various effects. Consider this stretch of text (from a newspaper) that Sacks uses (1992) to make the case that descriptions of sorts of people have powerful implications:

> How did he feel about knowing that even with all the care he took in aiming only at military targets someone was probably being killed by his bombs? "I certainly don't like the idea that I might be killing anybody," he replied. "But I don't lose any sleep over it. You have to be impersonal in this business. Over North Vietnam I condition myself to think that I'm a military man being shot at by another military man like myself." (205)

For our purposes I want to dwell on just one part of Sacks' analysis: "We may see one crucial matter here and that is that he [the pilot] takes it that there are alternative ways that he and those he is dealing with (bombing, being fired at by) may be categorically formulated" (1992: 205). By saying "I certainly don't like the idea that I might be killing anybody," the pilot is explicitly acknowledging that an alternative construction of the case might exist (that he might be "killing anybody"). The fact that he doesn't like that idea is testament that he has at least considered it; he is no careless automaton. And now that he has established that he knows what he is not, he can say what he is; that is, a military man being shot at by another military man like himself. The point, then, is that the pilot is designing his talk so as to make it clear that he knows that there are other ways of describing what he's doing. Once that's done, he then offers an alternative description of himself that now can't be heard as being mindlessly egocentric. He has been seen to acknowledge another view about who he is and what he does.

I want to extrapolate from that concern with other descriptions of one's categorical description to a statement about any matter, that is, to extend Sacks' insights to bear now on views about anything, not just one's own category membership and its implications. And in doing so I want to show how a caricature, absurd description can be smuggled into the proceedings.

Using an acknowledgment of others' views to smuggle in an absurd description

Let us see first how acknowledging the existence of another's views gives a good handle to give your own, absurd, spin on what they say. Consider this example:

Extract 8 (Appendix: New Zealand Interview 2: 245)

```
1.  R:   Uhm (1.2) I would li:ke to see apartheid done away with (1.0) but can
2.       anybody come up with a- [a (.) positive way of saying "This is how
3.  I:                            [Mm mhm
4.  R:   it can be done"
5.  I:   Mm mhm
6.  R:   It's all very well to turn round and say "Give 'em a vote"
7.  I:   Yes
8.  R:   I mean the majority of them (1.0) don't know what a vote is
9.  I:   Mm mhm
10. R:   I mean ya know the bright ones that have (.) been to school and
11. I:   °Mm mhm°
12  R:   run around the streets [ . . . ]
```

R uses a rhetorical question, studded with an extreme case formulation (can *anybody* come up with) to get across the view that apartheid can't be done away with. Perhaps later on we might see the interviewer offer a neutral gloss as part of her way of conducting the interview, and then we would have a clear pair of versions. But we don't need to wait that long. See how the respondent himself signals his appreciation that there is an alternative. One could, indeed, give blacks the vote: he has thought about that. In fact he has thought it through comprehensively, perhaps taken advice; all this is suggested by his question "Can anybody come up with a positive way of saying 'This is how it can be done?' "

Once he has got it on record that he has thought about it, he can then give his own view, without being accused of being blindly dogmatic. So he has built a fence of fairmindedness that might protect what he will now go on to say from the accusation that it is prejudiced. And look what he does say. He answers his own question with evidence that blacks cannot and should not be given the vote. To give them a vote would not be to do so after due deliberation, but to "turn round and" do it; that expression, very common in British English certainly, and seemingly used in the same vein here, has the sense of doing something on the spur of the moment, unthinkingly and against sober judgment. So to give somebody the vote on that basis, though it is possible, is clearly not very sensible. Moreover, R goes on to give still further grounds to reject the idea: most of them don't know what a vote is.

So, like the Navy pilot in Sacks' account, R has first inoculated himself against an accusation of partiality (as Edwards and Potter 1992 put it, in their descriptions of people's ways of preserving their neutrality in talk). He has shown that he knows that another view exists. Then he has gone on the attack, as it were, and got his own view across, but his description of the other view has helped his case along nicely. The general form of this way of building one's talk is to put it into a sequence where there is, first, a proposition or view, say:

And the protest movement *overstepped the mark* in my opinion.

then to follow this up with what is marked (by *ok, it's all right to*, and so on) to sound like a concession. For example:

Oh it's fine to march up and down the street protesting, I'm all in favour of that, it's an essential democratic right.

And finally to reprise the original with a contrastive "but":

but when *it steps over the mark* into the destruction of property into denying me my rights um then I think *it went too far* and the police had to step in with the inevitable scenes of violence.

Putting them into the sequence as it unfolded:

Extract 9 (New Zealand Interview not included in Appendix)[2]
1. R: And the protest movement *overstepped the mark* in my opinion.
2.   Oh it's fine to march up and down the street protesting, I'm all in favour
3.   of that, it's an essential democratic right.
4. I: yes
5. R: but when *it steps over the mark* into the destruction of property into
6.   denying me my rights um then I think it went too far and the police had
7.   to step in with the inevitable scenes of violence.

There is more detail about this structure, and how it pans out, in a paper by Antaki and Wetherell (1999), but you can see that it has a simple proposition, concession, reprise sequence. The view is stated, a concession is allowed, and the view is reprised (in the same sort of words, in the example above: *overstepped the mark* and *it steps over the mark*). The interesting thing from our point of view is the concession. It is at this point that the speaker smuggles in an absurd description. The respondent reduces the protest movement to one, rather silly, activity: they "march up and down the street protesting." This description is hardly what you would expect from someone genuinely sympathetic to the movement's aims. And compare it with the weighty description "the destruction of property," which the speaker sets against it. Clearly the concession form is being exploited to cradle a not-very-generous view of the other side of the argument.

Perhaps this is still clearer in the following example, where the concession is all the more obviously a caricature:

Extract 10 (New Zealand Interview not included in Appendix)

1. R: we're in an age (.2) now we're
2.   living in an age where um.hhh
3.   er (.5) people either want a
4.   physical or: a or a verbal
5.   at<u>tack</u> on- [on the authority (.2)
6. I: [yeah
7. R: and the authority is the police
8. I: yes
9. R: er they see that er this is where
10.   er the other portfolio where I come
11.   <u>in</u>
12 I: yes yuh
13. R: er they er- we had to maintain law
14.   and order
15. I: Yes yes. What hh er was there this
16   sort of a little (.2) group of Maori
17.   activists out there [>people like<
18. R: [yup
19. I: Donna Awatere and Ripka Evans and
20. R: .hh yes they are and er of course
21.   they er they've <u>got</u> a place er
22.   they keep the Minister
23.   for Maori Affairs on er (   )
24. I: ye(hh)ah
25. R: his toes otherwise what else would
26.   he have to do
27. I: tha(hh)t's right yes-=
28. R: =°yes° so they've got they've got
29.   their points of view but they are
30.   trying to apply it to *today's conditions*
31.   and it's what happened in eighteen forty
32. I: yeah
33. R: er was <u>tot</u>ally different.

We hear the speaker as conceding that Maori activists have a place. But why? Because otherwise the Minister responsible would have no function. This is, obviously, an absurd caricature. More than a mere extreme case formulation, it is one of those trumping, ludicrous descriptions that must demean what it is describing. It is not like saying that, without these Maori activists dominating his attention, the Minister would have less work to do, which is, in principle, possible (if very unlikely). It is saying he, a Government Minister, would have *nothing* to do, which is absurd, and hearably so. It certainly prompts a laughing reaction from the interviewer (lines 24 and 27).

But notice again that it is the bracketing show of concession that protects the absurdity. Without it, the absurdity might have been too nakedly
offensive. Being set up to be a concession, however, that is meant to be
(or sound as if it means to be) a positive, indeed rather jolly, thing to say
guards it against hostile fire. So the speaker ends up having gotten his
view on record, but not "seriously." If the only reason why one should
support these activists is that it keeps the Minister in a job, why, that is
an absurd reason, and so no reason at all.

Concluding comments

Speakers can use absurdity to get something on record (their own views,
their description of others' views) in such a way that they won't be held
seriously accountable for it. Such talk signals to any listener (be it the
people actually there or the sociologist who looks in later) that the expressed view is just the kind of sensitive thing that would attract criticism and argument. So absurd description can do three things. It can
be a sort of protective flag that lets the world know that the speaker is
aware of the arguableness or controversy of what he or she is saying. It
gets the description down. And it protects against someone "taking it
seriously."

How good is the protection? In all of the examples above, the speaker's
absurdity, even if not enclosed in the fairminded shell of a concession,
has elicited a cooperative laughter response form the interviewer. So
the protective coloring has "worked," for those speakers, in those interviews. But it might not. Perhaps elsewhere, where a listener is not
fulfilling an interviewer's institutional norms of neutrality, things can be
different.

Consider this, from the London-Lund corpus of largely middle-class
British conversation:[3]

Extract 11 (Svartvik and Quirk 1980: 638–639)

[Two couples, A and B and C and D, are talking]

1. B: but wait till you have a <u>baby</u> cos you'll find sort of dirty
2.   <u>nappies</u> in every <u>corner</u> and sort of banana skins all
3.   over the <u>place</u> (. .) I have a cousin a bit like you actually he
4.   used to throw his children bananas to eat (.) when they were
5.   hungry (he seems [to have)
6. C: [(gjum) (   ) ((*laughs*))

One can hear B to be casting her description not just extremely (in *every*
corner, *all over* the place) but absurdly: the image of throwing children

bananas conjures up the zoo keeper and a troupe of chimpanzees. It is laughable, yet the speaker has managed to get on record, jocularly or not, that she has some sort of discouraging view of what babies mean.

Does the protective coating of absurdity work? If we follow this conversation a bit longer, evidence begins to emerge that C, at least, is taking B "seriously":

```
7.  B:  yes -((it really looked like that)) just casually toss ((them))
8.      a ba:nana to a three month old child -tossed across the
9.      room- carry on writing his thesis (- - - laughs) it was
10.     an absolute pigsty -.
11. C:  I don't think this place is a pigsty
```

We are handicapped by the London-Lund corpus not notating things like "smile voice," so we don't know if C's comment is hearable as a loose-voiced, jokey admission, or, much more arrestingly, as a tight, offended rebuttal. Still, there is no outright laughter (which the LLC does include, for all speakers). So it is at least possible that C can be heard to take B "seriously" about the disorder in the house. C seems to be calling B's protective bluff of absurdity.

The immediate effect is that D offers a tentative laugh, then B comes in with a series of disclaimers, and the company makes explicit the gaffe she has made.

```
12. B:  it's not a pigsty [don't be so silly of course it's not
13. D:                    [[er:m] (- laughs)
14. B:  no this is. just.
15. C:  just a few piles of [newspaper around I suppose
16. B:                      [((don't be stupid)) no no I mean it's
17.     very nice I mean it's perfectly all right for two _people
18. A:  [(laugh)
19. C:  [(laugh)
20. D:  [(laugh)
21. A:  Deb you're digging a deeper and deeper pit - .and
22.     shortly you [will be forced
23. B:              [((yes)) actually I wish I wish ((you were a help))
24.     actually Arthur ((and you could)) sort of come in with some some
25.     amazingly diplomatic remark instead of in[s] in instead of.
26. A:  oh darling it's fun watching people
27.     [((people digging bigger)) pits
28. D:  [you're putting your foot in it again
29. C:  [yes I know. oh yes the only diplomatic way out
30.     is to change the subject very interestingly -(- laughs)
```

A makes the gaffe explicit, and B acknowledges it. The gaffe, on the reading I am suggesting, is for B's absurd description to have come across as a "serious" one. A speaker, then, might design her or his words to pass as madcap, non-accountable absurdity, but the protection is not water-tight. There is a risk that the absurd description comes over as extreme case formulation (which *seriously* establishes a case). If that happens then, like B, they might have to hope for help in the form of someone coming up with "some amazingly diplomatic remark," which will "change the subject very interestingly."

Absurd description, then, is not a foolproof way of getting your views on record without challenge. We could ask why it is that there is no such challenge in the New Zealand interviews, nothing that comes close to C's direct contradiction (in smile voice or not) of B's description. The New Zealand interviewer tends to offer laughter, or neutral formulations ("it's a very complex issue," and the like). Perhaps, as I say, that has something to do with the norms of interviewing, especially when the aim is to elicit the respondent's "own view."

Have we ended up then with a feature of these respondents' own views? Certainly I think we can say that here is a way in which the speakers set up a way of talking that simultaneously signaled something as controversial or offensive and got it on record, while pulling some cover over their heads in the process. We don't know, and can't know, whether they carry away from the interaction a disposition to do so again, or whether they have done so before, and in what company and with what effect. But if the aim of the research is to discover something about how strong views, about *anything*, are managed in the speakers' own interests, then we have something under our belt.

NOTES

1. In another interview from the New Zealand corpus not presented in the appendix, I only spotted one occasion where the respondent said something along those lines, but on inspection the delivery is more complex:

   I   . . . next part's about um New Zealand as a multi-cultural society and directions there.
        What do you think . . . I mean some people talk about a sort of renaissance of Maori culture
        [apparent in the language and so on?
   R   [Oh well that's a good thing, as long as they're not silly about it . . .
        Um you know they want their land back and this sort of thing; well that's all very nice
        but it's happened everywhere in the world for years

   "As long as they're not silly about it" nicely gets across the idea that they are nearly "being silly" about it, but not quite. So the speaker manages to hint (pretty strongly) that the opposition is being absurd, without quite putting her or himself on record as actually saying so.

2. Extract 9 is, like extract 10, selected from other interviews belonging to the New Zealand corpus not reprinted in the appendix.
3. Notation has been considerably simplified from the LLC conventions.

References

Antaki, C. and Wetherell, M. 1999. Show concessions. *Discourse Studies* 1: 1–32.
Atkinson, J. M. 1984. Public speaking and audience responses. In *Structures of social action: studies in conversation analysis*, edited by J. M. Atkinson and J. Heritage. Cambridge: Cambridge University Press.
Billig, M. 1989. The argumentative nature of holding strong views: a case study. *European Journal of Social Psychology* 19: 203–223.
    1991. *Ideology and opinions*. London: Sage.
Cuff, E. C. 1994. *The problem of versions in everyday situations*. Washington, DC: International Institute for Ethnomethodology and Conversation Analysis and University Press of America.
Drew, P. and Heritage, J. 1992. Analysing talk at work. In *Talk at work: interaction in institutional settings*, edited by P. Drew and J. Heritage. Cambridge: Cambridge University Press.
Drew, P. and Holt, E. J. 1988. Complainable matters: the use of idiomatic expressions in making complaints. *Social Problems* 35: 398–417.
Edwards, D. 1995. Sacks and psychology. *Theory and Psychology* 5: 579–596.
    1997. *Discourse and cognition*. London: Sage.
Edwards, D. and Potter, J. 1992. *Discursive psychology*. London: Sage.
Hester, S. and Francis, D. 1994. Doing data: the local organization of a sociological interview. *British Journal of Sociology* 45: 675–695.
Hutchby, I. and Wooffitt, R. 1998. *Conversation analysis*. Cambridge: Polity Press.
Jayyusi, L. 1984. *Categorization and the moral order*. Boston and London: Routledge and Kegan Paul.
Pomerantz, A. M. 1986. Extreme case formulations: a way of legitimizing claims. *Human Studies* 9: 219–230.
Potter, J. 1996. *Representing reality*. London: Sage.
Potter, J. and Wetherell, M. 1987. *Discourse and social psychology: beyond attitudes and behaviour*. London: Sage.
Sacks, H. 1992. *Lectures on conversation*, vols. 1 and 2, edited by G. Jefferson. Oxford: Basil Blackwell.
Silverman, D. 1993. *Interpreting qualitative data*. London: Sage.
Svartvik, J. and Quirk, R. 1980. *A corpus of conversational English*. Lund, Sweden: Gleerup.
Torode, B. 1996. Humor as impossible description. Paper delivered at the 5th International Pragmatics Conference, Mexico City, Mexico.

6   Multiple voices in talking race: Pakeha reported speech in the discursive construction of the racial other

Richard Buttny

Starting from the premise that "the racial other" is a discursive object socially constructed through talk, this chapter examines a particular kind of talk, reported speech, and how it is used to articulate Pakeha positions. Reporting speech, for example, quoting another's words, can be a powerful conversational practice due to "the double-voiced quality" of those words (Bakhtin 1984), in that the words of the original speaker are given voice by the reporting speaker. In giving voice to another's words through reported speech, the current speaker also assesses that speech and discursively positions him/herself in relation to it. In this chapter, Pakeha talk about the other is examined through a consideration of reported speech and its surrounding sequential context.

Discursive constructions of the racial other

Racial categories are commonly thought of as reflecting natural groupings of peoples based on cultural or physiological differences. Contrary to this common-sense view, there seems to be a growing consensus that such categories are discursive constructions rather than natural categories reflecting inherent (essentialized or genetic) differences among peoples (Miles 1989; Sanjek 1994; Winant 1994). As a discursive construction, the notion of "the other" involves the ways people talk and represent social realities about difference, particularly racial, ethnic, or cultural difference (Houston 1994; Verkuyten, DeJong, and Masson 1995; Wetherell and Potter 1992).

In the literature, most discourse analyses have examined Whites' (e.g., Northern Europeans, North Americans, New Zealanders) talk about racial others. A recurring finding is that much of the Whites' talk draws on a rhetoric that emphasizes the differences between Whites and the ethnic/racial/cultural other (Van Dijk 1987). These differences are the source of Whites' criticisms or complaints about the behaviors or qualities of the other.

In these studies, however, there are few explicit, old-style racist comments from Whites due to proscriptions against sounding prejudiced
(Billig et al. 1988). As a solution to this dilemma of wanting to criticize
but not wanting to be heard as prejudiced, participants design their comments to be heard as reasoned. One way to do this is to present arguments
to justify their criticisms (Van Dijk 1987; Wetherell and Potter 1992). For
instance, narratives may be told in which Blacks' actions create a com-
plication that remains unresolved, thereby implicating that they are the
continuing source of problems for Whites (Van Dijk 1993). Narratives
and concrete examples give the discourse a seemingly "factual" basis
(Potter 1997).

Other interpretative repertoires (e.g., descriptions, metaphors, vivid
images) have been studied to show how difference becomes discursively
constructed (Wetherell and Potter 1992). The racial other is largely represented in critical or stereotypical ways, as responsible for crime and
disorder, as receiving undeserved advantages from government policies,
or as having attributes that prevent their assimilation into society (Mehan
1997). Whites describe themselves in favorable terms, as "reasonable,"
"well-intentioned," or "tolerant" (Verkuyten, Dejong, and Masson 1995;
van Dijk 1987). In forming their arguments, Whites can be heard to be
drawing on preexisting discursive formations on ethnicity and race (Omi
and Winant 1994), and institutions may be heard to speak through individuals (Mehan 1997).

Reported speech as a conversational practice

The idea of using reported speech in this analysis grew out of my reading
of Basso's *Portraits of the Whiteman* (1979), in which a Native-American
people, the Western Apache, recounted stories of their encounters with
Whites and ridiculed and made fun of them by drawing on their words
and actions. Reported speech seemed to be a useful lens for studies in
talking race on campus (Buttny 1997; Buttny and Williams 2000). What
someone has purportedly said can be reconstructed in our own talk. The
issue of accuracy is bracketed, and reported speech is taken as serving
the reporting speaker's own purposes.

This practice of using another's words to make one's own point reflects
a "double-voiced discourse" (Bakhtin 1984). As Bakhtin (1986: 89) puts
it, "Our speech . . . is filled with others' words . . . (t)hese words of others
carry with them their own expression, their own evaluative tone, which we
assimilate, rework, and re-accentuate." This "assimilat[ing], rework[ing],
and re-accentuat[ing]" of another's words into our own suggests a

"dialogic relationship" between our speech and that of the other (Bakhtin 1984). That is, our speech is dialogic; it draws on multiple voices that are juxtaposed. So in reported speech, we have the voice of the teller, the report*ing* speaker, and the voice of one quoted, the report*ed* speaker (Volosinov 1971).

In talking about race, people can draw on a variety of conversational resources: they can tell narratives of incidents, make general claims about the state of relations, give examples from their own experiences, draw on images from the media, or propose common-sense explanations. Participants can also draw on what another said as a part of a narrative or claim about racial/ethnic conditions as a resource. This practice of reporting another's, or one's own, speech seemed to me to be a particularly rich phenomenon for investigating how the other is discursively constructed.

There are various types of reported speech (Goffman 1974; Tannen 1989; Volishonov 1971). The familiar distinction between direct and indirect speech breaks down (for a discussion see Sternberg 1982). For our purposes, two types of reported speech appear in the New Zealand data: *direct reported speech* and *prototypical speech* (adapted from Payne n.d.). Direct reported speech involves supposedly quoting the speech of the original speaker. So in 1, A directly reports the speech of "one of the guys" in lines 2–3.

Extract 1 Two African Americans (Buttny 1997: 495–496)
1. A: It killed me that one of the guys said (.) he said something like
2.   where do you see Black people at you don't see them on
3.   campus where do you meet them at
4.   I felt like I was an alien you know

A speaker may wish to summarize a group's discourse through a quote of a prototypical group member, prototypical reported speech. This resource allows the reporting speaker to epitomize the group through their characteristic utterances. For example, in extract 2 C draws on the prototypical voice of "the White students" in saying "well I didn't put it out" (line 2).

Extract 2 Four Latinos (Buttny 1997: 485)
1. C: it was ridiculous the way the White students reacted
2.   was like well I didn't put it out
3.   and it became an individual thing
4.   and it wasn't a matter of
5.   someone of my race offended you and something should be done
6.   and the students were taken out of the dorm . . .

Direct reported speech purports to quote the words of an individual, while prototypical speech purports to capture the words of the group, as articulated through the prototypical individual.

Reported speech may be seen as a *conversational resource* that speakers can draw on in reconstructing events. Of course narratives could be told, and arguments could be made, without the use of reported speech. But given the fact that reported speech is used, we need to specify what it is doing and how it functions. Reported speech can work as a way to provide evidence (Hill and Irvine 1993). By directly quoting another's speech, the reporting speaker supposedly removes his/her own interpretation and "objectively" reports what another said (Holt 1996). Also, invoking another's words is a way to hold them accountable (Buttny 1993) or responsible. Many of the instances of reported speech quote out-group members in order to criticize or complain about some troublesome incidents. Reported speech can help to involve recipients (Tannen 1989) since they are shown, rather than told, what happened through the reported actor's own words (Sternberg 1982). Reported speech also allows reporting speakers to distance themselves from the message (Macaulay 1987), since they position themselves as merely the animator, but not the source, of what is being said (Goffman 1981). In discussing contested topics such as race, this distancing function of reported speech seems especially salient.

Reporting speech is not simply a "reporting." It also involves making evaluations or assessments of what was said. Reported speech makes relevant an assessment from the teller or recipient. The assessment component tells interlocutors how to interpret or frame the reported speech; it displays the teller's positioning toward the quote. These assessments most explicitly reveal the discursive reasoning in talking race.

Analytic perspective and methods

Given that I want to look at what reported speech can tell us about race as well as reported speech as a conversational practice, methods that combine discursive analysis with conversation analysis seem most useful: discursive conversation analysis. Conversation analysis provides analytic tools to describe practices such as reported speech, and discursive analysis allows us to get at participants' positioning and their discursive construction of the other.

The data for this study are transcribed interviews. Instead of taking interviews in the empiricist tradition as answers (e.g., attitudes, opinions) to specified questions, these interview transcripts are taken as conversation (Mishler 1986). Interviewer and interviewee are seen as co-producing the conversation. I use conversation analytic methods (Heritage 1984; Pomerantz and Fehr 1997) not to look at the issue of race as such, but to describe reported speech as a practice. The following questions are posed of the interview materials: What are the identifying characteristics of reported speech? How does reported speech fit within larger conversational structures such as narratives or argument sequences? What does reported speech sequentially implicate?

In addition to reported speech as a conversational practice, I am interested in what reported speech is being used to do in making discursive claims about race. Initially I was struck by how reported speech was used to construct a portrait of the other. That is, participants were ascribing words to out-group members as a way to criticize their actions, so I was interested in what kind of claims or discursive positions participants were taking in talking race. Discursive action methods (Edwards and Potter 1992) are useful for describing how actions and persons are socially constructed through talk. Reported speech is used by participants as a communicative practice to reconstruct what was said so as to convey a version of events and the persons involved in doing them.

Reporting speech is not a neutral, disinterested activity; reporting speech is sequentially connected to assessing or evaluating it. Such evaluative components are useful for discursive analysis methods, in that they allow us to hear how the speaker wants the recipient(s) to take the actions and persons portrayed through the reported speech. To put this another way, I look at how the reporting speaker evaluates the reported speech as a way to understand how the actors being quoted, and what they did, are being framed. In short, I want to see *how* people use reported speech to talk race, and in doing so, *what* they say: their presentation of racial claims.

Reported speech in talking race

Given our focus on discursive construction, we want to know how Pakeha respondents take the racial other. That is, how these interviewees' notions of race, and related constructs, are oriented to and used in context. In particular, we examine the voice of, or about, the racial other as articulated through reported speech and its surrounding context. From an examination of the reported speech materials, Pakehas portray the racial other in two main ways: (1) as involving certain characteristics or behaviors that are cast as not only different (from the presumed Pakeha norm), but also deficient, and (2) as involving extreme or unreasonable political positions.

The racial other as deficient

In Pakeha discourse one sense of the racial other is as not only different, but also deficient, in the sense of not being able to live up to "White standards," perform middle-class jobs, or pass as White. Consider how this deficiency view is discursively achieved in specific cases. In the following excerpt, we see the interviewer asking about job discrimination against Maoris and the respondent giving a justification for not hiring a Maori for office work.

Extract 3 (Appendix: New Zealand Interview 16: 283)

```
1.  R:   ( . . . ) if you had a Maori candidate who was as good
2.       ([.) or better [I would say that they would get the job
3.  I:        [Yeah        [°Mm mhm°
4.  I:   °Mm mhm°
5.       (0.6)
6.  R:   It's normally that-  Okay that argument gets put in that
7.       Maoris never get the jobs okay but you look .hh when they
8.       turn up for an interview
9.  I:   Yes
10. R:   What's he wearing? How's he sitting?
11. I:   Yeah
12. R:   How's he talking? >ya know what I mean< an' there's no
13.      point in having a receptionist who picks up a phone "Yeah
14.      g'day, 'ow are ya" ((strong New Zealand accent))
15. I:   Ye:s (0.4) [mm mhm
16. R:                  [I mean they want someone that is- (0.4) that is
17.      gonna put their clients at ea:se
```

Using the lens of reported speech to examine this excerpt, we see the respondent draws on a mock voice of a strong New Zealand accent (lines 13–14), with the point being that such pronounced accents do not fit in an office environment (lines 16–17). This strong accent epitomizes the Maori deficiency, implicates other shortcomings for doing office work, and can be heard as a justification for not hiring the Maori for such jobs.

It is interesting how this argument against the charge of discrimination in hiring gets developed. The respondent switches footings from making general descriptive claims envisioning a typical job interview (lines 1–8) to drawing on the voice of someone assessing the hypothetical Maori candidate, "What's he wearing? How is he sitting? How is he talking?" (lines 10 and 12). The mock accent of the prototypical Maori (discussed above) illustrates the final question/complaint of this three-part list, "How's he talking?" (line 12). It is not clear if the respondent is using the prototypical voice of a Pakeha manager/interviewer or if this is his own evaluation.

In either case, it is clearly the voice of Pakeha authority, and it is designed
to undermine the acceptability of the Maori candidate.

The conversational practice of drawing on stereotypical prosody to
portray the other is used only a few times throughout these materials. In
the following we see a mock accent of an African's speech (lines 8–9).

Extract 4 (Appendix: New Zealand Interview 2: 244)

1. R: I've <u>been</u> to West Africa
2. I: Mm mhm
3. R: I mean one of my <u>bêtes</u> noirs is uh (0.4) (Abraham Or<u>di</u>yo)
4.   with his [<u>bloody</u> m- <u>smiling</u> (0.6) blooming Ibo face
5. I: [Y(h)eah
6. R: coming out on the
7. I: Yeah
8. R: screen tellin us what a <u>beau</u>:tiful country Nige<u>ri</u>a is
9.   ((prior a sort of mimic of a Nigerian accent))
10. I: ((laughs))
11. R: (I mean I) went into Nu- Nigeria for eight years s[o
12. I: [Yes
13. R: I know how b(h)ad Nigeria
14.   was then and it's a darn sight worse now

Here we see the vocal and physical qualities of the other becoming the
object of comment by the respondent (lines 3–8). These differences are
comically exaggerated as a resource for portraying the other. Here the
interviewer laughs following the respondent's vocal imitation or parody. There may be a facial imitation here as well. Such stereotypical
resources can be drawn on, in a sense, to perform the other in a mocking
manner.

The prosody of this direct speech is not illustrating any deficiency of
the sort seen in extract 3 above. The criticism arises in the respondent's
next utterances (lines 11–14) as he contradicts the claim voiced in the
direct speech of the African. Reported speech opens up a slot for the
reporting speaker to comment on or to assess those words. This format
(reported speech + assessment) is also apparent in extract 3. Following
the prototypical speech of the Maori receptionist's phone voice (lines 13–
14), the respondent adds the assessment justifying hiring practices (lines
16–17). This format reflects Bakhtin's point about the dialogical character of voices juxtaposed with each other (1984). In each case the reported
voice of the other comes first, followed by the teller's voice of negative
assessment.

The respondent's critical assessment of the African's reported speech
is bolstered by his report of having been to Nigeria for eight years. The
respondent's report of "having been there" is a way of displaying "how

I know" (Pomerantz 1984). In extract 3, "how I know" is shown, not through having been there, but through the reported speech as being prototypical or representative of Maori demeanor and Pakeha sensibilities. Reported speech is commonly drawn as a resource to exhibit one's claims to knowing.

The following excerpt uses prototypical reported speech to illustrate differences in Maori and Pakeha cultural practices concerning personal property. How these cultural practices are evaluated, as different or as deficient, becomes an issue between the respondent and interviewer.

Extract 5 (Appendix: New Zealand Interview 16: 285)
1. R: But then that comes down- (0.4) i:n Ma:ori culture
2. I: °Mm mhm°
3. R: (People think that uh) "Well everything belongs to everybody"
4. I: [Yes
5. R: [They're jus borrowing it.
6. I: °Mm mhm°
7. R: So you can turn around an' ask ( ) when a Maori (.) takes
8.   something "Why did you take it." "I was just borrowin' it"
9. I: Ye:s (0.4) yeah
10.   (0.6)
11. R: "He wasn't using it so I borrowed it"
12.   (0.6)
13. I: Yes so the problem is different- diff- different cultural
14.   definitions of theft
15. R: (°Tha[t's right/of theft°)
16. I: [°that Maoris have mm mhm°
17. R: What do you do about it? Well I mean you can't let 'em take
18.   this out on the street (0.4) cause they'd do it all the ↑time [. . .]
19. R: but you've still got to educate the people that they
20.   live in a white society now

Prototypical speech is drawn on to articulate the Maori moral reasoning. This Maori reasoning is presented as a general proposition in reported thought, "(People think that uh) 'Well everything belongs to everybody'" (line 3), then again as a prototypical exchange: a Pakeha question (or accusation) and a Maori account for taking something from another (lines 7–8 and 11).

What do the participants make of this cultural difference? The interviewer responds to this prototypical exchange by formulating it as a version of cultural relativism, as "different- diff- different cultural definitions of theft" (lines 13–14). The respondent picks up on the "theft" part of the interviewer's formulation and raises the question, "What do you do about it?" (line 17). The respondent assesses this cultural difference as problematic, as an issue of the Maori as unassimilated, "but you've still got to educate the people that they live in a <u>white</u> society now" (lines 19–20). We have competing models suggested in this excerpt. The position that Maoris need to assimilate into White society implies that this cultural practice of "borrowing/stealing" is deficient. If the cultural relativism model is taken, then the practices of how material possessions are treated is merely different from that of the Pakeha.

Another kind of ascribed deficiency of the other is the inability to speak English. This deficiency is also based on an assimilationist model. In the following excerpt, the Pakeha respondent distinguishes between groups; here he is criticizing immigrant islanders, not the Maori. A prototypical quote is used to illustrate the consequences of not speaking English (line 7).

Extract 6 (Appendix: New Zealand Interview 16: 276)

1. R: At <u>ho:me</u> Mum and Dad can't speak English
2.   [so the kids don't
3. I: [Mm mhm
4. R: speak English
5. I: Right [yeah
6. R: [They go to school an' suddenly they are confronted with
7.   English "We can't speak that language what'll we do?"
8. I: Yes
9. R: Nothing!
10. I: Mm mhm
11. R: An' so by the time they get to fifteen they just drop out
12.   they've had it up to here with school
13. I: Yeah
14. R: And it's not (.) <u>school</u>'s fault
15. I: Yeah
16.   (1.4)
17. R: They had brilliant lives

In presenting his argument, the respondent changes footings from general descriptive claims (lines 1–6) to a prototypical quote (lines 7–9) to illustrate a recurring problem. In drawing on the voice of the immigrant islander (somehow translated into English), he epitomizes both the deficiency of islanders and how this deficiency gets passed on from generation to generation. He portrays the immigrant islander in high school as asking, "We can't speak that language what'll do we do?" (line 7), to which is answered "Nothing!" (line 9). This answer of "Nothing!" epitomizes a basic deficiency of the immigrant islander for life in contemporary society. The respondent says as much as he switches footings back to general descriptive and evaluative claims about this other: "they just drop out . . . (of) school" and "They had brilliant lives."

Ascribed political positions of the racial other

For these Pakeha respondents, the ethnic, racial, or cultural other not only possesses characteristics portrayed as deficient, but also holds political opinions assessed as unreasonable, extreme, or radical. Reported speech is drawn on to articulate or to criticize such discursive positions.

Extract 7 (Appendix: New Zealand Interview 44: 299)

```
 1.  R:   Aw'right a lot of them sold land for very little (0.4) and
 2.        (0.4) for axes an' (1.4) and whatever (.) wasn't it
 3.  I:   Yes
 4.  R:   Blankets
 5.        (2.2)
 6.  R:   But (0.4) when (1.0) my: (.) ancestors came here (1.2) and
 7.        (0.4) (an' land) and made up (0.4) uhm (0.4) ya'know
 8.        just pastoral land and then sold it
 9.        it was sold for very low- little ↑too
10.  I:   Yes
11.  R:   But you can['t go back and say "Well I want to be compensated"
12.  I:                [Ye(h)ah (0.4) yes
13.  R:   for what-
14.        (1.0)
15.  R:   A::nd (1.0) I think you've got to go o::n
```

Here we see prototypical speech drawn on to voice a Maori demand for compensation (line 11). This prototypical Maori quote is used as part of a historical narrative by the Pakeha respondent. The way the narrative is told makes the Maori demand seem backward looking and unreasonable. The Maori are not the only people who have sold land for very little; the respondent's European ancestors have as well. The respondent assesses the Maori demand by saying, "I think you've got to go o::n" (line 15), with the implication that going back to remediate land claims is unreasonable and extreme. In the next extract, another case is brought up regarding Maori land claims, but here we see the ascription that outsiders are causing the trouble. Indeed, locals are quoted as saying there is no problem. The prototypical speech used here portrays the relations between the narrator and the Maori as one that is amiable but gets stirred up by an outside political leader.

Extract 8 (Appendix: New Zealand Interview 2: 257/258)

```
1.  R:   ( . . . ) a lot of the (.) racial (0.[4) prejudice I-
2.  I:                                        [(Uh huh)
3.  R:   I think is brought on you know by the Eva Rickards that a
4.  I:   Yes (0.4) [mm mhm
5.  R:             [that stand up=I::'ve been out (.) time after time
```

6.   and played golf at- at [[place name]
7.   I: [[place name]
8.   I: Yes yeah
9.   R: And (0.2) eh playing on the golf course there I've played
10.   with Maori
11. I: Mm mhm
12. R: people and they've said "Oh ya'know this the- this is the old
13.   burial- burial ground, =Hi'ya Roger" and ya'know an'
14. I: Yes
15. R: and ya'know "nobody minds you playing golf?" an' I'll say
16.   "No no no (.) It's fin[e"
17. I: [Yes
18. R: And it takes Eva Rickards to[c(h)ome down from somewhere else
19. I: [((laugh))
20. I: Yeah
21. R: and ah to stir the whole blooming pot (. . .)

The reported speech exchange between the Maori and the Pakeha narrator (lines 12–16) displays congenial relations among the locals. The
Pakeha interviewee invokes the voice of the prototypical Maori to display how he knows that the locals do not care about this golf course's
location. This firsthand knowledge of the locals' views is contrasted with
the outside political leader, Eva Rickards, who raises the controversy
over the old Maori burial ground. The notion of the outsider coming in and causing trouble is, of course, a common trope in political
discourse.

This is the first case in which the prototypical speech of the Maori is
not presented in a critical light. Instead, contrast is drawn between Maori
locals and outsiders. Indeed, the voice of the locals is used to undermine
the position of the outside political leader. In the following excerpt we see
a similar kind of distinction between Maori friends and extreme Maori
political positions. The respondent's Maori friends are presented as not
agreeing with the extreme political views.

Extract 9 (Appendix: New Zealand Interview 44: 297/298)

1.   R: U::hm (1.6) they're ma:king New Zealand a racist cu- country
2.   uhm but ya'know you usually feel (.) think that racism is
3.   uhm (1.4) putting th- putting (.) [the darker people down
4.   I: [Yes
5.   R: [but really they're doing it (.) the other way around
6.   I: [(   )
7.   I: A sort of [reverse [racism
8.   R: [I feel [Yes
9.   I: Yeah
10. R: U:hm (1.4) everything (0.6) seems to be to help (0.2) the

11.   Maori people, (1.0) a::nd ya'know (0.4) I think (1.4) at the
12.   moment sort of (0.6) the Europeans are sort of (0.4) They're
13.   just sort of watching [and putting up with it
14. I: [Yeah
15. I: Yeah
16. R: But (.) they'll only go so fa:r
17. I: Right yeah
18. R: U:hm (1.0) tsk (1.0) ya'know we- we've got (.) Maori friends
19.   out he:re uhm who we have into the house so yu- ya'know
20.   they're friends
21.   (0.6)
22. R: U:hm (2.0) but when things happen an' they- they suddenly say
23.   "Oh they're going to make (.) M- Maori language
24.   compulsory"
25. I: Yeah (.) yeah
26. R: U:hm (0.4) but that is an- antagonizing
27. I: Yeah
28. R: And- (1.4) the Maori friends that we::'ve got (1.0) they
29.   don't agree with it
30. I: Yes (.) yeah
31. R: U::hm (0.2) okay yu- you've got extremists there too

In this excerpt, the respondent's use of the indexical term "they" ("they're" and "they'll") as the agents pushing extreme positions is interesting, for instance, "they're ma:king New Zealand a racist cu- country" (line 1; also line 5). As the respondent moves from making general claims about race and identity politics to a particular case, she draws on reported speech to cite an example of a radical policy (lines 22–24). Who are the persons quoted by the initial use of "they" in: "they- they suddenly say 'Oh they're going to make (.) M- Maori language compulsory' "? Seen in the sequential context of lines 18–20, the "they" could be heard as referencing her Maori friends, or as referencing unidentified extremists. There is no ambiguity about the "they're" in the reported speech (lines 23–24), however. It clearly refers to the purported unnamed extremists.

Another point about the quotive: the use of "suddenly" in "they suddenly say" suggests the policy was proposed, or came about, too rapidly. In the respondent's next slot after the reported speech (following the interviewer's acknowledgment tokens, "yeah"), the respondent assesses the reported speech as "antagonizing" (line 26). She reports further that even her Maori friends "don't agree with it" (lines 28–29), a way of assessing its radical character.

As we have seen, reported speech seems to work within larger discourse units (e.g., narratives, claim-evidence sequences) to present the speaker's

discursive position. In the following excerpt we see the respondent draw
on the voice of the political extremist to articulate that position.

Extract 10 (Appendix: New Zealand Interview 2: 244/245)

1. R: They ↑want ↑separate de↑ve:lopment.
2. I: Mm mhm
3. R: They want (0.6) a Minister of Ma- Maori A↑ffairs,
4. I: Mm mhm
5.   (0.4)
6. R: ↑Where's the Minister of ↑Pakeha Affairs
7. I: Mm mhm
8. R: Can you give me his a↑ddress
9. I: Y(h)es ↑.hhh [yeah
10. R: [And (0.4) >ya'know< they want the Maori ↑All Blacks.
11. I: Yes [yeah
12. R: [Where is the Pakeha All Blacks.
13. I: Mm mhm
14. R: Well you can't have Pakeha ones that's- (.) that's racial↑ist
15. I: Mm mhm
16.   (1.0)
17. R: Now chhm. (0.6) to me they're- [that's wha- they're trying to
18. I: [°Mm mhm°
19. R: do they're trying to get separate de↑ve:lopment

In this excerpt the interviewee presents his argument with a dialogical
character: the racial political position is presented through attributions
with a "they want X" format (lines 1, 3, 10). Who "they" are is not specified, though contextually it is understood as those who hold an extreme
political, racial position. The respondent challenges the latter two of these
positions in the slot following with a "where's the Y" parallel structure.
For instance, the respondent attributes a political viewpoint (lines 3, 10)
and then switches footings to directly respond to these viewpoints as
though the other were present (line 6 and 12).

The interviewee then draws on prototypical speech (line 14) to voice
the racial political position in response to his criticism. This is the third
part of a constructed dialogue argument sequence. The respondent does
not leave it at that; typically the teller has the final word. As we have seen
before, prototypical speech gets assessed by the teller in the following
slot. Here the respondent switches footing from constructed dialogue to
making a general claim about "separate development" (lines 17–19). The
prototypical speech and "they want X" format epitomizes this "separate
development" position. The very word choice, "separate development,"
implicates his critical assessment.

Discussion

In reflecting on how Pakeha respondents use voices and reported speech in talking race, two points stick out. First, the reported speech works as part of a larger argument or narrative to criticize various behaviors, deficiencies, or positions. Here the racial other is presented as behaving in ways inconsistent with mainstream society (extracts 3, 5, 6), as making false claims (extract 4), or as avowing extreme positions (extracts 7–10). Even when local Maori are portrayed as congenial or as friends, their political leaders or positions are cast as problematic (extracts 8–9). The Pakeha interviewees explicitly or implicitly portray their own group practices as normative or as the standard, and as resisting extreme political currents.

The second main point involves the notion of voices: most of the reported speech used here was formed as prototypical reported speech of the racial other. Of the ten instances of reported speech, only one case is unambiguously direct discourse, and it is a quote from a television figure. Prototypical quotes involve reporting the speech of an individual speaker, while simultaneously purporting this speech to be typical of the group of which the individual is a member. That is, it ascribes speech to the group through the words of an (apparent) individual. Prototypical quotes work to epitomize the group's ways of speaking, for example, mock prosody of the Maori (extract 3), or extreme political positions, for example, land compensation (extract 7).

These instances of prototypical speech of the racial other typically are followed by the Pakeha's voice in the same or next available turn to respond to or to assess the voice of the other. This is consistent with the finding that reported speech involves not only a reporting but also an editorializing (Buttny 1997). The Pakeha voice commenting on or assessing the voice of the other reflects the presumed Pakeha position of being normative. Given that much of the reported speech of the racial other is portrayed as deficient or extreme, it also shares similarities with the discourse of social accountability (Buttny 1993).

To conclude with a reflexive caution, at times I wonder about my analysis, given the fact that I have never been to New Zealand, nor do I know much about its history. As a North American, I am struck by the similar issues and discourses current in both the USA and New Zealand. There is probably less analytic difficulty with looking at reported speech as a conversational practice. The area that I worry about is the discursive analysis: without local knowledge of the scene, the possibility of not hearing implicated meanings or positions seems more likely. For instance, in an initial draft of this chapter, I claimed that the preponderance of prototypical quotes over direct speech reflected an intergroup distance, a lack of face-to-face contact, between the Pakeha and Maori. One of the editors, Margaret Wetherell, a New Zealand native, pointed out that in fact there is considerable contact between these groups, which falsified my intergroup distance inference. Why then so much prototypical speech? To take a second crack at this, prototypical quotes allow the teller to epitomize the group by invoking the characteristic words of a prototypical individual's speech. As such, it seems more suited to the argumentative, critical stance often taken by respondents.

References

Bakhtin, M. M. 1984. *Problems of Dostoevsky's poetics*, translated and edited by Caryl Emerson. Minneapolis: University of Minnesota Press.

1986. *Speech genres and other late essays*, translated by V. W. McGee, edited by V. C. Emerson and M. Holquist. Austin: University of Texas Press.

Basso, K. 1979. *Portraits of "the Whiteman": linguistic play and cultural symbols among the Western Apache*. Cambridge: Cambridge University Press.

Billig, M., Condor, S., Edwards, D., Gane, M., Middleton, D. and Radley, A. 1988. *Ideological dilemmas*. London: Sage.

Buttny, R. 1993. *Social accountability in communication*. London: Sage.

1997. Reported speech in talking race on campus. *Human Communication Research* 23: 477–506.

Buttny, R. and Williams, P. L. 2000. Demanding respect: the uses of reported speech in discursive constructions of interracial contact. *Discourse and Society* 11: 111–135.

Edwards, D. and Potter, J. 1992. *Discursive psychology*. London: Sage.

Goffman, E. 1974. *Frame analysis*. New York: Harper and Row.

1981. Footing. In *Forms of talk*. Philadelphia: University of Pennsylvania Press. 124–159.

Heritage, J. 1984. *Garfinkel and ethnomethodology*. Cambridge: Polity.

Hill, J. T. and Irvine, J. T. 1993. Introduction. In *Responsibility and evidence in oral discourse*, edited by J. H. Hill and J. T. Irvine. Cambridge: Cambridge University Press. 1–23.

Holt, E. 1996. Reporting on talk: the use of direct reported speech in conversation. *Research on Language and Social Interaction* 29: 219–245.

Houston, M. 1994. When Black women talk with White women: why dialogues are difficult. In *Our voices: essays in culture, ethnicity, and communication*, edited by A. Gonzalez, M. Houston, and V. Chen. Los Angeles: Roxbury. 133–139.

Macaulay, R. K. S. 1987. Polyphonic monologues: quoted direct speech in oral narratives. *Papers in Pragmatics* 1/2: 1–34.

Mehan, H. 1997. The discourse of the illegal immigration debate: a case study in the politics of representation. *Discourse and Society* 8: 249–270.

Miles, R. 1989. *Racism*. New York: Routledge.

Mishler, E. 1986. *Research interviewing: context and narrative*. Cambridge, MA: Harvard University Press.

Omi, M. and Winant, H. 1994. *Racial formation in the United States: from the 1960s to the 1990s.* New York: Routledge and Kegan Paul.

Payne, M. E. (n.d.) Spoken quotation: an analysis of quoted talk in conversation. Unpublished manuscript. Department of Communication, SUNY.

Pomerantz, A. (1984). Giving a source or basis: the practice in conversation of telling "How I know." *Journal of Pragmatics* 8: 607–625.

Pomerantz, A. and Fehr, B. J. 1997. Conversation analysis: an approach to the study of social action as sense making practices. In *Discourse as social interaction*, edited by A. van Dijk. London: Sage. 64–91.

Potter, J. 1997. *Representing reality*. London: Sage.

Sanjek, R. (1994). The enduring inequalities of race. In *Race*, edited by S. Gregory and R. Sanjek. New Brunswick, NJ: Rutgers University Press. 1–17.

Sternberg, M. 1982. Proteus in quotation-land: mimesis and the forms of reported discourse. *Poetics Today* 3: 107–156.

Tannen, D. 1989. *Talking voices: repetition, dialogue, and imagery in conversational discourse.* Cambridge: Cambridge University Press.

van Dijk, T. A. 1987. *Communicating racism: ethnic prejudice in thought and talk.* London: Sage Publications.

(1993). Stories and racism. In *Narrative and social control*, edited by D. K. Mumby. Newbury Park, CA: Sage. 121–142.

Verkuyten, M., De Jong, W. and Masson, C. N. 1995. The construction of ethnic categories: discourses of ethnicity in the Netherlands. *Ethnic and Racial Studies* 18: 251–276.

Volosinov, V. N. 1971. Reported speech. In *Readings in Russian poetics*, edited by L. Matejka and K. Pomorska. Cambridge, MA: MIT Press.

Wetherell, M. and Potter, J. 1992. *Mapping the language of racism: discourse and the legitimation of exploitation.* New York: Columbia University Press.

Winant, H. 1994. *Racial conditions.* Minneapolis: University of Minnesota Press.

7   Contradictions in interview discourse

Harry van den Berg

Variability in interview discourse: a problem or a source?

In the course of a research interview, and especially in an open interview, an interviewee may construct very different, and often irreconcilable, positions and lines of argument regarding a single topic. Such variety and contradiction can be explained by appealing to the notion that discourse is essentially incoherent. This explanation isn't a very attractive one, however. After all, abandoning the assumption of coherence implies abandoning the assumption of any rationality in social interaction, and ultimately giving up the goal of trying to understand discourse. The crucial question is therefore: How to approach and analyze the discursive variety and contradiction that occurs within an interview?

Variability as a problem

In mainstream research methodology, variability is approached as a problem. Differences, and especially contradictions, in interview discourse are viewed as indicators of some kind of "measurement error" due to biasing factors, such as the possible inadequacies of the interviewer's behavior. After "purifying" interview discourse as much as possible from such errors (for example, by correcting for the supposed effects of social desirability), several procedures are recommended to construct an estimation of the "real" opinion or attitude of the interviewee. In the attempt to measure attitudes (or, more precisely, to construct estimations of supposed attitudes), these procedures transform different or contradictory interviewee statements into a consistent position that can be recorded on an attitude scale. These procedures accomplish this transformation by introducing speculative assumptions into the analysis, assumptions that revolve around the idea that discourse has to be viewed as an expression of something else, such as attitudes, cognition, emotions, and so on.

Variability as a source

There are other methodological approaches, however, that don't dismiss discursive variability as a problem of measurement. Rather, these approaches try to read variations and contradictions as relevant information about the discourse to be analyzed. These approaches are based on the assumption that discourse is a form of social action. From this viewpoint, variability is intrinsic to discourse. Because discourse is always locally constructed, it must be analyzed as context dependent. Variations and contradictions in interview discourse are thus valuable sources that can be used to get more insight into this context dependency. Several models are used to conceptualize this variability, such as schemata (D'Andrade 1995; Rumelhart and Ortony 1977), scripts (Schank and Abelson 1977), frames (Goffman 1974, Tannen and Wallat 1993; Van den Berg 1996), and interpretative repertoires (Gilbert and Mulkay 1984; Potter and Wetherell 1987; Wetherell and Potter 1992).

In the field of discourse analysis, the concepts of interpretative repertoire and frame are often used when analyzing variability in discourse. The concept of interpretative repertoire is closely linked to the understanding of discourse as a social activity. It draws attention to the phenomenon that ordinary talk is simultaneously systematic and flexible. Ordinary talk is systematic because terms and linguistic constructions used in talking about a specific topic show recurrent patterns. These patterns result from the fact that people use a limited number of mutually related terms and linguistic constructions in discussing a topic. Very often these patterns are due to the structuring force of specific metaphors and figures of speech (Potter and Wetherell 1987). But ordinary talk is also flexible. People may use different interpretative repertoires and may switch between repertoires in talking about a topic. The interviewee has different interpretative repertoires at his or her disposal. The use of a specific interpretative repertoire will be dependent on situational characteristics, such as the course of the interaction between interviewer and interviewee. From this viewpoint, the interviewee's discourse must be analyzed primarily as a co-production of interviewer and interviewee.

The concept of frame is related to the devices people use in processing and organizing experiences in everyday life. Following Goffman's work on framing, Deborah Tannen (1993) defines these devices as patterns of expectation that are socio-culturally determined. As a consequence, framing is often a routine activity, and social actors are seldom aware of the fact that, in framing the (interview) situation or the (question) topic to be discussed, they are making specific choices. In several respects the concept of frame is akin to the concept of interpretative repertoire. Both concepts point to the variability and context-dependency of talk.

The main difference between these concepts concerns the domains to which they apply. The concept of interpretative repertoire points predominantly to different ways of talking about a topic, and especially to the cultural/ideological resources for building arguments about the topic in question. The concept of frame points predominantly to different ways of defining the social interaction and the relation between those involved in the interaction, such as the interviewer and the interviewee. These concepts also differ in terms of their theoretical perspectives on the phenomenon of variability in (interview) discourse, which I discuss in more detail elsewhere (Van den Berg 1997).

More or less apart from differences in origin, domain of application, and theoretical perspective, each of these concepts is used in various ways in empirical research concerning discursive variations and contradictions. Therefore it is important to focus on the "logic-in-use" (Kaplan 1964) of discourse analytical research on variability. In the next section I will focus on one of the characteristic tendencies of the logic-in-use up till now, i.e. the tendency to resort to functionalist accounts of variations and contradictions in (interview) discourse.

Functionalist accounts of variability

A functional analysis of what conversationalists do can be very fruitful in understanding the dynamics of (interview) discourse. But recognizing the value of functional analysis doesn't necessitate the acceptance of functionalism as the general paradigm for discourse analysis. Functionalism is based on the questionable paradigmatic presupposition that any social action can be (and must be) explained by the functions of that action for the reproduction of the social system in question. Therefore, discursive phenomena should be analyzed in relation to the smooth functioning of ordinary and institutional conversations, the upholding of structural relations between conversationalists, and/or more general power relations in society.

In the field of discourse analysis, the functionalist paradigm is at the root of the idea that discourse must be viewed as a product of strategic interaction. And indeed, from an action-oriented viewpoint, it is tempting to embrace functionalism and to view interview discourse as a product of the strategic interaction between interviewer and interviewee. Besides, functionalism seems to offer a clear-cut explanation of contradictions in (interview) discourse. From a functionalist perspective, the behavior of both participants has to be analyzed as functionally related to specific strategic goals, i.e. goals that the participants try to achieve by participating in the interview. In addition to communicating "convincing" and "credible" answers, interviewees' behavior is also oriented to communicating positive self-presentations. Orienting to these different strategic goals may create a communicative dilemma for an interviewee. This is especially the case if the interviewee wants to communicate a message that could interfere with another communicative goal, such as positive self-presentation.

From this viewpoint, contradiction in an interviewee's discourse can be analyzed as a functional device employed to solve a communicative dilemma. For example, an interviewee's discourse may contain statements that could be interpreted as racist, as well as statements that could be interpreted as clearly antiracist. From a functionalist viewpoint, vehemently denying racism on the one hand, while telling racist stories on the other hand, can be read as a face-saving strategy. But in order to conclude that denying racism functions as a disclaimer (Hewitt and Stokes 1975) to solve the supposed communicative dilemma, it isn't sufficient to analyze only how these statements are embedded in interviewee's discourse, and how they are discursively related to each other. Such a conclusion also requires the introduction of certain assumptions, such as (1) racism is at odds with dominant social norms concerning social equality and tolerance, and (2) the interviewee expects that some statements may be considered by the interviewer as racist. Of course, these assumptions should be demonstrated in analysis. Unfortunately, in the practice of functionalist research, such assumptions are often taken for granted.

To summarize, approaching the interview as a form of strategic interaction requires that contradictions in an interviewee's discourse be conceptualized not as "errors" or as indicators of cognitive incompetence, but as careful constructions on behalf of the strategic goals of the interviewee. As a consequence, contradictions in interviewee's discourse are ultimately viewed as only apparent contradictions. According to this viewpoint, contradictions have to be read on two levels. On one level, communication is functionally related to the expression of the substantive information (the "real" opinions, etc.) the interviewee wants to communicate. But on another level, communication is functionally related to the presentation of self the interviewee wants to communicate, a self that conforms to social norms.

Critical discourse analysis and functionalist accounts of variability

In the field of critical discourse analysis, the functionalist approach plays a dominant role in accounting for variability in (interview) discourse. The studies of Van Dijk (1987, 1989, 1991, 1993), Van Dijk et al. (1997), and Essed (1991) are well-known examples of this approach. Contradictions in discourse (including interview discourse) on racial issues are accounted for in terms of impression management strategies. Denying racism and avoiding explicit negative statements about minorities are considered rhetorical methods for presenting implicit negative statements about these minorities in socially acceptable ways. In other words, according to Van Dijk, racism is presented in very subtle forms.

This approach relies on the premise that contradictions are ultimately only apparent. Denying racism and making positive statements about ethnic minorities are merely rhetorical devices used to hide a deep-seated racism. The assumed existence of this deep-seated racism is based upon a more general theory, according to which the social structure of Western societies is fundamentally racist. The proposition that denying racism is a careful strategic device is also based upon a more general theory, according to which interviewees are calculating, and potentially even manipulating, actors. It is assumed that an interviewee's behavior is guided by a system of coherent, and prejudiced, opinions and attitudes. Therefore, contradictions in an interviewee's discourse cannot be "real," but rather must be the results of deceptive presentations of the hidden reality of prejudice.

The central weakness of this functionalist approach to discourse analysis is the speculative presupposition concerning the functions of discourse and the role of this presupposition in empirical analysis. If it is postulated that everyday discourse is functional in reproducing the social structure of Western societies and the assumed characteristics of this social structure, such as structural racism, then denying racism can only be interpreted as a device to hide racism. As a consequence, the empirical analysis of (interview) discourse tends to produce what was already postulated in advance. This circularity is characteristic of any essentialist theorizing.

Discourse analysis should avoid this circularity by sticking to the methodological rule that any interpretation of discourse in terms of specific functions cannot be grounded through reference to speculative social and/or cognitive theories, but must be grounded in the data itself. As a consequence, the interpretation of discursive contradictions as merely apparent contradictions, due to the use of rhetorical devices (such as disclaimers) to solve conflicts between the different strategic goals of the speaker, must be demonstrated instead of postulated. The analyst should be open-minded in trying to account for the variations and contradictions in (interview) discourse.

Research question

The research question I want to answer by using the interviews selected as the exemplary data for this volume concerns the meaning of contradictions in interviewees' discourse. The main question I will focus on is simply: How to make sense of contradictions in interview discourse? Avoiding the trap of essentialist theorizing necessitates that this question cannot be answered beforehand. In other words, depending on the way contradictions are embedded in an interviewee's discourse, and taking into account the context of the interview, the analyst has to find out what these contradictions mean. They may fulfill functions in the interaction other than resolving a communicative dilemma. It may even be impossible to interpret contradictions in terms of functions related to the interactional goals of the interviewee. In other words: the analyst has to be open minded to the different types of work contradictions may, or may not, do in specific instances.

The kind of contradictions I'm interested in are more or less systematic contradictions in interviewees' talk, i.e., contradictions between or within interpretative repertoires used by interviewees in talking about a topic. The social relations between different ethnic groups in New Zealand (especially the relation between Pakehas and Maoris) constitute an important topic of the interviews. Therefore, the research question will be restricted to contradictions in interviewees' talk about this topic and issues related to this topic, such as race relations in general, or in other countries such as South Africa.

Systematically scrutinizing contradictions in the three interviews about racial issues in New Zealand offers the opportunity to get more insight into the variety of meanings of these contradictions. Of course it is impossible to go into detail and to discuss all the instances of contradiction in these interviews in depth. Therefore only some of the main results of my analysis will be presented. The attention will be focused on different types of contradictions.

The function of contradictions for face-saving strategies

Self-presentation is an important aspect of ordinary conversation, as well as institutionalized conversation such as the research interview. Carefully monitoring the image of oneself during the interaction is based on expectations concerning the social norms and opinions attributed to the conversational partner, i.e., the interviewer. In the case of possibly conflicting norms and opinions, there are two options to preserve a positive image of oneself: (1) conforming to the norms and opinions attributed to the interviewer (i.e., giving a social desirable answer), or (2) negotiating with the norms and opinions attributed to the interviewer. Negotiation implies that the interviewee is giving an answer that doesn't conform to the norms and opinions attributed to the interviewer, but at the same time, the interviewee wants to prevent the interviewer from making inferences that could be detrimental to the interviewee's self-presentation. In other words, negotiation is like walking a tight rope between two conflicting goals: presenting a positive image of oneself and presenting a view that may damage that image. This tightrope walk requires a carefully constructed contradiction in an interviewee's discourse, in which plausible inferences from a statement are explicitly denied by the interviewee. There are different forms in which a statement and a denial of plausible inferences from this statement are combined on behalf of saving one's face.

Presenting a disclaimer

A common face-saving device is the structure in which a denial of plausible inferences precedes the statement the interviewee is going to present. In other words, the denial is presented as a disclaimer to be used by the recipient (i.e., the interviewer) to interpret the subsequent statement(s): "I'm not a racist/sexist, BUT I endorse X (X = a statement that could be interpreted as racist/sexist)." Interview 2 contains a clear example of this construction of contradictions (extract 1, lines 1–2): "I would li:ke to see apartheid done away with (1.0) but . . ." (followed by a lengthy exposition about the problems and risks of abolishing apartheid).

Extract 1 (Appendix: New Zealand Interview 2: 245/246)

```
 1.  R:  Uhm (1.2) I would li:ke to see apartheid done away with (1.0)
 2.      but can anybody come up with a- [a (.)
 3.  I:                                 [Mm mhm
 4.  R:  positive way of saying "This is how it can be done"
 5.  I:  Mm mhm
 6.  R:  It's all very well to turn round and say "Give 'em a vote"
 7.  I:  Yes
 8.  R:  I mean the majority of them (1.0) don't know what a vote is
 9.  I:  Mm mhm
10.  R:  I mean ya'know the bright ones that have (.) been to school and
11.  I:  °Mm mhm°
12.  R:  run around the streets telling everybody else "Now you know
13.      [shout this throw- throw tha[t"
14.  I:  [°Mm mhm°                    [hh.
15.  R:  E:hm (0.6) but- (1.0) I mean what African country
16.  I:  °Mm mhm°
17.  R:  that u:sed to have European ru:le
18.  I:  °Mm mhm°
19.  R:  that is now ruled (0.6) totally by the blacks
20.  I:  Mm mhm
21.  R:  What (.) one can you hold up as an example and say "We would like
22.      South Africa to follow that (one)?"
23.  I:  Mm mhm
```

24.   (1.0)
25. I: [°Yes°
26. R: [Nigeria? Ghana? (1.0) Sierra Leone?
27. I: °Y(h)es°
28. R: °a:ny of them°
29. I: °Yeah°
30. R: Zem- Zimbabwe or- >an' I don't know the names of half of them<
31.   it's [a long time since I was the[re
32. I: [yes   [yes
33. R: Any of them I mean [they are absolute diabolic places
34. I: [yes

A few minutes later, R further develops his argument that apartheid cannot be easily done away with. The argument concerning the problems and
risks of abolishing apartheid are now supplemented by a strong defense
of the rationality of apartheid (extract 2):

Extract 2 (Appendix: New Zealand Interview 2: 247/248)

1.   R: They're keeping apartheid going because as .h they see it over
2.   [there that's the only way that they're gonna (0.2) kee:p the good way
3.   I: [°Mm°
4.   R: of life
5.   I: Yes (0.2) mm mhm
6.   (0.6)
7.   R: I m[ean ya'know if somebody came round to me and said
8.   I: [(   )
9.   R: "Look (1.0) we're gonna m- move a whole pile of these (0.4) Maoris
10.   off Bastion Point [.hh and they're gonna take over this part of
11.   [suburb name]
12. I: [Mm mhm
13. R: just this corner here going round these block a houses here" ((sounds
14.   like he's gesturing during end of prior))
15. I: Mm mhm
16. R: I'd sa:y ((three hand strikes to a table or chair arm)) No they're not!
17. I: Yeah
18.   (1:0)
19. R: And <[ya'know> (0:2) not matter what happens ther- (0.4)
20. I: [Mm mhm
21. R: THEY'RE NOT GONNA DO IT
22. I: Mm mhm
23. R: I shall take such steps a(h)s a(h)re necessary to
24. I: Yes [yeah
25. R: [(a-) avoid it
26. I: Mm mhm
27. R: Now (0.6) if somebody said "Oh yeah but you know this is how it's
28.   gonna be"
29. I: Mm mhm

30.   (1.0)
31. R: I'd go <u>FLAT</u> out I mean I don't care whether it was apartheid or
32.   whatever yo[u call it or. hh (0.4) build the barricades up there and' a
33. I: [Yeah
34. R: [you know put machine guns on the top
35. I: [>Mm mhm<
36. I: Mm mhm
37.   (0.6)
38. I: Ri[ght S[o,
39. R: [( ) [And <u>then</u> this is what I see that they're just pre<u>serv</u>ing

The very first statement of extract 1 ("I would li:ke to see apartheid
done away with") is not further developed or substantiated. On the contrary, this statement is a mere introduction to the argument that apartheid
cannot easily be done away with. In the second extract this argument is
further developed and turns into a straightforward defense of apartheid.
The use of "BUT" as a link between the first statement and the argument
leading to the conclusion about the necessity of apartheid shows that the
interviewee is aware of the fact that he's going to tell something that isn't
compatible with the wish to abolish apartheid. By starting his account
with a statement against apartheid, the interviewee shows his orientation
to the fact that the statements he's going to develop might be considered
by the interviewer to be controversial, or perhaps racist. Therefore it may
be concluded that this statement in extract 1 functions as a disclaimer in
order to prevent undesirable inferences.

Reversing possible blame

Another device that may be used to deny plausible inferences that could
be detrimental to one's self-presentation is more implicit. By blaming
their opponents for something their conversational partner (i.e., the interviewer) might infer as applicable to them, interviewees employ an implicit method of preventing such inferences: "They (those who pretend to
be antiracist) are themselves racist, prejudiced, etc." In the interview presented above (interview 2) the interviewee uses this device several times.
An example is presented in extract 3, an extract that precedes extracts 1
and 2 from the same interview:

Extract 3 (Appendix: New Zealand Interview 2: 244/245)

1. R: U:[hm (0.4) I mean they say (0.6) (I a) you know do away with
2. I: [°Mm mhm°
3. R: apartheid
4.   (1.2)
5. I: Yes
6. R: Eh but in my opinion (0.8) he:re (0.4) these marches to

```
 7.  I:   °Mm mhm°
 8.  R:   eh Waitangi [are ↑trying to get A↑par↑theid ↑he:re
 9.  I:              [°Mm mhm°
10.  I    Yes ye[s they
11.  R:        [They ↑want ↑separate de↑ve:lopment.
12.  I:   Mm mhm
13.  R:   They want (0.6) a Minister of Ma- Maori A↑ffairs,
14.  I:   Mm mhm
15.       (0.4)
16.  R:   ↑Where's the Minister of ↑Pakeha Affairs
17.  I:   Mm mhm
18.  R:   Can you give me his a↑ddress
19.  I:   Y(h)es ↑.hhh [yeah
20.  R:               [And (0.4) >ya'know< they want the Maori ↑All
21.       Blacks.
22.  I:   Yes [yeah
23.  R:       [Where is the Pakeha All Blacks.
24.  I:   Mm mhm
25.  R:   Well you can't have Pakeha ones that's- (.) that's racial↑ist
```

We may conclude that contradictions do fulfill a role in face-saving devices used to solve a communicative dilemma of the interviewee. In the three interviews about ethnic and racial issues, examples can be found of this type of contradiction. But interview discourse may contain contradictions that cannot be analyzed in terms of face-saving devices.

The function of contradictions for constructing a convincing argument

In addition to contradictions that are part of face-saving devices, I found contradictions that fulfill other rhetorical functions in interview discourse. Especially relevant is the use of contradictions to construct an argument that starts from a position assumed to be akin to the viewpoint of the conversational partner (i.e., the interviewer) and that gradually moves to a position that the speaker (i.e., the interviewee) wants to defend. In the following excerpt from interview 16 (extract 4), the interviewee takes a long break before answering the question concerning his expectations of race relations in the future. Initially, the answer is rather moderate, or even ambivalent.

Extract 4 (Appendix: New Zealand Interview 16: 284/285)

```
1.  I:   Do you feel positive about'a:: or optimistic about the future? (.) of race
2.       relations in this country or do you think we're gonna see race riots and
3.       (0.4) difficulties (0.6) that affect- as in say America
4.  R:   Phhh.
5.  I:   in the: (0.4) sixties?
6.       (8.0)
```

7. R: U:hm (1.0) I don't <u>know</u>. Sometimes <u>yes</u> an' sometimes <u>no</u>
8. I: Mm mhm
9.   (1.2)

In survey interviewing, this answer would be a very clear cue for the interviewer to choose a response category situated in the middle of the range of possible responses and to switch to the next question. But after some repairs, the interviewee goes on to develop a line of reasoning that results in a far more extreme position.

Extract 4 (continued)

10. R: They're gonna ha- you're gonna ha- they're gonna have problems with
11.   <u>gangs</u>
12. I: °Mm mhm°
13.   (0.6)
14. R: But (0.4) that is jus because they've got nothing better to do
15. I: Mm mhm
16.   (0.8)
17. R: And they're not gonna do anything. They're not gonna- they don't
18.   <u>wanna</u> do anything
19. I: Mm mhm
20. R: More than l(h)ike↑ly A lot of'em come he:re (0.4) because it's easy
21.   money, they can live off the ↑dole
22. I: °Mm mhm°
23. R: They can (0.4) rent a state house
24. I: °Mm [mhm°
25. R: [Whereas in the Islands they've gotta ↑work
26. I: [Yes
27. R: [Ya'know they can come here an' don't have to work
28. I: °Mm mhm°
29.   (1.0)
30. R: U:hm (3.4) they can bring all their friends over an' charge them (some)
31.   rent for houses (or something like- like that)
32. I: °Mm mhm°
33. R: An' where <u>does</u> all the money go
34. I: Yes
35. R: Back to the Islands
36. I: Yeah
37.   (1.2)
38. I: °Mm mhm°
39.   (0.6)
40. R: U:hm (2.2) <u>Ye:s</u> I could <u>see</u> problems (0.6) if they did-=<u>if</u> (0.6) they
41.   do all get fired up it would be a frightening force
42. I: Yes
43.   (0.6)
44. R: There'd be no other choi- ya'know I don't know what you'd do with
45.   them.
46. I: Yeah (0.4) [mm mhm
47. R: [Cause there's so many mixed marriages an' it would

48.   be ones in the mixed marriages that would suffer
49. I: Yes
50. R: A lot of the time because they'd be <u>trapped</u>
51. I: Yeah
52. R: They'd be <u>caught</u> into- between two cultures
53. I: Mm mhm
54.   (1.0)
55. R: So I don't know what they're gonna do
56. I: Yeah
57. R: (I mean)
58.   (2.6)
59. I: So you think they could- (.) it could come to violence?
60. R: It <u>could</u> come to violence [yes
61. I: [Yeah
62.   (0.6)
63. R: I mean well it's not safe at this- It's not safe in Otara (right/at night)
64.   now
65. I: Yeah

The ambivalence in the respondent's initial reaction to the question about the future of race relations has disappeared, to be replaced by an alarming pessimism. This contradiction is part of a carefully constructed device that takes the interviewer along with the development of the argument.

Integrating incompatible repertoires

It is impossible to interpret all contradictions in interview discourse in terms of face-saving devices or other rhetorical devices, however, unless the analyst resorts to pure speculation. The concept of interpretative repertoire offers the analyst the opportunity to analyze contradictions in terms of the different repertoires used by the interviewee to make sense of a question topic presented by the interviewer. One possibility is that the interviewee selects elements from incompatible repertoires and combines these elements in a new, more or less integrated, repertoire.

In extract 5 the interviewee combines elements of two well-known interpretative repertoires concerning race relations. Initially, the interviewee presents the core element of a cultural racist repertoire in which cultural differences between "them" (i.e., Maoris) and "us" are presented as valuable and, at the same time, irreconcilable. This cultural irreconcilability is subsequently strengthened by an argument derived from a biological racist repertoire: the supposed "danger" of mixed marriages. Notwithstanding this "smooth" combination, both repertoires are in fact incompatible. The inherent superiority of certain racial categories that is assumed in biological racism isn't compatible with the positive evaluation of different cultures that is characteristic of cultural racism.

Extract 5 (Appendix: New Zealand Interview 44: 302/303)

1. I: What- what do you think are the em (1.2) the sort of positive aspects
2.   of Maori culture that we should (0.4) take out and adopt an' e:hm
3. R: WELL I DON'T [THINK WE SHOULD- WE: SHO:ULD take out
4. I: [if any
5. R: and adopt <u>any</u> of them.
6. I: Yes
7. R: Their- their Maori culture is their <u>OWN</u>
8. I: Yes
9. R: And it's <u>uni</u>que to them u:hm: (1.2) I mean there's <u>noth</u>ing I think
10.   more <u>sti:r</u>ring than- than to go along (0.6) uhm (0.8) to a Maori
11.   concert and hear them singing it [and doing
12. I: [YEAH
13. R: An' that's <u>THE::M</u>
14. I: Yes (.) [yeah
15. R: [I don't want to COPY them that- that's something that's
16.   unique and it's- it's terrific
17. I: Yes (0.4) yeah
18. R: U::hm (1.0) I think they <u>must</u> keep their own identity
19. I: Yes (0.6) Right Mmm
20. R: I- I am against Maoris and whites (0.4) marrying and having ch[ildren
21. I: [Yes
22. R: because I- I- I feel it's <u>aw</u>ful for the children
23. I: Mm mhm
24. R: And they never become whites
25. I: Yes
26. R: They always become Maoris
27. I: Yes
28. R: A:nd (.) just the [colour
29. I: [(That's right) Yeah
30. R: So therefore they should stick to their own race
31. I: [Mm mhm
32. R: [uhm (.) they are <u>uni</u>quely ([.) Maoris
33. I: [Yeah
34. R: [They- they've got something that we can ne:ver have
35. I: [Yeah

Switching between incompatible repertoires

In addition to integrating elements from different repertoires, the interviewee may also make use of different repertoires that remain more or
less unconnected or compartmentalized in the interviewee's discourse.
In other words, the interviewee switches between these repertoires. An
important example is the discourse about apartheid in interview 2.
Extracts 1, 2, and 3 presented above show how the interviewee uses different devices to present pro-apartheid statements in a way that diminishes
the risk of damaging a positive self-presentation. But that's not the whole

story. In the second part of the interview, the interviewee mentions that he didn't attend the rugby matches of the Springbok tour "as a protest against apartheid."

Extract 6 (Appendix: New Zealand Interview 2: 249)

```
1. I:   ( . . . ) What- Did you attend any rugby matches or, (0.8)
2. R:   E::h (0.6) No: I dec(h)ided- .hh I decided as a protest I wouldn't go to
3.      any of the matches
4. I:   Mm mhm why as [a protest
5. R:                 [I-
6.      (0.4)
7. R:   Th- [A protest against apartheid
8. I:       [(begin as a) protest
9. I:   Oh right I see
```

After this rather unexpected move that contradicts the pro-apartheid statements in the first half of the interview, apartheid remains a recurring theme in the rest of the interview. But apartheid is now mainly presented as something undesirable (extracts 7 and 8).

Extract 7 (Appendix: New Zealand Interview 2: 252/253)

```
1.  I:   tsk .hh Ri:ght. ↑U:hm you said- (1.0) I- it sounds to me like you (1.0)
2.       e:h (1.0) y- you don't a- you think that- there's too much of (that/like)
3.       positive discrimination in New Zealand in favor of, of Maoris, The
4.       things like having four Maori parliamentary seats and the Department
5.       of Maori Affairs, you think it's sort of undemocratic or that
6.  R:   Well I think the Maor- Maor- Maor- the hh. Maori se:ats (0.4) should be
7.       abo:lished [I mean that's: (0[.6) an' that's always been my ([.)
8.  I:              [Yeah        [Mm mhm              [Mm mhm
9.  R:   opinion e:h
         [ . . . ]
10. R:   an' it's a- and (th- the day as well) To me it's a↑partheid
11. I:   Mm mhm (.) yes (.) mm mhm
12. R:   I mean ya'know they- they're grizzling it out in South Africa with it's
13.      eh .hh it's COLORED PARLIAMENT no:w
14. I:   Mm mhm
15. R:   Well we've got our colored parliament ya'know all four of them
```

Extract 8 (Appendix: New Zealand Interview 2: 256)

```
1. I:   Yes Right But what do you- Do you think there's been disadva:ntages
2.      for Ma:oris i:n the European culture that they have lost out?
3.      (2.2)
4. I:   at [all?
5. R:      [Ehh. They've got'ta li:ve (1.0) in (.) a (0.4) European culture
6. I:   Mm mhm
7. R:   They're a mino:rity .hh They cannot take over the country.
```

8.   [If they want Stewart Island I'd be quite [willing to give it them.
9.   I: [Mm mhm   [((out breath laugh))
10. R: Set up the <u>home</u>land for them <u>then</u> in Stewart Island. And they could-
11.   they- [they could all move in
12. I: [y(h)es
13. I: Y(h)es
14. R: And run it themselves. I mean ya'know there are plenty'a mutton birds
15. I: ((la[ugh))
16. R: [They- hh. But they're uhm (2.2) Chh. It's like when they- a few
17.   years ago there was all this- [eh screaming an' ranting about <u>Wales</u>
18. I: [Yeah
19. R: ya'know every-everybody in Wales has got to speak Welsh
20. I: That's right that's right
21. R: Now I mean what (.) on <u>earth</u> use is it to them.
22. I: Mm mhm
23. R: If they <u>wan:t</u> to speak Welsh if they want to (0.6) bring up the culture
24.   <u>li:ve</u> the culture
25. I: °Mm mhm°
26. R: FINE
27. I: Mm [mhm
28. R: [If they're gonna work in a <u>bank</u> (.) the bank manager's gonna
29.   come along and tell them what to do in English (0.4) an' he's gone pay
30.   them in English pounds

At the end of the interview, the interviewee sums up his viewpoint by opposing "getting on together" to "apartheid," and makes the unambiguous
statement, "I don't believe in apartheid."

Extract 9 (Appendix: New Zealand Interview 2: 259)

1. I: Um this is a bit repetitive you've probably already answered it, but uhm
2.   that do you think um do you feel optimistic about race relations in this
3.   country, thinking particularly of the Maori/Pakeha, Polynesia/Pakeha?
4. R: Yes, I I I do because I think that uhm the majority of people want to get
5.   on together.
6. I: Yes.
7. R: You've just got the ten percent hard liners on both sides um you know
8.   the ones that are going to march up to Waitangi

Extract 10 (Appendix: New Zealand Interview 2: 259)

1. I: Yes, so you think um you think the best hope's going to come through
2.   assimilation really the sort of fusing of the best cultures together.
3. R: Yes
4. I: Rather than what's called you know pluralism, or the separate
5.   development.
6. R: Yes, I don't believe in apartheid ((laughs))
7. I: Yeah(hhhh)

The intriguing question is: How to make sense of such a variety of statements about the same topic in one interview? It is highly improbable that the relevant statements in the latter half of the interview are rhetorical devices used to prevent undesirable inferences from the pro-apartheid statements in the first half of the interview. We can only make sense of the incompatible statements on apartheid if we look for the different repertoires used by the interviewee. A close inspection and systematic comparison of the relevant extracts shows that "apartheid" has different meanings throughout the interview, depending upon the interpretative repertoire within which it is used.

In the first half of the interview (extracts 1–3), "apartheid" is mainly used as a metaphor for European rule, in contrast to rule by Blacks. The latter is associated with "diabolic places" and "dictatorships." In the second half of the interview (extracts 6–10), however, "apartheid" has a totally different meaning, because it is constructed as the opposite of "Getting on Together." In fact, the interviewee uses two well-known in-terpretative repertoires concerning race relations. The first repertoire is based on the logic of segregation, while the second repertoire is based on the logic of assimilation. Both repertoires differ in terms of modes of expression and membership category devices (Sacks 1992). The interpre-tative repertoire of segregation is characterized by a dichotomy between "us" ("Europeans") and "them" ("blacks," "Maoris"). In contrast, the interpretative repertoire of assimilation is characterized by a dichotomy between an all-embracing and unified "we, the majority" ("the people") and "they, the minorities" ("the ten percent hard liners on both sides").

The question remains as to why the interviewee is switching between these repertoires. A comparison of the extracts on apartheid shows that each interpretative repertoire is used in a specific context. The assimi-lation repertoire is used in the context of criticism of positive discrim-ination and, more generally, of any politics to install specific collective rights for minorities. Within this context, the term "apartheid" functions as a disqualification of such policies. The segregation repertoire is used in the context of fear of possible Black rule. Within this context the term "apartheid" is associated with the defending of the European way of life. Of course, the common denominator of both interpretative repertoires is the preoccupation with the preservation of European culture. Neverthe-less, these repertoires are fundamentally incompatible. The interviewee switches between these repertoires depending on the discursive context.

Discussion

The virtue of the functionalist approach in the field of discourse analysis is that it draws attention to discourse as a form of goal-oriented social interaction. As demonstrated above, this approach is fruitful in analyzing variability in interview discourse. Sometimes, contradictions in interview discourse can validly be interpreted in terms of (1) face-saving devices, such as using disclaimers or shifting possible blame to one's opponents, and (2) argument-building mechanisms. But that's not the whole story. The functionalist approach has its limits. The co-occurrence of racist statements and denials of racism in an interviewee's discourse isn't always a matter of the careful use of rhetorical devices on behalf of strategic goals. On the contrary, contradictions in interviewee's discourse may point to a "real" or substantive dilemma, i.e., a dilemma that can't be solved by rhetorical means, because it is part and parcel of the interpretative repertoires used by the interviewee in talking about the topic in question. For example, the co-occurrence of racist and antiracist statements in an interviewee's discourse may imply that the interviewee is really developing a kind of dialogue between a repertoire articulating negative feelings (anxiety, distrust, etc.) about ethnic minorities and a repertoire articulating values of non-discrimination, equality, and tolerance. Therefore, it is fruitful to return to the notion introduced by Billig (1985, 1991; Billig et al. 1988), and further developed by Wetherell and Potter (1992), that contradictions in everyday discourse are quite natural, because these contradictions reflect the dilemmatic nature of common sense.

From this viewpoint, it is quite normal that an interviewee's discourse contains contrary themes and statements. The concept of "repertoire" can be used to take into account that contradictions in interviewees' discourse may reflect very different ways of combining incompatible repertoires. As demonstrated above, an interviewee may integrate elements from different repertoires, or the interviewee may switch between repertoires. The common-sensical stock of knowledge contains a variety of different, often contrary, ways of defining, arguing, and talking about an issue. Everyday discourse is dependent on this common-sensical stock of knowledge.

But this dependency doesn't mean that people are just the mouthpieces of the available cultural sources of different interpretative repertoires. On the contrary, these sources are used in creative ways. In addition to the possibility that social actors systematically select one of the available repertoires, there are three other possibilities: (1) social actors may select (elements of) a socially respectable repertoire as a rhetorical device to present another repertoire in a convincing or acceptable way, (2) they may negotiate between incompatible repertoires in constructing a new repertoire based on a specific combination of elements from the constitutive repertoire, and (3) they may switch between incompatible repertoires dependent on situational characteristics, such as the issue at hand in the conversation.

This variety of ways of combining contradictory repertoires could be depicted in terms of a scale, ranging from fully integrated to fully compartmentalized, as Claudia Strauss suggests in her analysis of conflicting discourses (Strauss 1997). But in contrast to Claudia Strauss' approach, it seems rather speculative, or even unlikely, to assume that a specific point on this scale reflects a specific cognitive schema or structure of the individual's belief system. On the contrary, each individual may use all the possibilities of selecting and combining contradictory repertoires mentioned above. The analysis of the contradictions in the discourse of interview 2 demonstrates this flexibility. Choosing a specific way of combining contradictory repertoires is a local activity dependent on the concrete social context. Relevant contextual aspects include, among others, the course of the interaction within which the discourse is produced, the way the participants frame the interaction situation and the relation between the participants, the goals of the participants, and the topic of discourse. The dilemmatic nature of discourse isn't a pre-given characteristic of assumed belief systems. Rather, it is accomplished in the concrete circumstances of social interaction. So, the notion that discourse has to be approached as a social activity is not only relevant in analyzing rhetorical aspects of (interview) discourse, but also in analyzing other aspects, such as the way dilemmas are constructed and dealt with.

References

Billig, M. 1985. Prejudice, categorization, and particularization: from a perceptual to a rhetorical approach. *European Journal of Social Psychology* 15: 79–103.
    1991. *Ideology and opinions; studies in rhetorical psychology*. London: Sage.
Billig, M., Condor, S., Edwards, D., Gane, M., Middleton, D. and Radley, A. 1988. *Ideological dilemmas: a social psychology of everyday thinking*. London: Sage.
D'Andrade, R. 1995. *The development of cognitive anthropology*. Cambridge: Cambridge University Press.
Essed, P. J. M. 1991. *Understanding everyday racism; an interdisciplinary theory*. London: Sage.
Gilbert, G. N. and Mulkay, M. 1984. *Opening Pandora's box: a sociological analysis of scientists' discourse*. Cambridge: Cambridge University Press.
Goffman, E. 1974. *Frame analysis*. New York: Harper and Row.
Hewitt, J. P. and Stokes, R. 1975. Disclaimers. *American Sociological Review* 40: 1–11.
Kaplan, A. 1964. *The conduct of inquiry*. Scranton, PA: Chandler Publishing Company.
Potter, J. and Wetherell, M. 1987. *Discourse and social psychology: beyond attitudes and behaviour*. London: Sage.

Rumelhart, D. E. and Ortony, A. 1977. Representation of knowledge. In *Schooling and the acquisition of knowledge*, edited by R. C. Anderson, R. J. Spiro, and W. E. Montague. Hillsdale, NJ: Lawrence Erlbaum.

Sacks, H. 1992. *Lectures on conversation*, edited by G. Jefferson. Oxford: Blackwell.

Schank, R. C. and Abelson, R. P. 1977. *Scripts, plans, goals, and understanding; An inquiry into human knowledge structures*. Hillsdale, NJ: Lawrence Erlbaum.

Strauss, C. 1997. Research in cultural discontinuities. In *A cognitive theory of cultural meaning*, edited by C. Strauss and N. Quinn. Cambridge: Cambridge University Press.

Tannen, D. 1993. What's in a frame? In *Framing in discourse*, edited by D. Tannen. Oxford University Press: 14–55.

Tannen, D. and Wallat, C. 1993. Interactive frames and knowledge schemas in interaction. In *Framing in Discourse*, edited by D. Tannen. Oxford University Press: 57–75.

Van den Berg, H. 1996. Frame analysis of open interviews on interethnic relations. *Bulletin de Methodologie Sociologique* 53: 5–32.

1997. Discours analyse van alledaags racisme [Discourse analysis of everyday racism]. In *De interpretatieve benadering in de communicatiewetenschap* [The interpretative approach in communication studies], edited by V. Frissen and J. Servaes. Leuven: Uitgeverij ACCO. 183–206.

Van Dijk, T. A. 1987. *Communicating racism: ethnic prejudice in thought and talk*. London: Sage.

1989. Structures and strategies of discourse and prejudice. In *Ethnic minorities; social psychological perspectives*, edited by J. P. van Oudenhoven and T. M. Willemsen. Amsterdam: Swets and Zeitlinger. 115–138.

1991. *Racism and the press*. London: Routledge.

1993. *Elite discourse and racism*. London: Sage.

Van Dijk, T. A., Ting-Toomey, S., Smitherman, G. and Troutman, D. 1997. Discourse, ethnicity, culture, and racism. In *Discourse as social interaction*, edited by T. A. Van Dijk. London: Sage. 144–180.

Wetherell, M. and Potter, J. 1992. *Mapping the language of racism*. New York: Harvester Wheatsheaf.

8   Racism, happiness, and ideology

Maykel Verkuyten

In 1775 Thomas Jefferson wrote in the famous opening words of the American Declaration of Independence: "We hold these truths to be self-evident, that all men are created equal, that they are endowed by their Creator with certain unalienable rights, that among these are life, liberty and the pursuit of happiness." The pursuit of happiness has become a fundamental individual right laid down in several key ideological texts. People have a right to be happy, and if they are not happy something has to be done about it. In this chapter I am interested in the way that this old notion of happiness functions in present-day racist talk, that is, in discourse that explains and justifies the exclusion of minority groups.

In general a distinction can be made between analytical approaches that focus on the structure of a text or talk, and those that focus on the content. Although structure and content cannot be easily separated, such a distinction is often made. For example, in his book *The uses of argument*, Toulmin (1958) distinguishes between the structure or procedure of argumentation, which he considers independent of the topic under discussion, and the kinds of justifications used in argumentation, which are topic dependent (see also Perelman and Olbrechts-Tyteca 1971). An emphasis on structure may involve a study of discursive devices, linguistic forms, and the sequential organization of texts and talk, whereas an emphasis on content may focus on cultural meanings used to define and justify specific representations. So we can look at the organization of talk, but also at the content, when analyzing how specific arguments become persuasive and bolster particular representations and claims. The present analysis focuses on content in examining how the notion of happiness functions as an argument for the exclusion of minority groups. In doing so, I try to take the broader society and its ideological history into account. This raises the question of context.

Context

In discourse analyses the problem of context is a recurrent one (see Auer and Di Luzio 1992; Goodwin and Duranti 1992). Context not only means quite different things within different approaches, but these approaches also have a different stance toward the role context should play in analyses. Context is often seen as a frame, which itself is constituted in discourse, that provides resources for the appropriate interpretation of the talk that is being examined. Anthropologists examining discourse find it necessary to take as much ethnographic material into account as possible. In contrast, linguists and conversation analysts tend to restrict context to the text or discourse itself. They stress that only the information the participants themselves orient to and make relevant in their talk should be used by the researcher. The practices and reactions of the speakers are used as the ground for determining meaning.

This emphasis on the way that the participants themselves orient to talk prevents the implicit use of unreflexive analytical categories, as in critical discourse studies (e.g. Essed 1991; Hodge and Cress 1993; Van Dijk 1987). These studies often use as an explanatory foundation for analysis a taken-for-granted approach to reality and identity. Critical analyses of racism are combined with realist accounts of the racialized or racist social system. There is a tendency to treat existing power relations and domination as a priori, as a backdrop for analysis, and thereby as unproblematic and given, whereas the phenomenon selected for analysis, such as race talk, is made problematic. In addition, identities such as "white" and "black," or majority and minority group member, are often also prior to the analysis (see Bonnett 2000). They are predominantly treated as determined by existing discourses that constitute subject positions. However, "reality" and "identity" can be considered situated and occasioned accomplishments designed to do interactional tasks. The study of these accomplishments is central in conversational analysis. Schegloff (1997) has argued that priority should be given to the "technical" analysis of the details of situated talk before more critical analysis is conducted.

In the present paper, I will try to stay close to the actual talk for examining how the notion of happiness features in the interviews. However, studying race talk with only an emphasis on details raises the question of the possibility of social critique. In a more conversation analytic approach, context is predominantly understood as being neutral (Cicourel 1992, Lindstrom 1992). Aspects of context are examined in terms of frames, scripts, perspectives, or some other analytical tool used for "entextualization" (Silverstein and Urban 1996). However, context can also be seen as a "set of cultural rules, conditions and practices that govern how people talk" (Lindstrom 1992: 102). What speakers make immediately relevant by the sequential organization of their talk often does not elucidate why a particular argument works as an adequate justification. It also does not tell us much about the nature and origin of the resources from which people construct discourses. Speaker orientations go beyond the previous turns in a conversation by drawing on "argumentative threads" (Wetherell 1998) in organizing accounts and formulating accusations and justifications. Some arguments are culturally more self-evident and pervasive than others, and therefore can be more easily mobilized in racist talk.

Talk can be situated within the speakers' cultural horizon and examined in terms of existing cultural discourses, interpretative repertoires, or arguments that are flexibly used as building blocks for constructing specific representations and justifying claims (Billig 1997; Durrheim 1997; Gramsci 1973; Wetherell and Potter 1992). In this way utterances can be linked to ideological traditions. Identifying the history of the conceptual resources that people take as natural and self-evident can be used to show their contingent origin. A historical dimension links the analysis to questions about ideology and shows how people's talk is connected to their political and moral culture. So the present analysis will examine the situated interaction on the one hand, and will look at the ideological history of the resources that shape argumentation on the other.

History and ideology

The concept of ideology is a contested one (Purvis and Hunt 1993). However, in general, theories of ideology are concerned with the way individuals or groups are reconciled to power relations that are not in their interest, or the way that power is transformed into domination and status quo (Thompson 1986). Language is increasingly seen as the main location of ideology. The traditional conception of ideology in terms of consciousness has been replaced more and more by the study of everyday discourse (Eagleton 1994). The discursive study of ideology examines the practices and resources that people use to justify their versions and accounts of the social world and to challenge those of others. The primary interest is in how distinctions and versions of reality are constructed and legitimated, in particular by making them natural or self-evident. In this way ideology is the common sense of society. Ideological themes can be examined in revealing what is taken for granted in common sense and how these themes are used for justification or criticism (Billig 1997).

Analyses of ideology have the danger of portraying individuals as passive recipients of socially determined ideas. People are easily cast as helpless victims who are subject to the ideological themes that proliferate within society. The result is that the individual person is denied agency and stripped of any personal ownership, and thereby stripped of any moral accountability or responsibility. Hence, "the 'Achilles' heel' of critical theories of ideology has been to show how ideologies penetrate the self, while at the same time retaining for normative reasons a conception of the self with capacities for reasoned political discourse and autonomous choice" (Warren 1990: 599). What is needed are notions that mediate between the constraining and determining effects of discursive regimes or dominant discourses identified by critical discourse analysis and the highly situated and occasioned talk examined by conversation analysis.

Theoretically the notions of lived ideology and ideological dilemmas, as developed by Billig and colleagues, are useful here (Billig et al. 1988). These notions were introduced as part of a more general claim about the nature of common-sense reasoning. Billig and colleagues argued that common sense is often organized through contrary themes and is dilemmatic in character. They talk about lived ideology, because ideology does not preclude thought, but rather provides the resources for thinking in and about ordinary life. Common sense does not merely reproduce a unified dominant system of integrated beliefs, but draws upon different, and often contradictory, ideological themes that have roots in Western philosophical and moral debates.

People are seen as actively using these themes for justifying and criticizing descriptions, explanations, and claims. Justifications and accounts are fashioned from these resources that have the status of socially accepted clichés, and therefore act as commonplaces (Billig 1997). Commonplaces are shared within a community and are often expressed in values, such as equality, liberty, and rationality. These values are predominantly treated as obvious and self-evident. They speak for themselves and are not questioned as such, although they can be made the topic of discussion. The result is that using them in an argument is often self-sufficient; it provides a basic accountability where no further warrant needs to be given.

Commonplaces are not only ready-made enough for discourse to be intelligible for its users, but also sufficiently flexible and vague to perform a variety of situated actions. For example, Wetherell and Potter (1992) have shown how arguments in terms of individual rights and equality are not only starting points of anti-racism, but are used also in a racist discourse. Further, in a focus group study in Rotterdam, it was found that ethnic Dutch local residents used notions such as equality, freedom, human rights, and rationality self-sufficiently in arguing about ethnic minorities living in the neighborhood (Verkuyten, De Jong, and Masson 1994). These principles were acknowledged and used by all participants in this study: that is, by those who presented themselves as anti-racist, as well as those who described themselves as more racist. The general principles were not questioned, but what gave rise to debate were the interpretations of these principles, as well as the question of whether and when such principles apply to a specific case.

The present chapter could focus further on equality, freedom, and similar core principles of liberal democratic thinking. It seems obvious to do so, because these are central notions in the political and everyday debate about ethnic minorities. However, there are several studies on the use of these principles, including Wetherell and Potter's (1992) book that is based on the interviews that are examined here. Therefore, I prefer to focus on happiness as a common-sense notion that can be linked to utilitarian moral philosophy. This notion plays a specific role in arguing about minority groups, and I found some of this in all three interviews.

In what follows I want to do two things. First, I present a short historical description of the idea of happiness in philosophical and political thinking. This description is important for analyzing the kind of conceptual resource the idea of happiness provides for argumentation and its contingent origin. Second, I examine how the notion of happiness is actually used in the interviews for arguing for the exclusion of minority groups. By addressing these two points I want to explore the relationship between ideological resources and situated talk.

Utilitarianism and happiness

The ideal of promoting happiness is an old one and a recurrent theme in the history of Western moral philosophy. The notion dates back to the ancient Greeks, and has been around ever since. Greek ethics revolved around two terms, "eudaimonia" and "arete," which are traditionally rendered as happiness and virtue.

The Greeks, however, attributed *eudaimonia* to someone with reference rather to what would normally be the source of such feelings, i.e. the possession of what is thought to be desirable, which looks more like an objective judgement. Thus someone may be called *eudaimon* because he or she is rich, powerful, has fine children and so on. (Rowe 1991: 122, his italics)

In modern English, residues of this past use of the word can still be found, although nowadays "happiness" seems more often to connote a subjective feeling of contentment or pleasure. In this change from references to social actions and circumstances to references to mental states, the word "happy" shows a similar historical transformation as other emotion words (Harr and Gillett: 1994).

At the end of the eighteenth century, the notion of happiness obtained a firm foothold, and at the beginning of the nineteenth century it became dominant in Western philosophical thinking with the British utilitarians Bentham and Mill. For utilitarians the principle of utility is the ultimate source of appeal for the determination of the moral value of actions. Bentham and Mill had a strong political and social commitment and used the principle of utility for criticizing the then existing moral convictions and social institutions.[1] Utilitarianism was an important force behind changes in nineteenth-century Britain. The utility principle was thought to be very useful because it made more rational decisions possible. The utility calculus would guaranty an objective decision-making process and an optimal outcome. This principle has survived as one of the ideological ingredients of current Western welfare states and public policy making. Decisions are often justified by utilitarian calculations, that is, they produce more good than any alternative would. Utilitarians think that these kinds of calculations simply make explicit and systematic what is already implicit in common-sense thinking. Utilitarianism provides a justificatory framework, and the utilitarian approach has filtered down from a philosophical system into common sense and practical policy decision making (Beauchamp 1991).

Utilitarianism is one of several ethical theories that assess the worth of actions by their consequences. These teleological theories are more or less the opposite of deontological ones. These latter theories argue that the rightness of actions cannot exclusively be determined by their consequences because other features of acts, such as duty and obligations, make them right or wrong. In the Western world, deontological theories have become less prominent than they are, for example, throughout much of Asia, where the emphasis is more on the desirability of duty and the moral obligation to others.

The basic idea of utilitarianism is simple in that the moral value of conduct is considered to be dependent on its effects. Actions that are useful are considered right.[2] This of course raises the question, "Useful for what, or how are we to determine what things are valuable?" The answer that Bentham and Mill gave was that we ought to look for things that are intrinsically rather than extrinsically valuable, and according to them happiness is the only thing that is good in itself. However, different interpretations of the utility principle exist. Griffin (1982) argues that there are two kinds of approaches. The first one defines utility in terms of mental states, whereas the second one emphasizes states of the world.

The first approach follows Bentham and Mill in arguing that actions are right to the extent that they promote pleasure and the absence of pain. This hedonistic utilitarianism is based on the empirical proposition that people are by nature driven by the experience of pleasure and pain, and that a moral theory should not ignore this basic fact. Bentham (in Beauchamp 1991: 139) wrote, "Nature has placed mankind under the governance of two sovereign masters, pain and pleasure. It is for them alone to point out what we ought to do, as well as to determine what we shall do." This idea was not new and is, for example, central in several psychological theories of motivation and learning. It also has had considerable influence on thinking about psychological well-being and individual rights.[3] The value of pleasure and pain is considered natural, and thereby non-moral. However, the production of happiness assumes moral and not merely personal significance when the consequences of actions importantly affect pleasurable or painful states of existence for others. From this, the well-known Greatest Happiness Principle was formulated, which has been very influential in political thinking. For example, it has been claimed that governments are responsible for promoting the greatest happiness of the largest number of people. Though not unchallenged, this view still enjoys considerable support.[4]

Bentham and Mill did not make a clear distinction between happiness and pleasure. Others, however, have argued that a distinction is necessary because statements of pleasure refer to subjective mental states, whereas happiness can have a more objective side to it, referring to states of the world. What matters is not only how one "feels from the inside," but also how these feelings are related to the world. This perspective raises the question of the relationship between the world and well-being. An answer to this question is found in individual preferences. For this approach the concept of utility refers to actual preferences. What is intrinsically valuable is not the pleasantness of experiences, but what people prefer to obtain. Utility is translated into satisfying or providing what a person has chosen from among the alternatives. The good is interpreted in terms of what is desired or wanted in the world. This preference utilitarianism approach links individual desire and choice with actions and states of the world.

Analysis

Extracts from the three interviews will be examined in which the notion of happiness is explicitly used. In the first extract the participant is talking about immigrants from the Islands. Immediately before the extract he has drawn a contrast between Maoris and immigrants, and he has given an elaborated and layered causal story explaining why immigrants cause problems (see Potter and Wetherell 1988). Then he goes on.

Extract 1 (Appendix: New Zealand Interview 16: 276/277)

1. R: They had brilliant lives, they had brilliant lives back in-
2.   family lives, back in the Islands
3. I: Yeah
4. R: That's where they should be
5. I: Right yeah so it's just causing social problems
6.   (0.6)
7. R: Mhmm, they're coming here (.) looking like- well like the (.)
8.   Ita:lians [we:nt to: N:ew York
9. I: [(°Yeah°)
10. I: °Mm mhm°
11. R: The streets are paved with gold
12. I: [Yeah
13. R: [That's what they're coming here for
14. I: Mh mhm
15.   (0.6)
16. R: But they're not
17. I: Mm mhm
18. R: An' dey- Yeah they're probably all quite happy living in
19.   their- living in Otara or living in their [little communities
20. I: [Mm mhm
21. I: Yes
22. R: But hhhh. (1.2) do we really want them?

Different interesting things can be said about this extract, for example, the us–them distinction that forms the major backdrop of the talk. This distinction was an intrinsic aspect of the topic of the interviews and was sometimes prompted by the interviewer.

Here I am concerned with the way in which certain views are justified, in the first part, the view that immigrants should return to their country of origin, and, in the second part, the view that "they" should stay in their little communities. The central claim in this piece of talk is in line 4, where it is stated that immigrants should be in their place of origin. A first argument to substantiate this claim was made in the talk preceding this extract and is repeated by the interviewer in line 5: it [immigration] is just causing social problems. "They" are coming with the idea that the "streets are paved with gold," whereas, the participant stresses, this is not so.

A second argument is that immigrants had brilliant and happy lives back in the Islands. The claim that "they" should return to or stay in their place of origin is related to the factual claim that "they" had brilliant and happy lives back there. In lines 1–2 this latter claim is presented as a mere fact. A similar line of argument is in lines 18–19, where it is stated that "they" are happily living in Otara, which is a suburb of Auckland where most Pacific Island immigrants live. Here the qualifying term "probably" is used before asking whether "we really want them" (line 22).

These factual claims about life in the place of origin or residence function as arguments for "them" living there, because happiness is implicitly used as the principle for evaluating situations. It is this principle that provides the justification for the link between the facts as presented and the claim made. The principle of happiness and the good life is used here self-evidently, apparently needing no further explanation or discussion. It functions as a sort of bridge between presented facts and claim. This is not specific for this piece of talk, but can be found also in the other two interviews (see also Verkuyten 1997).

In the extract, happiness is related to real geographical places, which brings in the notion of belonging. People are happy in a certain place, the place they belong. In the extract this is the Islands of origin where their family is or their little communities in Otara. These constructions make it possible for arguing that it is in their own interest to live there instead of here. So a specific interpretation of happiness is provided: happiness as belonging to a place of origin or residence.[5]

The argument of happiness can also do some discursive work. The familiar argument of the problems that "they" cause for "us" only takes the perspective of the majority group into account, and therefore is easily subject to criticisms and accusations. The reference to happiness in a way softens the negativity of this argument by stressing the positive effects for the immigrants. It is to their benefit, and in particular their well-being and happiness, to return to their islands or to stay in their communities. The use of both arguments helps to manage the potential conflict of interest between us and them. Interests are presented as complementary: what is in our interest is also in their interest. This presentation makes the argument for return-migration and the question of whether "we really want them" (line 21) more acceptable and defensible. It also makes the argument one that can not be discounted easily as a mere product of self-interest.

Moreover, the definition of their lives in the Islands as brilliant and happy, together with the claim that immigrants come for material reasons, provides an argument for their return without questioning the speaker's or society's moral status. This definition does not question the general willingness to accept others who, for example, are political refugees or live under deplorable, "unhappy" circumstances in their place of origin. Rejecting these kinds of immigrants would mean a threat to one's status as a moral and responsible human being when arguing for return-migration.

The next participant uses quite a similar line of reasoning when talking about immigrants and why they should return. At the end of the interview, the question from the interviewer was whether New Zealand could cope with some more immigrants, and the answer from the respondent was "no." New Zealand should not have an "open door policy with the Islands." Then the participant explains herself.

Extract 2 (Appendix: New Zealand Interview 44: 305/306)

```
 1.  R:   U::hm because really they seem to be causing more
 2.        problems than anything
 3.  I:   Right [yeah
 4.  R:          [An' I would rather we had immigrants in from England
 5.  I:   Right [yeah
 6.  R:          [U::hm (0.2) than (0.4) leaving it just open to (.)
 7.        just anyone coming in from the Is[lands.
 8.  I:                                      [( )
 9.  I:   Ri[ght
10.  R:     [just because they just happen to have a relation (0.2) or just
11.        com↑ing
12.  I:   Yes (0.4) yeah
13.  R:   I think that's wrong
14.  I:   Mhm [yeah
15.  R:        [Because they're not happy here. It's- it's no good for
16.        the:m
17.  I:   Right [yeah
18.  R:          [as- as well as uhm they create problems (0.4) for ↑us
19.        (1.0)
20.  I:   Right
21.        (.)
22.  R:   Yeah
23.        (0.4)
24.  I:   Yeah
25.  R:   I certainly don't think they're happier here
```

Again we see a strong us–them distinction that is emphasized. Also we see the same two factual claims that function as arguments against immigrants from the Islands, separately introduced by the term "because" (lines 1 and 15). First they create problems for us. This situation stands in contrast to immigrants from England, and this contrast underlines the general willingness to accept immigrants. Second, they are not happy here so it is not good for them to come to New Zealand. In line 25 the participant explicitly uses "happiness" as a criterion for evaluating immigration from the Islands. In this extract the focus is on their soon-to-be-realized unhappiness here, rather than their assumed happiness in their country of origin. This difference is understandable because the talk is about potential new immigrants and not about return-migration. This difference shows that the notion of happiness can function in arguing for return-migration as well as against further immigration. In both cases happiness is related to a geographical place of belonging, a place where people should stay. However, this argument of geographically related happiness is not applied to potential immigrants from England.

As in the previous extract there is also an implicit calculation, whereby their not coming to New Zealand brings the greatest good for the greatest number, for us as well as for them. Both "their" and "our" happiness is an important issue. In this calculation a relative notion of happiness is used. The talk is about being "happier" and "much happier," and not happiness in an absolute sense.

Let us turn to the third participant, who is also using the notion of happiness when talking about immigrants. The next extract is from a passage where this participant states that restrictions on immigration are unfortunately necessary. Then he continues to talk about return-migration.

Extract 3 (Appendix: New Zealand Interview 2: 261)

1. R: I think you know there's one thing I can't see
2. is why when the Cook Islanders work their life
3. in New Zealand and want to go back to Cook, Rarotonga
4. and draw their pension their old age pension there,
5. it would be good for the economy of the country out there.
6. They're going to get the same money from New Zealand,
7. you know the government's going to pay the same pension,
8. why they won't pay it to them while they're in Rarotonga
9. they'd be much happier back there and you know they
10. wouldn't be um taking up housing, you know cheap flats
11. or state housing and anything like that here.

Here I only want to draw attention to the way that the notion of happiness is used. As with the previous participants, we see at the end of the extract how on the one hand it is good for us when they return to their island, and on the other hand it is good for them because they will be much happier back there. So the interests are presented as complementary, and this representation is strengthened by presenting the government as blocking a return that would be beneficial for all. Note that in this extract the participant is talking about islanders who want to go back, and not that they should go back. It is their own preference, and providing what they prefer would lead to them being much happier.

These three examples are about immigrants who have an island of origin and therefore in principle can return to a specific geographical place. This situation of course is different for the Maoris. However, also in relation to the Maoris, the argument of happiness can be used for exclusion.

Extract 4 (Appendix: New Zealand Interview 16: 278)

1. I: (. . .) Finally (.) the last section of questions (1.0) is about'em
2.   (0.6) New Zealand as a multi-cultural society (.) Do you
3.   think there's still differences between Maori and Pakeha
4.   people in terms of temperament and interests (0.6) or are we
5.   really (.) o:ne- (0.4) one nation, one people
6.   (2.2)
7. R: There is a lot of difference (1.0) uhm New Zealand is
8.   basically a whi:te (1.0)
9. I: °Mm mhm°
10. R: a white society a::nd (1.0) some of the Maoris fit in
11. I: °Mm mhm°
12.   (1.6)
13. R: And the ones- some of the ones in the cities fit in the ones in the
14.   country (1.6) are quite happy where they ↑are
15. I: °Mm mhm°
16. R: Uhm (2.6) so it probly- (they don't/it may not) really bother
17.   them I don't really know.
18. I: Yeah
19. R: But then you've got the misfits that don't fit in.
20. I: Yeah

Three points can be made. First, we clearly see here the importance of a distinction between "us" and "them," and the factual claim that there is a difference. Further, the definition of New Zealand as basically a white society makes it possible to talk about the Maoris as "fitting in or not."

Second, in the extract the notion of happiness is related to fitting in and living in the country. It is unclear whether happiness refers to a geographical or a social place, but the former seems more plausible in relation to the "ones in the country." Then it is claimed that because they are happy they are probably not really bothered by general issues of race and interests. In this way the existing relationship is justified. They are happy where they are (and so are we), and therefore they should stay where they are, implying that change is not necessary.

On the other hand there are those that don't fit in, and in the talk that follows after this extract it becomes clear what is meant by this: a minority that expects and demands more and more, that wants to get their own way, which in the end will lead to an underground terrorist organization. Interestingly the ones that do not fit in are not described as unhappy but as self-interested and extremists. A definition of unhappiness would more easily lead to a legitimate claim for change.

Third, I want to draw attention here to the different qualifications that are made in this and the other extracts, such as "quite happy," "probably," and "I don't really know." These qualifications do some discursive work.

The expression of uncertainty qualifies the descriptions and thereby works against the suggestion that the talk is the mere result of the speaker's interests or racist views. Hence, these qualifications can be seen as functioning to head off a self-interested or racist imputation.

So in these extracts the notion of happiness is used for arguing for the exclusion of immigrants and minority groups. However, the use of "happiness" in justifying exclusion and domination can also be shown in relation to other topics. In the next extract the topic is women politicians.

Extract 5 (Appendix: New Zealand Interview 44: 291)

```
1.  I:   What do you think about the- the- the new breed of
2.       women politicians which have been emerging in
3.       the last uh
4.  R:   Like Annie Hercus
5.  I:   Ye:s and [(0.4) further back Marilyn Waring
6.  R:            [((throat clear/little cough))
7.       (1.0)
8.  R:   U:hm all right (1.0) they- they've got their opinions
9.       a:nd (0.6) but I think they went too fa:r
10. I:   Mm mhm
11. R:   and (1.2) because I believe that (0.6) u:hm any woman is
12.      as liberated [if she wants to be
13. I:                [Mm mhm
14. I:   Yes [yeah
15. R:       [There are a lot of women who don't want to be that-
16.      [they're quite happy being (.) [dominated
17. I:   [Yeah                          [(Right)
18. I:   Yes (.) [yeah
19. R:           [and (0.6) an' if a woman re:ally wants to get to the top in
20.      something (.) you can ↑do it
21. I:   Yes (0.4) yeah
```

Women politicians are accused of going too far, and it is interesting to see how a contrast is made whereby women politicians have their opinions, but so have others. Then it is claimed that every woman can be liberated, but that some do not want to be (lines 11–12, 15), and are even quite happy being dominated (line 16). When women prefer not to be liberated and are quite happy, then the situation is as it should be. So existing domination is justified by a claim on self-determined happiness that is presented as a more important goal than other possible goals. The notion of happiness is associated with a social space where women are being dominated and is related to the claim about existing possibilities for choice. This presentation makes the claim difficult to refute because such refutation has the danger of being related to notions of paternalism or to the distinction between true and false consciousness.

Discussion

Studying race talk (implicitly) involves social critique. In critical discourse analysis this critique is often based on a series of unquestioned assumptions, so that the analysis risks being undermined by the uncritical acceptance of "facts," which are assumed to be self-evident. Critical analyses are combined with a realist account of the racist social system and a fixation and reduction of identities by using racial identity as background knowledge that informs the analysis.

The present analysis tried to stay close to the actual talk by examining how the notion of happiness featured in the interviews. An emphasis on situated talk and speakers' own orientations helps to prevent the use of unreflexive analytical categories. It was demonstrated how "happiness" functioned as a commonplace resource for the justification of the exclusion of minority groups. In their talk the speakers made distinctions between "us" and "them," and the notion of happiness was not questioned as such. It functioned as a self-evident and self-sufficient argument that places a morally loaded frame of reference on the state of affairs. Happiness is good, and people should be happy and have a right to be happy.

The analysis was grounded in the talk itself. The notion of "happiness" was used and oriented to by the participants themselves. I tried to demonstrate empirically that this notion has relevance for the participants and functioned as an argument linking claims about exclusion and "facts" about life in specific places. However, it also seems necessary to examine the nature and origin of this notion for understanding why it is used and treated as an adequate and self-sufficient justification in these interviews. Restricting the analysis to the technical details, as in conversation analysis (e.g. Schegloff 1997), limits the possibility for plausible and insightful critical analyses of discursive patterning. From my perspective, analysis of race talk has to pay close attention to the organization and details of the talk, but also to the history and content of the arguments and commonplaces that are displayed in the participants' orientations (see Wetherell 1998).

Gramsci (1973) argues that elements of common sense have their own history, so that common sense is situated within a wider context than the actual situated talk. This context is not neutral and differs in this respect from the frames, scripts, or perspectives that are typically studied by linguists and conversation analysts. Present-day talk is full of elements of (moral) philosophy that have passed into common sense and are taken as natural and self-evident. A detailed analysis of situated talk does not tell us much about the nature and history of the resources from which people construct discourses. However, a reference to happiness can achieve its situated argumentative function not only because of the organization of the talk, but also because of its specific ideological nature and origin. An understanding of the ideological meanings involved requires a broad historical analysis. Talk of the present is linked to discussions of the past, making it possible for ideological notions to function as arguments. Hence, what is required in examining race talk critically is to "be prepared to look at the microprocesses of present interaction in terms of the long reach of history" (Billig and Sabucedo 1994: 141). On the basis of content elements in the talk, it can be assumed that there is access to ideological resources that makes particular arguments and definitions available. Further, by studying how these notions are actually and flexibly used, it can be examined whether they act as commonplaces that have consequences for race relations.

The historical background is important for another theoretical reason. Many studies examining situated interactions stress the flexibility and variability of talk and the indexicality of meaning. Words take on specific meanings relative to the actual situation of their utterance. This stress on situation is of course centrally important, but can lead to a neglect of the possibility of more stable meanings. In all the extracts discussed the underlying idea is that unhappiness implies a need for or a right to change, whereas happiness is an argument for the status quo, and even domination. Arguing that "they" will be less happy here (and thus are more happy there) is arguing against further immigration. Arguing that "they" will be more happy there (and thus are less happy here) is arguing for return-migration. Happiness is a basic individual right. Hence, certain definitions (unhappiness and change) are more likely to be accepted than others, and certain constructions (unhappiness and status quo) need much more discursive work to support them than others. Due to their specific history, notions may have cultural default values, which implies that more work has to be done to use them in another way. This does not mean that competing constructions are not possible. For example, happiness can be made problematic, such as in happy-go-lucky, or where happiness is related to a lack of responsibility or a lack of choice. Furthermore, there are also other moral notions available for criticizing an argument in terms of happiness, such as virtue and duty.

Thus the fact that its ideological history gives the notion of happiness often a self-evident meaning does not imply that challenges are not possible. As the history of utilitarian thinking shows there are always questions of interpretation leading to debate. For example, preference utilitarianism argues for a distinction between happiness and pleasure. Pleasure is considered a subjective state, whereas happiness refers to people's choices and desires in relation to actual situations in the world. For justifying domination, the participants made this relationship between choice and situation in talking about happiness. In the interviews, a reference to happiness also functioned as a justification for the exclusion of minority groups because a specific definition was given. In particular, happiness was related to a geographical (or social) place, a place of belonging (or "fitting in"). This is an important construction because it allows the argument that it is in "their" interest not to come here, to return to their land of origin, or to stay in their social place. It is in their own interest, which happens to be also in our interest, so that, for example, return-migration brings the greatest good for the greatest number.

In contrast, a definition of happiness in relation to the local living conditions would make it possible to argue in favor of minority groups. For example, in a focus group study in Rotterdam, two participants argued in favor of the position of ethnic minorities and for positive changes in their living conditions (Verkuyten 1997). These self-defined anti-racist participants argued that ethnic minorities live and belong in the neighborhood but were not happy at all. Their definition in terms of the local situation made it very difficult for the other participants to criticize the plea for changes for minorities. Happiness is a human right and something has to be done when people feel miserable in the place where they belong, including minorities.

NOTES

1. They also proposed concrete social improvements. A well-known example is Bentham's design for a new prison system, the Panopticum.
2. A distinction is often made between act and rule utilitarians. This concerns the debate on the question of whether the principle of utility should be applied to acts in particular circumstances or whether it should be applied to rules of conduct that themselves determine what is right or wrong.
3. For example, happiness is considered an important indicator for the quality of life. Therefore, measures that assess happiness are used for evaluating sociocultural conditions between groups, regions, and countries (e.g. Campbell 1981; Veenhoven 1984).
4. Later utilitarians argued that there are other kinds of intrinsic value besides pleasantness. In particular, pluralistic utilitarians reject a monistic conception of intrinsic value by arguing that values such as health, courage, and friendship have intrinsic worth.
5. Note also the reference to "family lives" (line 2). This is not only interesting because it is often a major (conservative) political topic, but also because the family-origin metaphor gives a genealogical definition of ethnicity (Roosens 1994). It is also tempting, although not unproblematic, to read in this extract residues of the old image of the "noble savage" that is available in common sense as a sort of stock character. Historically there are two somewhat contradictory images people can draw upon for such characterizations, and

anthropologists have shown that in the colonial period both images were useful for justifying all kinds of exploitation and atrocities. One is the dangerous,
sexual, and wild savage that should be controlled, and the other is the prim-
itive, ignorant man who happily lives in his original affluent, tight, and little
(line 19) community. References to this latter image were made by interviewee 2 (last 30 lines of the interview) in describing Australian Aborigines and
Maoris.

References

Auer, P. and Di Luzio, A., editors. 1992. *The contextualization of language.*
Amsterdam: John Benjamins.
Beauchamp, T. L. 1991. *Philosophical ethics.* 2nd edn. New York: McGraw Hill.
Billig, M. 1997. Discursive, rhetorical, and ideological messages. In *The message of
social psychology*, edited by C. McGarty and S. A. Haslam. Oxford: Blackwell.
36–53.
Billig, M., Condor, S., Edwards, D., Gane, M., Middleton, D. and Radley, A. R.
1988. *Ideological dilemmas: a social psychology of everyday thinking.* London:
Sage.
Billig, M. and Sabucedo, J. M. 1994. Rhetorical and ideological dimensions
of common sense. In *The status of common sense in psychology*, edited by
J. Siegfried. Norwood, NJ: Ablex. 121–145.
Bonnett, A. 2000. *Anti-racism.* London: Routledge.
Campbell, A. 1981. *The sense of well-being in America: recent patterns and trends.*
New York: McGraw-Hill.
Cicourel, A. V. 1992. The interpenetration of communicative contexts: examples
from medical encounters. In *Rethinking context: language as an interactive
phenomenon*, edited by A. Duranti and C. Goodwin. Cambridge: Cambridge
University Press. 291–310.
Durrheim, K. 1997. Cognition and ideology: a rhetorical approach to critical
theory. *Theory and Psychology* 7: 747–768.
Eagleton, T. 1994. *Ideology.* London: Longman.
Essed, P. (1991). *Understanding everyday racism.* Newbury Park, CA: Sage.
Goodwin, C. and Duranti, A. 1992. Rethinking context: an introduction. In
Rethinking context: language as an interactive phenomenon, edited by A. Duranti
and C. Goodwin. Cambridge: Cambridge University Press. 1–42.
Gramsci, A. 1973. *Selections from prison notebooks.* London: Lawrence and
Wishart.
Griffin, J. 1982. Modern utilitarianism. *Revue Internationale de Philosophie* 36:
331–375.
Harr, R. and Gillett, G. 1994. *The discursive mind.* London: Sage.
Hodge, R. and Kress, G. 1993. *Language as ideology.* 2nd edn. London:
Routledge.
Lindstrom, L. 1992. Context contests: debatable truth statements on Tanna
(Vanuata). In *Rethinking context: language as an interactive phenomenon*, edited
by A. Duranti and C. Goodwin. Cambridge: Cambridge University Press.
101–124.

Perelman, C. and Olbrechts-Tyteca, L. 1971. *The new rhetoric*. Indiana: University of Notre Dame Press.

Potter, J. and Wetherell, M. 1988. Accomplishing attitudes: fact and evaluation in racist discourse. *Text* 8: 51–68.

Purvis, T. and Hunt, A. 1993. Discourse, ideology, discourse, ideology, discourse, ideology . . . *British Journal of Sociology* 44: 473–499.

Roosens, E. 1994. The primordial nature of origins in migrant ethnicity. In *The anthropology of ethnicity*, edited by H. Vermeulen and C. Govers. Amsterdam: Spinhuis. 81–104.

Rowe, C. 1991. Ethics in ancient Greece. In *A companion to ethics*, edited by P. Singer. Oxford: Blackwell. 121–132.

Schegloff, E. A. 1997. Whose text? Whose context? *Discourse and Society* 8: 165–187.

Silverstein, M. and Urban, G. (1996). The natural history of discourse. In *Natural histories of discourse*, edited by M. Silverstein and G. Urban. Chicago, IL: University of Chicago Press. 1–17.

Thompson, J. B. 1986. Language and ideology: a framework for analysis. *Sociology* 35: 516–536.

Toulmin, S. E. 1958. *The uses of argument*. Cambridge: Cambridge University Press.

Van Dijk, T. 1987. *Communicating racism: ethnic prejudice in thought and talk*. Newbury Park: Sage.

Veenhoven, R. 1984. *Conditions of happiness*. Dordrecht, the Netherlands: Reidel.

Verkuyten, M. 1997. *"Redelijk" racism*. Amsterdam University Press.

Verkuyten, M., De Jong, W. and Masson, C. N. 1994. Similarities in anti-racist and racist discourse: Dutch local residents talking about ethnic minorities. *New Community* 20: 253–268.

Warren, M. 1990. Ideology and the self. *Theory and Society* 19: 599–634.

Wetherell, M. (1998). Positioning and interpretative repertoires: conversation analysis and post-structuralism in dialogue. *Discourse and Society* 9: 387–412.

Wetherell, M. and Potter, J. 1992. *Mapping the language of racism*. London: Harvester-Wheatsheaf.

9   The frame analysis of research interviews: social categorization and footing in interview discourse

Titus Ensink

Introduction

The three interviews that are central to this volume are part of a corpus of interviews collected by Margaret Wetherell. The corpus is described in Wetherell and Potter (1992: 98–100 and 221–224). These interviews were conducted from within a conversational perspective on social research:

> On the one hand, this involved the interviewer being an animated conversationalist, commenting and providing the sorts of "back channel" "ums" and "yes" responses that are characteristic of informal talk. On the other, this involved being prepared to be much more straightforwardly argumentative than would be appropriate in an orthodox research interview: offering counter examples, questioning assumptions and so on. (Wetherell and Potter 1992: 99)

This approach to research interviews acknowledges the intrinsic interactional nature of the interview situation. Interviews (even those that are conducted from the orthodox point of view) are conversations between an interviewer and a respondent. Hence they have properties that any human interaction has. They are open-ended, unpredictable, situation-bound, open to negotiation, and vulnerable to misunderstandings. In addition, the content of the interaction is influenced by emotional and relational factors (Cicourel 1964: chapter 3; Mazeland and Ten Have 1996). These properties preclude interactional materials from being fully interpretable out of context, within fixed interpretative coding schemata. The question then is, how to make use of interview materials in analysis?

    In this paper, I propose to answer this question by considering interviews as based on frames. First, I will sketch a framework for the description of interviews as framed activities. I will then argue that particular details of the way in which the interview participants formulate their questions, answers, and remarks are indicative of the way these frames operate. The formulations I will focus on are manifestations of the participants' footing and (self-) categorizing. In their footing, participants show on the basis of what authority they express their views. In the way they categorize self and others, they display their identification with or distance from others in society. I will analyze fragments of the interviews in order to show how the analysis of footing and (self-) categorizing sheds light on the issue of how ethnicity is constructed or expressed.

Interviews as framed activities

Frames

In this paper, I use the term "frame" in a double sense. Frames operate both on a social and a cognitive level. Whenever people interact, their behaviors may be considered as constructed in coherent patterns, which may be termed "frames" (Lee 1997; Tannen 1993). On the other hand, frames are independent cognitive psychological structures that "show themselves" in the behaviors of people (e.g. coherence phenomena based on script-like structures: Baddeley 1990: 335; Pan and Kosicki 1993; Schank and Abelson 1977). Of course, both senses of the term are related. In fact, the first sense is a specific instance of the second one. Social interactions get their meaning when they are interpreted, and their interpretation is guided by frames. It is useful, however, to distinguish both senses since they draw on different sets of theoretical connotations.

The social/interactional sense of frame is shown in example 1. A high school pupil asks her father to test her knowledge of French, because she is having an exam about French vocabulary the next day. Her father takes the list of vocabulary items and starts:

Example 1

F(ather):	Wednesday
D(aughter):	mercredi
F:	butcher
D:	le boucher
F:	car
D:	la voiture
F:	why
D:	[puzzled] well, "car" is just "voiture" in French

The daughter interprets "why" as a demand for explanation (which the utterance of the isolated word "why" undoubtedly is, in most cases), whereas it was meant as the next vocabulary item (so as to expect the daughter to mention the proper French word, "pourquoi"). People design their contributions to an ongoing interaction so as to fit in a frame, a known scheme or pattern. And people *expect* each other's contributions to fit into frames, the basic function of which is to create schemes of expectation (Tannen 1993). Application of a frame that is different from the intended one yields a form of misunderstanding that is not attributable to mishearing the spoken words, or applying different semantic meanings.

The second (cognitive) meaning of frame is shown in Example 2.

Example 2
Sudden death is a German specialty

The noun phrase "sudden death" has different meanings, depending on which knowledge is activated by the context, such as some medical context, or the context of an undecided sports contest (whoever scores the next point wins the game), or the context of a discussion about capital punishment. According to a news message (on August 15, 1996) in several Dutch newspapers, the utterance in example 2 was used as a slogan by the German chemical corporation Bayer in its Guatemalan advertising campaign for an insecticide. Apparently, the slogan is meant to invoke two knowledge frames. First, a frame related to sport events: one is supposed to remember that the German soccer team became world champion in the 1996 tournament, winning a tied game according to the sudden death rule. Second, a frame related to everyday life biology: irritating insects may be gotten rid of by using a poisonous spray. To many people, however, an unintended third frame was most dominant: historical knowledge about the holocaust. The juxtaposition of the third frame yields a highly cynical meaning. According to the newspaper message, Bayer decided to stop its campaign for that reason.

The meaning attributed to a behavior (example 1) or an otherwise identical phrase (example 2) is decided according to which general cognitive pattern is invoked. In general, all meanings are attributed on the basis of cognitive frames. When confronted with an unframeable perception, people literally are at a loss. Without frames, they *cannot make sense* of their perceptions (Goffman 1974: 21, 28–29).

Frames in interviews

The following frames may be shown to be operative in research interviews (Van den Berg 1996):
(a) the interview frame
(b) the social research frame
(c) the mutual relation frame
(d) the topic-related cognitive frame

(a) The basic interactional frame to which both interviewer and respondent orient themselves is the *interview frame*. The basic interactional pattern consists of questions and answers, related to the basic roles that interviewer and respondent play in the interview. This pattern is not only

fundamental to research interviews, but to any kind of interview, e.g. news interviews, job interviews, etc. (Schegloff 1988/89: 218; Heritage and Greatbatch 1991: 97–98). Both participants and analysts expect to see interactional patterns showing this Q–A sequence. The operation of this frame explains why several utterances of the interviewer are heard as questions, and why, by the same token, utterances by the respondent are taken to be answers.

(b) The goal of these interviews is to provide data for some research project. The data will be used to answer some research question. Furthermore, the interview is not an "autonomous" social occasion, but one within a series of similar occasions. Other respondents from the sample will be interviewed as well. Awareness of these facts is possibly relevant to the participants: the *social research frame*. (There is a parallel here to the awareness of the participants of news interviews that what they say is meant for an "overhearing" audience, Heritage and Greatbach 1991: 107.) In extract 1, the respondent shows some awareness that the interviewer is a researcher.

Extract 1 (Appendix: New Zealand Interview 2: 236)

```
1. R:  I think- what you (want/ought) to do is a- a thesis into the a
2. I:  Mm mhm
3. R:  operation of maritime u:nions
4. I:  .hh (0.4) Yes (.) that would be in- Yeah thad be very interesting. It'd
5.     probably be difficult for me to get access to some of the (1.0) the
6.     materials
```

Note that the interviewer's reaction is formulated from within two frames. The reaction is accommodating within the mutual relation frame ("thad be very interesting . . ."), but is evasive within the research frame ("difficult for me to get access . . ."). The interviewer also makes reference to the research frame, mentioning answers that *other* respondents have provided, e.g. in extract 2:

Extract 2 (Appendix: New Zealand Interview 16: 271)

```
1. I:  Some of the people I've talked to have suggested that the police possibly
2.     (0.4) escalated the violence through their actions. Is that a view that you
3.     agree with?
```

Obviously, "some of the people" are from the research sample, not from some other possible group the interviewer happens to have talked to. By the same token, "I've talked to" refers to interviews, not to some other social occasion. The research interview is not an autonomous social event, but an event within a sample.

(c) Both the interviewer and the respondent see each other on the basis of more than just the roles defined by being the interviewer and the respondent. Thus, a frame of *mutual relation* is active. The interview is a being-together of two persons who may or may not like each other, who show inevitably some form of social accommodation related to each other's age, sex, ethnicity, pronunciation, appearance, and so on. This frame is rather ambivalent in relation to methodological criteria. For one thing, this frame may help to establish a rapport between the interviewer and the respondent, thus encouraging the respondent to comply with the interview's demands (Babbie 1995: 289–290). On the other hand, the frame interferes with the methodological demands of neutrality and stability (Moser and Kalton 1971: 299). In some instances in the three interviews, we see the interviewer react (for example, expressing that a respondent's story is "marvelous") in a way that a neutral interviewer should not, but which is understandable within a human relationship of mutually sharing experiences.

(*d*) Both the interviewer and the respondent need to have mutually shared *topic-related cognitive frames* at their disposal. These frames may be used in order to describe the (organization of the) large amount of background knowledge people need to share in order to communicate effectively. The idea of a frame structure is common to several disciplines that are concerned with communication and knowledge, such as psychology (e.g. Baddeley 1990; Schank and Abelson 1977), discourse analysis, cognitive linguistics, and artificial intelligence (for an overview, see Brown and Yule 1983: 233–256; Tannen 1993; Lee 1997). People know what they are talking about because of the frames they share. Frames contribute to the "common ground" on the basis of which people are able to communicate (Clark 1996: chapter 4). Frames make it possible to leave many normal aspects of what one is talking about unmentioned, without the risk of not being understood.

Interference of frames

We are now in a position to characterize research interviews in terms of frames. The orthodox methodological view on research interviews is that frames *a* and *d* are prominent, in the sense that *a* is the means of getting a view of *d* and of attitudes and experiences related to *d*. And this is what research interviews *ought to* be. Frames *b* and *c* are a nuisance, and should be avoided. Within social reality, however, all frames interact. Hence, social reality does not allow one to get rid of this nuisance so easily. Implicitly, all methodologists are very well aware of this. Rules and guidelines in order to avoid, for example, answers according to social desirability presuppose the existence and pressure on behavior of frames *b* and *c*.

Of course, social desirability plays an important role in respondents' (and interviewers') behavior related to ethnicity. The editors of this volume have asked the contributors to suggest possibilities for dealing with ethnicity (and the extreme form of it, racism) as a topic in interviews. Especially concerning ethnicity, the view on interviews as a way of getting access to frame (d) by means of frame (a) is not sufficient. The answer that I should like to suggest is to follow the ethnomethodological adage to treat the "nuisance" (i.e., the working of the different frames) *as a resource*. This may be done by analyzing participants' footing and (self-) categorizing.

Footing and social categorizing

I borrow the term "footing" from Erving Goffman (1979, 1981). Footing may be decribed as "participants' interactional positions in any encounter. Whenever people interact, verbally or not, they take up some sort of position with respect to others" (Wortham 1996: 332). The concept applies especially to the involvement of participants in the interview.

Speakers may take up various footings in relation to their own remarks. By employing different "production formats" they may convey distinctions between the animator, author and principal of what is said. The "animator" is the person who presently utters a sequence of words. The one who originated the beliefs and sentiments, and perhaps also composed the words through which they are expressed, is the "author." Finally, the "principal" is the person whose viewpoint or position is currently expressed in and through the utterance. (Clayman 1992: 165. See also Ensink 1997, Levinson 1988)

In their footing, people show the authority their words are supposed to have. I will argue that participants' footing is a major source of social information (Wortham 1996).

The "position with respect to others" in research interviews is of course initially determined by the interview situation itself. Frame (a) as described above is the basis for the behaviors and the perceptions of both interviewer and respondent. Any change relating to this frame thus is a change in footing. A case in point is when the respondent gets a phone call and temporarily changes from "respondent" into whatever role the telephone talk puts him. However, such cases are rather trivial. More interesting are cases in which the respondent subtly changes his own role as respondent. For example, a respondent may formulate an answer not on his own behalf, but in a quasi-quoted way, so as to make a fictitious non-existing other liable as the author of the words uttered. (In extract 2 we have already seen an example of a change in the interviewer's footing: the point of view expressed is not her own, but quoted from other respondents, possibly in order to show a neutral position, Clayman 1992.) Examples of these footing phenomena have been described in standardized survey interviews by Houtkoop-Steenstra (2000: 44–54), and in news interviews by Clayman (1992) and Heritage and Greatbach (1991). Wortham (1996) has shown a procedure for the systematic analysis of participants' footing; the procedure focuses on the use of deictics, especially the use of personal pronouns.[1]

Since footing is the way in which participants show or display their own position within the interaction, it is a manifestation of the way people categorize themselves and the world they live in. This categorization has more manifestations than footing phenomena. Participants also *talk about* themselves and the outside world, and either formulate or presuppose their relation to that world, thus showing the way in which they apply categories (Jayyusi 1984; Schegloff 1991, 1996). The application of these categories may be used as a second source of information. The interviews may be analyzed regarding the way in which participants categorize and evaluate themselves in relation to that world. The motive for this approach may be found in the following statement from Schegloff (1996: 465):

Most significant in this regard is its inclusion of all the category terms for types of persons in a culture's inventory, by reference to which are composed a society's understanding(s) of "the sorts of people" there are, what they are like, how the society and the world work – in short, its culture.

Interviewer and respondent present themselves to each other not as autonomous persons in their own right, but as belonging to, representative of, or related to several social categories. I have summarized these categories schematically in figure 9.1. The interview situation itself is represented in box 3. Both participants know that research is going on and that this interview is not a unique event, but one that belongs to a set of similar events (box 4). Since both interviewer and respondent display themselves as being citizens (or at least normal inhabitants) of New Zealand, and since New Zealand and recent developments within the country are the interview topic, their being part of box 1 is represented in figure 9.1 as well. In box 2, relevant and stable subgroups of New Zealand society are represented; among these subgroups at least the Maori should be mentioned in view of the topic and goal of these interviews. From within the interview situation, both participants (but mostly the respondent) are able to refer to any group that is relevant at that moment (e.g., "our family," "the neighborhood," "me and my colleagues at work," "our sports team," and so on). This is represented in box 5.

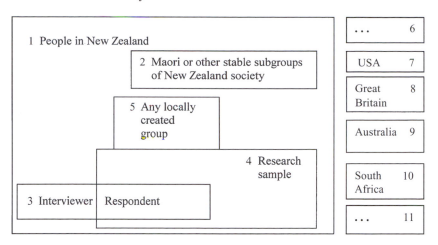

Figure 9.1 Reference to groups from within the interview situation

From within New Zealand, references to other countries and societies are possible (boxes 6 through 11), and occur frequently.

Two examples will suffice to demonstrate the relationship of the interview participants to (some of) the different categories:

Extract 3 (Appendix: New Zealand Interview 16: 265)

1. I: Do you think that New Zealand should (0.2) keep fostering its links with
2.   Britain or that really we (0.4) should (.) orientate ourselves towards Asia
3.   and the Pacific now that it's (0.2) past history

This question, one compound sentence, switches easily between the components of figure 9.1. "You" ("Do you think") is from box 3, "New Zealand" is a non-deictic reference to box 1, which is related to box 8 ("its links with Britain"), "we" is a deictic reference to box 1, which is related to an instantiation of box 11 ("Asia and the Pacific"), in view of the fact that the relation between box 1 and box 8 is "past history."

In extract 4, we find another example of the close relationship of deictic categories with the country (box 1) in general, as well as parts (Mangere and Remuera) thereof.

Extract 4 (Appendix: New Zealand Interview 2: 242)

1. I: Do you think there's equal opportunities here so that (0.6) almost
2.   irrespective of where you're born say if you're born in Mangere that you
3.   have a chance- a bigger chance with (1.0) a child born in Remuera you
4.   know that'em (0.6) we're sort of a sufficiently mobile country to

The first pronoun "you" (in "Do you think") clearly refers to the respondent, and hence belongs to box 3. In the subsequent formulation of this question, there is a switch to box 1. "Here" (in "equal opportunities here") is not the place of the interview, but, rather, New Zealand, and "you" (in "irrespective of where you're born") does not refer to the respondent himself, but rather to "anyone living in New Zealand." Again, "we" in "we're sort of a sufficiently mobile country" refers to box 1. Thus, interviewer and respondent are taken as the referential starting point for making reference to New Zealand in general. It is not clear, however, whether box 2 (containing the Maori part of the population) is intended to be contained in the New Zealand that is talked about here. Presumably, when participants talk about box 1, its default value is that of a white, Western, "European" country. Ethnic attitudes may become manifest in the way in which persons relate box 2 to box 1.

Analysis of ethnic and racial categories

Where ethnicity as a research topic is concerned, footing and categorizing phenomena are informative about the basic ethnic and racial categories people hold and the way people relate to them. In relation to ethnicity, two questions should be asked:

1. How do participants use their situation (as in box 3) in order to identify themselves with or distance themselves from other boxes? (Concerning this question, the analysis of the use of deictic expressions is particularly relevant.)
2. On the basis of what authority, as shown in their footing, do participants express their views?

I will demonstrate the relevance of this approach in the discussion of the following fragments of the interviews.

Extract 5 (Appendix: New Zealand Interview 44: 288/289)

```
 1.  I:   ↑Uhm (0.8) what are the things that you: value about living in
 2.       New Zealand (0.6) things that (0.8) really appeal to you about life
 3.       here or (1.0) that you see as the most positive aspects
 4.  R:   Well we're not poo:r, none of us are
 5.  I:   Yes
 6.  R:   A:[nd
 7.  I:     [Mm mhm
 8.       (0.6)
 9.  R:   You might think "O:h that's okay for her she's on a farm" But we're
10.       not I mean we're only employed
11.  I:   Mm mhm
12.  R:   Ya'know (0.2) U:hm (0.4) but there's no nee:d for anyone in
13.       New Zealand (0.6) to be ↑poo:↓r
14.  I:   Mm mhm
15.       (0.8)
```

16. R: A::nd (0.4) there's still plenty of ro:om (0.4) in New Zealand ya'know
17.   (0.2) and (.) if you want to live in the country you ca:n (0.4) even if
18.   that means going and renting a [place you can do it
19. I: [°Mm mhm°
20. I: Yes (0.2) yeah
21. R: A:nd (4.0) [I don't think we're- we're at it- we're not-(0.2)
22. I: [( )
23. R: uhm spoilt (2.0) in the sense I- as I think Americans are
24. I: Y(h)eah
25. R: U:hm
26.   (0.6)
27. I: What too much material
28. R: Ye:as
29. I: goods
30. I: Yeah
31. R: All right [then there's always- you- (1.0) ehm your extremes
32. I: [Yeah
33. R: [I suppose
34. I: [Yeah
35. R: There are a few but- but basically the- (0.6) the average New Zealander
36.   is (1.8) is [ya'know unspoiled
37. I: [Yeah
38. I: Yes ye[ah
39. R: [I like to think that
40. I: Yes
41. R: Perhaps I'm wrong
42. I: Oh no I(h) [th(h)ink that's quite right Yeah
43. R: [((laughs))
44. I: ↑.hh[h yeah
45. R: [Uhm (2.0) O::h (3.0) I think at the moment we're still a fairly
46.   happy country
47. I: Mm mhm
48. R: and there- there are undertones of- of racial (1.0) uhm disharmony
49.   which could come (1.0) to- out here you can see that they could
50.   possibly come to feeling (what way) (.) the
51.   [government and other (1.2) people act=But at the moment
52. I: [Mm mhm
53. R: I think really we're- we're a rea:sonably happy country
54. I: Yes (0.4) yes Mmm
55.   (1.0)

This fragment begins with the question "what are the things that you: value about living in New Zealand (0.6) things that (0.8) really appeal to you about life here or (1.0) that you see as the most positive aspects." The first reference ("New Zealand") makes use of a descriptive term, and the interviewer then moves to the deictic reference "here." Similarly, the respondent starts with the deictic "we," saying "Well we're not poo:r, none of us are." Both interviewer and respondent thus show in their use of deictics that there is a close link between New Zealand and themselves, since there is an easy shift (similar to what we see in extracts 7 and 8) between the descriptive term and the deictic formulation. In addition, the respondent in her answer (Well we're not poo:r) shows a footing in which the three major footing roles (author, animator, and principal) coincide.

In the subsequent lines of this fragment, we see once again the shift between descriptive terms and deictics:

"there's no nee:d for anyone in New Zealand (0.6) to be poo:r"
"there's still plenty of ro:om (0.4) in New Zealand"
"if you want to live in the country you ca:n"
"I don't think we're- we're at it- we're not uhm spoilt (2.0) in the sense I- as I think Americans are"
"I think at the moment we're still a fairly happy country"

In the last two quotations we also see again that the respondent is speaking for herself. Immediately following the last utterance above, however, the respondent remarks, "and there- there are undertones of- of racial (1.0) uhm disharmony which could come (1.0) to- out here you can see that they could possibly come to feeling (what way) (.) the government and other (1.2) people act=But at the moment I think really we're- we're a rea:sonably happy country." Where negative racial aspects ("disharmony") are concerned, referring expressions which do not imply any personal involvement are used. At the same time, the respondent acts merely as the animator of this utterance and leaves open the footing roles of author and principal ("there are undertones of racial disharmony"; "you can see that . . ."). Thus it is conceded that these phenomena exist somewhere, without conceding a personal relation to them. Personal involvement ("we") is shown again when New Zealand is concerned in a positive way ("we're a rea:sonably happy country").

Extract 6 (Appendix: New Zealand Interview 2: 247/248)

```
1.  R:  I m[ean ya'know if somebody came round to me and said
2.  I:      [(    )
3.  R:  "Look (1.0) we're gonna m- move a whole pile of these (0.4) Maoris
4.      off Bastion Point [.hh and they're gonna take over this part of
5.      [suburb name]
6.  I:                          [Mm mhm
7.  R:  just this corner here going round these block a houses here"
8.      ((sounds like he's gesturing during end of prior))
9.  I:  Mm mhm
10. R:  I'd sa:y ((three hand strikes to a table or chair arm)) No they're not!
11. I:  Yeah
12.     (1.0)
```

13. R: And <[ya'know> (0.2) not matter what happens ther- (0.4)
14. I: [Mm mnm
15. R: THEY'RE NOT GONNA DO IT
16. I: Mm mhm
17. R: I shall take such steps a(h)s a(h)re necessary to
18. I: Yes [yeah
19. R: [(a-) avoid it
20. I: Mm mhm
21. R: Now (0.6) if somebody said "Oh yeah but you know this is how it's
22.   gonna be"
23. I: Mm mhm
24.   (1.0)
25. R: I'd go FLAT out I mean I don't care whether it was apartheid or
26.   whatever yo[u call it or.hh (0.4) build the barricades up there and'a
27.   [you know put
28. I: [Yeah   [>Mm mhm<
29. R: machine guns on the top.
30. I: Mm mhm
31.   (0.6)

In contrast to the respondent in extract 5, the respondent in extract 6 is quite outspoken in his ethnic attitudes. He makes some remarkable utterances about how far he is prepared to go in order to defend his possessions, saying "I'd go FLAT out (. . .) build the barricades up there and'a you know put machine guns on the top." He also displays awareness of the extreme attitude he is showing. He says, "I mean I don't care whether it was apartheid or whatever you call it." Even here we find mitigating behavior, however. Note the way in which the respondent states the problem. A hypothetical person is introduced ("if somebody came round to me and said") who says, "Look (1.0) we're gonna m- move a whole pile of these (0.4) Maoris off Bastion Point and they're gonna take over this part of Remuera (. . .)." It is unclear who "we" is here, (probably "weak" authorities who follow a policy that is friendly to ethnic groups), whereas the rather distancing and deprecatory formulation "a whole pile of" is used in reference to Maoris. The responsibility for the deprecatory formulation, however, is with the hypothetical person. The respondent makes use of the footing phenomenon that the author of some talk is a fictitious person, and thus the animator is not responsible for the deeds and words of that fictitious character.[2]

Explicit expressions of negative attitudes such as in extract 8 are rare. If we compare extract 6 to extract 7, we see a fragment in which a possibly sensitive ethnic topic is discussed: the rising crime rates. Points of view and attitudes are expressed much more subtly and indirectly. (Extract 7 is also discussed in Wetherell and Potter 1992: 96–97.)

Extract 7 (Appendix: New Zealand Interview 16: 275/277)

```
 1.  I:   Tsk ↑right .hh Do you think New Zealand can be described generally
 2.       as a violent socie↑ty (0.4) in terms of crime rate an',
 3.  R:   °Yes it has got a very high crime rate°
 4.  I:   °Yeah°
 5.  R:   (°around there°)
 6.       (3.0)
 7.  R:   Ye:s I think so, it's not as bad as some places though
 8.  I:   Ye:s
 9.       (1.4)
10.  R:   But (.) the crime rate i:s going up
11.  I:   Mm mhm
12.       (1.0)
13.  I:   Why do you think- wa-what's responsible there an' what could be done
14.       about it (.) (do you think)
15.       (3.4)
16.  R:   Pphhh. To:: re:ally answer that we'd have to look at (2.4) u:hm the type
17.       of crimes you've got (0.6) uhm and who's committing them
18.  I:   Ye:ah (0.4) mm mhm
19.  R:   There've been ya'know (0.4) u:hm (1.4) ideas put about that- ya'know
20.       >what is it< the majority of the rapes are committed by Islanders
21.       or [Maoris
22.  I:      [°Mm mhm°
23.  I:   That's right [mm mhm
24.  R:                [U::hm (1.4) then you- an' a lot of house burglaries I
25.       would imagine are committed by kids
26.  I:   Mm mhm
27.  R:   And the majority of the kids that are hanging around on the streets
28.  I:   Yes
29.  R:   are Islanders. They not the Maor-=well-
30.  I:   Mm mhm
31.  R:   It's unfair to say the Maoris because the Maoris that I know are quite
32.       nice really
33.  I:   Yes (0.4) mm mhm
34.  R:   The Maoris (1.0) are quite good. It's the Islanders that come here an'
35.       have nothing.
36.  I:   Yeah
37.       (2.2)
38.  I:   Yes so it's partly sort of immigration- it's related to immigration
39.  R:   Mmmm
40.  I:   Yeah.
41.  R:   We don't- (0.4) seeing them coming through (.) off the air craft
42.       [at night
43.  I:   [Mm mhm
44.       (1.2)
45.  R:   half of them can't speak English
46.  I:   Yeah
```

47. R: A::nd (2.0) if they can't speak English they're not gonna be able to get
48.   a job they're gonna go an' they're gonna be little communi↑ties
49. I: Yeah (0.2) mm [mhm
50. R: [A::nd (2.0) they're not gonna be able to contribute
51.   anything to the country.
52. I: Mm mhm
53. R: And they're gonna get frustrated and they're gonna get <u>bored</u>
54. I: Yes
55.   (0.6)
56. R: And they're gonna- ya'know (.) there's nothing for them to do so
57.   the kids'll start hanging out in the streets
58. I: Mm mhm
59. R: At <u>ho:me</u> (0.4) Mum and Dad can't speak English [so the kids don't
60. I: [Mm mhm
61. R: speak English
62. I: Right [yeah
63. R: [They go to school an' suddenly they're confronted with English
64.   "We can't speak that language what'll we do?"
65. I: Yes
66. R: Nothing!
67. I: Mm mhm
68. R: An' so by the time they get to fifteen they just drop out they've had it
69.   up to here with school
70. I: Yeah
71. R: And it's not (.) <u>school</u>'s fault
72. I: Yeah
73.   (1.4)
74. R: They had brilliant lives, they had brilliant lives back in- family lives,
75.   back in the Islands
76. I: Yeah
77. R: That's where they should be.
78. I: Right yeah so it's just causing social problems.
79.   (0.6)
80. R: Mhmm they're coming here (.) looking like- well like the (.) Ita:lians
81.   [we:nt to: N:ew York
82. I: [(°Yeah°)
83. I: °Mm mhm°
84. R: The streets are paved with gold
85. I: [Yeah
86. R: [That's what they're coming here for
87. I: Mm mhm
88.   (0.6)
89. R: But they're <u>not</u>
90. I: Mm mhm
91. R: An' dey- Yeah they're probly all quite happy living in their- living in
92.   Otara or living in their [little communities
93. I: [Mm mhm

94. I: Yes
95. R: <u>But</u> hhhh. (1.2) do we really <u>want</u> them?
96. I: [°Yes°
97. R: [We've got <u>ten</u> thousand Niueans living in New Zealand
98. I: °Mm mhm°
99. R: three thousand of them live in- three thousand Niueans left in Niue
100. I: Ye(h)ah
101. R: Is that <u>right</u>? Or should we turn around an' send'em all back again.

This rather extended fragment starts with the question, "Do you think New Zealand can be described generally as a violent society (0.4) in terms of crime rate." The respondent answers, "Yes it has got a very high crime rate." In contrast to extracts 4 and 5, both interviewer and respondent use descriptive, non-deictic formulations ("New Zealand," "it"), possibly due to the negatively evaluated topic. The interviewer subsequently asks who is responsible and what could be done about it. The respondent does not provide an answer immediately. First, the respondent makes a statement suggesting that the question calls for an objective approach, saying "To:: re:ally answer that we'd have to look at (2.4) u:hm the type of crimes you've got (0.6) uhm and who's committing them." In this answer, "we" and "you" are used as general references to persons (equivalent to "one"), rather than as situated, deictic references. Second, the respondent makes a shift in his footing. He quotes unidentified sources, saying "There've been ya'know (0.4) u:hm (1.4) ideas put about that . . ." Only then is the respondent prepared to relate crimes to Islanders (i.e., Polynesian migrants to New Zealand, according to Wetherell and Potter 1992: 96) and Maoris by stating that ". . . the majority of the rapes are committed by Islanders or Maoris." The effect of this shift in footing is that the respondent acts as the mere animator of this statement, leaving the roles of author and principal open.

In his next remark, the respondent shifts his footing again by taking responsibility for the utterance (only mitigated by "I would imagine"). On the other hand, the respondent uses a form of indirect, "chained" categorizing. Crimes are attributed to kids, and most kids are Islanders: "an' a lot of house burglaries I would imagine are committed by kids And the majority of the kids that are hanging around on the streets are Islanders They not the Maor-=well- (. . .) It's unfair to say the Maoris because the Maoris that I know are quite nice really."

In the final utterance of this fragment, the respondent makes a reservation, saying "It's unfair to say the Maoris because the Maoris *that I know* are quite nice really." Although negative views are expressed toward box 2 (Maori and other relevant subgroups, i.e., the Islanders), this box is subcategorized. One (smaller) subcategory is personally related to the respondent and positively evaluated. The other part is negatively evaluated, and referred to in descriptive expressions that do not give rise to the supposition of any personal relationship. In some analyses (e.g. Van Dijk 1987), it is noted that such a reservation is a frequent phenomenon in racist discourse. In this fragment, the status is not quite clear, due to the unclear meaning of the utterance after "the Islanders," "They not the Maor-=well-."

The respondent makes a distinction between the Maoris and the Islanders, and goes on to discuss the fact that the Islanders have a weak command of English, the social effects of which are enumerated: a low chance of getting jobs, boredom, and bad schooling. These effects are mentioned in a factual way by the respondent. When discussing the effects on schooling, the respondent for a moment even speaks from the point of view of these children (thus taking *their* footing), saying "Mum and Dad can't speak English so the kids don't speak English They go to school an' suddenly they're confronted with English 'We can't speak that language what'll we do?' " But it becomes immediately clear that the respondent does not adopt this footing from a personal identification, but rather in order to make the position of these children dramatically clear. He says, "Nothing! An' so by the time they get to fifteen they just drop out they've had it up to here with school," and sums up with "They had brilliant lives, they had brilliant lives back in- family lives, back in the Islands. That's where they should be." The respondent then concludes by saying "they're coming here (.) looking like- well like the (.) Ita:lians we:nt to: N:ew York . . . Yeah they're probly all quite happy living in their living in Otara or living in their little communities . . . But hhhh. (1.2) do we really want them? . . . Is that right? Or should we turn around an' send'em all back again."

In analyses of discourse about group antagonism (to which racist discourse belongs), the "we"/"them" distinction is characteristic (e.g., Van Dijk 1987, 1993). In this fragment, we now find such an opposition between boxes 1 (New Zealand) and 2 (Maoris or other relevant subgroups). The formulations presuppose that on the referential or cognitive level, box 2 is a part of box 1, but on the level of social identification, the respondent signals distance between the two. The deictic expressions "here" ("they're coming here") and "we" ("do we really want them?") characterize the position with which the respondent identifies. This position is related to box 1 (consider "We've got ten thousand Niueans living in New Zealand"). In contrast, "they" belong in another place, to which only a negative deictic relationship exists ("send'em all back again").

Extract 8 (Appendix: New Zealand Interview 44: 297/298)

1. I: >One of the-< The other thing that (.) I'm interested is the (0.4)
2.   multiculturalism and (0.6) what people think about sort of race
3.   relations (0.4) scene. >Sort of< There's been quite a change in that
4.   over the six years I've been away, There's a much greater emphasis now
5.   on ehm Maori culture and the use of the Maori language (1.0) an' so
6.   on. (0.6) Do you think in general that's been (0.4) uh constructive or
7.   (1.4) what do you feel about the way things are going (0.2) on that
8.   front?
9.   (2.0)
10. R: I think they'll end up having Maori w:ars if they carry on the way
11.   [they have I mean no it'll be a Pakeha war
12. I: [((laugh))
13. I: Yes
14. R: U::hm (1.6) they're ma:king New Zealand a racist cu- country uhm
15.   but ya'know you usually feel (.) think that racism is uhm (1.4) putting
16.   th- putting ([.) the darker people down
17. I: [Yes
18. R: [but really they're doing it (.) the other way around
19. I: [( )
20. I: A sort of [reverse [racism
21. R: [I feel [yes
22. I: Yeah
23. R: U:hm (1.4) everything (0.6) seems to be to help (0.2) the Maori
24.   people, (1.0) a::nd ya'know (0.4) I think (1.4) at the moment sort of
25.   (0.6) the Europeans are sort of (0.4) They're just sort of watching
26.   [and putting up with it
27. I: [Yeah
28. I: Yeah
29. R: But (.) they'll only go so fa:r
30. I: Right yeah
31. R: U:hm (1.0) tsk (1.0) ya'know we- we've got (.) Maori friends out he:re
32.   uhm who we have into the house so yu- ya'know they're friends
33.   (0.6)
34. R: U::hm (2.0) but when things happen an' they- they suddenly say
35.   "Oh they're going to make (.) M- Maori language compulsory"
36. I: Yeah (.) yeah
37. R: U:hm (0.4) but that is an- antagonizing
38. I: Yeah
39. R: And- (1.4) the Maori friends that we::'ve got (1.0) they don't agree
40.   with it
41. I: Yes (.) yeah
42. R: U::hm (0.2) okay yu- you've got extremists th[ere too
43. I: [Mm mhm
44. R: the ones who feel that ya'know that everyone should learn it but
45.   u:hm (2.0) I think the average Maori sort of perhaps is worried ↑too
46. I: Yeah So there's a sort of split in the Maori com[munity

47. R: [Yes
48.   (0.6)
49. I: between the: yeah (.) yeah
50.   (2.0)
51. I: Yes
52.   (1.0)
53. R: An' I- I know that uhm (2.0) you know there is a- a problem in the
54.   schools here (.) the- the blacks and whites sort of thing a::nd (1.0)
55.   there's a Maori lady down the corner down here (1.4) an' she's got
56.   two boys (1.0) well she was thrilled that her boy was going to a class
57.   with a lot Europeans
58. I: ((lau[gh)) yes
59. R: [Because she was worried [uhm that he would get into a class
60. I: [( )
61. R: with quite a few Maoris and therefore they'd form a gang
62. I: Yes ([.) and he'd stop worki[ng yeah
63. R: [And   [and once they're a gang [then
64. I: [Yeah
65. R: they- they (loll it not seem to apply) themsleves
66. I: Yes
67. R: If they (.) ya'know are not interested- got more interested agitating
68.   in the classroom than
69. I: than working
70. R: Mmm
71. I: Yeah (.) Right (.) I know

In extract 8, the issue of racism is explicitly formulated in the interviewer's question. Again (compare extract 7), this question avoids deictic
formulations ("we" or "here"), and does not address the respondent directly. The respondent's answer reflects this. The respondent's reaction
is both outspoken and personally distanced. She says, "I think they'll end
up having Maori w:ars if they carry on the way they have I mean no it'll
be a Pakeha war . . . they're ma:king New Zealand a racist cu- country."
There is no "we" in this answer, or any other explicit indication of being personally involved. A few moments later, the respondent uses "we"
in constructing an instantiation of box 5 (a locally created group), into
which persons from box 2 are inserted, saying "ya'know we- we've got
(.) Maori friends out he:re," and adding, "who we have into the house
so yu- ya'know they're friends." The mere categorizing as friends is not
sufficient. The information that these Maoris actually come into the respondent's house has to be added so as to substantiate their categorization
as friends. This additional information is remarkable, since in other cases
a mere categorization "we've got friends who . . ." would do. Obviously,
the additional information is needed so as to cancel out the tacit presupposition that friendship between persons from box 1 (New Zealanders)

and persons from box 2 (Maori or other subgroups) is unlikely. This presupposition thus makes clear that the respondent considers box 1 to have white people as its "default value."

Subsequently, these "Maori friends" serve as a source for expressing the point of view (which thus is not expressed on the basis of the repondent's own footing) that Maori language should not be made compulsory, and for making the inference that the Maori themselves are divided. This inference is reinforced by information the respondent supplies when she says, "there's a Maori lady down the corner down here." This lady is introduced by means of deictic reference, thus making her close to the respondent: "down here." This lady also makes a negative evaluation of Maoris. The negative evaluation thus is not presented as one that the respondent authors. The evaluation is (literally) *authorized* by absent Maoris themselves, to which the respondent more or less closely relates.

Extract 9 (Appendix: New Zealand Interview 44: 299)
```
 1.  I:   What do you think- there's all this discussion going on at the moment
 2.       about Waitangi Day and uhm (0.6) ya'know whether (0.4) we should
 3.       (.) celebrate it at all or celebrate it- in what- what way should we
 4.       celebrate it and all the rest of it. What do you feel about (.) that (.)
 5.       that topic? (0.4) Do you feel that that we should ta keep on with
 6.       Waitangi Day or that we should have some other
 7.       day for a national holiday
 8.       (3.2)
 9.  R:   Well each year there seems to be (1.0) quite a fuss over it and really
10.       uhm (0.2) I mean (3.2) it's just another day I mean (.)
11.       [ya'know you don't sort of think "Oh! the Treaty
12.  I:   [Yes
13.  R:   of Wai[tangi Day's today ya'know
14.  I:         [((laugh))
15.  I:   Yeah
16.  R:   and think about how they all got together an' so on I mean you just
17.       think "Oh! [It's a holiday on Monday ya'know
18.  I:              [It's a holiday ye(h)ah .hhh
19.  I:   Yeah
20.  R:   I think it's- it's lost it's
21.  I:   Yeah
22.       (1.0)
23.  R:   ya'know to people
```

In the three interviews, respondents' answers are not often formulated as direct statements, possibly prefaced by "I think." Rather, they tend to be formulated in a more distanced manner. We have an instance of this in extract 9. The repondent reacts to the question about the meaning of Waitangi Day (Wetherell and Potter 1992: 108–110) in general terms, not on the basis of her own authority. She says, "Well each year there seems to be (1.0) quite a fuss over it," and similarly a few moments later, she says "to people" instead of "to me": "I think it's- it's lost it's (. . .)ya'know to people." Furthermore, the answer is formulated in a "you" format. "You" means the same here as "I" from a purely referential point of view, but it does not put the speaker herself to the front. Thus, the meaning of Waitangi Day and its implications to ethnic groups and their attitudes are kept at a personal distance.

Concluding remarks

In the previous section, I demonstrated some phenomena related to participants' footing and categorizing in the three interviews. In these phenomena, there is a continuous interplay between different frames, notably the frames that I identified in the first part of this paper. It appears then that interviews yield data that may be taken for granted to some extent: utterances in which respondents give their points of view or formulate their attitudes on an explicit level. When footing phenomena are taken into account, interviews yield data on a second level as well. This level may be described as the level of the ongoing interaction as related to society at large. Participants, notably respondents, show social presuppositions, social categorizations, and the evaluations related to those, on this level. Part of what respondents display is on a routine, implicit level. Since basic presuppositions, attitudes, and evaluations appear on this level, it may be considered informative about social relations within a particular societal context. These phenomena may be characterized as not the explicit formulation, but as the interactional manifestation of ethnic attitudes, opinions, and categorizations. Hence, this approach uses not only explicitly stated, but implicitly displayed, positions (notably toward ethnic categories) as well.

Although the emphasis is on the respondent, the role of the interviewer should be taken into account as well. There are two reasons for doing this. First, the interviewer's behaviors are related to footing as well. Second, since one of the frames identified in the first part of this paper, frame (c), pertains to the relationship between interviewer and respondent, it must be assumed that the person of the interviewer and the footing behavior displayed by her has influence on the respondent's behaviour (Van den Berg 1996).

I have not provided a complete analysis with regard to the three interviews. A complete analysis should have the form of a matrix of explicit statements on the one hand, and categories, deictic references, and implicit evaluations as demonstrated in participants' footing behaviour on the other (similar to the approach by Wortham 1996). The value of the approach as proposed here can only be assessed on the basis of such a full analysis. In this chapter, I have only provided an indication of the data that would be provided by this approach.

One question is beyond the scope of this chapter: Do interviews yield materials suitable for the analysis of ethnic relations? I agree with Wetherell and Potter's remark (1992: 98–99):

> In many ways we would have preferred to have participants' everyday, unsolicited talk about race – what they said over family dinners, in discussion in pubs, in the course of doing their ordinary jobs. However, the technical and practical difficulties in collecting a large, comparative body of such material led us to do interviews instead.

From the point of view of ecological validity, interview materials are only second best. But, since they are easier to get, we will have to work with them.

NOTES

1. Deictics are formulations such as "I," "you," "now," "here," which refer *immediately* and non-descriptively to elements of the situation in which people communicate, cf., Brown and Yule 1983: 50–51.
2. Compare the possible formulation in which the respondent would have taken full responsibility for the authorship: "when a whole pile of these Maoris would be moved off Bastion Point and they're gonna take over this part of [suburb name] just this corner here going round these block a houses here." It is clear that this formulation would be more blatantly racist than the one he used in the interview.

References

Babbie, E. 1995. *The practice of social research*. Belmont, CA: Wadsworth.

Baddeley, A. 1990. *Human memory. Theory and practice*. London: Lawrence Erlbaum.

Brown, G. and Yule, G. 1983. *Discourse analysis*. Cambridge: Cambridge University Press.

Cicourel, A. 1964. *Method and measurement in sociology*. New York: Free Press.

Clark, H. H. 1996. *Using language*. Cambridge: Cambridge University Press.

Clayman, S. 1992. Footing in the achievement of neutrality. In *Talk at work*, edited by P. Drew and J. Heritage. Cambridge: Cambridge University Press.

Ensink, T. 1997. The footing of a royal address. An analysis of representativeness in political speech, exemplified in Queen Beatrix's address to the Knesset on March 28, 1995. In *Analysing political speeches*, edited by C. Schäffner. Clevedon: Multilingual Matters.

Goffman, E. 1974. *Frame analysis. An essay on the organization of experience*. New York: Harper and Row.

1981. *Forms of talk*. Oxford: Basil Blackwell.

Heritage, J. and Greatbatch, D. 1991. On the institutional character of institutional talk: the case of news interviews. In *Talk and social structure. Studies in ethnomethodology and conversation analysis*, edited by D. Boden and D. H. Zimmerman. Cambridge: Polity Press.

Houtkoop-Steenstra, H. 2000. *Interaction and the standardized survey interview. The living questionnaire*. Cambridge: Cambridge University Press.

Jayyusi, L. 1984. *Categorization and the moral order*. Boston, MA: Routledge and Kegan Paul.

Lee, D. A. 1997. Frame conflicts and competing construals in family argument. *Journal of Pragmatics* 27: 339–360.

Levinson, S. C. 1988. Putting linguistics on a proper footing: explorations in Goffman's concepts of participation. In *Erving Goffman. Exploring the interaction order*, edited by P. Drew and A. Wootton. Cambridge: Polity Press.

Mazeland, H. and Ten Have, P. 1996. Essential tensions in (semi-) open research interviews. In *The deliberate dialogue*: *qualitative perspectives on the interview*, edited by I. Maso and F. Wester. Brussels: VUB University Press.

Moser, C. A. and Kalton, G. 1971. *Survey methods in social investigation*, 2nd edn. London: Heinemann.

Pan, Z. and Kosicki, G. 1993. Framing analysis. An approach to news discourse. *Political Communication* 10: 55–75.

Schank, R. C. and Abelson, R. P. 1977. *Scripts, plans, goals and understanding. An inquiry into human knowledge structures*. Hillsdale, NJ: Erlbaum and Wiley.

Schegloff, E. A. 1988/89. From interview to confrontation: observations of the Bush/Rather encounter. *Research on Language and Social Interaction* 22: 215–240.

Schegloff, E. A. 1991. Reflections on talk and social structure. In *Talk and social structure. Studies in ethnomethodology and conversation analysis*, edited by D. Boden and D. Zimmerman. Cambridge: Polity Press.

1996. Some practices for referring to persons in talk-in-interaction: a partial sketch of a systematics. In *Studies in anaphora*, edited by B. Fox. Amsterdam: John Benjamins.

Tannen, D., editor. 1993. *Framing in discourse*. Oxford: Oxford University Press.

Van den Berg, H. 1996. Frame analysis of open interviews on interethnic relations. *Bulletin de Méthodologie Sociologique* 53: 5–32.

Van Dijk, T. A. 1987. *Communicating racism. Ethnic prejudice in thought and talk*. Newbury Park: Sage.

1993. *Elite discourse and racism*. Newbury Park: Sage.

Wetherell, M. and Potter, J. 1992. *Mapping the language of racism. Discourse and the legitimation of exploitation*. New York: Harvester Wheatsheaf.

Wortham, S. E. F. 1996. Mapping participant deictics: a technique for discovering speakers' footing. *Journal of Pragmatics* 25: 331–348.

10 Affiliation and detachment in interviewer answer receipts[1]

Tom Koole

Interviewer's conflicting interactional tasks

The interviewer in research interviews on ethnic and racial relations faces potentially conflicting interactional tasks with regard to the interviewees and the topics of the interview. The interviewer aims to have the interviewees express themselves on issues where disagreement and conflict are around the corner, even between interviewer and interviewee. On the one hand, the interviewer may want to create an atmosphere of confidence in which the interviewee feels free to express possibly controversial views, while on the other hand the interviewer as a person holds views on the interview topics that may not be in agreement with those expressed by the interviewee. The potential interactional conflict that arises from this is that the interviewer may want to establish an interpersonal rapport with the interviewee without identifying at the same time with the views the interviewee expresses. In this paper I will argue that this interviewer problem is particularly precarious since one of the discursive means to establish interpersonal rapport is precisely a content-oriented affiliation with the other's prior contributions.

I will discuss three open interviews on ethnic identity and ethnic relations in New Zealand and be concerned with one aspect of the interview as a reciprocal activity; namely, the ways in which the interviewer responds to the answers given by the interviewee. I will show that the interviewer uses different types of answer receipts, ranging from utterances in which the interviewer comments on the answer just given, to minimal responses such as "mm hmm" and "yeah."

I will argue that these interviewer answer receipts often gain an affiliating or detaching character in that they signal affiliation with or detachment from the answer to which they respond. Sometimes this signaling is done more overtly, especially when agreement is signaled, but I will argue that the signaling may also result from withholding the tokens of affiliation or detachment that occur in similar sequential positions in response to previous answers.

The method I will use in this analysis is primarily conversation analytic (cf. Atkinson and Heritage 1984; Boden and Zimmerman 1991; Drew and Heritage 1992; Pomerantz and Fehr 1997; Psathas 1995; Ten Have 1999). This method, or array of methods, finds a basis in its treatment of interactional discourse as a there-and-then achievement of the participants in which these participants are constantly and interactively producing the order of the discourse (for instance, in terms of the right to speak or listen) and the meaning of the produced utterances. In my present analysis, this method and perspective on interactional discourse will enable me to show how participants may treat utterances such as answer receipts as signaling affiliation with or detachment from the content of prior discourse.

The analytical procedure

The analytical procedure I am using here consists of essentially two elements. First I will make a sequential analysis of the interviews in order to establish where and with what interactional meaning the answer receipts of the interviewer are produced. Then I will look at the different types of answer receipts that are produced in these sequential positions.

Sequential analysis

Interactional discourse is produced in sequences. Participants speak in turns and thus produce sequences of turns in which each turn is a response to the prior utterance of another speaker, while at the same time each turn builds a context in which the subsequent utterance must be understood. The meaning of utterances in discourse can therefore be characterized as interactional meaning; it is not the meaning of the utterance in isolation, but the meaning of the utterance understood as responding to the prior one(s). To a large extent, therefore, utterance meaning in interactional discourse can be characterized in terms of the position of the utterance in a sequence of utterances.

Another aspect of sequences in interactional discourse is that they can be relatively fixed. The most common example of such relatively fixed sequences is the two-utterance sequence that has been labelled *adjacency pair* (Schegloff and Sacks 1973). Examples of such two-part sequences are the exchange of greetings (A: "good morning" B: "good morning") and some question–answer sequences. The relatively fixed character of such sequences does not mean that greetings are always returned or that questions are always followed by answers, but it means that following the first part of such a sequence (for instance, a question) a subsequent utterance will be interpreted in the light of the expected second part (for instance, an answer).

Thus the meaning of an utterance following a question is in part occasioned by the fact that the question has established the expectation of an answer. Within such relatively fixed sequences, the production of one utterance opens up a slot for the next utterance, thereby establishing an aspect of that next utterance's meaning, regardless of the actual utterance that is produced in that slot. If, for instance, a question is followed by an utterance that is not interpretable as an answer to that question, then one aspect of the interactional meaning of that utterance is the "noticeable absence" (Schegloff and Sacks 1973) of the expected answer.

The pair is not the only sequence with rather fixed character. Several researchers have described ways in which one utterance can open up a three-, four-, or even five-part sequence. In the case of the much-researched area of questions and answers, for instance, it has been established that it is rather exceptional for question–answer sequences to consist of only two parts. More often the answer will be structurally followed by some sort of answer receipt produced by the one who asked the questions. In fact, Greatbatch (1988) and Heritage and Greatbatch (1991) note as a special feature of the institutional character of British news interviews that the news interviewers do *not* produce answer receipts, thereby signaling that they, as questioners, are not the primary party who is addressed by the answer, but rather the audience. Since I aim to focus my present investigation of research interviews on answer receipts produced by the interviewer, my first step will have to be to describe the sequence in which these receipts are produced and to establish whether and how the receipts figure as a structural part of this sequence.

Slot related variation

The second step is to investigate the slot related variation, that is, the types of utterances that can be produced to fill a particular sequential slot. Conversation analytic researchers of interactional discourse have acknowledged the potential meaningfulness of such variation. Jefferson contrasts the work "mm hmm" does with, for instance, "news receipts," such as "Oh really," that might have been produced in the same sequential position (1984: 202). Drummond and Hopper state that "encounter partners interpret items within slots by comparing a response to other items that might have appeared in that slot" (1993: 162). Moreover, Schegloff (1982) proposes in the analysis of minimal responses to focus on the question what a speaker *does not* do by producing the minimal response. In his analysis of "uh huh" he distinguishes two analytical procedures for investigating the meaning of utterances such as "uh huh" that can be used to fill a particular slot (Schegloff 1982).

The first procedure looks at the local sequential context in order to establish what kind of action is made locally relevant by the immediately preceding discourse. Having established which actions are potentially relevant following a certain utterance, the analyst is in a position to conclude what type of action the production of a "uh huh" is withholding. Following the pun of a joke, for instance, the production of an "uh huh" can be said to be withholding laughter, while subsequent to an invitation the same "uh huh" is withholding an acceptation. Thus, the variation of utterances produced to fill a particular sequential slot is meaningful, with its meaning depending on the preceding discourse.

The second procedure looks at a more general level at actions that are relevant independent of the local sequential context. One such action is the repair initiator, with which the speaker indicates that the preceding utterance contains a trouble source of some kind, causing a form of not-understanding. Schegloff (1982: 87) argues that if indeed these actions are potentially relevant following each utterance, then the production of an utterance other than a repair initiator implies that the speaker treats the prior utterance as understood.

Also in the present analysis of research interviews I will use the analytical procedure of slot related variation, in particular the first procedure distinguished by Schegloff. In order to establish the range of potentially relevant actions that might have been produced in a particular sequential position, I will compare the sequences analyzed in the first step of my analytical procedure. This comparison enables me to propose answers to the question of what could have been, but was not, produced by the interviewer in response to the answers of the interviewee. These answers in turn can lead to a discussion of the withholding aspect of the interactional meaning of answer receipts in these interviews, or phrased more simply: to a discussion of what the interviewer *does not* do by producing this particular answer receipt.

The resulting analytical procedure deviates slightly but importantly from Schegloff's proposition. Rather than taking only the immediately preceding discourse as an indication of the interactional meaning of the utterance under analysis, as Schegloff proposes as a first procedure, I have additionally included an analysis of comparable sequences in the same interview. In other words, in addition to analyzing the sequential context as proposed by Schegloff, I have also analyzed the context of the discourse of which the sequence is a part. The reason for this adaptation is that, in order to know what participants perceive as potentially relevant actions, we must look at the actions they actually perform on different occasions. If, for instance, in a particular interview the use of minimal responses to answers is alternated by the use of tokens of agreement, the minimal response may be interpreted as withholding agreement. If, alternatively, the minimal response is alternated by tokens of disagreement, the interpretation may be the opposite.

A sequential format for topic management

I will now turn to the analysis of the New Zealand interview data, starting with the analysis of the sequential status of the interviewer's answer receipts. Both interviewer and interviewee in the interviews seem to deal with topics according to a certain format. This format can be illustrated with the opening sequence of one of the interviews:

Extract 1 (Appendix: New Zealand Interview 2: 232)

```
1.  I:   U:hm (1.0) have you travelled a↑t'all or
2.       (1.2)
3.  R:   I go to sea for a living
4.  I:   ↑DO: you now
5.  R:   Ye(h)ah
6.  I:   Ahaa This is gonna be interesting.
7.  R:   So
8.  I:   So: you- what you::'re a merchant seaman [or what
9.  R:                                            [Yes
10. I:   Yeah
11.      (1.0)
12. R:   [mhm
13. I:   [U:hm (1.0) which country would you say that (0.8) New
14.      Zealand is (1.0) clo:sest to >sort of< (.) culturally
15.      in ter- terms of outlook and attitude and so on.
```

Topics are typically initiated by the interviewer, not surprisingly with a question. This question in turn is often preceded by a transition marker such as "U:hm" (line 1). The interviewer then responds to the answers provided by the interviewee with a variety of minimal responses (line 10: "Yeah"), news receipt tokens (line 4: "Do: you now"), and the like, which I will come back to extensively below. Also the interviewer performs further questions expanding on the topic and shifting it (line 8: "So: you- what you::'re a merchant seaman or what").

There seem to be mainly two ways in which the participants manage a topic change, that is, a transition to a new interview question. One is a sequence in which the interviewer acknowledges the answer, after which there is a pause (or two pauses) and a transition marker, in varying linear orders. In extract 1 the answer "Yes" (line 9) is followed by the interviewer's "Yeah" (line 10), after which there is a considerable one-second pause (Jefferson 1989). Mazeland (1992) analyzes what he calls the "post-answer trajectory" in research interviews as a space in which participants negotiate the completeness of the answer (1992: 224). Following an answer, the participants have to agree whether the answerer will elaborate on this answer, or whether the questioner will proceed by asking another question. In the New Zealand interviews considered here, such answer elaborations sometimes take the form of narratives by the interviewee.

In extract 1 the interviewer produces the minimal response "yeah," followed by a pause, but the answerer does not use that pause as an opportunity to elaborate on his answer. Apart from collaborating in creating the pause, he subsequently produces a "mhm"; both can be understood as indications of his preparedness to listen (or his unwillingness to elaborate). The interviewer in turn agrees that the answer is complete by moving to a new question: she[2] overlaps R's "mhm" with the transition marker "U:hm" (line 13; see also line 1), then pauses and asks a new question. The "U:hm" marks the end of the post-answer trajectory, and the pause following it is therefore not an appropriate place for the interviewee to come in: it is a turn-internal interviewer's pause (which is not to say that participants will never act inappropriately).

A second way of managing a topic change is for the interviewer to leave little or no space to the interviewee to possibly elaborate on the answer provided. An example of this can be seen in extract 2:

Extract 2 (Appendix: New Zealand Interview 2: 233)

1. I: How long have you been living here?
2. R: E:hh. nearly [number of years specified] now.
3. I: Quite a time.
4. R: [Mhm
5. I: [Mmm
6. I: .hh What- (1.2) Do you think that one can talk about
7.   a sort of national character for New Zealand (. . .)

In this sequence the interviewer responds to the answer in line 2 with the commentary "quite a time," and subsequently leaves no pause for possible elaboration of the answer: immediately following this commentary she produces first an acknowledgement (line 5: Mmm) and then an audible in- breath (line 6: .hh) projecting a turn at talk. Since the 1.2 second pause (line 6) follows the in-breath and the cut off "what-", both projecting more to come, it is to be considered in the same way as the one-second pause in line 13 of extract 1: as a turn-internal pause, not as an invitation to the interviewee to come in. The topic change to the question about national character has thus been accomplished by the interviewer in not giving the interviewee the opportunity to elaborate.

Even though the interviewer does not leave the interviewee the space to elaborate, this does not mean that the interviewer does not respond to the answer, as is the case for instance in British news interviews (Greatbatch 1988). Indeed, we see that the interviewer responds twice, first with a commentary and then with an acknowledgement. Answer receipts can thus be seen to have a relatively fixed place in the topical question blocks of these interviews. Answers or parts of answers are followed by answer receipts. Variation does not lie in the presence or absence of answer receipts, not even in sequences in which the interviewer does not provide the interviewee with space to elaborate, but lies in the tokens used as answer receipts. This variation is the topic of the next section.

Variation in answer receipts

In this section I will be concerned with three types of answer receipts that are found throughout the three interviews. The first is the "joint answer construction," the second and third are two types of assessment, the "confirmation" and the "topic assessment." The use of minimal responses such as "yeah" and "mm hmm" will be discussed in the next section.

Joint answer construction

One type of answer receipt is what I will call the joint answer construction, where the interviewer responds by adding to the answer of the interviewee. An example can be seen in the following extract:

Extract 3 (Appendix: New Zealand Interview 2: 242/243)

```
 1.  I:   Do you think there's equal opportunities here so that (0.6)
 2.       almost irrespective of where you're born say if you're born
 3.       in Mangere that you have a chance- a bigger chance with
 4.       (1.0) a child born in Remuera you know that'em (0.6) we're
 5.       sort of a [sufficiently mobile country [to
 6.  R:            [Hhh.                         [CHmm.
 7.  R:   N::o. (.) Uhm If- (1.4) everything- If you had two children
 8.       (.) that [were identical twins [one was born in Mangere and
 9.  I:            [°Mm mhm°              [°Mm mhm°
10.  R:   one was born in (0.2) Remuera I would say that the- the one
11.       who was born in Remuera (0.4) ya'know [(with affluent parents)
12.  I:                                         [would do better
13.  R:   [would finish up better because he [would have been given all
14.  I:   [yeah                              [yeah
15.  R:   the better opportunities.
```

Following R's "I would say that the- the one who was born in Remuera
(0.4) ya' know" (lines 10–11) the interviewer adds: "would do better"
(line 13). By doing this, the interviewer adds a crucial element to the
answer. The interviewer completes a syntactic unit the interviewee has
initiated (cf. Lerner 1991, 1996). Moreover, the interviewer adds the
"new" element, the "rheme" of the given-new (theme-rheme) structure
of the answer: the answer provided thus far by the interviewee has been
little more than a rephrasing of the question. The "real" answer in terms
of new semantic content is provided by the interviewer and subsequently
confirmed by the interviewee by repeating "better." The account the
interviewee provides for that view ("because he would have been given
all the better opportunities") shows that the interviewee is confirming
rather than merely acknowledging the prior utterance.

In one of the other interviews, the interviewer to a large extent answers her own question, but not before she has an indication from the
interviewee that they are in agreement on the matter.

Extract 4 (Appendix: New Zealand Interview 44: 287)

```
1.  I:    . . . How far do you think that should go, Do you think
2.        perhaps that we should go (0.6) the whole way an'
3.        seek a political union (1.0) with Australia and become
4.        one big
5.  R:    No I don't think so [no
6.  I:                        [No [yeah
7.  R:                            [Right
8.  I:    That would be a sort of loss of identity,
9.  R:    I think so (.) [yes definitely
10. I:                   [(       )
11. I:    Yeah
12. R:    Right uhm (1.2) An' I think there's a- there's a rivalry
13.       always there between Australia and New Zealand
14. I:    Y(h)es [.hhh yeah
15. R:           [ya'know that uhm thad be ↑lost
16. I:    Yes
17. R:    An' I- [I wou- I think that's: good for competition
18. I:           [Yeah
19. I:    Yeah
20. R:    Really
21. I:    Right
22.       (1.2)
23. I:    ↑Uhm I mean because overseas people see: (0.2) Australia and
24.       New Zealand as very interchangeable but of course to a New
26.       for a New Zealander there's a great (1.0) you know we're
26.       quite separate from Australia (0.4)
27.       [I mean we like to think that we are
28. R:    [Mm mhm
```

In this extract the interviewer is doing work to get the interviewee to expand a given answer. The interviewer asks the question of whether a political union between New Zealand and Australia would be desirable and gets the answer "No I don't think so" (line 5). She produces a minimal reponse (line 6: "No yeah"), but the interviewee also responds minimally with a "right" (line 7). Then the interviewer herself proposes an extension of the answer: "That would be a sort of loss of identity" (line 8). This extension can be analyzed as a question of the Labov and Fanshel (1977) B-event type (i.e., a statement on an issue from the knowledge domain of the addressee), and it is also treated that way by the interviewee (line 9: "I think so (.) yes definitely"), but the result is that the content of the information we get is presented not by the interviewee, but by the interviewer. The answer is a co-production of both participants. This co-production goes even further in lines 23–27, where the interviewer displays her own perspective on these matters, linked to the prior discourse as an "explanation" or "account" (line 23: "I mean because"), and receives a minimal reponse from the interviewee (line 28: "Mm mhm"), which possibly, but certainly not overtly, signals agreement.

A last example of this type of responding to answers is the co-construction of the topic of rape. The topic evolves out of the topic of violence in New Zealand and the question of desirability of capital punishment. The rape topic is introduced by the interviewee:

Extract 5 (Appendix: New Zealand Interview 44: 296)
1. R: But loo:k at what ra:pists are do:ing I mean we didn't
2.   he:ar of ra:pists [even a fe:w years ago
3. I: [Yeah
4. I: That's right (0.2) yeah

The interviewer does not respond with a mere display of active listenership or understanding, but indeed with a confirmation of this statement ("that's right"). A bit further in the interaction this confirmation takes on the form of a co-constructed answer:

Extract 6 (Appendix: New Zealand Interview 44: 297)
1. R: Or do they not- (.) believe that it- it I:s an enormity to- to
2. I: Right
3. R: to- (.) to a woman to be raped?
4. I: Yes that's right I mean it- to me it must be one of the
5.   worst things that can ever happen to a- (0.4) to you
6.   I imagi[ne yeah   [yeah
7. R: [It must be [surely
8.   U:hm
9.   (0.2)
10. I: Mm mhm

```
11.       (0.4)
12. I:    Particularly uh ya'know if it's sort of (0.4) some of
13.       these awful gang rapes [and that kind thing which
14. R:                          [Ye::s
```

The interviewer proceeds from an elaborate confirmation (lines 4–6: "Yes that's right". . ."it must be one of the worst things that can ever happen to a- (0.4) to you") to co-constructing the answer by adding to it the new element of "gang rapes" (line 14).

Confirmation

The second type of answer receipt I want to discuss is one that we have seen an example of already in extract 5, namely "confirmation." Confirmations are agreeing assessments of a view put forward by the prior speaker, in these cases the interviewee. As Pomerantz (1984) has shown, assessments are extremely common in everyday conversational discourse. In the discourse of the research interviews I am dealing with here, they are, however, much less frequent.

The combination of confirmation and joint answer construction that we have seen in the previous example occurs more often. The next extract is taken from a discussion of the visit of (apartheid) South African rugby teams to New Zealand and the unrest which resulted from the visit. After having introduced the topic the interviewer asks:

Extract 7 (Appendix: New Zealand Interview 44: 293)

```
1. I:    . . . did you think that'a (0.4) the teams should have come
2.       (0.4) o:r
3. R:    Yes I did (0.2) I felt the teams should've come (0.2) u:hm
4.       (4.0) I think u::hm (0.6) the news media (2.0) u:hm made the
5.       most of it (0.4) an' perhaps stirred up a lot
```

Following this exchange the interviewee elaborates on the role of the media and finally concludes:

Extract 8 (Appendix: New Zealand Interview 44: 293/294)

```
1.  R:   And that's why I think it really
2.       was something that was (0.4) orchestrated between (1.2) uhm
3.       the extre:me groups
4.  I:   Yes [(yeah)
5.  R:       [And the media
6.  I:   Yeah
7.       (1.0)
8.       ( . . . )
9.  R:   the media's a- [a powerful thing
10. I:                  [People are very suggestible aren't [they
11. R:                                                      [Yes they
```

12.   [are I mean w(h)ell how el- else did- did Hitler
13. I: [Yeah
14. I: Yes
15. R: u:hm [(0.8) ever do what he did
16. I: [Yeah
17. I: Yes!
18.   (0.6)
19. I: That's right yes
20.   (2.0)
21. I: Yeah

The interviewee displays her view that the protests against the South African tour were orchestrated between extreme groups and the media. Her conclusion that "the media's a powerful thing" is supported by the interviewer who mentions the "'suggestible people'" as the other side of the "powerful media" coin. After the interviewee subsequently brings up Hitler as an example of the suggestibility of people, the interviewer produces a series of answer receipts: "Yes (0.6) That's right yes (2.0) Yeah." The repeated "yes," in combination with "that's right," gives this utterance the nature of a confirmation. The interviewer confirms that the Hitler example is appropriate in this context.

The next extract is another part of the discussion on rapists we examined in the previous section. The discussion follows a question on violence and punishment in New Zealand. At some point the interviewee states:

Extract 9 (Appendix: New Zealand Interview 44: 297)
1. R: A:nd (1.2) I'm not afraid but I take precautions.
2. I: Ye:s right [it's sensible isn't it [Mm mhm
3. R: [Ya'know   [I mean some people
4.   wouldn't bother- wouldn't go to work at night I know [that
5. I: [Yeah
6. R: And they wouldn't stay in the house on their own but
7. I: Yeah
8. R: I believe [you can't live like that
9. I: [Yeah
10. I: That's right I mean it's like giving in in a way

In this extract the interviewer twice provides a positive assessment of the actions reported by the interviewee. First she confirms the appropriateness of the "precautions" reported by the interviewee: "Ye:s right it's sensible isn't it" (line 2). Secondly, she expresses her agreement with the interviewee's view that you cannot live with too many precautions (such as not working at night and not staying alone in the house): "That's right

I mean it's like giving in in a way" (line 10). Also here, as in extract 4 above, the explanation "I mean it's like giving in in a way" removes the possible interpretation of "That's right" as just an acknowledgement.

Sometimes the interviewee actively invites the interviewer's confirmation of her views. In reply to the question "What are the things that you value about living in New Zealand," the interviewee mentions a number of things:

Extract 10 (Appendix: New Zealand Interview 44: 288)

```
1. R:   There are a few but- but basically the- (0.6) the average
2.      New Zealander is (1.8) is [ya'know unspoiled
3. I:                            [Yeah
4. I:   Yes ye[ah
5. R:         [I like to think that
6. I:   Yes
7. R:   Perhaps I am wrong
8. I:   Oh no I(h) [th(h)ink that's quite right Yeah
9. R:              [((laughs))
```

Here the interviewer is invited to either confirm or disconfirm the idea that "basically the average New Zealander is unspoiled" (lines 1–2) and responds with a confirmation of this idea.

Topic assessment

The third type of answer receipt that deserves attention in my present argument is a specific type of assessment the interviewer uses. Indeed, it is a type of assessment that shares characteristics with what has been called a "formulation." A formulation is a meta-characterization of the prior discourse (Heritage and Watson 1980). In a formulation a participant presents a locally relevant interpretation of a preceding part of the interaction. In many cases formulations are used to display the speaker's understanding of, for instance, the result of interactional decision making or of an answer of the interviewee.

The type of assessment I want to discuss here presents both the speaker's understanding and her assessment of the way a topic has been discussed. It is not a proper "formulation" since it does not provide a characterization of what has been said or done, but rather a characterization on top of what was said: an assessment of the way a topic has been dealt with. I have glossed this as "topic assessment."

The three examples I will discuss here all characterize the topic of the prior discourse as complex or problematic in cases where there is no clear indication in the prior answer that the interviewee considers the topic to be complex or problematic. Consider the following extract:

Extract 11 (Appendix: New Zealand Interview 2: 245/246)

1. R: E:hm (0.6) but- (1.0) I mean <u>what Af</u>rican country
2. I: °Mm mhm°
3. R: that <u>u:sed</u> to have European rule
4. I: °Mm mhm°
5. R: that is <u>now</u> ruled (0.6) <u>totally</u> by the <u>blacks</u>
6. I: Mm mhm
7.   (1.0)
8. R: <u>What</u> (.) <u>one</u> can you <u>hold</u> up as an example and say
9.   "We would like South Africa to follow that (one)?"
10. I: Mm mhm
11.   (1.0)
12. I: [°Yes°
13. R: [Nigeria? Ghana? (1.0) Sierra Leone?
14. I: °Y(h)es°
15. R: °a:ny of them°
16. I: °Yeah°
17. R: Zem- Zimbabwe or- >an' I don't know the names of half of
18.   them< it's [a long time since I was the[re
19. I: [yes   [yes
20. R: <u>Any</u> of them I mean [they are <u>absolute</u> (0.6) dia<u>bolic</u>
21. I: [yes
22. R: places
23.   (0.6)
24. I: Well it's a very complex [problem isn't it that whole [thing
25. R: [(ghh.)   [I mean

In this extract the interviewee discusses the apartheid system in South
Africa by comparing it to the government of other African countries.
A formulation of the interviewee's argument could have been: "so you
believe they're not doing any better than South Africa." The topic assessment produced by the interviewer in line 24, however, does not refer
to anything that has been observably said or done in the prior discourse,
but rather characterizes the topic of that discourse as "a very complex
problem."

The second example is taken from the same interview, where the interviewer responds to a statement about white South Africans:

Extract 12 (Appendix: New Zealand Interview 2: 248)

1. R: e:hm what they've got °o:ka:y° (1.4) maybe it isn't the <u>best</u>
2. I: Mm mhm
3. R: °But it's far from being the worst°
4. I: Mm mhm
5.   (1.0)
6. I: Right
7.   (1.0)
8. I: Yes I mean an' the whole thing's such a co:mplex issue.

Also here the topic assessment does not refer directly to what the inter-viewee has just stated, but characterizes the topic of his statement as "a co:mplex issue" (line 8).

The third example is taken from interview 16, where the interviewer responds to a statement on Polynesian immigrants and unemployment, which the interviewee finishes in lines 1–8:

Extract 13 (Appendix: New Zealand Interview 16: 278)

```
1.   R:   So ya' know however many you bring in here (0.6)
2.        that's what the unemployment's gonna go up [by
3.   I:                                              [°up by°
4.   I:   °Mm mhm°
5.        (0.4)
6.   R:   An' it's gonna cost the state more
7.   I:   Yes (0.4) °mmm°
8.   R:   to pay for them.
9.        (2.2)
10.  I:   Yea:h it's a difficult problem isn't it?
```

Again the formulation in line 10 does not refer to anything the interviewee has just stated. On the contrary, while the interviewer characterizes the topic of Polynesian immigration as "a difficult problem," the interviewee presents the issue straightforwardly as a relatively transparent calculus.

The topic assessments I discussed here have in common that their characterization of the prior discourse is not directly based on the inter-viewee's answer. This is first evidence of how the interviewer employs such characterizations as a means of detaching herself from the opinions uttered by the interviewees: the characterizations are not in line with the interviewer's stated opinions. Moreover, these formulations assess issues as "complex" or "difficult," that is, as "hard to form an opinion on," which in this respect contrasts with the clear opinions stated by the in-terviewees. Thus the topic assessment is used to characterize a topic as sensitive, and in doing so it contrasts the interviewer's perspective on the topic with that of the interviewee. The topic assessment is therefore a to-ken of the interviewer's detachment from the opinion of the interviewee.

The use of answer receipts as tokens of affiliation or detachment

The three types of answer receipts I discussed above are interesting for my present analyses because they are evidence of the interviewer's affili-ation with or detachment from a position taken by the interviewee. As I argued just now, the topic assessments I analyzed here are used as tokens of detachment. The joint answer construction and the confirmation, on the other hand, are tokens of affiliation with the stance taken by the in-terviewer. It is therefore not surprising that we have seen these response types co-occurring in several parts of the interviews. In producing a confirmation the interviewer displays her agreement with the view present in the interviewee's prior utterance. In producing a joint answer, the distinction between the interviewee's perspective on an issue and that of the interviewer practically disappears. In some cases, as we have seen, this content-oriented alignment is reinforced by syntactic co-construction.

As perhaps may be expected from the interactional need to create interpersonal rapport, the occurrences of affiliation tokens grossly outnumber the occurrences of tokens of detachment, the two types of affiliation tokens being largely in a quantitative balance. This observation brings me to the fourth and most frequent type of answer receipt, the minimal response, which, as I will argue, can derive meaning in terms of withholding affiliation.

Affiliation and detachment in minimal responses

The most frequent type of answer receipt is the minimal response. Receipts such as "mm hmm" are seemingly without semantic content, which renders them apparently neutral with regard to either affiliation or detachment. However, research carried out with regard to this reponse type casts serious doubts on their presumed contentless character.

The back-channel category

Yngve (1970) proposed the category of "back channel" action to analyze situations in which one speaker holds the floor (the "front channel") and a second speaker produces turns in the "back channel" without disputing the primary speaker's right to the floor. Yngve's category of back-channel actions is a broad one. It includes both minimal responses such as "uh huh" or "mm hmm" and potentially more elaborate responses, such as assessments and repair initiators, that do not compete for the floor.

Although the interactional feature of being non-floor-competitive appears to be shared by all members of the back-channel category, it is clear that the interactional work done by different back-channel actions may at the same time be quite diverse. Drummond and Hopper therefore rightly criticize those quantitative studies of the use of back-channel actions in which it is assumed that they are one functional category (1993: 161).[3]

Still, for the analytical purpose of my investigation of research interviews, it suits me to treat the interviewer's answer receipts for the time being as one theoretical category. The subsequent analysis of the interview data may reveal relevant functional differences. The danger of proposing a functional differentiation at this pre-analytical stage is that such a differentiation could be based on formal characteristics of the answer receipt rather than on their position in discourse.

Meaning of minimal responses

A major analytical question with respect to answer receipts is whether minimal responses such as "hm" can have any relation to the content of the prior utterance or whether their function is strictly one of organizing the speech exchange. In other words, can the relation between minimal responses and prior utterances be characterized as a semantic one? Existing research provides contradictory answers.

Most linguistic semantic theories would claim that responses such as "hmm" and "uh huh" do not have semantic properties since they are words without content. There are also conversation analytic studies that support this view. Mazeland, in his study of research interviews (1992), treats the production of minimal responses as a "pure formal, talk organising activity" (1992: 297) on the part of the interviewer, as opposed to the activity of content processing, which is apparent when the interviewer draws conclusions from the answer of the interviewee. In line with this view, he calls minimal responses such as "hmm" "neutral with regard to content" (1992: 296).

This view seems to be in line with Jefferson's (1984, 1993 [1983]) analysis of "yeah" and "mm hmm" as "acknowledgment tokens." Jefferson speaks of acknowledgment tokens principally in the analysis of overlapping talk. Acknowledgment tokens are then responses that do not pick up the topic of the overlapping talk, nor proceed on a different topic, but simply acknowledge the overlapping talk. It seems, then, although Jefferson does not explicitly say this, that this functional notion of acknowledgment implies the absence of a semantic relation.

Schegloff's (1982) analysis of "uh huh" as a "continuer" differs from Jefferson's notion of acknowledgment tokens in this respect. With the use of a minimal response such as "uh huh" as a continuer, the producer of that response exhibits "an understanding that an extended unit of talk is underway by another, and that it is not yet, or may not yet be (even ought not yet to be) complete" (1982: 81). Even though the term "continuer" points towards the discourse organizing function of minimal responses, Schegloff takes care to note that this organizing function is only "apparently lacking semantic content" (1982: 74). He argues that "continuers do not merely claim an understanding without displaying anything of the understanding they claim" (1982: 81). A continuer "does not claim understanding in general, but displays a particular understanding through production of an action fitted to that understanding"

(1982: 81). In other words, a continuer does not merely invite the other to continue, but through its sequential placement it also shows aspects of *how* the producer of the continuer understands the turn-so-far. The methodological importance of the point Schegloff makes is that he shows how contentless linguistic elements, such as many minimal responses, can have a semantic relation to other parts of the discourse.

This view is supported by researchers who claim that, although minimal responses may be lacking verbal content, they may have different relations with prior discourse depending on their prosodic realization, especially pitch movement. Ehlich (1979) distinguishes different intonation movements related to different interactional functions in the realization of "hm" in German. Gardner (1997) distinguishes between different uses of "mm" on the basis of intonation. One of the uses he distinguishes is the use of "mm" as an "assessment" of prior discourse. This research thus uses the argument of prosodic features to show that seemingly contentless elements such as many minimal responses may have semantic relations with prior utterances.

A number of researchers of answer receipts focus on the presence or absence of minimal responses in different types of question–answer activity. In the preceding section I mentioned Greatbatch's (1988) and Heritage and Greatbatch's (1991) analyses of the meaningful absence of interviewers' minimal responses in British news interviews. This notion of the meaningful absence or presence of minimal responses is also found in Atkinson's (1992) study of different types of question–answer exchanges in court. He concludes that, for a judge in one specific court,[4] his "practice of acknowledging receipt is a way of avoiding a range of alternative and more disaffiliative responses" (Atkinson 1992: 207). At the same time, in comparison with what could be expected in everyday conversation, "it also has the effect of avoiding various more affiliative options" (Atkinson 1992: 207).

Affiliation or detachment

As mentioned above, Schegloff (1982) argued that minimal responses are used in sequential positions where some other action might have been performed. Indeed, in the preceding section I have shown three such possible actions, namely joint answer construction, confirmation, and topic assessment, or, characterized from a different perspective: tokens of affiliation and tokens of detachment. From the occurrence of these tokens as answer receipts in the interviews, we can conclude that a minimal response potentially occurs in a position where either a token of detachment or a token of affiliation might have been relevant. In the same way that a minimal response, as Schegloff argues, may sometimes be doing "withholding laughter," it may, in the case of these research interviews, be withholding affiliation or withholding detachment. Such instances of minimal responses can no longer be called contentless. Even though their linguistic form does not reveal semantic content, their position within the discourse relates them to the content of the utterances to which they respond.

The all-important question is of course: when are minimal responses doing "withholding affiliation," and when are they doing "withholding detachment"? The answer seems to lie in what I will call the "context of discourse." The research interviews I am concerned with are organized as a series of topic-centered sequences of the type I discussed in section 3. For each single sequence, all other sequences together form the "context of discourse." It is the similarity or contrast with these other sequences in terms of the use of types of answer receipts that I believe are responsible for the possible treatment of minimal receipts as withholding affiliation or detachment.

As an example I want to discuss the overall structure of interview 44. The first half of this interview contains sequences in which both joint answer constructions and confirmations are not infrequent. For instance, on the topic of the relation between New Zealand and Australia, the interviewer responds by co-constructing an answer, as we saw in extract 4. Later on the interviewer does the same when she and the respondant discuss the rape topic (extracts 5 and 6). The confirmations shown in extracts 8, 9, and 10 are also taken from the first half of this interview. In the second half, however, the tone of the responses changes. In this second half the major topic is the relation between different ethnic groups in New Zealand and the positive discrimination measures the New Zealand government has taken to improve the position of Maoris, the native New Zealanders. In this second half, a vast majority of the interviewer's contributions are restricted to minimal responses and follow-up questions.

The contrast thus established between different parts of the interview is a contrast in the use of answer receipts, yet it is not a contrast between single receipts. The occurrences of joint answer constructions and confirmations in the discussion of different topics in the first half of the interview makes the overall restriction to minimal responses in the second half interpretable as withholding affiliation. It does not, however, make one specific minimal response interpretable as such. The context of discourse provided by the first half of the interview with its frequent tokens of affiliation causes the second half of the interview with its minimal responses to be interpretable as withholding affiliation, and thus as showing the interviewer's detachment from the views of the interviewee.

Conclusion: affiliation and detachment in research interviews

In this chapter I have discussed interactional functions of answer receipts in research interviews. In particular I have addressed the question of how different types of answer receipts by the interviewer can be used to signal affiliation with or detachment from the answers given by the interviewee. I first discussed three types of non-minimal responses, namely joint answer construction, and two types of assessments, confirmation and topic assessment. In this discussion I concluded that joint answer constructions and confirmations from the interviewer serve to signal affiliation with the views expressed by the interviewer. Topic assessments, however, which qualify the topic discussed as complex or problematic, signal detachment from the interviewee's views in which these qualifications were absent.

From this discussion I moved on to a discussion of minimal responses. Although researchers have claimed that these responses are neutral with respect to the content of the utterance to which they respond, others have argued that the sequential environment of minimal responses may lend them a character of withholding certain actions, thus giving them the quality of commenting on the content of prior discourse. In line with this argument, I have argued that, in research interviews, the contrast between phases with relatively many tokens of affiliation and phases with relatively many minimal responses may lend these latter phases the character of signaling the interviewer's detachment from the views of the interviewee. In this line of reasoning, it is conceivable that minimal responses may serve to withhold the detachment present in other phases of the interview. However, in the interviews investigated here, such phases of detachment were not found.

An important question is then raised regarding what these tokens of affiliation and detachment do to the open interview as a research method. Do such tokens affect the validity of the interview, and, if so, in what direction? It can be argued that the interviewer should act as neutrally as possible to avoid the risk of influencing the answers of the interviewee. From this argument it would follow that interviewers in open interviews are best advised to refrain as much as possible from tokens of either affiliation or detachment. Still, there is reason to believe that the use of tokens of affiliation or detachment in research interviews should not be assessed altogether as negative, especially when controversial and sensitive topics such as ethnicity and race are concerned. It seems unnatural for an interviewer in an open interview wishing to dig into such issues to act as a completely neutral recipient of the views of the interviewee. Moreover, in order to establish the kind of interpersonal relationship necessary to have the interviewee express him or herself on these issues, it may be required for the interviewer to take a stance on some issues and to affiliate with positions of the interviewee (in the way the interviewer does in interview 44), and perhaps even to show detachment on other issues. Indeed, in regular talk it is very common for participants to perform assessments of the views and situations discussed (Pomerantz 1984). This may imply that signaling affiliation or detachment are ways in which the interviewer can contribute to lending the interview a less formal, conversational character.

More generally speaking, the interactional work the frequent answer receipts in the interviews investigated here are doing is indeed to signal the attentive listening activity of the interviewer. It is perhaps a contrast with many news interviews (where interviewees often act "in function") that the interviewee's motivation for engaging in an open research interview to discuss sensitive issues must in part be established in the interview itself. The constant monitoring of the interviewee's contributions by the use of answer receipts can work as such a motivating means, since it displays the interviewer's interest in what the interviewee has to say.

The three types of answer receipts I discussed in section 4 show that such displays of interest are oriented to the content of the interviewee's contributions. Although they are not the only interactional means for establishing interpersonal rapport (think, for example, also of claims of empathy), the content-oriented answer receipt is the principal means used by the interviewer in these interviews to create an atmosphere in which the interviewees can present possibly controversial views: the affiliation tokens, and possibly also the tokens of detachment I discussed in this chapter.[5] Indeed, it seems to be virtually impossible for an interviewer in open inteviews to contribute to such an atmosphere without commenting on the content of the interviewee's contributions.

Whether this is a methodological problem for researchers using the open interview as a research instrument is not a question I will attempt to answer. This is where the social science methodologist should take over from the discourse analyst. The question of whether or not to use certain types of answer receipts is not the question I have aimed to answer in this paper. I have been concerned with a discourse analytic study of the interactional status of the interviewer's answer receipts, and I have shown how they can be used as tokens of affiliation or detachment. Furthermore, I have provided some arguments as to why research interviews could possibly benefit from interviewers taking a stance toward the topics of the interview. As Schegloff (1982) argued, the contributions of one participant cannot be fully understood if we do not look at the contributions surrounding them. The answers of interviewees are not just a look at the content of their thought; they are a product of the interview as an interactional process. In my analysis I have attempted to contribute to our insight into what surrounds these answers.

NOTES

1. I would like to thank several persons for valuable comments on earlier versions of this paper: Anita Pomerantz, the members of the Utrecht University research group "lokale praktijken," and, most of all, the editors of this volume.
2. Since the interviewer in all three interviews is Margaret Wetherell, I will be using female references.
3. For a similar argument, compare James and Clarke's (1993) critical discussion of studies in which it is assumed that the category of "interruption" is functionally coherent.
4. The court in question was the Small Claims Court, where the "judge" is called the "arbitrator."
5. Brown and Levinson (1987) also discuss content-oriented strategies such as "claim common opinions/attittudes/etc." and cooperative actions (joint construction) as positive politeness strategies. The idea that the tokens of detachment also possibly contribute to an atmosphere for expressing controversial views seems to go against Brown and Levinson's politeness intuitions.

References

Atkinson, J. M. 1992. Displaying neutrality: formal aspects of informal court proceedings, in *Talk at work: interaction in institutional settings*, edited by P. Drew and J. Heritage. 199–211.

Atkinson, J. M. and Heritage, J., editors. 1984. *Structures of social action: studies in conversation analysis*. Cambridge: Cambridge University Press.

Boden, D. and Zimmerman, D. H., editors. 1991. *Talk and social structure: studies in ethnomethodology and conversation analysis*. Cambridge: Polity Press.

Brown, P. and Levinson, S. C. 1987. *Politeness: some universals in language usage*. Cambridge: Cambridge University Press.

Drew, P. and Heritage, J., editors. 1992. *Talk at work: interaction in institutional settings*. Cambridge: Cambridge University Press.

Drummond, K. and Hopper, R. 1993. Back channels revisited: acknowledgment tokens and speakership incipiency. *Research on Language and Social Interaction* 26, 2: 57–177.

Ehlich, K. 1979. Formen und Funktionen von "hm": eine phonologisch-pragmatische Analyse, in *Die Partikeln der Deutschen Sprache*, edited by H. Weydt. Berlin: de Gruyter. 503–517.

Gardner, R. 1997. The conversational object "mm": a weak and variable acknowledging token. *Research on Language and Social Interaction* 30, 2: 131–156.

Greatbatch, D. 1988. A turn-taking system for British news interviews. *Language in Society* 17: 401–430.

Heritage, J. and Greatbatch, D. 1991. On the institutional character of institutional talk: the case of news interviews, in *Talk and social structure: studies in ethnomethodology and conversation analysis*, edited by D. Boden and D. H. Zimmerman. 93–137.

Heritage, J. and Watson, D. 1980. Aspects of the properties of formulations in natural conversations: some instances analyzed. *Semiotica* 30: 245–262.

James, D. and Clarke, S. 1993. Women, men, and interruptions: a critical review, in *Gender and Conversational Interaction*, edited by D. Tannen. Oxford University Press. 231–280.

Jefferson, G. 1984. Notes on a systematic deployment of the acknowledgement tokens "yeah" and "mh hm." *Papers in Linguistics* 17: 197–216.

1989. Preliminary notes on a possible metric which provides for a "standard maximum" silence of approximately one second in conversation, in *Conversation: an interdisciplinary perspective*, edited by D. Roger and P. Bull. Clevedon: Multilingual Matters. 166–196.

1993 (1983). Caveat speaker: preliminary notes on recipient topic-shift implicature. *Research on Language and Social Interaction* 26, 1: 1–30.

Labov, W. and Fanshel, D. 1977. *Therapeutic discourse*. New York: Academic Press.

Lerner, G. 1991. On the syntax of sentences-in-progress. *Language in Society* 20, 3: 441–58

1996. On the "semi-permeable" character of grammatical units in conversation: conditional entry into the turn space of another speaker, in *Interaction and grammar*, edited by E. Ochs, E. A. Schegloff, and S. A. Thompson. Cambridge: Cambridge University Press. 238–276.

Mazeland, H. 1992. *Vraag/antwoord-sequenties* (question/answer sequences). Amsterdam: Stichting Neerlandistiek VU.

Pomerantz, A. 1984. Agreeing and disagreeing with assessments, in *Structures of social action: studies in conversation analysis*, edited by J. M. Atkinson and J. Heritage. Cambridge: Cambridge University Press. 57–101.

Pomerantz, A. and Fehr, B. J. 1997. Conversation analysis: an approach to the study of social action as sense making practices, in *Discourse studies: a multidisciplinary introduction*, edited by T. A. van Dijk. London: Sage. 64–91.

Psathas, G. 1995. *Conversation analysis. The study of talk-in-interaction*. London: Sage.

Schegloff, E. A. 1982. Discourse as an interactional achievement: some uses of "uh huh" and other things that come between sentences, in *Analyzing discourse: text and talk*, edited by D. Tannen. Wahington DC: Greorgetown University Press. 71–93.

Schegloff, E. and Sacks, H. 1973. Opening up closings. *Semiotica* 7: 289–327.

Ten Have, P. 1999. Doing conversation analysis: a practical guide. London: Sage.

Yngve, V. H. 1970. On getting a word in edgewise. *Papers from the Sixth Regional Meeting of the Chicago Linguistics Society* 6: 657–677.

11 Interviewer laughter as an unspecified request for clarification

Tony Hak

Introduction

In interviews, an interviewer and a respondent meet at an arranged time for an encounter with an agreed aim. Both parties must do quite a lot of work to achieve this aim, which is the production of "interview data." In a technical sense, the aim of the interview has been achieved if the respondent's talk during the interview has been recorded. The recording then can be taken away from the interview setting to the researcher's workplace, where it can be manipulated (transcribed, interpreted, analyzed) by the researcher. From the respondent's perspective, the aim of the interview has been achieved if she has been able to express her ideas about the topics of the interview, and if she is satisfied that the recorded talk represents what she wanted to tell the interviewer and how she wanted to represent herself. From the researcher's perspective, the aim of the interview has been achieved if she has been able to elicit (and record) talk from the respondent that can be transformed (transcribed and reduced) into the data that she wants to get for analysis.

In this volume we deal with data produced in interviews aimed at eliciting talk that would exhibit the ways in which white New Zealanders (Pakehas) make distinctions between their own group and others, and that in the subsequent analysis could be analyzed as instances of "the language of racism" (Wetherell and Potter 1992). Interviewees were asked to discuss the 1981 Springbok rugby tour of New Zealand and to express their views and opinions on different topics related to race relations (Wetherell and Potter 1992: 224). From the respondents' perspective, the aim of the interview was achieved when they expressed their views and opinions on race relations in such a way that they could be reasonably satisfied that the interviewer had understood them. From the interviewer's perspective, the aim of the interview was achieved when she had been able to elicit (and record) talk from the respondents that could be transformed (transcribed and reduced) into data that represent "the language of racism."

What do such data look like? The following example is a data extract taken from pages 76–77 of the published report (Wetherell and Potter 1992):

In this extract someone we have called Joan Wood gives her response to recent attempts in New Zealand to establish a "renaissance" of Maori culture.

Wood: I think we'll end up having Maori wars if they carry on the way they are. I mean no it'll be a Pakeha war (yes). Um (.) they're making New Zealand a racist country. Um but you know you usually feel, think, that racism is um (.) putting the darker people down but really they're doing it the other way around, I feel. Um, everything seems to be to help the Maori people, um, you know. I think at the moment sort of the Europeans sort of they're just sort of watching and putting up with it, but they'll only go so far. Um you know we've got . . . [The remaining part of Wood's discourse is omitted from this quotation.]

There are a number of categories introduced in this strongly racist account of recent events: . . .

In this fragment a data extract is presented, labeled as a "strongly racist account," and analyzed in terms of the categories used in it. It is important to note that this data extract is an edited transcript from the interview. The effect of the editing is that, as is usual in production processes in general, traces of the production process itself have been removed. The topic of this chapter is the actual process (interaction) by which the interviewer in cases such as this has co-produced the talk from which these "data" could be extracted.

The interviewer as a co-producer of interview data

Let us look at the interview transcript that corresponds to the data extract above:

Extract 1 (Appendix: New Zealand Interview 44: 297/298)

1. I: (. . .) There's a much greater emphasis now on ehm Maori culture
2.   and the use of the Maori language (1.0) an' so on. (0.6) Do you think
3.   in general that's been (0.4) uh constructive or (1.4) what do you feel
4.   about the way things are going (0.2) on that front?
5.   (2.0)
6. R: I think they'll end up having Maori w:ars if they carry on the way
7.   [they have I mean no it'll be a Pakeha war
8. I: [((laugh))
9. I: Yes
10. R: U::hm (1.6) they're ma:king New Zealand a racist cu- country uhm but
11.   ya'know you usually feel (.) think that racism is uhm (1.4) putting th-
12.   putting ([.) the darker people down
13. I: [Yes

14. R: [but really they're doing it (.) the other way around
15. I: [( )
16. I: A sort of [reverse [racism
17. R: [I feel   [yes
18. I: Yeah
19. R: U:hm (1.4) everything (0.6) seems to be to help (0.2) the Maori people,
20.   (1.0) a::nd ya'know (0.4) I think (1.4) at the moment sort of (0.6) the
21.   Europeans are sort of (0.4) They're just sort of watching [and putting
22. I: [Yeah
23. R: up with it
24. I: Yeah
25. R: But (.) they'll only go so fa:r
26. I: Right yeah
27. R: U:hm (1.0) tsk (1.0) ya'know we- we've got (. . .)

Extract 1 demonstrates that (and how) the interviewer is actively involved in the production of the respondent's talk. This involvement begins
with presenting a question for response: "What do you feel about the way
things are going on that front?" and subsequently ranges from actively
demonstrating the expectation that the respondent will continue her talk
("Yes" and "Yeah") to formulating the gist of what the respondent has
said ("A sort of reverse racism"), a formulation that is accepted and ex-
pounded upon by the respondent ("Everything seems to help the Maori
people"). Thus we can see that, and how, respondent talk is produced in
a local interactional context in which the interviewer plays an important
role. In this specific case, this extract demonstrates that a "strongly racist
account of recent events" (Wetherell and Potter 1992: 77) is not only
provided by a respondent for the interviewer, but also co-produced by
the interviewer. Obviously this does not mean that the interviewer is a
co-author of this account, which is clearly the respondent's own. It does
mean, however, that the interviewer is showing a willingness (and a com-
petence) to appreciate the respondent's viewpoint to such a degree that
the latter is helped to express it.

In this chapter, it is discussed, first, how the interviewer's discourse
in extract 1 can be analyzed as supporting the respondent in producing pertinent accounts. Next it is shown that the instance of interviewer
laughter in this extract – ignored in the published report – can be analyzed as a signal that the interviewer has problems with "appreciating"
the respondent's viewpoint. Finally, through a comparison of different
instances of interviewer laughter, it is concluded that instances of uninvited single-party interviewer laughter function as unspecified requests to
the respondent to provide for some clarification or justification of what
has just been said.

Appreciative interviewer discourse

Acknowledgment of receipt ("Yeah," "Yes") and back channelling ("Mm") are very common features in these interviews. In a large number of question–answer sequences, "Mm" and "Yeah" (or "Yes") are the only ways by which the interviewer shows her appreciation of the respondent's talk. Such instances could be called the *basic question-answer sequence* figure (11.1).

I: [question]
R: [answer]
I: mmm
R: [answer]
I: yeah *or* yes
R: [answer]
I: mmm *or* yeah *or* yes
     [next question]

Figure 11.1 The basic question–answer sequence

In the three interviews there are many instances of question–answer sequences in which formulation–agreement sub-sequences are added to this basic pattern (see figure 11.2).

I: [question]
R: [answer]
I: mmm
R: [answer]
I: [formulation]
R: [acceptance]
     [expansion]
I: yeah *or* yes
R: [answer]
I: mmm *or* yeah *or* yes
     [next question]

Figure 11.2 The formulation sequence.

An example of such a formulation–acceptance–expansion sub-sequence is the "reverse racism" sequence in extract 1a below (which is a fragment from extract 1 above). When formulating, the interviewer does not just show an interest in the respondent's talk (as with back channelling and acknowledgment of receipt), but also explicitly shows an understanding of its gist by providing a version of it.

In extract 1a, the gist of the respondent's talk is formulated as "a sort of reverse racism." The respondent *accepts* this formulation as correct, not just by agreeing ("Yes"), which in isolation could be heard as a mere acknowledgment token, but also by *expanding* upon this formulation by providing another, more extreme, version of the same phenomenon ("Everything seems to be to help the Maori people").

Extract 1a (Appendix: New Zealand Interview 44: 297/298)

1. R: [but really they're doing it (.) the other way around
2. I: [( )
3. I: A sort of [reverse [racism
4. R: [I feel [yes
5. I: Yeah
6. R: U:hm (1.4) everything (0.6) seems to be to help (0.2) the Maori people,
7.   (. . .)

Formulation–acceptance–expansion sub-sequences are a rather frequent phenomenon in these interviews, which suggests that they form a routine part of the interviewer's interactional work. The same applies to a less frequent, but still quite prevalent, interactional phenomenon: namely, the use of a seemingly positive evaluation ("Right" or "Good") as signaling the closing of a sequence and the announcement of a topic shift (figure 11.3).

> I: [question]
> R: [answer]
> I: mmm
> R: [answer]
> I: yeah *or* yes
> R: [answer]
> I: right *or* good
>   [next question]

Figure 11.3 Sequence ending with an evaluation

Although "Right" or "Good" in this position can be heard as a (positive) evaluation of the content of the respondent's utterance, both interviewer and respondent seem to treat it as an unambiguous instance of sequence closing and topic shift. If "Right" and "Good" are heard as *evaluations* at all, it is the production of "good" interview talk that is evaluated, not the content of what has been said. These utterances signal that "enough" talk has been produced about the current topic, and that another topic can be addressed.

Interviewer laughter

Back channelling, acknowledgment of receipt, formulating, topic-shift announcements, and the introduction of new topics followed by new

questions cover almost all the interactional work performed by the interviewer as observed in the three transcripts. These interviewer utterances
are described above as unambiguous contributions to the smooth running of the interview, characterized by a division of interactional labor
in which the respondent provides opinions and viewpoints and the interviewer provides topics for discussion as well as positive evaluations of the
respondent's talk as "good" data. There is, however, one other kind of
rather frequent interviewer discourse in the three transcripts that does not
fit easily into this framework: namely, interviewer laughter. An example
of interviewer laughter is present in extract 1 above (see extract 1b).[1]

Extract 1b (Appendix: New Zealand Interview 44: 297)
1. R: I think they'll end up having Maori w:ars if they carry on
2.   the way [they have I mean no it'll be a Pakeha war
3. I: [((laugh))
4. I: Yes
5. R: U::hm (1.6) they're ma:king New Zealand a racist cu- country

This instance of interviewer laughter immediately precedes the beginning
of a clarification on the part of the respondent ("I mean"), which is
interrupted by self-repair ("no it'll be a Pakeha war"). This, in turn, is
followed (after a supporting "Yes") by what seems to be an explanation of
why a "Pakeha war" will happen ("They're making New Zealand a racist
country"). In order to make sense of this interaction, it is necessary, first,
to ascertain what the respondent is doing here and, next, how this can be
seen as the result of this instance of interviewer laughter.

Apparently, the respondent considers her preceding statement ("I think
they'll end up having Maori wars if they carry on the way they have") as
something to be clarified. Two candidates for clarification can be identified. One candidate is the prediction of (new) "Maori wars" itself. The
(original) "Maori wars" are the nineteenth-century rebellions by Maori
tribes against the colonists. Most people in New Zealand think that such
wars are a thing of the past and that they will not take place again. Therefore, the prediction of further Maori wars is itself in need of supporting
evidence. The second candidate is the reason given for these wars ("If
they carry on the way they have"). This utterance, which can be heard as
placing the blame for these possible future wars upon the recent behavior
of the Maoris, calls for further explanation.

We will never know what the respondent was going to clarify, however,
because just after beginning her explanation ("I mean"), she interrupts
herself with a repair. She amends the label "Maori wars" to "Pakeha war."
It seems the Pakeha will be provoked to start this war "because they're

making New Zealand a racist country." The respondent thus treats her statement "I think they'll end up having Maori wars if they carry on the way they have" as a gloss to be unpacked. Her utterance, "I mean no it'll be a Pakeha war" is (only) the beginning of this unpacking. If this is so, how then can the interviewer laughter that occurs just before the (beginning of this) unpacking be interpreted?

One possible approach to this question assumes that this instance of interviewer laughter influences the respondent's turn substantively and, therefore, can be seen as a request for clarification to which the respondent complies. In this way, this instance of laughter can be seen as an invitation to unpack the gloss. An alternative approach to this instance of laughter treats it as a (mere) acknowledgment token and, as such, as a (mere) invitation to the respondent to continue her talk. How can we decide between these two interpretations?

One way of approaching this problem is by analyzing similar instances. In extract 2, from the same interview, the interviewer receives the respondent's statement that "she'd cut their" with laughter. If the transcript is correct – which we assume here – the respondent pauses for a moment before completing her sentence. Then she uses the same phrase ("I mean") as in extract 1, apparently as an introduction to the clarification that follows.

Extract 2 (Appendix: New Zealand Interview 44: 296)

```
1.  R:  But loo:k at what ra:pists are do:ing I mean we didn't he:ar of ra:pists
2.      [even a fe:w years ago
3.  I:  [Yeah
4.  I:  That's right (0.2) yeah
5.  R:  And now every weekend- I'd cut their [(0.4) whats its off
6.  I:                                        [((laughs))
7.  R:  I mean I think that's dre::ad↑ful
8.  I:  Yea:s
9.      (0.6)
10. R:  And to think that this bloke Pa:lmer has actually let two: rapists out of
11.     prison
```

Though the clarification in this extract is completed without self-repair, this clarification follows a pause, which apparently signals the searching for what could be "cut off," and next, a completion ("whats its") of the sentence that was interrupted by the laughter. Common to extracts 1 and 2 is the phrase "I mean," which follows the interviewer laughter. In both instances, thus, this laughter seems to be interpreted by the respondent as an invitation to clarify or, rather, in extract 2, to justify. A little bit later in the same interview, there is another instance of interviewer laughter followed by "I mean" and a clarification (extract 3).

Extract 3 (Appendix: New Zealand Interview 44: 296/297)

1. R: And to <u>let</u> two rapists- and one was a <u>third</u> time convicted
2. I: O::h that's right ([.) yeah
3. R: [That- that's shocking I mean that's just ah making it
4.   a real mockery
5. I: Yes (0.4) yeah
6. R: U:hm (0.4) ya'know I feel like going out an' shooting ↑hi:m
7. I: ((laughs)) yeah
8. R: I mean it makes you wonder <u>if</u> he's got any <u>daugh</u>ters
9. I: Yes (0.2) [what if that's [right
10. R: [or   [what- would he care if wife was raped?
11. I: Yeah (0.4) really
12. R: Or do they not- (.) believe that it- it i:s an eno:rmity to- to
13. I: Right
14. R: to- (.) to a woman to be raped?
15. I: Yes that's right I mean it- to me it must be one of the worst things that
16.   can ever happen to a- (0.4) to you

This instance is very similar to the one in extract 2. The statements "I feel like going out and shooting him" and "I'd cut their (whats its) off" both seem to invite interviewer laughter. Also, in both instances, this interviewer laughter is followed by a justification by the respondent.

Thus, we can see that, despite the superficial similarity in interactional effect (the respondent continues talking), instances of interviewer laughter accomplish a more specific interactional outcome than do instances of acknowledgment tokens. The result of interviewer laughter is that the respondent expands upon her previous statements. The respondent is not (merely) invited to continue talking, but to do so in a specific way, namely, by clarifying or justifying. In this way, the format of the resulting sequence is similar to the formulation sequence (figure 11.4).

	Formulation sequence	Interviewer laughter sequence
I:	[question]	[question]
R:	[answer]	[answer]
I:	mmm	mmm
R:	[answer]	[answer]
I:	[*formulation*]	[*laughter*]
R:	[acceptance]	[acceptance as request to expand]
	[expansion]	[expansion]
I:	yeah *or* yes	yeah *or* yes
R:	[answer]	[answer]
I:	mmm *or* yeah *or* yes	mmm *or* yeah *or* yes
	[next question]	[next question]

Figure 11.4 The formulation sequence and the interviewer laughter sequence

Although they might have a very different origin and, therefore, a very different meaning for the interviewer, both formulations and interviewer laughter are for all practical purposes ways in which the interviewer invites further expansion of respondent talk. An important difference is that formulations are themselves substantive contributions to the construction of the respondent's talk with which the respondent must engage, whereas interviewer laughter does not restrict respondents in their next utterances in this same way. Laughter does not specify what it is that should be clarified or justified. It's up to the respondent to decide what this is.

Interviewer laughter as an ambiguous response

What is it in the respondent's talk that invites an "unspecified" request for clarification, rather than a mere back channelling, or a formulation, or an explicit question? In beginning to answer this question, it is important to note that, in the report on this study, this piece of talk is labeled as "a strongly racist account." The least that can be claimed here is that, in the research report, it is taken for granted that this account is immediately recognizable as racist to the participants (interviewers, analysts) in this study. It is a safe assumption, thus, that this account was recognizable as a racist account to the interviewer when she heard it. It is obvious that the interviewer cannot explicitly respond to the respondent's talk by calling it "racist," however. The interviewer's approach throughout the interviews, which is evident in the three transcripts and also in the extract discussed here, is one of "appreciation" and of supporting respondents in expressing their opinions and views. It is therefore quite understandable that the interviewer's response is minimal and takes a form in which her stance is expressed without being "said" in so many words.

Through the interviewer's laughter, the respondent is signaled that something in her utterance is "wrong," without getting information about what this is exactly. Consequently, it is the respondent's task to uncover the problem. Apparently, the respondent hypothesizes that there is nothing wrong with the content of what she has said, but rather with the clarity with which she has expressed it. At least, this is what she seems to indicate when she starts unpacking and clarifying her utterance. In this way, both parties save face. The interviewer distances herself from the respondent's "racist" account without jeopardizing the smooth running of the interview, and the respondent is able to ignore a potential criticism of her account as in some way improper.

This analysis applies to all three extracts discussed thus far. The problem with this analysis, despite its intuitive plausibility, is that it brings interpretations to bear on the data that are derived from outside the interview and its transcript; namely, from the research report that has been published much later. This problem applies in particular to the assumption that the interviewer cannot (and does not want to) respond explicitly to an obvious "racist account" by calling it the same. It treats her as a party with a "hidden agenda."

Received opinion in conversation analysis (and, for that matter, in discourse analysis) is that interpretations of transcripts should entirely and solely rely on what the parties in the interaction make observable to each other. Apart from invoking the plausibility of the above analysis, it is not possible to demonstrate here why the received opinion, and in particular the rules for analysis deduced from it, are misguided. Such a demonstration can be found in Hak (1995), where it is shown that the discovery and analysis of the effects of "hidden agendas" on an interaction can be based, among other things, on an analysis of speakers' orientations to *past* instructions as well as to *future* audiences. Speakers design their utterances not only for parties present in the current interaction, but also for non-present audiences, particularly audiences to which "reports" about the interaction will be made.

Summarizing the analysis so far, interviewer laughter in extracts 1, 2, and 3 has been interpreted as an interactional device through which the interviewer signals to the respondent that a statement is in some way improper or at least is in need of some further clarification or justification. Among all instances of laughter in the transcripts, instances of uninvited single-party interviewer laughter, as the ones discussed above, are the most common. They can all be analyzed in this way. To make this point, just one other, randomly selected, example is presented here (extract 4).

Extract 4 (Appendix: New Zealand Interview 2: 256)
```
1.  R:  They're a mino:rity .hh They cannot take over the country
2.      [If they want Stewart Island I'd be quite [willing to give it
3.  I:  [Mm mhm                                   [((out breath laugh))
4.  R:  them. Set up the homeland for them then in Stewart Island. And they
5.      could- they- [they could all move in
6.  I:               [y(h)es
7.  I:  Y(h)es
8.  R:  And run it themselves. I mean ya'know there are plenty'a mutton birds
9.  I:  ((la[ugh))
10. R:      [They- hh. but they're uhm (2.2) Chh. It's like when they (. . .)
```

This extract contains two instances of uninvited single-party interviewer laughter.[2] These two instances are not, as in the extracts 1, 2, and 3, followed by instances of "I mean," but they seem to have a similar function as invitations for expansion. In this instance, it can again be argued that the interviewer's uninvited laughter signals her recognition of a racist account which, on the one hand, is more or less repulsive to her but, on the other hand, is also (and precisely for that reason) "good data." As in extracts 1, 2, and 3, the respondent is signaled that an unspecified something in his utterance needs clarification or justification.

Respondent-initiated laughter

Not all instances of interviewer laughter can be analyzed this way. In this section, examples of respondent-initiated laughter will be discussed in order to highlight the difference between uninvited and invited interviewer laughter. In extract 5, the respondent delivers, with a "smile voice," the statement that he tends to think of Australian Aborigines as people "standing on one leg and looking into the sunset."[3]

Extract 5 (Appendix: New Zealand Interview 2: 258/259)

```
1.   R:  And (2.0) hh. I think (0.4) basically (0.2) e:h (1.0) the Maori as a
2.       people (1.4) >or the better ones< a:re [e:h an excellent people
3.   I:                                         [°Mm mhm°
4.   R:  [Ya'know they're a lo:vely people
5.   I:  [Yes
6.   I:  Yeah
7.   R:  E:h (0.4) I don't kno:w many Aborigines
8.   I:  Mm mhm
9.   R:  I always tend to think of them as long an' bony and standing on one leg
10.      [and looking into the sunset ((smile voice))
11.  I:  [((laugh))
12.  I:  Yes (0.2) yeah
13.  R:  (°a::nd°)
14.      (1.0)
15.  I:  Yes I mean it's (1.0) yeah I think that's probably true it's something to
16.      do with the character of the Maori people an'
17.  R:  ↑Mhm
```

The respondent presents his statement about Aborigines as something the interview parties can laugh about, demonstrating this very point by starting the laughter himself. As Jefferson, Sacks, and Schegloff (1987) have demonstrated, teller-initiated laughter is on many occasions an interactional move by which tellers pursue intimacy. Sharing something "improper" that cannot be shared with just anyone further substantiates this intimacy. Teller's laughter marks the told event as "improper" and, at the same time, demonstrates that the teller knows this. However, the categorization of the told event, or its telling, as "improper" is qualified: although it is marked as something "improper" for others, it is at the same time presented as proper for the interaction at hand. Treating something as proper on this occasion that is not proper in other situations creates intimacy.

This does not imply, however, that parties must agree on what exactly is "not proper" in a specific case. For instance, in extract 5 the interviewer might think that they have agreed on the improperness of thinking such things about Aborigines. From this perspective, the laughter marks the improperness. On the other hand, the respondent might think that they have agreed that sensible people (such as they obviously are) find these thoughts quite proper among themselves, and that this marks their being different (in a positive way) from other people. From this perspective, the laughter marks the conspiratorial nature of this agreement. In either case, the laughter is seen as supportive and, therefore, the respondent can continue his discourse, which in this specific case results in a comparatively positive description of the Maoris, as compared to less likeable peoples who tend to stand on one leg (see figure 11.5).

> I: [question]
> R: [answer]
> I: mmm
> R: [answer with laughter]
> I: [laughter]
> R: [expansion]
> I: yeah *or* yes
> R: [answer]
> I: mmm *or* yeah *or* yes
>   [next question]

Figure 11.5 Respondent-initiated laughter sequence

There are several reasons why it is difficult for the interviewer to not accept the intimacy offered by the respondent in extract 5. One of them is the cunning way in which the derogatory remarks about the Aborigines, marked as improper in an unspecified sense, are embedded in the construction of a relatively positive description of the Maoris.

There are occasions in which the interviewer does not respond to respondent-initiated laughter, however. In extract 6, the respondent presents with laughter – which is marked in the transcript by the symbol (h) in "th(h)ere's" and "r(h)ight" – the statement that "the headmaster there has got the right idea." The interviewer does not respond to this laughter, but rather produces a back-channel token and maintains a supportive attitude throughout the subsequent talk by means of expressions such as "Yes" and "Yes right." This dismissal of the laughter invitation might be explained by the laughter's placement. The "improper" part, the headmaster's statement, has yet to follow, and is delivered itself without any hint of laughter.

Extract 6 (Appendix: New Zealand Interview 2: 253)

1. I: So why do you think there is such a gap then and what what'em can be
2.   done about it (1.0) between eh Maori children and (0.4) Pakeha
3.   children which is .hh
4.   (2.0)
5. R: .hh Well I'd se:nd, (0.2) send them to [school name] where the
6.   headmaster there's got th(h)ere's got the r(h)ight idea
7. I: Mmm
8. R: He said if- if they're eh- if they're forced to work they work
9. I: Y[es
10. R: [If they don't- if they're not forced to work they'll dole it
11. I: Ye:s right

Respondent-initiated laughter is much more rare in the interviews than laughter initiated by the interviewer, although it is very difficult to substantiate this claim with a precise number due to the difficulty of recognizing such instances unequivocally on the tapes or in the transcripts. Extract 6 is a point in case. Whereas I have presented the way in which the respondent delivered the words "th(h)ere's" and "r(h)ight" as indicating laughter, another analyst might treat them as just hearable breathing. If we discard such equivocal cases, we are left with only a negligible number of cases of full-blown laughter initiated by the respondent. This makes the rather frequent occurrence of single-party interviewer laughter more striking, and supports the claim that such interviewer laughter functions as a signal of distancing rather than as an invitation to create intimacy around an "impropriety."

Conclusions

In qualitative research, researchers usually collect data themselves, rather than hiring interviewers to do this (as is usual in survey research). One of the often-quoted advantages of this practice is that "analysis" begins in the interview itself. Respondent discourse is continuously monitored for its value as data for the study's purposes. In a sense, collecting the interview data is the first step in the writing of the research report. Therefore, it is not only counter-intuitive, but also plainly wrong, to treat interviewer utterances in these transcripts as if they are only relevant and explainable as local moves in the ongoing interaction. This does *not* imply that attributing pre-existing, determining intentions to the interviewer in the analysis of these transcripts is acceptable, but it *does* imply that inspecting interviewer utterances for their orientation to being received by other audiences (which can and must be specified) in non-local future contexts is justifiable. Therefore, we must inspect interviewer discourse in these transcripts not only for how it "appreciates" respondent discourse in the local context of the interview itself (i.e., as "appreciative" to the respondent), but also for how it can be seen to "appreciate" respondent discourse in the future context of analysis and reporting.

In this chapter it is argued that a large part of interviewer discourse in these transcripts can be analyzed as locally functional as "appreciative" to the respondents' viewpoints and as supporting them in expressing their opinions and views. It is argued that single-party uninvited interviewer laughter is different in the sense that it signals a request from the interviewer to clarify or also to justify something that just has been said. This laughter does not signal receipt of "good" interview data (as signaled by means of back-channelling and acknowledgment tokens) or understanding of what was said (as demonstrated by a formulation of a candidate gist). Instead it signals non-understanding or, possibly, non-acceptance of what was said and, therefore, the need to clarify or justify. The artfulness of laughter as a device for signaling a difficulty in appreciation on the part of the interviewer without threatening the smooth continuation of the interview is that it is non-verbal and that, therefore, respondents are free to interpret the signaled "problem" in their own way. This allows both parties to save face.

In the small but impressive body of conversation analytic research on laughter, which began with the seminal study by Jefferson, Sacks, and Schegloff (1987), there is no mention of this "unspecified distancing" function of single-party hearer-initiated laughter, as identified in this chapter. Further research might identify instances of such recipient-initiated laughter, not only in other types of social science interviews, but also in other types of institutionalized encounters (as in news interviews, psychiatric and other medical interviews, job interviews, and court hearings) and in informal conversations. In such research, this type of laughter as a face-saving, distancing act might be seen to be particularly "functional" in contexts in which a party for some reason is obliged to demonstrate an "appreciation" of politically or morally "improper" talk. This reason might be institutional, e.g., in the work of interviewers, physicians, judges, etc.

One of the achievements of conversation and discourse analytic studies is that they have highlighted the artfulness of participants in both "ordinary" and less ordinary types of interaction. In the case discussed in this chapter, the interviewer's measured use of uninvited laughter as a device to signal some unspecified "problem" in her appreciation of respondent talk, next to and different from the routine use of back-channelling signals and acknowledgment tokens, demonstrates her artfulness in elic-iting the data on which an impressive analysis of the "language of racism" was based.

1. It is very difficult to transcribe laughter precisely, and, therefore, this transcript can only be taken as the transcriber's interpretation of the recording. However, because this transcript is the best approximation of the recording we have, it is taken in the analysis as a "true" rendering of the interaction in the interview. It is assumed in particular that the timing of the laughter – for example indicated by the symbol [in the transcript that laughter starts while the other speaker is still talking – is correct.

2. Some inbreaths ("hh" and "Chh") in the last line of the transcript could be seen as instances of reluctant laughter on the part of the respondent, but it is certainly not the case that the respondent fully joins the interviewer's laughter. Moreover, this would still leave the first instance of interviewer laughter in this extract as an instance of single-party laughter.

3. It is very difficult to identify laughter from a tape, and the same applies to a "smile voice."

References

Hak, T. 1995. Ethnomethodology and the institutional context. *Human Studies* 18: 109–137.

Jefferson, G., Sacks, H. and Schegloff, E. A. 1987. Notes on laughter in the pursuit of intimacy, in *Talk and social organization*, edited by G. Button and J. R. E. Lee. Clevedon: Multilingual Matters. 152–205.

Wetherell, M. and Potter, J. 1992. *Mapping the language of racism*. Hempel Hempstead: Harvester Wheatsheaf.

12   Perspectives and frameworks in interviewers' queries[1]

Anita Pomerantz and Alan Zemel

> *It is futile to search for truly neutral questions. They don't exist. Every question carries presuppositions, so every question establishes a perspective. So for each question we must ask: Is the perspective taken really the one from which we want the respondent to answer? If the answer is yes – if we can justify the perspective – then we can also justify the question.*
>
> (Clark and Schober 1992: 30)

One use of in-depth interviews is to determine the respondents' attitudes, beliefs, and/or opinions on controversial issues. Race is one such controversial issue. When an interviewer asks questions about racial issues (or controversial issues more generally), a fundamental organization comes into play: (1) asking about a racial issue reflects and implicates a position or perspective with respect to the controversy; and (2) an interviewer can construct a query that aligns to a greater or lesser extent with a position or perspective, or he or she may work to avoid aligning with a particular position or perspective.

When an interviewer asks about a particular racial matter, the interviewee might presume that the interviewer endorses the perspective implicated by the query. Likewise, when an interviewee responds to a query about a particular racial matter, the interviewer might presume that the interviewee endorses a perspective implicated by the response. The possibility of the interactants' making inferences about each other's perspective presents certain problems for both the interviewer and interviewee in terms of how to formulate and interpret queries and responses.

Interviewers attempt to structure their interviews so as to allow interviewees to display their understandings of, feelings about, or perspectives on a controversial matter. On some occasions, an interviewer may ask about an issue or problem that is not of interest or concern to the interviewee. When this happens, the interviewer and interviewee might make adjustments that enable the interviewee to display his/her own perspective on that issue or problem.

In examining three interviews in which the interviewer elicited the interviewees' attitudes, beliefs, and/or opinions on controversial matters, our objectives were (1) to illuminate some features of interview queries and (2) to show how these features operate when interviewers elicit interviewees' views on controversial issues like race. After presenting the analysis, we discuss how our findings may be useful to those who employ in-depth interviews as a research tool.

Interviewers' queries[2]

In eliciting responses from interviewees, interviewers are faced with the practical problem of asking questions that interviewees can understand *and* answer. This involves organizing the interview and constructing queries in ways that make the questions intelligible to interviewees and that provide interviewees with ways of organizing their own experiential resources to produce responses (Holstein and Gubrium 1995).

When interviewers formulate their queries, they unavoidably incorporate particular interpretive frameworks, presumptions, and/or perspectives.[3] Clark and Schober (1992) discuss how perspectives are necessarily part of constructing queries.[4] "Perspectives usually get established automatically, without notice, as the participants in a discourse proceed with what they have to say" (20). Interviewers incorporate a perspective when they construct their queries: "Perspectives get established more generally by how speakers *frame* what they say" (21). Generally, interviewers choose perspectives they judge their interviewees will accept (20).

The incorporation of perspectives in interviewers' queries affects the interviewees and their responses.[5] The perspective incorporated within a query sets a perspective for the interviewee's response. Much of the time the perspective or framing of the issue goes unnoticed by, and is unproblematic for, the interviewees. When interviewees respond to the questions as formulated, they implicitly endorse the framing or perspective as valid for them. However, there are occasions when interviewees display some problem with the assumptions associated with, or the framing of, an interviewer's question. In order to avoid accepting and/or being seen as accepting the perspectives incorporated within the interviewer's query, an interviewee would need to put forward a new perspective. "You must express your answer from some perspective, and unless you create a new one, the questioner will interpret your answer, by default, from the perspective she has established" (Clark and Schober 1992: 29). In other words, it takes the special effort of objecting to, rejecting, or shifting the framing.

Our concern in this chapter is to discuss some of the ways that perspectives, assumptions, and/or frameworks are implied by the interviewer's queries. We examine two query packages: *This is a publicly known problem;*

What is your solution? and *This is a matter of public debate; What is your position?* We will show how each of the query packages deals with associated implicit perspectives, assumptions, or frameworks. Through this analysis, we hope to shed light on how the participants, themselves, analyze interview queries on controversial issues as reflecting particular stances on those controversial issues.

Summary of related empirical research

In this report we investigate how interviewers incorporate or implicate perspectives when they construct queries. Of particular interest are those queries for which interviewees seem to author alternative assumptions and frameworks. There is empirical research relevant to this issue. We will describe briefly research by Buttny (1998), Schegloff (1992), and Bergmann (1992) as it bears on methods of building perspectives into queries. While not addressing interviewing or questioning directly, Buttny and Schegloff do investigate ways that speakers build frameworks and perspectives into utterances that contextualize reported speech and stories. Bergmann actually investigates ways that physicians build in perspectives and insinuate moral assessments into questions in psychiatric intake interviews.

Buttny's research (1998) on reported speech describes ways that framing utterances are used to contextualize speech and actions in the current interaction. These framing utterances provide recipients with a context for an upcoming report (Buttny 1998). In analyzing a couple's therapy session, Buttny describes how a client tells a story to provide a context for describing his feelings. According to Buttny (1998: 52): "The story – the characters, circumstances, and what occurred – puts the narrator's feelings into context by making those feelings and emotions understandable, as a response to certain contingencies." In a similar way, we have observed that the interviewer brackets certain questions with prefaces in ways that establish interpretive frameworks that provide for the intelligibility of the interviewer's question and make it possible for an interviewee to respond appropriately.

Schegloff (1992) examines ways that speakers produce contextualizing utterances that allow recipients to hear a story as sensible, warranted, and intelligible. Specifically, he examines how storytelling prefaces, particularly characterizations such as "funny," "awful," etc., "provide recipients with an interpretive key or context by reference to which the story may be monitored and understood step by step in the course of its telling, and by reference to which recipients may recognize the story's possible completion" (Schegloff 1992: 202). Similarly, we observe that the interviewer uses query prefaces to procedurally implicate both that a question is going to be asked and how that question ought to be understood by the interviewee.

Bergmann (1992) examines how a psychiatrist's questions can be produced as "discreetly exploring utterances" that implicate both a medical and a moral assessment of the respondent. Discretion is accomplished through the use of litotes, indirection, and my-side-telling strategies in the formulation of psychiatrists' questions. As Bergmann describes it, "a discreetly exploring utterance can be regarded as a prototypical carrier of insinuation – insinuating in the official medical version some trouble, and in the unofficial moral version some improper behavior. The seemingly innocent, helpful, and affiliative utterances with which a psychiatrist attempts to induce a candidate patient to disclose his feelings and opinions have structurally an inbuilt hidden or veiled morality" (1992: 156). In other words, the formulation of a question may implicate multiple participation frameworks for respondents as well as multiple and possibly conflicting standards of evaluation by which both respondents and their responses may be evaluated. Furthermore, Bergmann's study demonstrates that, at least in psychiatric intake interviews, respondents monitor the production of a psychiatrist's questions for features that implicate these alternative standards of evaluation.

It is not always the case that the interviewer's interpretive frameworks and/or assumptions are consistent or compatible with those of the respondent. When a respondent finds the interviewer's interpretive frameworks and/or assumptions to be inconsistent with his/her own, the respondent may attempt to negotiate a new set of frameworks and/or assumptions. Very little work has been done to examine how respondents accomplish this negotiation. Of the studies considered, only Bergmann (1992) observes interactions in which respondents try to negotiate a framework or set of assumptions different from those of an interviewer. Specifically, he explores circumstances in which candidate patients may not accept "the veiled morality and the incipient suggestions of wrongdoing" in the discreetly exploring utterances of physicians at intake interviews. He goes on to note that differences between a recipient's and a speaker's implicit interpretive frameworks may be profoundly consequential:

Discreetly exploring utterances are extremely vulnerable to being heard by the recipient in moral terms and may therefore trigger *uncontrollable, interactionally disastrous social situations.* That is, an utterance which not only looks quite innocuous but also seems sympathetically to assist the recipient may lead to a kind of *explosive reaction.* Since such reactions in the psychiatric intake interview will unavoidably lead the psychiatrist to the judgment that the candidate patient is showing strange if not aggressive behavior, and in any case is in need of treatment, *the psychiatric discretion which triggered that reaction may be called fatal.* (157, emphasis ours)

These studies support the proposal that queries may incorporate frameworks and/or imply assumptions that are relevant to how the questions are to be understood by interviewees. They support the notion that recipients may respond not only to the explicit query but also to the implicit frameworks or assumptions associated with the query. They also point to the fact that recipients may treat the production of a response to an interviewer's question as a delicate matter, because how one responds to a question may implicate one's alignments with publicly available and commonly known positions regarding the matter being investigated.

Methods

Assumptions

Rather than seeing the interview as an instrument to uncover the respondents' attitudes and beliefs,[6] we see the interview as an interactional occasion in which respondents' expressed views are partially shaped by the respondents' perceptions of: the reasons for the interview, the sympathies of the interviewer, previous interview talk, anticipated upcoming topics, etc. The methods that we used for this analysis allow us to make claims about the participants' conduct within these interviews. We cannot make claims about how the respondents talk about racial issues in other circumstances. Nor can we address the consistency between the respondents' conduct with respect to racial matters and their expressed views during the interviews.

Selection of data extracts

We were given three complete interviews conducted by the same interviewer with three different interviewees. We limited and narrowed the analysis in two ways. The first way involved concentrating on only a subset of the query–response units present in the three interviews. We did this in several steps. First we identified all of the instances in which the interviewer seemed to be asking the interviewee about his or her opinion or perspective on a matter related to public policy. Using that collection, we then divided the cases into two groups: (1) those in which interviewees answered the questions in the terms in which they were asked, and (2) those in which it seemed that the interviewees shifted the framing of the queries while responding. We selected three cases in which it seemed relatively clear that the interviewee, in responding, shifted the perspective incorporated within the query. The second way in which we limited the scope of the analysis was to focus only on the interviewer's queries, not her queries along with the interviewees' responses. In this way, we limited the materials on which we concentrated to the query segments in the three cases we had selected.

Identifying the presuppositions, assumptions, or framing of the inquiry

As indicated earlier, queries necessarily have presuppositions or perspectives incorporated within them. Rather than attempting to analyze all of the assumptions that are associated with the queries, we elected to discuss only the assumptions with which the interviewee took issue. Methodologically, this involved working "backwards" from interviewee's response to interviewer's query. We used the interviewees' shifts of perspective to identify perspectives incorporated in the interviewers' queries. Because the topic of the interview queries involved racial issues, the assumptions associated with the queries also involve racial issues.

Analysis

This is a publicly known problem; what is your solution?

One way for an interviewer to investigate an interviewee's position on a publicly known and controversial matter is to formulate a query that casts the controversial matter as a problem with possible solutions. Particular problems are recognized and made coherent in relation to a backdrop of particular assumptions, attitudes, and beliefs. A state of affairs is recognized as a "problem" only inasmuch as it is different from what is assumed to be the way things should be. Understanding a state of affairs as a problem relies upon an assumption of a normative order, one that is not being satisfied or fulfilled in the problematic state.

An interviewee's assumptions of the way things should be may or may not be compatible with the normative state of affairs implied by a "problem" posed within an interviewer's query. If the interviewee's perspective is compatible with the normative perspective associated with the "problem" posed in the query, the interviewee would operate within the same frame in addressing solutions. However, the interviewee may subscribe to a perspective that does not support a view of the matter as a problem. In such cases, the interviewer would need to make certain adjustments in the query if he or she is attempting to investigate an interviewee's perspective.

In this section, we examine two queries from two different interviews in which the interviewer formulates as a problem that there is disproportionately low representation of Maori children at higher levels of educational achievement. The normative order that provides the backdrop for seeing this state of affairs as a problem is that there ought to be proportionate representation of Pakeha and Maori children at all levels of educational attainment. In both interviews, the interviewees took issue with the interviewer's treatment of the matter *as a problem*. However, the interviewer used different strategies in each interview to deal with the incongruity between the assumptions associated with the query and the interviewee's assumptions.

Query 1. In extract 1, the interviewer formed the query by describing a problem that pertained to racial issues and asking the interviewee to discuss her view of a possible solution.

Extract 1 (Appendix: New Zealand Interview 44: 300)

```
 1.   R:   I think you ma- you're making (0.6) a worse- a different situ[ation
 2.   I:                                                                 [Mm mhm
 3.          So really we have to sort of work together
 4.   R:   Yeah
 5.   I:   [into the future
 6.   R:   [Yeah
 7.   R:   [Mmmm
 8.   I:   [( )
 9.          (1.0)
10.   I:   One of the big problems seems to be with ehm sort of
11.          educational difference because it's very noticeable that at sixth and
12.          seventh form levels an' in universities that there was very few (.) Maori
13.          students ([.) left in the classrooms
14.   R:                    [Yes
15.          (1.0)
16.   I:   D'you think that u:hm (1.2)
17.          what do you think can be done about that
18.          Do you think we should change the school system
19.          (0.4) u:hm (0.4) as a result
20.          or (0.8) uhm is that something that really ca:n't be ah (0.2)
21.          solved that way
22.   R:   The Maoris who wa::nt to get on and do:: things do it
23.   I:   Yeah
24.          (1.4)
25.   R:   They a:re a lazy ra:ce most of [them.
26.   I:                                  [( )
27.          (1.2)
28.   R:   U:hm (1.0) how can you change a- a race that's uhm (0.4) what?
29.          inheritance uhm
30.   I:   Ye(h)ah
31.   R:   Re:ally
32.   I:   Yes
```

The interviewer introduced her query with a preface in which she described the discrepancy in the level of educational attainment of Maori and Pakeha students as a problem (lines 10–13). She portrayed the state of affairs as a problem, not only with the explicit characterization of the matter as "One of the big problems," but also by portraying the educational difference as "very noticeable." This implied that the current circumstance, i.e., low numbers of Maori in the higher grades, stands in contrast to a normative standard that there *ought* to be proportionate representation of *all* children, both Pakeha and Maori, at *all* levels of educational achievement. Accordingly, in presenting the problem in this way, the interviewer implied that the described educational difference calls for a remedy that would yield a greater representation of Maori in the higher grades.

The relevance of race is provided by the interviewer's use of the category "Maori" in her formulation of the problem. Had she used an alternative formulation, such as "it's very noticeable that at sixth and seventh form levels an' in universities that there was very fe:w (.) *low income* students (.) left in the classrooms," a very different basis for interpreting the nature of the problem would be relevant. With the actual formulation, the interviewer cast the problem as a racial contrast and made race a relevant framework for interpreting the problem.

The normative standard that was used in conceptualizing the characterized state of affairs as a problem was implicit. In that it was implicit, it was not a matter focused upon in the query preface nor a matter asked about in the ensuing question. In contrast, the interviewer explicitly pointed to low Maori student representation as a problem, and thus set up a frame in which she could reasonably ask about the interviewee's solution to the problem.

Having laid out the problem in the query preface, the interviewer asked a question about solutions to the problem (lines 16–21).[7] In her formulation of the question, the interviewer put forward, as a possible solution, a proposal to "change the school system." With this proposed solution, the interviewer identified the school system as a site for effective policy intervention.

There are two points to be noted. First, the proposed remedy constituted an example of the type of response the interviewer was looking to obtain from the interviewee. It suggested that the interviewee ought to formulate remedies as policy interventions.[8] Secondly, the interviewer implicitly elaborated the nature of the problem by proposing that *this is a problem for the schools to solve*. By identifying the schools as agents for change who may remedy the problem, the interviewer extended and clarified the scope of the problem. This was more than an internal Maori problem to which they alone should attend. Instead, it was cast as a problem for the school system as an institution of society at large, which serves both Maori and Pakeha students alike.

As suggested earlier, when an interviewee responds to a query in the terms provided by the query, he or she implicitly endorses the assumptions associated with the query. If an interviewee withholds a response, that may be read as indicating that he or she has some order of problem with the query. In this case, the interviewee did not respond to the interviewer's proposed solution (see line 18). While the interviewee's silence at this point suggests that she may have had trouble with some aspect of the query, there is no audible indication as to what the source of that trouble might have been.[9]

The interviewer responded to the interviewee's hesitation by putting forward a second question, "or: (1.0) °uhm (0.8) is that something that really ca:n't be ah (0.2) solved that way°" (lines 20 and 21). This second question seemed designed to remedy a trouble that the interviewee might have been having in responding to the initial question (Pomerantz 1984). Specifically, this question incorporated an assertion that rejected not only the specific solution but also the type of solution that was offered in the prior question. The interviewer thus opened the possibility that the interviewee may reject not only the proffered solution but also the framework or perspective implied by the interviewer's first question.

In this case, the interviewee put forward a position (line 22), an assessment (line 25), and a question (lines 28 and 29) consistent with a perspective different from the one implied by the interviewer's first question. Rather than accept that the schools were a site for effective policy intervention, the interviewee implied that this is a problem for the Maori to take care of by themselves.

Query 2. As with the previous query, in this query the interviewer used the *This is a publicly known problem; What is your solution?* package. In constructing the query, the interviewer designed it in ways that displayed that she anticipated the interviewee's disaffiliation with her treatment of the matter as a problem.[10]

Extract 2 (Appendix: New Zealand Interview 2: 253)

1. R: I mean ya'know they- they're grizzling it out in South Africa
2.   with it's eh .hh it's COLORED PARLIAMENT no:w
3. I: Mm mhm
4. R: Well we've got our colored parliament ya'know all four of
5.   them
6. I: Yeah ((burst laugh)) Yeah
7.   So: (0.4) >well< what about- I mean is ch- there is a
8.   large gap between Maori and Pakeha
9.   achievement= educationally (0.2) Maori
10.   kids aren't doing so well in schools. .hh
11.   So what abou:t some: (.) special education measures to help them.
12.   Do you think that's similarly (0.6) [(not right)

13. R: [Is it gonna do them any good.
14. I: Yeah
15.   (0.4)
16. I: Mm mhm
          [. . .]
17. R: If- (0.4) I believe that every chi:ld should be educated
18.   (0.4) to the ability that [they can receive education.
19. I: [Mm mhm
20. I: Mm mhm
21.   (1.0)

In several ways, the organization of this query is similar to the one considered previously. As with the first query's preface, the interviewer described the difference in the level of educational attainment of Maori and Pakeha students as a problem. By characterizing the described educational difference as a "large gap," the interviewer implied that the poor educational achievement of Maori children stood in contrast to the normative standard that Maori children should display comparable levels of achievement with Pakeha children. By casting Maori representation in the higher levels of school as a problem, the interviewer's query implicitly called for improved Maori representation at those levels. As with the first query's question, the interviewer put forward a candidate solution consistent with her treatment of the matter as a problem. By proposing a school-based intervention, the interviewer again implied that this was a problem for the schools to solve and not a problem only for the Maori to solve.

In a manner similar to the first query, the interviewer established the relevance of race by using the categories "Maori" and "Pakeha" in her formulation of the problem: "there is a large gap between Maori and Pakeha achievement educationally." The interviewer commented on the performance of Maori children ("°Maori kids aren't doing so well in schools.°"), whereas the performance of Pakeha children was treated as thoroughly unremarkable. With this treatment, the interviewer cast the problem as a racial contrast and made race a relevant framework for interpreting the problem.

This query differs from the first in that the interviewer formulated the preface and posed questions in ways that oriented to the interviewee's likely disaffiliation with the perspective implied by her query. This is indicated in a variety of ways. In asserting that there was a discrepancy in educational attainment, the interviewer noticeably emphasized the "is" in line 7: "Yeah ((burst laugh)) Yeah So: (0.4) >well< what about- I mean is ch- there is a large gap between Maori and Pakeha achievement educationally." By emphasizing the "is," the interviewer put forward an assertion that supported a position she anticipated would be contrary to one the interviewee would hold. In so doing, she displayed an understanding of the interviewee's position or perspective as contrary to the one implied by her query.

Also, by latching this first question to a second, the interviewer eliminated any possible turn-transition relevance following the first question so that she could present both questions as a single discursive unit. Moving without pause to a question that affirmed the rejection of the proposed solution displayed that the interviewer anticipated that such a rejection was likely. Furthermore, by asking if the candidate solution is "similarly (0.6) (not right)," the interviewer presumed that the interviewee's as-yet-to-be-formulated position on the Maori in this query was similar to the unsympathetic stance toward the Maori he displayed in responding to previous queries. In other words, the interviewer put forward a possible solution as an example of a remedy appropriate to the perspective of the interviewer's query, but which the interviewee was likely to reject.

In asking, "Is it gonna do them any good." the interviewee affirmed his rejection of the perspective advanced in the interviewer's query. The interviewee literally called into question the point of view, implied in the interviewer's query, that the gap in Maori educational achievement was a problem for which special education measures or other school-based interventions could be solutions.

This is a matter of public debate; what is your position?

Another way for an interviewer to investigate an interviewee's position on a publicly known and controversial matter is to formulate a query that casts the controversial matter as a matter of public debate, with various positions represented within that debate. While a normative stance is implicated in the respective parties' views of the problems related to the public issue, an interviewer's framing the issue as a matter of public debate may be an attempt to be even-handed with respect to the various positions within the debate.

Generally holding a position is seen to be related to, or an outcome of, having beliefs that support the position. In a publicly known controversial matter, there are sets of beliefs that serve as typical bases for the known positions in the debate. When an interviewer asks an interviewee for his or her position on a matter of public debate, the interviewer and interviewee may know the typical bases of the various positions. The interviewer may intend the query, and/or the interviewee may hear the query, to be about not only a position, but also a basis for holding the position.

Query 3. In the following extract, the interviewer first reported on a matter of public debate, the celebration of Waitangi Day, and followed this report with questions about the interviewee's position on the issue.

Extract 3 (Appendix: New Zealand Interview 44: 299)

```
1.  R:  I'm sure there are
2.  I:  Yes yeah
3.      (1.0)
4.  I:  What do you think- there's all this discussion going on at
5.      the moment about Waitangi Day and uhm (0.6) ya'know whether
6.      (0.4) we should (.) celebrate it at all or celebrate it- in
7.      what- what way should we celebrate it and all the rest of it.
8.      What do you feel about (.) that (.) that topic? (0.4) Do you
9.      feel that that we should ta keep on with Waitangi Day or that
10.     we should have some other day for a national holiday
11.     (3.2)
12. R:  Well each year there seems to be (1.0) quite a fuss over it
13.     and really uhm (0.2) I mean (3.2) it's just another day I
14.     mean (.) [ya'know you don't sort of think "Oh! The Treaty
15. I:           [Yes
16. R:  of Wai[tangi Day's today" ya'know
17. I:        [((laugh))
18.     Yeah
19. R:  and think about how they all got together an' so on I mean
20.     you just think "Oh! [It's a holiday on Monday ya'know"
21. I:                      [It's a holiday ye(h)ah.hhh
22.     Yeah
23. R:  I think it's- it's lost it's
24. I:  Yeah
25.     (1.0)
26. R:  ya'know to people
```

In her query preface, the interviewer introduced the topic of Waitangi Day as a matter of public discussion and offered examples of the types of questions that are part of the debate (lines 4–10). Questioning the celebration of Waitangi is consistent with certain normative assumptions pertaining to racial issues. Based on a limited search on the web, we understand that a basis for questioning the practice of celebrating the Treaty of Waitangi is the claim that the Treaty, which was intended to guarantee certain rights to the Maoris, has not been honored and that Maori rights have been violated. While raising the issue of celebrating Waitangi Day is associated with certain perspectives (that Maori rights, as guaranteed by the Treaty, have been violated), the interviewer attempted to put forward the query without affiliating with that normative view, avoiding this affiliation in several ways. First, she used a *This is a matter of public debate; what is your position?* package, acknowledging the existence of different positions within the discussion.[11] Second, she offered two questions as illustrations of the types of questions asked in the public discussion, each representing a somewhat different perspective, and she indicated that there were other questions being asked in the debate.

[question 1]   whether (0.4) we should (.) celebrate it at all
[question 2]   in what- what way should we celebrate it
[gloss for other questions]   and all the rest of it.

By including the option of not celebrating Waitangi Day at all as an illustrative question, the interviewer gave voice to the position that the current practice of celebrating Waitangi Day is wrong. By problematizing how to celebrate Waitangi Day, the interviewer's second illustrative question was formed with the presumption that Waitangi Day would be celebrated. While these two questions illustrated different positions in the public discussion and operated with different presumptions, they both questioned the celebration of Waitangi Day at present. The gloss referencing the other questions in the debate ("and all the rest of it") seems to provide the interviewer some distance from being affiliated or aligned with those wanting a change from the current practices. This formulation implies that there are many additional questions and arguments in the debate, yet it does not elevate them as worthy of specification or enumeration.

In sum, the interviewer used the query preface to introduce the issue of celebrating Waitangi Day. The raising of this issue is associated with those who view the rights of the Maoris, as guaranteed by the Waitangi Treaty, to have been violated. However, while the interviewer introduced an issue associated with a particular stance toward racial issues, she also somewhat distanced herself from aligning with that stance. The interviewer used the query preface to provide a context for asking the interviewee to give her position on the issue of celebrating Waitangi Day. Following the preface, the interviewer directed several questions to the interviewee, forming the questions in a way that seemed to anticipate the interviewee's perspective as one that would conflict with that of those who question the celebration of Waitangi Day.

In her first question, "What do you feel about (.) that (.) that topic?" she constructed an open question without incorporating possible positions for confirmation or disconfirmation. In addition, she remained as neutral as possible by referencing the matter of public debate as "that topic" (and hence avoiding a formulation of the issue). After a four tenths of a second gap, the interviewer offered two positions for the interviewee's confirmation or disconfirmation: "Do you feel that that we should ta keep on with Waitangi Day or that we should have some other day for a national holiday." In contrast to the earlier illustrative questions that referred to changes in the current practice of celebrating Waitangi Day, this question offered the interviewee the position of "keeping on with" Waitangi Day. Thus the initial position she offered to the interviewee implied a stance toward racial issues that was discrepant with the stance implied by raising the issue itself.

The interviewer also offered a contrasting position within the question: ". . . or that we should have some other day for a national holiday." While the expected contrast with "keep on with Waitangi Day" would be some form of "not keeping on with Waitangi Day," this proffered position was not put in terms of something being wrong with Waitangi Day, but rather in terms of maintaining the same number of national holidays. We tentatively suggest that this proffering may allow the interviewee to confirm a version of "not celebrating Waitangi Day" without positioning herself on the issue of whether Maori rights, as guaranteed by the Treaty, have been violated.

In her response, the interviewee indicated her position on the issue of celebrating Waitangi Day and her basis for that position. She indicated her position was to keep celebrating Waitangi Day as a national holiday and proffered a basis that could be seen to be different from the typical basis or stance toward racial issues associated with the position she took. In contrast to the typical basis of supporting the current practice of celebrating Waitangi Day (that is, the belief that the rights of the Maoris had not been violated), the interviewee claimed that she supported celebrating Waitangi Day because the holiday no longer had symbolic value.

Even though the interviewer did not explicitly ask about the basis of the interviewee's position, the interviewee felt it relevant to provide it. It seems that she was orienting to the presumption she inferred that the interviewer would make concerning the basis for her position. Interviewees may find themselves being asked about positions that others may assume are based on particular beliefs and attitudes. This is not always a problem. However, interviewees may be uncomfortable when their bases are different from what they assume others may attribute to them. Interviewees may counter the bases they anticipate other will attribute, but it takes interactional work to do so.

Discussion

We believe that our findings should be useful to those who use interviews as a research tool. Two areas of particular interest are (1) query packages and (2) the kinds of problems that emerge related to perspectives and inferences and the adjustments that are made.

Query packages

As we have shown, the query packages we identified consist of two parts: a preface and one or more questions. We have shown how the preface provides a context or frame for an upcoming question and how both the preface and the questions are thematically connected. For example, the *This is a publicly known problem; what is your solution?* query package casts the issue as a problem, which plays off a normative order or a sense of how things should be but are not. In this way a problem formulation implicates a perspective that is associated with it.

On the other hand, the *This is a matter of public debate; what is your position?* query package casts the issue as a debate or discussion, which implies the existence of multiple positions or perspectives. This query format also recognizes multiple perspectives in allowing contrary perspectives to be put forward. In this way, the query package somewhat avoids aligning with the perspectives associated with raising the issue.

Interviewers are practitioners who have expertise in query formulations. We believe they can use our analyses of the two query packages to identify and analyze other query packages. We would expect query packages to differ with respect to the degree to which they align with perspectives and the types of inferences interviewers and interviewees are likely to make.

Adjustments

During interviews, interviewees enact that they are having difficulty, often without articulating the source of the difficulty. We have seen two kinds of difficulties: (1) the interviewee's perspective differs from the perspective implied by the query, and (2) the interviewee's basis for a position is other than what he or she thinks the interviewer will take it to be. When difficulties arise, both interviewers and interviewees are in a position to make adjustments.

We have described several conversational practices that are used when interviewers question interviewees whose perspectives are at odds with the perspective implied by the query. We have described some ways interviewers adjust their questions in the course of asking. For example, the interviewer may ask a subsequent question that allows the interviewee to confirm a perspective different from the one implicated in the original query. This type of adjustment is designed for an interviewee who may be having trouble with the assumptions implicated by the query. We have also described adjustments interviewers can make in their queries to display their anticipation that the interviewee's perspective is different from the queries' perspective.

A second difficulty occurs when the interviewee's basis for his or her position is different from what he or she assumes the interviewer will infer as his or her basis. Interviewees may counter the assumed basis for their position by explicitly offering a basis. If there is no opportunity for the interviewee to counter an assumed basis, interactional difficulties may emerge. Interviewers need to know that such problems can arise if they are to make adjustments.

NOTES

1. We wish to thank the editors for their insightful comments on an earlier draft.
2. We use the term "query" to identify the entire discourse unit through which the interviewer introduces and asks a question.
3. The incorporation of frameworks, presumptions, and/or perspectives within queries operates not only during interviews but in other circumstances and situations as well.
4. While Clark and Schober's chapter is about survey research, they discuss surveys in relation to ordinary, social discourse. Many of their observations about survey questions apply to open-ended qualitative interview questions as well.
5. Saying that a question embodies a perspective does *not* imply that it is, in some sense, "loaded," i.e., directs the recipient to produce a particular response. Perspectives and interpretive frameworks are unavoidable and, in many instances, may be frameworks and perspectives that the interviewer unproblematically shares with the interviewee.
6. A common assumption of those who employ interviews is that people have stable attitudes and beliefs and these attitudes and beliefs determine or, more modestly, influence people's choices of conduct.
7. Actually, this utterance consists of two questions joined together as a single unit. The first part of this utterance, "what do you think can be done about that" (line 17), does two things. First, it explicitly topicalizes remedies for the problem as the matter about which the interviewer will elicit responses from the interviewee. Second, it alerts the interviewee to monitor this part of the question as a preface that frames the interviewer's subsequent question, "do you think we should change the school system (0.4) u:hm (0.4) as a result" (lines 18–19).
8. See Sacks (1992: 21–25) for a discussion of the "correction-invitation device" that allows a speaker to offer a member of a class in order to obtain, as a "correction," another member of the class.
9. Based only on the audio data, it is difficult to assess what else might have occurred between the interviewer and interviewee at this point in the interaction.
10. Immediately prior to this query, the interviewee had displayed an unsympathetic stance toward the Maori. For example, the interviewer had asked about "positive discrimination" and if the interviewee considered "things like

having four Maori parliamentary seats and the Department of Maori Affairs" to be "sort of undemocratic." The interviewee responded with "Well I think the Maor- Maor- Maor- the hh. Maori se:ats (0.4) should be abo:lished I mean that's: (0.6) an' that's always been my (.) opinion e:h." This allowed the interviewer to infer that the interviewee is not likely to be supportive of any social policies that give the Maori any special advantages over the Pakeha.

11. A normative stance would be implicated had the interviewer used a "*this is a publicly known problem; what is your solution*" query package. A hypothetical example using this query package might be the interviewer's asking the interviewee for her solution to the problem of celebrating Waitangi Day. The current practice of celebrating Waitangi Day thus would be portrayed as a problem to be remedied.

References

Bergmann, J. R. 1992. Veiled morality: notes on discretion in psychiatry. In *Talk at work: interaction in institutional settings*, edited by P. Drew and J. Heritage. Cambridge: Cambridge University Press. 137–162.

Buttny, R. 1998. Putting prior talk into context: reported speech and the reporting context. *Research on Language and Social Interaction* 31, 1: 45–58.

Clark, H. H. and Schober, M. F. 1992. Asking questions and influencing answers. In *Questions about questions*, edited by J. M. Tanur. New York: Russell Sage Foundation. 15–48.

Holstein, J. A. and Gubrium, J. F. 1995. *The active interview*. Thousand Oaks: Sage.

Pomerantz, A. 1984. Pursuing a response. In *Structures of social action*, edited by J. M. Atkinson and J. Heritage. Cambridge: Cambridge University Press. 152–163.

Sacks, H. 1992. *Lectures on conversation*. Vol. 1. Cambridge, MA: Blackwell Publishers.

Schegloff, E. A. 1992. In another context. In *Rethinking context: language as an interactive phenomenon*, edited by A. Duranti and C. Goodwin. Cambridge: Cambridge University Press. 193–227.

Interview transcripts

These face-to-face interviews were collected by Margaret Wetherell in the mid-1980s in New Zealand, as part of a joint project on discourse and racism conducted by Margaret Wetherell and Jonathan Potter (for further details of the method and analysis, see Wetherell, M., and Potter, J. 1992. *Mapping the language of racism.* London: Harvester Wheatsheaf). Wetherell and Potter would like to acknowledge financial support from the UK Economic and Social Research Council for the original transcription and to thank the participants for giving up their time to this project.

The interviews were retranscribed for the current project by Barbara Fehr and Marjon Vos van der Born. Edits have been made to the transcripts to remove personal details that could compromise the anonymity of the participants. Please note that no part of these interviews should be copied or used for any purpose without prior permission from Professor Margaret Wetherell, Social Sciences, Open University, Walton Hall, Milton Keynes. MK7 6AA UK.

NEW ZEALAND INTERVIEW 2

I: U:hm (1.0) have you traveled a↑t'all or (1.2)
R: I go to sea for a living
I: ↑DO: you now
R: Ye(h)ah
I: Ahaa This is gonna be interesting.
R: So
I: So: you- what you::'re a merchant seaman [or what
R: [Yes
I: Yeah (1.0)
R: [mhm
I: [U:hm (1.0) which country would you say that (0.8) New Zealand is (1.0)
     clo:sest to >sort of< (.) culturally in ter- terms of outlook and attitude and
     so on.
R: England.
I: England.
R: Yeah.
I: You don't think we're becoming Americanized (1.0)
R: No:t really

232

I: (Right) (0.6) Yes.hh and sa:y (.) although a lot of overseas people would
      tend to bunch us up with Australia an' see us as (1.0) interchangeable,
      you [think there's (1.0)
R: [mhm
I: pretty clear cut differences between us an' Australia (1.2)
R: O:wl yes I de- I definitely think there is
I: Yeah
[. . .]
I: How long have you been living here?
R: E:hh. nearly [number of years specified] now.
I: Quite a time.
R: [Mhm
I: [Mmm .hh What- (1.2) Do you think that one can talk about a sort of
      national character for New Zealand the way you can talk about a sort of
      British (0.8) person a British character (0.6) or an American character
      (1.4)
R: Ye::s but they're ah- (0.4) they're no more (1.0) ehm true
I: Mm mhm
R: ah as a group a: [as a whole than you know the British bulldog
I: [Mm mhm
I: Mm mhm
R: type or ya'know and the American Uncle Sam
I: Mm mhm
R: eh type
I: [Yeah
R: [They eh (0.6) You can have a type I mean ya'[know
I: [Yeah
R: and I think it's a (1.0) the rugby racing an' bee[r
I: [Mm mhm
R: (0.4) outlook or [ya'know
I: [Mm mhm
R: Right but it- it
I: Mm mhm
R: it only applies to ten percent of the (0.2) [population
I: [Ri:ght Yes, yeah (0.6)
      What do you value most about living in New Zealand (1.4)
R: E::h hh. I don't know that's a difficult one.hh e:m (1.0) chm. I came here to
      make my fortune in the colonies (0.4)
I: [((little out breath laugh))
R: [and'a (.) I'm still here
I: ((little out breath laugh))
R: a::nd (3.4) I just like the (2.4) way of life and [a the style of life
I: [Mm mhm
[. . .]
I: D'you- Do you see any di- disadvantages in living here things that are
      negative from your point of view (0.4) things you'd like to a change if (1.0)
      if you had the °power to change them° (2.4)

R: Well I've noticed that hh. in the last ten or fifteen- well ten ye:ars (1.0) the whole country has gone backward

I: Mm mhm

R: a:nd (1.0) as you say I

I: Mm mhm

R: chm. travel aro(h)und quite a bit

I: [Yeah

R: [and (0.4) and ten (1.4) ten years ago (1.0) e:hm (0.8) we could affo:rd (1.0) to (0.4) >take the whole family< (.) and go 'round the world

I: Mm mhm

[. . .]

R: We could afford it

I: Yes (.) right

R: Now I'm doing the ↓same ↑job

I: °Ye:as°

R: (1.4) and (0.4) uhm you know I could no more [↑dre:am of going

I: [(Yes)

R: to A↑merica (0.4) [(when I looked)

I: [With the de- devaluation in particular or [just general cost of living.

R: [When I went there we got I think it was a- a dollar thirty American [for every dollar (.)that we ↑had

I: [Yeah

I: Mm mhm

R: Now I've got to pay out two dollars to get a- [a dollar American

I: [Mm mhm

I: That's right Yes Mm

R: I mean I was on the (0.4) eh (quite a good) of salary and eh

I: Mm

R: .hh in the States (1.0) ↑I was on a good salary in the ↑States when you: translated ↑it

I: Mm mhm

R: Ya'know an' everybody said "Gee" you know "Do they pay that amount [down in-"

I: [Yeah I know=

R: =Ya'know "Where was that place?" ((laugh))

I: ((laughs))

R: And em

I: ((continues laugh)) yeah

R: I said "Yes" you know ["I-it's ↑great!"

I: [Yeah

R: You have to ↑work for it but it's ↑good

I: Mm mhm

R: and ehm (1.0) ↑no:w (0.4) if I went to the ↑States I'd be on [the ↑dole on the pay I'm get↑ting

I: [Mm mhm

I: Ye:s so we've sort of gone behi- backwards in contrast to [Australia and America are sort of (0.6) booming economically

R: [Mhm
I: in a way that we aren't do you think
R: chhm. I mean ya'know and a- (.) I- (2.2) in a (1.0) ya'know a sea going
    fra[ternity
I: [Mm mhm
I: Mm mhm
R: I could get a job hhh. well you know not quite as much over the last two
    years. .hh There's been a general turn down but
I: °Mm mhm°
R: Prior to that I could get a job sailing out of Hong Kong
I: Mm mhm
R: sailing out of Canada or [England,
I: [Mm mhm
    (1.0)
R: anywhere in the world
I: Mm mhm
R: I mean my >[qualifications[< were good for all round the world
I: [Yes   [°Mm mhm°
R: and'em (1.0) use to th- (.)
    [think this an' say "Oh you're- it's not really worth goin over
I: [°Mm mhm°
R: there we- ya'know th-the pay we get here is eh quit[e adequate"
I: [Yes
I: Yeah (1.0)
R: But eh (1.0) providing you- if you cut [out Bangladesh and eh the
I: [°yes°
R: Phillippines
I: Mm mhm
R: and'a a few countries like that
I: Mm mhm
R: we're the next cheapest (0.6)
I: Mm mhm
R: eh laborer as far a seafarers are concerned
I: Really Eu::a
R: W- phh. They've got [a (0.4) a fairly (0.4) ridiculous- well not
I: [(°Yes°)
R: ridiculous but a
I: Mm mhm
R: a very generous
I: Mm mhm
R: e:hm leave system
I: Yeah
[. . .]
R: But'em (1.4) I mean the rate of eh the [money I get [paid for that
I: [(Right)   [Mm mhm
R: although it's good by New Zealand standards (0.6) e:m is about half what
I: Yeah
R: half or less than what an American (0.6)

I: would do
R: eh would get [paid doing similar work[
I: [But-   [why do you think that's happening.
      What's going wrong with our economy that's causing (1.4) this (1.0)
R: hhh.
I: or our outlook
R: O:h.hh E:HM (4.4) I don't know unless I- unless I start- you start getting
      into politics [a:nd'em ya'know saying that
I: [Yeah
R: (0.6) I think the u:nions have- have done this and the
      un[ions [have'a have done that ehm
I: [Yeah [Mm mhm
R: (0.4) I mean we see it on the- (0.4) on the ships this a- I was complaining
      very bitterly just the other day
I: Mm mhm
R: We have an absolute useless drunk on the ship
I: Mm mhm
R: and he's a ni:ce fellow but he's drunk [utterly totally
I: [Yeah
      he needs [treatment
R: [incapable by [ten o'↑clock And all- >every morning<!
I: [Yeah
I: ((ironic laugh)) Yes that's a bit off isn't it [.hh
R: [and ah he's getting paid twenty
      odd thousand dollars a year
I: Ohh.
R: and only from six months of the year to get it
I: [Yeah
R: [And he's never sober after ten o'↑clock (0.6)
I: That's terrible isn't it
D: Yeah
I: So you can't get rid of him.
R: No (I mean   ) the way the unions are a[t the moment
I: [Mm mhm
I: [Yes
R: [I think- what you (want/ought) to do is a- a thesis into the a
I: Mm mhm
R: operation of maritime u:nions
I: .hh (0.4) Yes (.) that would be in- Yeah thad be very interesting. It'd
      probably be difficult for me to get access to some of the (1.0) the
      materials
[. . .]
R: I mean (.) you know the e:h (0.6) the control of employment
      [is: (.) I've always considered (0.4) as being
I: [Mm mhm
R: one of the (0.6) bosses preogatives I [mean ya'know
I: [Yeah

I: Mm mhm
R: you either employ them or you <u>don't</u> employ them
I: Mm mhm
R: Somebody comes along and you s[ay "<u>Yes</u> you can have a <u>job</u>"
I: [Mm mhm
I: Mm mhm
R: ((little laugh)) But (0.2) ah as far as the sea- ah the em
I: Mhm
R: <u>seamen</u> are concerned ya'know an' the cooks [an' stewards
I: [Mm mhm
I: Mm mhm
R: They are totally employed by the <u>union</u>
I: Mm mhm
R: If my son wanted to go to sea as an a-[as an <u>AB</u>
I: [Yes
I: Yes (0.6)
R: The ↑first thing he would have to do would [be to get into
I: [Mm mhm
R: the [name of organization] (0.8)
     An' with me as his father he'd never stand a chance ((smile voice))
I: ((burst of laughter)) So there's a sort of patronage system
R: [Mhmmm
I: [Yeah mm
R: I mean (I-id)- <u>back</u> in the eighteenth <u>century</u> [with it
I: [Yes (1.4)
R: Ya'know where- where- where was it back in Ireland or something like that
I: Yes
R: Or- or in the eh eighteenth century the ah.hh various people used to have
     hi::ring rights
I: Yes
R: Y'know somebody'd be going a<u>ro:und</u>
I: Mm mhm
R: <u>doing</u> something and they'd have hi:<u>ring</u> rights for the [big <u>firm</u>
I: [Yeah
I: Mm mhm
R: So ya'know if [you did something <u>right</u> for them
I: [So:
R: they'd "Oh we'll get you a job down at the
I: Right
R: at the works"
I: So it's our working practices partly that are (0.6) to blame for the
     [productivity's lowering and
R: [( )
R: Proda- Productivity's [just diabolic
I: [Yeah
I: Yeah
R: A:nd'e:m (0.8)

I: Mhmm
R: Ya'know nobody wants to (0.6) <u>change</u> it
I: Yes (1.6) Mhmm (1.4) So uhm (1.2) I- If I asked you to think of (0.6)
      particular New Zealanders that you admire or you'd like to (0.6) say have
      your children use as models for their own behavior wha- what people (0.6)
      stick out in your mind as great New Zealanders (1.4)
R: Well of course there's always Sir Edmund Hillary I[::
I: [Yeah
R: I've always got a hh. soft spot for him [an'
I: [Yes
R: [John Marshall
I: [Right
I: yeah
R: ([ya'know) Sir John Marshal[l
I: [Yes   [Mm mhm
R: E::hm (0.4) People (0.4) <u>never</u> to follow ya'know my friend Jim Knox
I: Ye(h)ah ((laugh))
R: A:nd (2.4) the ah (2.0) <u>Actually</u> there're whole <u>lot</u> of tre<u>men</u>dous
      New Zealand[ers   [and (0.6) you meet them everywhere
I: [°Mm [Mm mhm°
I: [Mm mhm
R: [I mean we've got (0.6) lots of friends and I think the majority of them are
      tremendous. Some of them go to sea, some of 'em are farmers
I: Mm mhm
R: Some run their own businesses
I: Mm mhm
R: Some wo:rk for (0.4) for wag[es
I: [Yes
I: Mm mhm
R: And'em (0.6) and I- and they're tremendous New Zealanders
I: Yes
R: and in their own way they all do a tremendous job
I: Mm mhm (1.0)
R: [And-
I: [So someone like Sir Edmund Hillary because of his eh sort of
      independence and his courage and those sorts of features
      [(that you think or)
R: [Well chh. he-
      (0.4) a<u>chie</u>ved (0.4) something that he set out [to do
I: [Yeah
R: Ya'know so there's a- a sense of achievement And <u>then</u> he went ba:ck and
      put something <u>ba:ck</u> into the <u>coun</u>try
I: Mm mhm (0.6) Mm mh:m
R: Now that's::- that's what I like
I: Yes y[eah
R: [a- about it You know he didn't just wave a big flag and say "Yeah oh
      yeah I was (0.[4) I was there I did this"
I: [Mm mhm

I: Mm mhm
R: He- he went down and saw that (0.4) [there was a necessity an'
I: [°Mhm°
R: going back an'
I: Mm mhm
R: He kept going back an' starting sch[oo:ls an' ya'know that's tremendous
I: [Yes
I: Yes
R: A tre<u>men</u>dous thing that he a- that he did
I: Yes I saw a television pro<u>gram</u>me about him (that [spoke about that)
R: [Mhm
I: Yeah that's very a- I hadn't realized he'd done so much work in Nepal
D: Yeah
R: Mhm!
I: What about'uhm (0.4) John Marshall what are the qualities there that you
     admire
R: [chhhmm.
I: [(particularly)
R: His basic <u>hon</u>esty for a pol<u>it</u>ician I t[hink is absol(h)utely
I: [Yeah
I: Yeah.hh
R: I mean ya'know nor- normally I consider that (0.6) ah I'm not quite
     <u>dishon</u>est <u>enough</u> to think of becoming [a politician myself
I: [((laughs)) Yeah
[. . .]
I: Yes but John Marshall sort of stood out as someone that was different °sort
     of (.) a more [decent honest person°
R: [Mhm.
R: ↑Mm↓mm
I: Yeah (0.6) Mhmm
R: I didn't say he'd make a terribly good politician because ya'know he
I: Mm mhm
R: he wasn't <u>ruth</u>less enough
I: Mm mhm (0.4) Yea
R: But'ehm (1.2) Y'know I just admired him for wh(h)at h(h)e d(h)id
     [an' what he- what he <u>wa:s</u>
I: [Mm mhm yeah
R: at the time and what he [<u>still</u> speaks out <u>now</u> I mean
I: [(°Yeah°)
I: °Mm mhm° (0.8)
R: if he sees- (0.4) [sees anything that's only going one way
I: [°Yeah°
     (1.4)
R: I mean my politics are slightly (.) [right of Ghengis <u>Kahn</u>
I: [°Mm mhm°
I: ((laugh))
R: The ah
I: Is this what your son tells you ((laugh))

R: ((laugh))
I: [Yeah
R: [He ehm-
I: Hh. heh.hh
R: Ya'know when you get'ta (.) somebody like (.) Roger Douglas an' the (.)
    Labour ([0.4) Party ehm
I: [Yeah
I: Mm mhm (0.6)
R: e:hm (0.4) y'know Minister of ehm [Finance
I: [Finance yes
R: eh having- he's- he's right wing of ↑me
I: ((laugh))
R: He's ↑totally right [wing [ya'know
I: [yeah [Yes
R: Can't see h(h)ow h(h)e g(h)ot into the Labour P(h)arty
I: So do you think that ah the Labour National distinction, it's not the same as
    the right wing and left wing in Britain where it seems much more clear cut
    (0.6) a sort of socialist conservative government
R: No well I think the- the Labour ([0.6) Pa:rty (1.0) and the (0.4)
I: [Mm
R: um if you- well if the Labour Party spans from about mid-ri:ght
I: Mm mhm
R: down to far-left
I: Y(h)es
R: and the e:m th- [the National Party's from mid-left right up to
I: [Yes
I: Far-right
R: Nn:o I don't think they've got any real [far-right
I: [So there's this sort of band of [a:
R: [There's a band I mean jus
I: K- where they're all the same [basically
R: [There all the s(h)ame
I: Yeah What do you think of Muldoon. Do you thi- What effect- Do you
    think he was a positive force for New Zealand or
R: .hh hh. I think he did a tremendous amount of good
    [but his public relations [image was absolutely ([   ) abysmal
I: [Yeah   [Y(h)eah   [↑.hhh
I: Yeas yeah
R: E:h [chmm.
I: [Was it just his personality do you think sort of abrasive
    (0.[6) personality
R: [Hhh. He didn't ca::re what everybody else
I: °Yeah°
R: thought (0.4) e:h (0.6) he was doin it(.) hi:s wa:y [and
I: [Mm mhm
R: (0.6) in a lot of the cases I think he was right (0.6)

I: Mm mhm (0.6)
R: E:hmm hhh. a:nd (1.0) this is where I think (.) he <u>fin</u>ally <u>lost</u>
I: Mm mhm
R: because he <u>kept</u> going more an' more left <u>wi:ng</u>
I: Mm mhm (0.6)
R: and <u>al</u>ienated his own party He- he shouldn't'a joined up (.) not quite with
     the SUP but [<u>nearly-</u>   <u>nearly</u> down that end of the scale
I: [((laughs))
I: ↑.Hhh [ahhh. (That's interesting)
R: [He was <u>tremen</u>dously left-wing
I: Yes (0.2) yeah
R: I mean h- ya'know holdin' down interest rate holdin' mo:rtgages down
                    ((some clamoring in background))
I: Mm mhm
R: D- Doing this doing that
I: Yea mm mhm
R: And eh (2.2) you know everything he <u>did</u>
I: Mm mhm
R: was a- a <u>socialist</u> bloomin' poi[nt of ↑view
I: [Mmm
I: Mm mhm
R: I mean Muldoon was <u>fi:ne</u> but you know we couldn't stand the <u>socialism</u>
I: Mm mhm Bu- I- Can I ask are you a National Party voter or
     (.) [eh
R: [I'm a member of the National [Party yes
I: [Party yes yeah Mhmmm (1.2)
I: Right (1.2) Yes what would- Can I- We(h)ll. Can I ask what's
     gonna happen do you think to Muldoon. Is he going to be sticking around
     or (0.4) is there a sort of groundswell in the National Party to eh
R: <u>Mister</u> Muldoon is a- is an <u>ex</u>ceptionally clever bloke
I: °Mm mhm°
R: and (1.0) ehm (2.2) he will (1.0) o:rganize things so that he's indispensable
I: °Mm mhm°
R: Buh'a come (0.4) [>ya'know January an' February when
I: [(Yeah)
R: everybody's back from their holidays and all feeling a lot better the sun has
     [been shining< (0.4) and everything like that (.) e:h He'll-
I: [Y(h)es ↑.hh yes
R: he'll- hh. on my thought heh heh he'll [<u>prove</u> himself
I: [Yeah
R: totally in[dispensable an' [he'll still stay there
I: [(   )   [°Mm mhm°
I: Yes
R: Now whether he'll hang in fer (1.0) ya'know two years
I: °Mm mhm°
R: so that he leads the Party into th- into the next

I: °Mm mhm°
R: election (1.0) I <u>don't</u> know [I think it depends on how <u>bad</u>
I: [°Mm mhm°
     (0.6)
I: °Mm mhm°
R: the uhm (0.6) the-[the ah Labour Party (0.4) carries on
I: [°Mm mhm°
I: Mm mhm
R: Cause (.) <u>I'm</u> dead scared
I: [Yes right
R: [that eh from <u>my</u> point of view (.) I'm gonna be <u>hit</u> (1.0) I'm gonna <u>lo::se</u>
     (1.2) something like (0.4) five to seven hundred dollars a year of my
     income
I: Mm mhm
     [what through inflation
R: [by the <u>tax</u> [tax policies tha- that are [coming out I [mean (.) ya'know
I: [Mmm   [Yeah   [Yeah
R: they keep tellin' you they're gonna take it from those that have <u>got</u> it
I: Mm mhm (1.0)
R: (   ) (1.0)
I: Yes. Right. (1.0) Do you see New Zealand as a (1.0) a kind of cla:ss society
     the way that people often talk about Britain as being a class society (1.0)
R: No it's a <u>different</u> kind of class society
I: °Mm mhm°
R: (over here) (0.6) In England (I mean) you're <u>bo::rn</u> with ([.) with your class
I: [°Mm mhm°
R: and it's very hard to climb from anywhere else
I: Yes
R: a:nd (1.0) <u>here</u> (0.6) eh you make your own
     ([0.4) class I mean if you <u>li:ve</u> in Remuera
I: [Mm mhm
R: you be[long to one class If you live in <u>Mangere</u> you- [you're- you're-
I: [Mm mhm   [you're in another
R: you're in another and then ya'know if you go to private schools an'
     (.) [and that
I: [°Mm mhm° (1.0)
R: You- you <u>make</u> within limits
I: Mm mhm
R: eh your o::wn (0.4) class
I: Yeah
R: a:nd and associate with them
I: Mm mhm (0.4)
I: Do you think there's equal opportunities <u>here</u> so that (0.6) almost
     irrespective of where you're born say if you're born in Mangere that you
     have a chance- a bigger chance with (1.0) a child born in Remuera you
     know that'em (0.6) we're sort of a suf[ficiently mobile country [to
R: [Hhh.   [CHmm.

R: N::o. (.) Uhm If- (1.4) everything- If you had two children (.) that
    [were identical twins [one was born in Mangere and one was born
I: [°Mm mhm°   [°Mm mhm°
R: in (0.2) Remuera I would say that the- the one who was born in Remuera
    (0.4) ya'know [(with affluent parents)
I: [would do better
R: [would finish up better because he would have been given [all the
I: [yeah   [Yeah
R: better opportunities. (1.0) But-
I: Mm mhm [so they're not complet[ely-
R: [(and)   [But there's- If you've got a real clever
    (0.4)
I: Mm mhm
R: person I think (every) born in the back end of Otara
I: Y(h)eah!
R: the a [ya'know (0.4) they could (0.4) still finish up
I: [Yes
I: yeah
R: eh you know a Rhodes Scholar or any[thing
I: [°Mm mhm° (1.0)
R: b[ecause ther- there's opportunity there
I: [Yes
I: Mm mhm
R: for them. (0.6) (I think   ) Hh. O:h well I know what we do for our kids
    (0.6) is (.) give them hh. every opportunity to a:h (2.4) achieve that much
    bet[ter
I: [better mm mhm
R: put every [opportunity in their way to e:h (0.6) to do better
I: [yea mm mhm
I: Mm mhm (1.4) Yes yeah (2.0)
I: ↑Right ↑ehm (2.0) the next set of questions are ehm (0.4) is about (1.2) uh
    well it's partly sort of (0.4) ho:me policies (0.6) and (0.4) mainly in relation
    to the Springbok tour cause that seemed sort of watershed in (0.6) events in
    New Zealand over the last five years or so. (0.6) Is that something that you
    felt strongly about or is it not something that concerned you (.) very much
R: E:h hh. I didn't feel terribly strongly abo[ut it
I: [mhm
R: e:h but yes I did fee:l
I: Mm mhm
R: about it
I: Mm mhm
R: E:hm (1.2) I'm one'a the (0.4) ones who believed it shoulda- should've
    occu:rred
I: Occurred yes [yeah
R: [And e:hm (1.4) of course on the ships we: were fairly evenly
    divided like the [rest of the country
I: [rest of the country yes

R: A:nd and seeing them nearly coming to blows at times and
I: (It was[ )   [Yeah
R: [I regret this y[a'know
R: Hh. people that are <u>friends</u> you <u>w(h)orked</u> with <u>s(h)ailed</u> with for <u>y(h)ears</u>
I: It was a very di<u>visive</u> [issue wa- wasn't it
R: [and
R: It was. It was a [<u>terribly</u> divisive [issue
I: [Yeah   [Yeah
R: and (that/it) (2.2) I don't think it hh. (0.6) <u>any</u>body that I know (0.4) came
    up with a <u>re:al goo:d</u> (0.4) <u>reason</u>
I: Mm mhm
R: for having it [or a real good for not having it
I: [Mm mhm
I: Mm mhm (1.0) yes
R: They were <u>a:ll</u> emotional
I: Mm mhm
R: issues.
I: Mm mhm
R: and (0.6) I mean I've <u>been</u> to (1.0) South Africa
I: Yeah. Mm m[hm
R: [I've <u>been</u> to West Africa
I: Mm mhm
R: I mean one of my <u>bêtes</u> noirs is uh (0.4) (Abraham Ordiyo) with his
    [<u>bloody</u> m- big <u>smiling</u> (0.6) blooming Ibo face coming out on the
I: [Y(h)eah
I: Yeah
R: on the screen tellin us what a <u>beau:</u>tiful country Ni<u>ger</u>ia is ((prior a sort of
    mimic of a Nigerian accent))
I: ((laugh))
R: (I mean I) went into Nu- Nigeria for eight years s[o I know how
I: [yes
R: b(h)ad Nig(h)eria was th[en and it's a darn sight [worse now
I: [yeah   [worse
R: U:[hm (0.4) I mean they say (0.6)(I a) you know do away with
I: [°Mm mhm°
R: apartheid (1.2)
I: Yes
R: Eh but in my opinion (0.8) he:re (0.4) these marches to
I: °Mm mhm°
R: eh Wai<u>tang</u>i [are ↑<u>try</u>ing to get a↑par↑theid ↑<u>he:re</u>
I: [°Mm mhm°
I: Yes ye[s they
R: [They ↑want ↑<u>sep</u>arate de↑<u>ve:</u>lopment
I: Mm mhm
R: They want (0.6) a <u>Min</u>ister of <u>Ma</u>- Maori A↑ffairs
I: Mm mhm (0.4)
R: ↑Where's the Minister of ↑Pakeha Affairs

I: Mm mhm

R: Can you give me his a↑ddress

I: Y(h)es ↑.hhh [yeah

R: [And (0.4)> ya'know< they want the <u>Maori</u> ↑All Blacks.

I: Yes [yeah

R: [Where is the Pakeha All Blacks.

I: Mm mhm

R: Well you <u>can't</u> have Pakeha ones that's- (.) that's <u>racial</u>↑ist

I: Mm mhm (1.0)

R: <u>Now</u> chhm.(0.6) to <u>me</u> they're- [that's wha- they're trying to do

I: [°Mm mhm°

R: they're trying to get separate de↑<u>ve:</u>lopment

I: R[ight

R: [They want <u>Maori</u> housing <u>Maori</u> (.) [Affairs <u>Maori</u> this yu you

I: [Mm mhm

R: know you [<u>name</u> it

I: [Mm mhm (1.4)

R: And (1.2) and the Maori language. If this is a mi:<u>no:</u>rity? (0.8) Now if you
     gave them everything (0.6) and they took o:ver

I: Mm mhm

R: we'd be in exactly the same state of- ([.) as South Africa

I: [Mm

R: except you know we poor whites would- [hh.

I: [Mm mhm

R: would be the poor whites

I: Right yes ye[ah uhm

R: [Uhm (1.2) I would <u>li:ke</u> to see apartheid done away with (1.0)
     but can <u>anybody</u> come up with a-[a (.) <u>positive</u> way of

I: [Mm mhm

R: saying "This is how it can be done"

I: Mm mhm

R: It's all very well to turn round and say "Give 'em a <u>vote</u>"

I: Yes

R: I mean the majority of them (1.0) don't <u>know</u> what a <u>vote</u> is

I: Mm mhm

R: I mean ya'know the bright ones that have (.) been to school
     and

I: °Mm mhm°

R: <u>run</u> around the streets telling everybody else "Now you know
     [shout this throw- throw tha[t"

I: [°Mm mhm°   [hh.

R: E:hm (0.6) but- (1.0) I mean <u>what</u> African country

I: °Mm mhm°

R: that <u>u:sed</u> to have European ru:le

I: °Mm mhm°

R: that is <u>now</u> ruled (0.6) <u>totally</u> by the <u>blacks</u>

I: Mm mhm (1.0)

R: <u>What</u> (.) <u>one</u> can you <u>hold</u> up as an example and say "We would like South
   Africa to follow that (one)?"
I: Mm mhm (1.0) [°Yes°
R: [Nigeria? Ghana? (1.0) Sierra Leone?
I: °Y(h)es°
R: °a:ny of them°
I: °Yeah°
R: Zem- Zimbabwe or- >an' I don't know the names of half of them<
   it's [a long time since I was the[re
I: [yes   [yes
R: <u>Any</u> of them I mean [they are <u>absolute</u> (0.6) dia<u>bol</u>ic places
I: [yes (0.6)
I: Well it's a very complex [problem isn't it that whole [thing
R: [(ghh.)   [I mean there are-
   [what is it I was readin (.) (somewhere there) <u>nineteen</u> of the
D: [yeah
R: (.) countries that [were <u>colonized</u>
I: [yeah (0.6)
I: [°Mmm°
R: [there (0.4) are <u>no:w</u> (0.4) dictatorships. [One party states
I: [Yes (0.6)
I: Mm mhm

   ((*phone rings*))
R: Excuse me

   ((*tape recorder temporarily shut off*))
R: Sorry about ↑that
I: That's o↑<u>kay</u> (0.6) Can't be ↑helped (2.2)
I: ↑U:hm (0.4) Yes so: (2.2) Did your attitude- D'you- say that this- the
   politics and sport argument is that one that you find (0.6) convincing you
   know that politics and sport should be kept separate
R: HHH.
I: o[r
R: [WELL I ah- (0.4) I would turn round (0.4) <ya'know> accept the end-
   the other d- alternative is they should build <u>bridges</u>
I: Yes Mm mh[m
R: [I'm- hh. (1.2) e:hm (1.2) I hate the feder(h)ation (h)of
   l(h)about there >you know< but- You'll always- always get a bite from me
   about the federa[tion of La-.hh but there's-
I: [y(h)eah
R: (0.4) [There's NO way I can influence the Federation of Labour
I: [(yes)
R: I might [HATE them you know [willing to out and shoot the
I: [yeah   [yeah
R: whole lot of 'em[I can't influence 'em
I: [((burst laugh))
I: Ye:s [yeah
R: [If I was a <u>friend</u> of theirs and went in and saw them occasionally

I: Mm mhm you might have some impact [on them   [yeah
R: [I might be ab[le to in- (0.6)
    influence them or say "Well look" ya'know "Don't- DON'T" (0.6) "Jim Jim
    my friend <u>don't</u> d(h)o that"
I: Yes (0.4) ↑.h[hh
R: [A::n
I: Yeah
R: So (1.2) hhh. I mean South Africa's a big country
I: Yes
R: It's a <u>ri:ch</u> country (0.6) and- (0.4) a:nd (1.0) everybody goes round the
    back door I mean they all might wave flags and say you know "Oh we don't
    believe in this"
I: Mm mhm
R: But I mean <u>who</u> supplies them with their oil Who
    buy[s their diamonds Who what-   Who bu[ys
I: [That's right who's trading with them   [yeah
R: You know who <u>trades</u> [with them
I: [Yeah
    It's a bit hypocritical ([isn't it. Yeah [Mm mhm)
R: [A:nd   [And if they want it. And then ya'know
    they say that ehm they're <u>doing</u>- that getting <u>sport</u> <u>JUST</u> to ge- to (.)
    ya'know
I: °Mm mhm°
R: keep APARTHEID GOING
I: °Mm mhm°
R: I don't think it is. They're keeping apartheid going because as.h as <u>they</u> see
    it over [there that's the <u>only</u> way that they're gonna (0.2)
I: [°Mm°
R: <u>kee:p</u> the good way of <u>life</u>
I: Yes (0.2) mm mhm (0.6)
R: I m[ean ya'know if somebody came round to me and said
I: [(   )
R: "Look (1.0) we're gonna m- move a whole pile of these (0.4) Maoris off
    Bastion Point [.hh and they're gonna take over this part of
I: [Mm mhm
R: [suburb name] just this corner here going round these block a houses here"
    ((sounds like he's gesturing during end of prior))
I: Mm mhm
R: I'd sa:y ((three hand strikes to a table or chair arm)) No they're <u>not</u>!
I: Yeah (1.0)
R: And <[ya'know> (0.2) not matter what happens ther- (0.4)
I: [Mm mnm
R: THEY'RE <u>NOT</u> GONNA DO IT
I: Mm mhm
R: I shall take such steps a(h)s a(h)re necessary to
I: Yes [yeah
R: [(a-) <u>avoid</u> it
I: Mm mhm

R: Now (0.6) if somebody said "Oh yeah but you know this is how it's gonna
    be"
I: Mm mhm (1.0)
R: I'd go <u>FLAT</u> out I mean I don't care whether it was apartheid or whatever
    yo[u call it or .hh (0.4) build the barricades up there and'a
I: [Yeah
R: [you know put machine guns on the top.
I: [>Mm mhm<
I: Mm mhm (0.6)
I: Ri[ght S[o,
R: [( ) [And <u>then</u> this is what I see that they're just pre<u>serv</u>ing
I: Mm mhm
R: e:hm what they've got °o:ka:y° (1.4) maybe it isn't the <u>best</u>
I: Mm mhm
R: °But it's far from being the worst°
I: Mm mhm (1.0) Right (1.0) Yes I mean an' the whole thing's such a
    co:mplex issue. What did you think about (1.0) the actions of the protesters
    during that period (.) in nineteen eighty one °when they were here?° (2.2)
R: Well hhh. (.) again I- (.) I thought that a <u>lot</u> of it was- (1.2) a lot of the
    (worsting) (.) [parts I'm sure em
I: [Mm mhm
R: (1.0) eh ya'know were planned.
I: Mm mhm (.) [Yeah
R: [I mean ya'know when they call in all the- all the bikey
    gangs with
                [their <u>hel</u>mets and tell them to (0.2) have it-
I: [Mm mhm
R: roll newspapers up round their arms so that
I: Yeah
R: an' carry wooden shields and everything like that .hh eh it's obviously (.)
    <u>pre</u>-planned
I: Mm mhm
R: And (0.2) the <u>peo</u>ple (1.0) the whole groups whole families
I: Mm mhm
R: that (.) <u>wa:</u>lked (2.0) to express their (1.0) displeasure I think
I: Mm mhm
R: I'm thinking they were blooming brave
I: Yes
R: For <u>those</u> that went out looking for a <u>fight</u>
I: Y[es
R: [I reckon that the police were far too (.)(lenient).
I: ((laugh))
R: [Eh Ya'know easy going on them
I: [(((laughter))
I: Ye(h)ah
R: A:nd (0.2) but'a (0.4) >ya'know ( )< (1.0) get into that <u>stage</u> of
    con<u>front</u>ation [they should just be <u>hauled</u> away and'a
I: [°Mm mhm°

R: ([0.6) and locked up
D: [Mm mhm
I: Yes (.) yeah
R: And just ya'know s- <u>send</u> somebody round in five years time an' see how
    they're [doin. "Oh we haven't taken you to court yet have we?"
I: [((burst laugh))
R: You know "Do come along."
I: ((laugh)) .hh What- Did you attend any rugby matches or, (0.8)
R: E::h (0.6) No: I dec(h)ided- .hh I decided as a protest I wouldn't go to any
    of the matches
I: Mm mhm why as [a protest
R: [I- (0.4)
R: Th- [A protest against a<u>p</u>artheid
I: [(begin as a) protest
I: Oh right [I see.
R: [Because you kno[w it was all (.) [it was all on at the time
I: [Mm mhm   [Yeah
R: and I said "Well-" (.) I said (1.0) "<u>if:</u> (1.0)
I: Mm mhm
R: everybody (.) refused to <u>go</u>
I: Mm mhm
R: (1.2) it would be the last one that ever'd be held."
I: Mm mhm .h[( )-
R: [because [<u>nobody</u>'d <u>go</u> there=
I: [( )
I: =Playing to [empty stands [(.) too
R: [Every-   [Every- Everybody had a- (0.6) ya'know if they
    had a <u>big</u> party and nobody turned up
I: Mm mhm (1.2)
R: [So hh.
I: [(Mmm) Yeah
R: U:hm I wouldn't say that I go to every (.) football match ya'know
    I go to the odd one
I: Mm mhm
R: And there I thought Oh hh.the best thing I can do is just not <u>go</u> to them
I: ((out breath laugh))
R: And (.) so I didn't
I: Mm mhm. (1.2) Right
R: That was my:: a (0.6) protest
I: Yes (1.2) But- (0.4) Do you think >(aside   )< why was there so much
    violence <<u>thi:s</u> ti:me>. Why: why this particular tour?
R: hh.
I: ( ) (0.4) Like you say you think there was: some sort of <u>planning</u> or that it
    was (1.4)
R: Woh yes the um (0.4) the Abraham Ordiyas the: u[m and'a the
I: [°Mm mhm°
R: Black Nationalists [the Council of Churches
I: [°Mm mhm°

I: °Mm mhm°

R: ah were a::ll doing their pla:nning (0.4) to try an' isolate (0.4) South
     Africa

I: Mm mhm

R: and'em tsk (0.4) I can never understand why they pick on New Zealand
     probably because I think New Zealand's (.) you know just
     ni[ce and small and can be kicked around

I: [Mm mhm

I: Mm mhm

R: and they haven't got any great clout I mean (.) so Engla:nds se:nds: <u>tours</u>
     down <u>their</u> place cricket down <u>there</u>=(nobody even would-) Well o:le you
     had th- the great Abraham Ordiya and all the rest of 'em [all come and

I: [Yeah it's-

R: THEY'LL RANT AN' RAVE ABOUT IT AN' IT'S- It's all over in two
     weeks!

I: That's right there wasn't any protest for the British Lions at all

D: Ye[ah

R: [I mean ya'know an' their- their- their idea of a protest is twenty five
     people at Heathrow when they fly out [or something like that

I: [Mm mhm (1.0)

R: So: um ya'know tsk (0.8)

R: Why? (0.6)

I: [Yeah

R: [Why pick on us (1.0)

I: Ri:ght. ↑u:hm (2.0) Do you think- would you describe New Zealand
     as a particularly violent society in comparison to other countries you've
     visited?

R: °No definitely not°

I: Yea'm. .hh But don't- But do you think that things are getting worse here
     I'm thinking say of crime now rather than'da (1.0) [(   )

R: [<u>Yes</u> I think <u>cri:me</u> a:nd
     (.) an' <u>vi:o</u>lence is (1.0) ehm (1.4) There is more <u>of</u> it

I: Mm mhm (0.6)

R: Eh but how do you measure it I mean (you have) per [head of population

I: [(mm)

I: Mm mhm

R: A:nd I mean ya'know (we would) There's probably more crime in New York

I: Mm mhm [((quiet laughter))

R: [than in the whole of New Zealand

I: Yes ((smile voice))

R: But okay they've got- they've got twice the population of New Zealand

I: Yeah

R: there

I: Ye:s

R: But then what do they- what do th[ey run to you know

I: [°Mm mhm yeah°

R: fifteen murders a day or something isn't it

I: [(something) ridiculous like that here[

R: [I don't know something like-   [Something like that

I: Yeah

R: Uhm hhh. (1.4) <u>Gen</u>erally (2.2) u:hm I ne:ver struck violence in New
     Zealand.

I: °Mm mhm°

R: I might have been lucky

I: °Mm mhm°

R: I mean it's the:re [and it's: u:m (1.0) you know bikey

I: [°Mm mhm°

R: gangs and things like that it's:: never fa- it's never far away

I: Mm mhm (0.4) that's right

R: I think our police do a (0.4) a reasonably good job

I: Yes (0.4) yeah

R: They're a (0.4) Ya'know they don- They don't pack a- (0.4)
     a [big <u>gun</u> to come out [an' start shooting like

I: [mm mhm   [((burst out breath laugh))

I: Like the Australian police or whatever

R: Or the <u>Americ</u>ans I- I'm always dead scared if I see a policeman I head the
     other way

I: [Yes

R: [Not- not because I'm scared of the police but I'm just scared that he might
     hur- [I mean pull his gun out and start sh(h)ooting at s(h)omebody.

I: [There might be some sort of accident (1.0)

I: Yes yeah .hh What eh- (.) Some people I've talked to have argued that the
     police (1.0) particularly say the Red Squad affair with the ah (.) some of the
     protesters, that the police acted in a (1.0) unnecessarily violent way
     themselves or (in an) oppressive way. Is that a view that you'd (0.4) support
     or agree with?

R: E::hm hh. (1.2) I can sympathize with it.
[. . .]

R: Ya'know people (1.0) argue an' argue an' argue you- you get so (0.2) mad
     with arguin'

I: Ye:s ((smile voice))

R: Now I mean if you will- if you were there and somebody's (0.4) <u>taunt</u>ing you

I: Mm mhm

R: day in an' day out

I: Mm mhm

R: an' you're not just expected to stand there

I: Yeah

R: and then all of a sudden somebody says "<u>GO GET 'EM!</u>"

I: Ye(h)ah

R: you know you can just imagine °"I'll get- I'll get that one over there."°
     ((whispered))

I: [Yes ((smile voice))

R: [(   ) "That one, that one over there!"

I: Yes

R: >Y'know<   you'd said to me it's a quite a natural reaction °I mean you
     know they say oh the police aren't supposed to do this but I mean the police
     have done the same°
I: Yes yeah [(They're just) hum[an yeah
R: [same reactions as [anything- as anything else
I: [That's right
R: [((cough)) I mean they have- they have great fun the police I mean
I: Yeah
R: There was a friend of mine once and he em (1.0) eh (1.0) one of their
I: Mm mhm
R: superintendents or (something) No not superintendent a bit lower down
     lieutenant or whatever he- [he was, police lieutenant .hh and
I: [Mm mhm
R: (.) he was out to the- at a dance
I: Mm [mhm
R: [and all his mates went an' e:h g- got whole bunches of keys, opened
     his blooming [boot of his car
I: [((laughs))
R: and put about three quarter a ton of eh of eh ba[g s of (0.6) em of
I: [(   )
R: gra:vel
I: Oh no: ((laugh))
R: in the boot.   Put a- put a couple of blocks under the back
I: Yeah (1.0)
R: and then when he drove off it just dropped off the blocks and sat straight
     down on his (knees) and he couldn't move so   ((laughs through))
I: ((laughs))
R: They thought this was a great idea
I: Yes! Yeah a little practical joke [sort of
R: [Yeh
I: Yeah
R: Mhm.
I: tsk .hh Ri:ght. ↑U:hm you said- (1.0) I- it sounds to me like you (1.0) e:h
     (1.0) y- you don't a- you think that- there's too much of (that/like) positive
     discrimination in New Zealand in favor of, of Maoris, The things like
     having four Maori parliamentary seats and the Department of Maori
     Affairs, you think it's sort of undemocratic or that
R: Well I think the Maor- Maor- Maor- the hh. Maori se:ats (0.4) should be
     abo:lished
     [I mean that's: (0[.6) an' that's
I: [Yeah   [Mm mhm
R: always been my ([.) opinion e:h
I: [Mm mhm (1.4)
R: Whe:n the National Party were in with just one or t(h)wo
I: Oh yes
R: .hh eh seats [I was glad they had them bec[ause the
I: [Yeah   [Right
R: (   ) keeps all the- all the- all the Mao:ri voters

I: Mm mhm
R: or if you like (.) all the <u>black</u> voters [ya'know <u>all</u> they can do is elect four
I: [Mm mhm
R: people now it's not gonna make much difference [to the par- to the party
I: [(That's- yeah)
I: Mm mhm
R: ya'know if they've only got <u>fo:ur</u>.
I: Mm mhm. But if they're spread [across (the elec-)
R: [I they were spread acro:ss you know
    (then that may-) an' they might (.) just have the three hundred (.)
    Maoris [in ea(h)ch in each electorate that put
I: [Mm mhm
R: another four or six eight ten seats in.
I: Yes (0.4) [Yeah
R: [an' it's a- and (th- the day as well)   To me it's a↑partheid
I: Mm mhm (.) yes (.) mm mhm
R: I mean ya'know they- they're grizzling it out in South Africa with it's eh .hh
    it's COLORED PARLIAMENT no:w
I: Mm mhm
R: Well we've got our colored parliament ya'know all four of them
I: Yeah ((burst laugh)) Yeah So: (0.4) >well< what <u>about</u>- I mean
    is ch- there <u>is</u> a large gap between Maori and Pakeha <u>achieve</u>ment=
    educationally Maori kids aren't doing so well in schools. .hh So what
    about some special education measures to help them. Do you think that's
    similarly (0.6) [(not right)
R: [Is it gonna do them any good.
I: Yeah (0.4) Mm mhm
    [. . .]
R: <u>If</u>- (0.4) I believe that every <u>chi:ld</u> should be <u>ed</u>ucated (0.4) to the a<u>bil</u>ity
    that [they can receive education.
I: [Mm mhm
I: Mm mhm (1.0)
    [. . .]
R: >I-mean it's no use< (1.0) <u>giving</u> them education unless it- unless it's (0.4)
    achieving something
I: Or supported at home really isn't it? That's the issue= question
D: (Yes)
R: [Mhm!
I: [So why do you think there is such a gap then and what what'em can be
    done about it (1.0) between eh Maori children and (0.4) Pakeha children
    which is .hh (2.0)
R: .hh Well I'd se:nd, (0.2) send them to [school name] where the headmaster
    there's got th(h)ere's got the r(h)ight idea
I: Mmm
R: He said if-   if they're eh- if they're forced to work they work
I: Y[es
R: [If they don't- if they're not forced to work they'll dole it
I: Ye:s right

R: E:hm (2.2) I be<u>lieve</u> that you know from the- (1.4) ya'know right from the
    start(1.4) if you're in a home like this (.) you <u>do</u> your homework you
    le[<u>arn</u> to (be-hh) before you go to school you can re[:ad
I: [Mm mhm   [Mm mhm
I: Yes yeah
[. . .]
R: So: (0.4) [I   don't know why there [is a gap (in it) It's- the
I: [( )   [So it's the home- the home background
    don't you think
D: Yes (1.0)
R: If the (3.0) I mean if the opportunity's there (1.2) I went to the (1.2) the
    Maori Girl's Queen Victoria [(.) School
I: [Mm mhm (1.4)
R: °The ↑girls ↑there are ↑tr::↓<u>men</u>dous°
I: Yes (0.6) Y[eah
R: [I mean they're putting- learning,   I mean ya'know they're on-
    (.) on a par with
I: Yes
R: any of the other
I: Mm mhm
R: first class girl's school
I: Mm mhm (0.8)
R: And ninety percent of them are Ma:ori
I: Mm mhm (0.6)
I: Ye[s they're a really good school[
R: [And I mean ya'know ac-   [academically they're do- doing
    tremendously well but I mean ya'know it's the parents there that have-
I: Yes (0.6)
R: either <u>put</u> them into that school or[- or seen that they have a<u>chieved</u>
I: [Mm mhm
I: Yes [yeah
R: [to get there
I: Yeah
R: I mean if the parents aren't gonna give a stuff whether the (0.6) eh kids are
    out running the streets all night
I: Mm mhm
R: E:hm (0.6) ya'know an' leave them (1.0) in the ca:r while they sit in the pub
    from (0.2) seven o'clock til mid- 'til ten o'clock
I: Yes
R: A:nd ([1.4) (Why don't/Well I don't) ya'know they're not-
I: [Mmm
R: there're no bad kids they say they're all bad parents (of)
I: Yes
R: E:hm (1.0) might've over<u>simpl</u>ified things but'ta (1.4) I think the hhhh.
    values that you put into the kids
I: Mm mhm
R: in the home

I: Are gonn[a influence what they [get out of their school
R: [( )   [gonna influence [how they- how
D: [Yeah
R: they go through life (1.4)
I: ↑So:: (0.4) do you think there's- (2.0) that there're any differences
     remaining between Maori and Pakeha a ehm culturally do you think
     (0.4) we have <u>one</u> nation if you like one- one set of people or do think
     there's some (.) quite big differences still the[re (1.0) <u>cul</u>turally and so
     on
R: [O::wl well there are tre<u>men</u>dous differences
[. . .]
R: .hh went an' spent a night on the (.) ma↑rae:
I: °Mm mhm°
R: At the last moment .hh I found out that'ta (0.6) they hadn't got'em (1.0)
     integration there [the women aren't allowed to <u>speak</u> on the marae
I: [°Mm mhm°
I: Mm mhm
R: So I was ro:ped into giving one of the speeches
I: Yes
R: And'em (0.6) ya'know <u>go</u>ing there, I'd never been on the mar(h)ae b(h)efore
I: Mm mhm
R: And'em (1.0) <u>go</u>ing there (.) an' seein' (0.6) what they did
     [and what <u>their</u> values
I: [Mm mhm
I: Mm mhm
R: were
I: Mm mhm
R: and <u>learn</u>ing (0.6) enough ta (.) get up an' talk for five minutes (1.0)
I: Mm [mhm
R: [A(h)nd (1.0) all in about an hour
I: Yes ((smile voice)) .h[hh
R: [I won't say it makes me an expert on <u>Maori</u> but I-
     (1.0) I <u>met</u> (.) what I consider there (0.4) a <u>beau</u>:tiful class of Maori
I: Yes yeah
R: >I mean< (.) they're not- economically they're (.)
     no[t in my (1.0) you know [not in my class (1.0) but <u>cul</u>turally
I: [Mm mhm   [Mm mhm
R: [they've got a class of their o:wn
I: [°Mm mhm°
I: Yes. So you think there's things that-   What kind of things do you think we
     could t- take or learn from Maori culture (1.0)
R: The way that- (0.6) the:ir (.) Maori wardens and the Maori
I: °Mm mhm°
R: eh (0.4) And (0.4) the fellow that (0.4) eh greeted us on the marae was (.)
     ah a carpenter
I: Yes (0.2) mm mhm
R: I mean ya'know working for wages

I: Mm mhm (0.4)
R: But hi:s ma:nner he- he's ehm (0.8) his <u>say</u> ([1.0) on what went on
I: [Mm mhm
R: at the ma↑rae
I: °Mm mhm°
R: was <u>damn</u> near absolute
I: °Mm mhm° (1.0)
R: E:hm (1.0) ya'know they heh hhh. <u>He:re</u> I mean if I- if I walked up the road
     and said something to a- a Pakeha kid he'd
I: °Mm mhm°
R: ya'know (0.4) [tell me where I could GO [<u>BUT</u> (0.4) with these ah
I: [((laughs))   [Yeah
R: these Maoris
I: °Mm mhm°
R: An if you like the Maori wardens an' the eh and their <u>leaders</u>
I: °Mm mhm°
R: they eh they have <u>great</u> (0.[6) con<u>TROL</u> over the kids
I: [Yes
I: There's a respect for author[ity   [Yeah
R: [Oh ya'know they- [There's a respect for for
     authority which (0.4)) ehm hhh. (I don't know) it needs playing up
I: Yes [mm mhm
R: [a <u>treme:n</u>dous amount (2.0)
I: Yes Right But what do you- Do you think there's been disadva:ntages for
     Ma:oris i:n the European culture that they have lost out? (2.2)
I: at [all?
R: [Ehh. They've got'ta <u>li:ve</u> (1.0) in (.) a (0.4) European culture
I: Mm mhm
R: They're a mino:rity .hh They cannot take <u>over</u> the country
     [If they want Stewart Island I'd be quite [willing to give it them.
I: [Mm mhm   [((out breath laugh))
R: Set up the <u>home</u>land for them <u>then</u> in Stewart Island. And they could- they-
     [they could all move in
I: [y(h)es
I: Y(h)es
R: And run it themselves. I mean ya'know there are plenty'a mutton birds
I: ((la[ugh))
R: [They- hh. but they're uhm (2.2) Chh. It's like when they- a few years
     ago there was all this- [eh screaming an'
I: [Yeah
R: ranting about <u>Wales</u> ya'know every- everybody in Wales has got to speak
     Welsh
I: That's right that's right
R: Now I mean what (.) on <u>earth</u> use is it to them.
I: Mm mhm
R: If they <u>wa:nt</u> to speak Welsh if they want to (0.6) bring up the culture <u>li:ve</u>
     the culture

I: °Mm mhm°
R: FINE
I: Mm [mhm
R: [If they're gonna work in a <u>bank</u> (.) the bank manager's gonna come
     along and tell them what to do in English (0.4) an' he's gonna pay them in
     English pounds
I: Yes
R: Or here ya'know New Zealand (0.4) dollars and he's gonna tell them (.) in
     Engli<u>sh</u> (0.6) what to do
I: Mm mhm
R: and he's gonna ex<u>pect</u> them (.) to talk to the (0.6) ninety nine percent of
     their customers
I: Mm mhm
R: in (1.0) English (1.2) So they- ya'know basically they've got to do their
     (0.2) English in English their maths in English
I: Mm mhm
R: [And- everything else so [ya'know
I: [Right   [Yes
R: this ([.) is a side line
I: [it's a harkening back (.) to [the past (really)
R: [you <u>ca:n't</u> go: ba:ck
I: Yeah yes=
R: =I mean you <u>ca:n</u> (1.0) I mean they can go back but I mean they're not
     gonna <u>live</u> in this ([0.4) in this day and age
I: [Yes
I: Mm mhm (0.6)
R: I mean I'd far sooner see them all learnin' Japanese
I: Yes
R: So that they can say "Ah so" when all the [visitors come
I: [((laughs)) (0.4)
I: Do you think there's any (.) racial discrimination in New Zealand Do you
     think there's sort of racial prejudice against Maoris?
R: .hhh Hhh. I think- (1.0) hh. to some extent but I think there's (0.4)
     principally economic
I: Mm mhm
R: e:hm ya'kno::w (.) lines
I: Mm mhm
R: e:hm (1.0) rather than racial prejudice
I: [Yes
R: [(rather) than in race
I: Mm mhm
R: And if <u>people</u> are going to li:ve in that style and e:hm (0.4) ya'know act in
     that way
I: Mm mhm
R: <u>I</u> don't want to know them whether they're
     [Maori (0.2) Pakeha or anything [else
I: [Yes   [Right (1.4)

R: E:hm (0.2) I think this:- an' that's the biggest division (1.0) a:nd (0.4) a lot
    of the (.) racial (0.[4) prejudice I-
I: [(Uh huh)
R: I think is brought on you know by the Eva Rickards that a
I: Yes (0.4) [mm mhm
R: [that stand up= I::'ve been out (.) time after time and played golf
    at- at [[place name]
I: [[place name] Yes yeah
R: And (0.2) eh playing on the golf course there I've played with Maori
I: Mm mhm
R: people and they said "Oh ya'know this the- this is the old burial- burial
    ground,=Hi'ya Roger" ya'know an'
I: Yes
R: and'a ya'know "nobody minds you playing golf?" an' I'll say "No no no (.)
    It's fi[ne"
I: [Yes
R: And it takes Eva Rickards to [c(h)ome down from somewhere else
I: [((laugh))
I: Yeah
R: to ah to [stir the whole bloomin pot (1.0) [and ehm ya'know
I: [( )   [°Mm mhm°
R: then the government gets in and'a
I: Yeah
R: buys the land (o:r well I don't know) they- they sorted it all
    [out an given the- given them all a brand new ehm golf
I: [Yes
R: course there an' [I haven't been down an' tried the new one
I: [((laughs)) yeah
    (1.0)
I: Yes (0.2) So ehm (1.0) why do think race relations are so good here in
    comparison even to say Australia where things have not been so- (0.4)
    there's not so much integration an' sort of mixing .hh of cultures and so on?
    (1.0)
R: Well (I mean me- he)(0.2) if you are talkin' about the indigenous
I: °Mm mhm°
R: native ya'know such as the Aborigine
I: °Mm mhm°
R: I mean Australia's got a magnificent mix it's almost like as good as the
    States [isn't it
I: [Yes so uhm
R: Ya'know your Spanish an' Greek an'
I: That's true ([0.2) yeah
R: [an everything [else I mean these are all foreigners as
I: [(these were foreigners)
R: well as the parents
I: Yes yeah

R: And (2.0) hh. I think (0.4) basically (0.2) e:h (1.0) the Maori as a people
   (1.4) >or the better ones< a:re
   [e:h an excellent people [Ya'know they're a lo:vely people
I: [°Mm mhm°   [Yes
I: Yeah
R: E:h (0.4) I don't kno:w many Aborigines
I: Mm mhm
R: I always tend to think of them as long an' bony and standing on one leg
   [and looking into the sunset ((smile voice))
I: [((laugh))
I: Yes (0.2) yeah
R: (°a::nd°) (1.0)
I: Yes I mean it's (1.0) yeah I think that's probably true it's something to do
   with the character of the Maori people an'
R: ↑Mhm
I: the way (1.0) they've accepted the situation an' made (.) the best of it really
   (.) °and uhm° (1.4)
R: The- you have they- They've gotta (0.4) a good life style ya'know an'
I: Mm mhm
R: go down the beach, pick a- pick ourselves a feed of
I: Right
R: of- of shell fish an' lie on the beach I mean that was great- that's a great way
I: Yes
R: And
I: I wouldn't mind doing a bit of that from time to time yeah ↑.hhh
R: Yeah but'ta ya'know ss:: eh (3.0) ya'know I mean s:a (.)they've got a

*The last part of the tape was deleted in copying. Therefore, the original, less detailed,
transcription of this part of the interview is presented below.*
I: Um this is a bit repetitive you've probably already answered it, but um that
   do you think um do you feel optimistic about race relations in this country,
   thinking particularly of the Maori/Pakeha, Polynesia/Pakeha?
R: Yes, I I I do because I think that um the majority of people want to get on
   together.
I: Yes.
R: You've just got the ten percent hard liners on both sides um you know the
   ones that are going to march up to Waitangi I mean I was talking to
   someone you know very nice girl, mid-twenties, Pakeha, she went to this
   march up to Waitangi she said the Maoris, they're cunning blooming lot,
   she said when we get up there there's Maori maraes just this side of the
   bridge, said all the Maoris were called in there you know to go and have a
   bit of a conference in the marae.
I: Yes.
R: Left all the Pakehas standing out, they came out and said okay on we go,
   they got onto the bridge the police blocked off both ends and got hold of
   the Pakehas, where were the Maoris, back in the marae, they knew what

was going to happen. You know she went up because she honestly thought you know that this would do something for race relations then you know she found out how she was used, that's the last time for those blooming lot.

I: Yes, so you think um you think the best hope's going to come through assimilation really the sort of fusing of the best cultures together.

R: Yes

I: Rather than what's called you know pluralism, or the separate development.

R: Yes, I don't believe in apartheid ((laughs))

I: Yeah(hhhh) So there's no future really in the sort of importing Maori language into the schools or

R: Not in my opinion no.

I: Right um some people I've talked to actually think it was er I talked to someone from the New Zealand Party, um who said that he objected to er commission for race relations and the Race Relation Conciliator and all the rest of it, because it prevented freedom of speech essentially, people become very self conscious about what they said or did and the result was was a sort of undemocratic loss of freedom.

R: Well to me it gets it gets so ridiculous, you've been in New Zealand a few months, did you hear the commentary in the rugby march?

I: O yes the Maori side step

R: The Maori side step

I: Yes

R: To me, I roared with laughter, I thought that's blooming marvellous you know, and of course somebody's got to bring it up at the Race Relations, I mean you know if they'd called it an Irish one all the Irish would have laughed at it as well wouldn't they? And you know to me when they can't laugh at themselves

I: Yes

R: Particularly some of it, there's no viciousness in it.

I: Yes.

R: You know it's uh, yes I think Hiwi Tauroa I mean the em there er I think it needs somebody like him just to have a little sit there just to make sure they're not being you know things aren't going too bad. I mean things that that you'd never think of, or the average person wouldn't I mean such as such as making a dish cloth with a Maori head on it, I mean I'd have probably tore out and bought one of those

I: Yes.

R: Never think a word of it you know but, And then you know to have any chief's head you know touching anything that's touched food, I mean it's a great nono.

I: Yes.

R: Yes, so you know keep us on the straight and narrow, tell us where we're upsetting you.

I: Yes.

R: And um I for one will try not to upset you.

I: Right.

R: But you know don't keep telling me I can't tell you that was a good Maori side step.

[. . .]

I: Yep. Um when er do you think there's if you like that British people have a stronger right to emigrate here than say people from the Pacific Islands?

R: No

I: No, d'you think there should be res- restrictions on immigration? How do you feel about

R: Oh yes, there's got to be.

I: Yeah

R: Unfortunately. I would love to see the whole world you know where you just go where you like m, which in the fifties is pretty well was er but I've been to most of the Islands around the Pacific and I think the people are marvellous.

I: Yes.

R: I think you know there's one thing I can't see is why when the Cook islanders work their life in New Zealand and want to go back to Cook, Rarotonga and draw their pension their old age pension there, it would be good for the economy of the country out there. They're going to get the same money from New Zealand, you know the government's going to pay the same pension, why they won't pay it to them while they're in Rarotonga they'd be much happier back there and you know they wouldn't be um taking up housing, you know cheap flats or state housing and anything like that here.

I: Right yes, so you don't think um, again some people I've talked to suggested that Pacific Island immigration has caused a lot of social problems and that we should think more carefully about immigration from the Pacific Islands than we should think about say immigration from Britain and Europe or America or Canada.

R: The um the big problem is of course that the islanders, the Melanesians the Polynesians, your Maoris, the Rarotongan Maoris, can't get on with each other, they hate each other's guts.

I: ((laughs))

R: You know while the average American and Canadian and Frenchman and German and Englishman could sit down and all get er form a group they're getting into war, I mean the er Cook islanders can't blooming live with the Samoans, the Samoans can't live with the Tongans. They're magnificent people

I: Yes

R: The Samoan, well I don't go for those so much, but I mean they're blooming people. Um all these things, but they can't bear each other. I mean it's like Africa used to be, I mean it was only because of the white man there that stopped the whole blooming country killing each other off years ago.

I: Right, yes, sort of tribal warfare really. Is there anything you'd like to add?

R: O no chatted away

NEW ZEALAND INTERVIEW 16

R: (Well what are/were we) talking about (1.0)
I: A:h (1.4) about the devaluation and'a (0.4) the need for (0.6)
   the [(expense of/expensive) imports and (1.2) so on.
R: [Yeah
R: Yeah (da violent-)(1.4) yeah it was probly- it was probly- it was probly
   necessary (0.4) from, (1.0) Again it's- it's difficult for the average man in the
   street to say what is ri:ght because [he has to rely: on what he's been to:ld.
I: [Ye:s
I: Ye:s
R: A:nd (0.4) example of that was you had Rob- Sir Robert Muldoon
   [telling people one thing, David Lange comes into
I: [Mm mhm
R: power an' says "Shockingly ridiculous state of affairs, I've never been so
   disgusted in all my ↑life"
I: Yeah
R: Same thing.
I: Yeah
R: Who: do you believe?
I: Ye(h)ah
R: Was- was [Robert Muldoon keeping the- [(0.6) or telling people
I: [Yeah   [°mm°
R: part of the truth?
I: Yeah
R: because it wa:s really bad and okay it's really bad there's no point in
   telling'em,
I: Ye:s (0.6)
R: O:r did David Lange come out an' say it is re:ally bad but that was just
   because he wanted to turn people against (0.4)
I: Muldoon
R: Muldoon and the National Party. Well Muldoon rather than the National
   Party (1.2)
I: Yes di- did you think (0.4) I mean some people I've talked to have argued
   that Muldoon's leadership style was very bad for the country ya'know
   irrespective of National Party politics (0.4) because he was so abrasive an'
   con- ya'know divisive (0.4) inflicting confrontation.=Is that a view that you
   (.) would agree with or not. (3.6)
R: ↑U:hm (2.0) his one good point (0.8) why he probably was- he probably was
   wrong in not consulting people and trying to take everything on [himself
I: [Mm mhm
R: He was probably wrong in doing that (1.4) But I think he: possibly expected
   a lot from the country and he knew that at least if he did it himself
I: Mm mhm
R: He'd be asking people the right questions
I: Yes
R: He'd be getting the right answers from people
I: Mm mhm

R: He wouldn't just be getting a fob off he'd be getting the answers he wanted
    (0.6) a:nd (1.2) possibly he could see that someone had to stand up to the
    unions
I: Ye:s (0.4) [mm mhm
R: [And so the action he took in confronting the unions
I: Mm mhm
R: Yes it did hurt them
I: Yeah
R: And (.) you only have to look at- wi:th thi:s voluntary unionism
    bill, the unions that have suffered (.) are the clerical workers and
    the shop [(.) employees' [unions
I: [Yeah   [yeah
R: Those are the ones that have suffered the engineers haven't
I: Mm mhm
R: All those other unions haven't suffered
I: Mm mhm (0.8)
R: But it's all- it's these (1.4)
I: The middle ranking [labour unions
R: [Yeah
R: Whe:re you've got a lot of women who are working who don't really wanna
    be part of the union. [All they wanna do is
I: [Yeah
R: go out an' work an' earn a bit of money
I: Yeah
[. . .]
R: They- it is a case of women or people like that have to go onto the union
    ledgers (0.4) just so the militants don't get their way
I: Yeah
R: Otherwise you gonna end up with them, ya'know they'll be out on strike
    every five months.
I: Yes (0.2) [mm mhm
R: [But the people that need the money
I: Mm mhm
R: that wanna work (0.4) can't get it
I: Right [yeah
R: [Which is what- (0.4) is why they've brought out this voluntary
    unionism [bill Yeah you ge- you can join the union
I: [Mm mhm
R: if you want to (.) You don't have to
I: Mm mhm (0.4)
R: And those that don't- that don't belong can just go an' work (whenever they
    like to)
I: [Yeah
R: [Aw'right they haven't got protection
I: Ye:s (0.6)
R: Bu:t >in a lot of cases with a lot of companies< >you play ball with them
    they'll play ball with you<

I: Ye:s (0.2) yeah (2.0) Mhmm. ↑So (1.0) if I asked you to pick out some New
      Zealanders that you admire (.) for their achievements what people (1.4)
      come to mind (1.2)
R: I don't know I've never really thought about it (1.0)
I: Well (.) I'll give [you a m(h)inute
R: [U:hm what sort of politically [or
I: [politically (0.4) e:hm
      culturally (1.0) people that you think have made sort of outstanding
      contributions (0.6) ya'know done- have done some- (0.6) the people that
      should be- (.) one should- you could almost use as a model for your own life
      (.) say (5.0)
R: That's difficult I've never really thought about (.) that
I: Yeah well don't worry if you can't ['em
R: [U:hm (4.6)
R: Right people that I might admire culturally an' through sport I suppose are
      at- at the Olympics so the- the people who did [well at
I: [Right
R: the Olympics They would've (helped.) .hh Kiri te Kan- te Kanewa
I: Mm mhm
R: does a lot (.)
I: Yes
R: with her singing (1.0)
R: A::nd (2.0)
I: It's interesting because when I've asked I've- I tend to find that (0.4) older
      age groups say (.) Edmund Hillary is a figure they say instantly (0.6)
      whereas younger people I've talked to that's not such a spontaneous
R: hhh.
I: Why is that is he just not such a meaningful figure for (0.4) the younger
      generation do you think?
R: No:: I don't think so (0.4) I don't really think so=I mean he- (0.6) u:hm
      (1.4) if- you may find in fifty years time ya'know if Ian Ferguson's the only
      one that's won-=ever won three gold medals for [New Zealand
I: [Yes
R: the:n u:hm (1.2) the- the older- the people that'll be older generation now
      that are [young now
I: [Yes
I: [(Mmmm mhmmm)
R: [The:n that are runk- young (.) now
I: Mm mhm
R: will say he:'s re:ally good
I: Mm mhm (1.0)
R: Whereas I think it's because (0.2) the older people were on- wer:e alive an'
      were (0.4) [young when Edmund Hillary [(0.4)
I: [Mm mhm   [Yes
R: climbed Everest They can remember him for th:at
I: Mm mhm
R: No:w all we see him- all we see him doing is running off to ya'know (0.4)
      u:hm (1.2) buildin schools in Nepal or

I: Yes (0.4) mm [mhm
R: [all that sort of- (1.4) ah which doesn't really strike people as
     (0.2) anything ↑great
I: Mm mhm (1.0) Do you think that New Zealand should (0.2) keep fostering
     its links with Britain or that really we (0.4) should (.) orientate ourselves
     towards Asia and the Pacific now that it's (0.2) past history (1.0) ou::r
     [links with Britain
R: [No: (0.6) we shouldn't. (1.2) We shouldn't. (0.4) There's too: much of our
     heritage (.) comes from Britain.
I: Mm mhm (0.4)
R: U:hm (1.6) an' we have to align ourselves with someone
I: Mm mhm (0.2) yes
R: Otherwise we're gonna find ourselves >non-aligned< and >cut off<
I: Yeah
R: And no: one would come to our aid=all right Britain always will come to
     our aid an say ya'know that they would [always come to our aid
I: [Mm mhm
I: Yes
R: But we shouldn't push them too far
I: Mm mhm (0.6)
R: [A:nd
I: [So you don't- what do you think about that in relation to the (0.4) recent
     discussions about ANZUS and nuclear ships coming to New Zealand and
     all the rest of it (1.0)
R: Personally I've got no worries about (1.6) nuclear ↑ships
I: Mm mhm
R: If they wanna come here (0.2) they're in. (0.6) In a way they're a
     necessa [ry evil to- to make sure that the Russians stay in line.
I: [Yeah
I: Yeah
R: Because the big- the biggest thing's okay they're gonna have a war in the
     Northern Hemisphere
I: Mm mhm (1.4)
R: You'll find whoever- then they'll be a mad race to get to New Zealand an to
     protect New Zealand.
I: Ye:ah
R: Because New Zealand (.) would be (1.0) Aw'right it may only last for
     another ten fifteen years after nuclear war [in the Northern Hemisphere
I: [Mm mhm (1.0)
R: A::nd before we get a situation like that (uhm) Neville Shutes' On the Beach
I: Yes
R: where you've got the dust cloud
I: °Mm mhm°
R: But in that time (2.0) they would have New Zealanders wo:rking (.) to
     produce food
I: Mm mhm
R: to go up to the Northern Hemisphere
I: Yeah

R: to feed their people (0.2) or to feed their (animals)
I: Mm mhm (0.6)
R: And then (0.8) I think the people who are turning round and saying
    "No no the Russians no they're not interested in New Zealand we don't-
    [they won't do anything about us"
I: [Yes
I: Yes
R: It's very narrow minded an' very short sighted.
I: Yeah (.) Mm mhm
R: They will! (0.6) They may not say they will but they will.
I: Yes
R: That's what- that's what they're here for.
I: [Mm mhm
R: [That's what they're there for. They just- they want to (0.2) take over
I: Mm mhm (0.6)
R: A::nd (1.2) from books that I've read (0.8) even- (0.4) even fiction books
I: °Mm mhm°
R: that are talking about Russia and they talk about the food (.) queues
    [and how (0.4) grain production and everything like that is down.
I: [Mm mhm
I: Yes
R: Why:: do people think that the Russians are so brilliant
I: Ye(h)ah .hh[[mm mhm
R: [when in fact they   [can't even feed their own country, they've
    got to go an' buy gra:in from the Americans [(again)
I: [Yes (0.4) yeah (1.4)
I: Right. (1.4) ↑So(1.0) do you think there is a sort of a- a New Zealand
    national character in the way that you can talk about a sort of British (0.8)
    national character or everybody has an image of what Americans are like,
    (1.0) or Australians or, (1.0)
R: It's developing.
I: °Mm mhm°
R: I would say. (1.0) U::hm (2.4) it's almost (1.2) a mixture of all three of
    those.
I: Mm mhm (0.8)
R: Ya'know that's where- that's whe::re (0.4) New Zealand's sort of (1.0)
    identity has come from, it's come from all three it comes from
    [everything that New Zealand has been through
I: [Yeah
I: °Mm mhm°
R: So that New Zealanders are kno:wn to be hard working an' they're
    [(ed)
I: [°Mm mhm°
R: a:nd (2.0) ya'know willing to get on with the job that's the thing they sort of
    try and push
I: Yes (0.4) [mm mhm
R: [for- >yeah for New Zealand to get back on it's feet< (0.4) and
    that is what New Zealand[er]'s would be- would be known for

I: Mm mhm
R: U:hm (3.0) so it's a-=yeah it would be a mixture of all three:
I: °Mm mhm°
R: Yeah we've had- we've had (0.6) people from (0.4) most- basically those
     countries [coming here
I: [Mm (0.6)
R: bringing their culture (0.4) and bringing their ide↑as
I: Yes (1.0)
R: An' plus of course then we've got the Islanders (0.4) and [the:n we
I: [yeah
R: have Maoris.
I: Mm mhm (1.0) Do you think eh (0.4) the sort of rugby racing and bee:r
     image that wa:s: so: associated with New Zealand male culture (1.0) (what)
     even ten years ago (is it- is it) still uhm prevalent (.) today? (1.0)
I: a (.) very masculine sort of cul [ture in that way.
R: [It's::- (1.0)
R: In so:me ci:rcles ye:s i::n (1.4) u:hm (4.0) in some Catholic circles yes
I: Mm mhm
R: especially the rugby an' the racing.
I: Yes
[. . .]
R: And it's'uhm (1.2) among a lot of guys I think it is losing the appeal.
I: Ye:s
R: U:hm (1.2) Right what's- What is it smoking statistics show that it's more
     women
I: Yes
R: between the ages of what about sixteen an: thir:ty that are
     smok[ing
I: [smoking mm [mhm
R: [when they tend to stop
I: Yeah
R: It's not such a (1.4) socially accepted
I: Mm mhm (1.0)
R: thing now °smoking°
I: Ye:s
R: But I think that just comes in with the whole change in
     culture=Like you look at ten years ago an' you look at the colours an' the
     type [clothing peoples wear-
I: [Yes
I: Mm mhm
R: were wearing (then) (0.6) a:nd (1.0) you think of the music that was around.
I: Yes
R: It's [all changed now it's- [everything has gone from being
I: [(changed mm mhm [Mm)
R: heavy and dark to [being light and colourful
I: [Yes
I: Mm mhm (0.8)
I: [(Yeah)

R: [A:nd u:hm (2.4) I don't <u>think</u> that the sort of the rugby racing and bee:r
I: Yeah
R: syndrome really fits in anymore.
I: Yes (1.2) tsk ↑Right okay well what'em (0.6) <u>On:e</u> thing that interested me
  (1.0) when I was in Britain was the Springbok Rugby Tour because that
  seemed like such a sort of unprecedented event in (0.6) New Zealand's
  history (1.0) U:hmm wa- was that something you felt strongly about or not.
R: Tsk (1.2) I felt more strongly (1.0) u:hm (2.2) tsk about the people who
  were protesting [(0.8) saying it shouldn't go ahead.
I: [Yeah
R: It was a little group of minori↑ty
I: Mm mhm
R: A::nd some opinionated <u>bigots</u> prob↑ly
I: Mm mhm
R: A:nd people- (0.4) just because people didn't agree with them
I: Yes (1.6)
R: the:y wanted to stop <u>it</u>
I: Mm mhm
R: Which is whatever protest is anyway.
I: Mm mhm
R: Jus- It's a minority group that wants to impose it's will (0.6)
I: Yeah
R: They talk about the freedom for the blacks in South Africa
I: Mm mhm
R: equal rights for the blacks well what about equal rights for the people in
  New Zealand.
I: Mm mhm
R: If they decide they wanna go an' watch (0.2) the Springbok play rugby (0.2)
I: Yeah
R: Why shouldn't you let them. Why [should a minority group
I: [Yeah
R: impose it's will on them.
I: Mm mhm (1.2) A:nd'em (1.0) so (1.0) in a sense you thought the
  Springbok <u>should</u> come here (1.2) to begin with or not?
R: It didn't bother me really one way or the other. If they wanna <u>come</u>, they
  <u>come</u>. If they don't wanna come,
I: Yeah (0.4)
R: that's <u>their</u> choice.
I: So: the government of the day's line was that really it was a matter for rugby
  union (.) to-
R: (It (tis a/doesn't) matter for the [rugby union (as/cause) rugby didn't matter)
I: [(right)
I: Mm mhm
R: A:n [d aw'right you can try an' mix politics and sport an' I
I: [°Yeah°
R: s'pose to a degree it i:<u>s</u> mixed.
I: Mm mhm (0.4)

R: <u>But</u> (1.4) for the government to turn'round and say what the pressure
   groups wanted to say
I: Mm mhm (1.4)
R: you're having almost a totalitarian
I: Mm mhm
R: sort of state where the government's coming in an' saying "You're gonna do
   <u>this</u>! You're <u>not</u> gonna do <u>that</u>!"
I: Yes (0.4) mm mhm
R: A::nd (0.4) you do that <u>any</u>where else with <u>any</u>thing else (0.6)
I: Yes
R: you'd have the civil liberties groups on your back
I: Mm mhm
R: An' you- you- you're not giving people their free- their freedom of choice
   their freedom of speech their free rights
I: Yeah
R: Their personal rights
I: Mm mhm
R: But yet when it comes to rugby (.) an' [comes to South Africa
I: [°Mm mhm°
R: they all forget it an' they "Oh- Oh no well we must look out for the ↑blacks"
I: Yes (1.0) So you think- (1.4) in your view that sort of <u>cut</u>ting
   sporting events with South Africa really isn't gonna have much impact
   upon (0.4) (what/war)(0.6) their sort of political structures in that
   country ([.) (that's your view point)
R: [No because we're still trading with them
I: Yeah
R: We still trade [(0.4) There was a letter in the Herald (1.0)
I: [Mm mhm
R: goin- saying that well no- if they're gonna cut- if they're gonna come- <u>cut</u>
   contact with South Africa
I: Yeah
R: they should do it across the board not just the things that uhm
I: Yeah (0.6)
R: People can <u>see</u> that we're still trading with them
I: Yeah (0.2) mm mhm
R: We're still gonna take South Africans into New Zealand
I: Yes (0.6)
R: So ya'know I mean (0.4) they just picked on ya'know they just picked on
   [the things that the pressure groups want
I: [Mm
I: Yes
R: The pres [sure groups want the South Africa consulate closed
I: [Mm mhm
R: so it's closed
I: Mm mhm (0.6)
R: They don't want the rugby here so (0.6)
I: Mm mhm

R: they complained.
[. . .]
I: What- i- hh. but what are the images that you hold of that time when you think an' remember it. What do- what kind of images do you see? (4.0)
R: Frus<u>tra</u>tion (1.2) a lot of frustration that a mi<u>nor</u>ity (1.0) that wanted to impose it's will on the majority for [once I mean all the
I: [Mm mhm
R: <u>peo</u>ple in New Zealand (0.4) started to wake up
I: Yes (0.6)
R: A::nd (1.4) there was a time when it could've (0.6) sort of blown itself ↑up
I: Y [eah
R: [I mean ya'know sort of gone inta (1.4) y'know ra:ce ri:ots an' uhm
I: Mm mhm
R: ya'know large pitched <u>batt</u>les in the streets type thing
I: Yes
R: A::nd (1.4) So I think (1.2) the majority of- >yeah=aw'right< the majority of the <u>pro</u>:-tour people
I: Mm mhm (0.6)
R: <u>bas</u>ically just wanted to go an' watch the rugby they weren't very interested in what the others had to say about it
I: Yes
R: An' they looked on the others as a <u>nui</u>sance.
I: Mm mhm
R: An' I think (they) possibly- possibly had even (if I would-) a picture would be like a- (0.4) a <u>fly</u> bothering a <u>lion</u>
I: Mm mhm
R: an' the lion being the <u>mass</u> of people that wanted to just go an' watch the rugby
I: Yes
R: An' the fly was gonna keep on <u>worry</u>ing it [an' <u>worry</u>ing it
I: [Yes
R: until the lion finally did something.
I: Yes
R: Well then they're gonna run off an scre:am (0.4) [all sorts of things.
I: [Mm mhm (2.2)
I: Yes (0.2) Well weren't- (1.0) weren't there sort of quite a wide range of people who'd gotten involved in the pro↑test I mean (0.4) it wasn't just
R: Ye:ah there was political there was (0.4) religious
I: Mm mhm
R: But I think- (0.6) the people that the- especially th- the <u>church</u> people that were going
I: Mm mhm (1.4)
R: u:hm (1.0) I (.) <u>won</u>der if they'd really thought it through
I: Yeah (0.2) mm mhm (0.6)
R: An they- they sort of go through and say "Oh (1.2) well it's not what Christ would'a done"=Okay it's not what Christ would'a done but Christ wouldn't have been out there protesting either

I: Yes (0.4) mm mhm

R: He wouldn't have been doing that=He wouldn't have been out in the forefront of a battle.

I: Yeah

R: So he wouldn't have been out causing a civil disturbance   He didn't cause civil disturbances

I: Yeah

R: And that is basically what (they've done).

I: Mm mhm (1.0)

I: [So:-

R: [Ya'know it says- it says- it says in the Bible that'em (.) you're to honour the government because the [government's been put there by God

I: [Yeah

I: Mm mhm

R: And sure okay (1.6) what the government (1.0) may do may not be right but you have to [honour what the government says

I: [Mm mhm

I: Yeah [mm mhm

R: [An' if the government says "okay" (.) they're welcome

I: Mm mhm (1.2)

R: You can't- yeah an' you should really go by that

I: Yes

R: They are supposed to be the elected members of- the elected representatives of the country

I: Yes (.) yeah (2.0) Some of the people I've talked to have suggested that the police possibly (0.4) escalated the violence through their actions. Is that a view that you agree with?

R: .hh From what I've heard the police showed great (0.6) [control

I: [Mm mhm

I: Mm mhm

R: A:nd gre:at (1.0) tolerance of the protesters

I: Mm mhm

R: From what I've heard that happened (0.6) to the front li::ne Well things that I've heard the front- happened to the front line of the police

I: Yes

R: with- they had women protesters that would go along an' fondle the police.

I: Mm mhm

R: And the police could not do a thing.

I: Mm mhm

R: They had to stand there and take it

I: Yeah (0.4) mm mhm

R: Wherever- wherever anything- (1.0) you get the u:hm (2.0) the police with their- with the miners in Britain

I: Yes

R: Very- you're beginning to now but five yea [rs ago

I: [°Mm mhm°

R: you never heard about the police casualties.

I: Yeah

R: All you heard about was five (.) protesters <u>bat</u>toned
I: Mm mhm
R: Well what about the five (   )- five policemen who were <u>cut</u> by flying glass or
    [<u>bot</u>tles?
I: [Yes
I: Mm mhm
R: All that sort of thing you never heard about that
I: Mm mhm (0.6)
R: No I think the poli- the poli- In (1.0) in South Africa they would have had
    dogs straight in, they would have had- they would've been in with rubber
    bullets
I: Yes (1.0) [Yeah
R: [And they would have been in with (rooks/rocks)
I: Yes
R: In New Zealand they just left them there
I: Mm mhm (0.8) So in a way (.) you think that they could have acted even
    ehm (1.2) cleared the crowd earlier and [more effectively perhaps
R: [(Mhm)
R: Yeah (.) [Well you look at Hamilton there were-
I: [°Yeah°
R: there were people there that were all set for the police to charge them
I: Yes (0.6)
R: <u>But</u> (0.6) Bob Walton said "No"
I: Mm mhm
R: "They're not going to achieve anything." [They <u>would</u>n't have
I: [Mm mhm
R: achieved anything.
I: Yes
R: They would have had a pitched battle an' okay (.) as soon as tho:se (0.2)
    protesters had started attacking the police
I: Mm mhm
R: the <u>cro::wd</u>, the rugby crowd would have been <u>in</u>.
I: Yeah
R: t- to defend the police (.) wh [ich is great
I: [Mm mhm
I: Mm mhm
R: But it's not right
I: Ye [ah
R: [It's not right so yeah okay jus leave'em jus surround'em an jus leave'em
       [(ya'know)
I: [Mm mhm So in fact that- that was the right sort of tactic (for the Hamilton
    police/to have handled the whole thing)
R: <u>Re:</u>ally yes
I: Yeah
R: At <u>no:</u> ti:me I would say, okay the police <u>ma:y</u> have (.) by their <u>presence</u>
    (1.0) pro<u>vok</u>ed people but they were just [there to be provoked
I: [Mm mhm

I: Yes (0.4) yeah

R: They were just there to yell an' to scream abuse at the police an' the police-
[and <u>force</u> the police to do something.

I: [Mm mhm

I: Yeah (0.4) mm mhm

R: And then soon as the police do some'um they cry "Wolf" ["Wolf"

I: [Yes (.) mm mhm

R: and <u>ru:n</u> (0.6) an' the police <u>cha:se</u> them an' that's where you get photos

I: Y(h)eah [yeah

R: [(ya'know) 1.2

I: So do you ↑think- (1.2) What would you have thought say (.) were the
worst (kind of sort of) episodes. As far I understand where rugby supporters
did <u>clash</u> with (.) demonstrators and protesters. D'you think the:re there
might have been (0.4) sort of ehm (0.6) tsk aggro on both sides, as it were,
that some of the rugby supporters acted (.) unreasonably ↑too or not.

R: Yes I s'pose there always is, there's always two sides to a story an' it's always
yeah

I: Yeah

R: it takes two to fight

I: Mm mhm

R: A::nd uhm (3.0) No I think if the protesters ju- had just protested silently

I: Mm mhm

R: it would have been aw'right

I: Y [es

R: [But I think (0.6) ya'know when they came along with uhm
(.) newspapers rolled up an' [crash helmets and all this sort of thing

I: [Mm mhm

I: Yes (1.4)

R: Had the::y (1.0) I don't know they sort of (1.4) they got themselves
organized an' it was no longer just a- ya'know just- just sort of the .hh man
on the street protesting.

I: Mm mhm

R: It was an organized protest

I: Yes (.) mm [mhm

R: [A::nd (3.0) [I think it just- (0.6) the ru-

I: [Mm mhm

R: ya'know if they had left the rugby fans it would have been all ↑right

I: Yeah

R: But they didn't they just wanted to worry them an' [play with them

I: [Yes

I: Mm mhm (1.0)

R: An so they got <u>thump</u>ed an' so ya'know they got (0.6)
[an' th- that's all you heard, you never (0.4) ya'know

I: [Mm mhm

R: there was very few articles (0.2) on the side of the rugby supporters.

I: Yes (0.4) Do you think the::- the media were biased in their presentation of
the (0.4) e↑vents? (2.8)

R: Yes I think so because I think (.) a lot of: a lot of reporters basically
    themselves are little stirrers
I: Yeah (0.4) mm mhm
R: Ya'know cause- the thing that is gonna <u>se:ll</u> is a- (0.2) is a <u>scandel</u>
I: Yes
R: I mean if you can get a photograph of- of- of a rugby supporter belting a
    protester yeah ↑great
I: Y(h) [eah ((laugh))
R: [Now here we have <u>proof</u> that it's the protes- it's the
    [supporters fault not the-
I: [Yeah

*Approximately 5 second gap in recording. The original, less detailed, transcription of
this part of the interview is presented below.*

1   R: Now here we have pr<u>oof</u> that it's the protest, supporters fault,
2   I: Yeah.
3   R: not the protesters. But they haven't shown all the other photos,
4   like those three clowns that
5   I: Oh yes, that was a strange affair wasn't it?

I: Oh yes that was a- (0.2) a strange affair wasn't it
R: Yeah you [don't hear what the clo:wns did to the police
I: [Yeah
I: Mm mhm
R: Ya'know I mean as far as they're concerned all they wanted to do was
    walking down the street
I: Yes
R: And they suddenly got set upon. Rub [bish
I: [Mm mhm mm mhm
R: The police I know wouldn't- ya'know they- they don't do that
I: Yes [yeah
R   [Not in New Zealand anyway (1.0)
I: Mmm [It must of been a very- Sorry
          [(   )-
R: There <u>will</u> have been a motive for the police to [do something about it
I: [Yeah
I: Yeah (1.2)
R: There <u>will</u> have been a motive=okay they may have used excessive force
I: Mm mhm (0.4)
R: But I think the police got frustrated
I: Ye:s well that was the third t [est wasn't it yeah
R: [Ya'know they- they were caught in the middle
I: Yeah (1.4)
R: An' to be hon- ya'know like to be honest i- it (0.4) got out of hand I mean
    (0.4) the average people at the beginning of the tour
I: Mm mhm
R: who were protesting like that an' <u>they</u> were ↑there

I: Yeah

R: The third test where they were turning over cars an' [(0.4)

I: [Yeah

R: demolishing police cars (1.0) that's not protest that's just anarchy

I: Yeah (0.4) mm m [hm

R: [That's mob rule

I: Ye:s (2.0) It must have been a rather difficult time .hhh partly ya'know sort
     of divisive time because you hear stories about fami [lies split down

R: [Mmm

I: the middle an' so on.hh an' places of work sort of split down the middle.
     So was it something that (0.2) during that period you debated a lot with
     other people o:r was it discussed a great deal or (0.2) not really.

R: Phh. Not really cause if i- I was still at school then. (.) No I wasn't. (.) °No I
     wasn't.° But- °Yeah that's right I was working° But the majority of the
     people at ↑work

I: Yeah (0.6)

R: we:re (1[.0) for the tour [They wanted the rugby

I: [Mm mhm   [Yeah

I: Yeah

R: An' basically you had a political- you had a group that were politically
     motivated

I: Yeah

R: the protesters against the people who wanted to watch it (.) were just out for
     the sport they [were just out for enjoyment. (0.4)

I: [Yeah

R: Ya'know guys that play rugby.

I: Y [eah

R: [there was no political

I: Ye[ah

R: [as far as they could see there was nothing an' so you had one group (ing)
     the game for one thing and the other group saying "Well we're not worried
     about that"

I: Yeah (0.4)

R: Ya'know (1.4)

I: Tsk ↑right .hh Do you think New Zealand can be described generally as a
     violent socie↑ty (0.4) in terms of crime rate an',

R: °Yes it has got a very high crime rate°

I: °Yeah°

R: (°around there°) (3.0)

R: Ye:s I think so, it's not as bad as some places though

I: Ye:s (1.4)

R: But (.) the crime rate i:s going up

I: Mm mhm (1.0) Why do you think- wa-what's responsible there an' what
     could be done about it (.) (do you think) (3.4)

R: Pphhh. To:: re:ally answer that we'd have to look at (2.4) u:hm the type of
     crimes you've got (0.6) uhm and who's committing them

I: Ye:ah (0.4) mm mhm

R: There've been ya'know (0.4) u:hm (1.4) ideas put about that- ya'know
    >what is it< the majority of the rapes are committed by Islanders or
    [Maoris
I: [°Mm mhm°
    That's right [mm mhm
R: [U::hm (1.4) then you- an' a lot of house burglaries I would
    imagine are committed by kids
I: Mm mhm
R: And the majority of the kids that are hanging around on the streets
I: Yes
R: are Islanders. They not the Maor-=well-
I: Mm mhm
R: It's unfair to say the Maoris because the Maoris that I know are quite nice
    really
I: Yes (0.4) mm mhm
R: The Maoris (1.0) are quite good. It's the Islanders that come here an' have
    nothing.
I: Yeah (2.2) Yes so it's partly sort of immigration- it's related to immigration
R: Mmmm
I: Yeah.
R: We don't- (0.4) seeing them coming through (.) off the air craft [at night
I: [Mm mhm
    (1.2)
R: half of them can't speak English
I: Yeah
R: A::nd (2.0) if they can't speak English they're not gonna be able to get a job
    they're gonna go an' they're gonna be little communi↑ties
I: Yeah (0.2) mm [mhm
R: [A::nd (2.0) they're not gonna be able to contribute
    anything to the country.
I: Mm mhm
R: And they're gonna get frustrated and they're gonna get <u>bored</u>
I: Yes (0.6)
R: And they're gonna- ya'know (.) there's nothing for them to do so the kids'll
    start hanging out in the streets
I: Mm mhm
R: At <u>ho:me</u> (0.4) Mum and Dad can't speak English [so the kids don't
I: [Mm mhm
R: speak English
I: Right [yeah
R: [They go to school an' suddenly they're confronted with English "We
    can't speak that language what'll we do?"
I: Yes
R: Nothing!
I: Mm mhm
R: An' so by the time they get to fifteen they just drop out they've had it up to
    here with school

I: Yeah

R: And it's not (.) school's fault

I: Yeah (1.4)

R: They had brilliant lives, they had brilliant lives back in- family lives, back in the Islands

I: Yeah

R: That's where they should be.

I: Right yeah so it's just causing social problems. (0.6)

R: Mhmm they're coming here (.) looking like- well like the (.) Ita:lians [we:nt to: N:ew York

I: [(°Yeah°)

I: °Mm mhm°

R: The streets are paved with gold

I: [Yeah

R: [That's what they're coming here for

I: Mm mhm (0.6)

R: But they're not

I: Mm mhm

R: An' dey- Yeah they're probly all quite happy living in their- living in Otara or living in their [little communities

I: [Mm mhm

I: Yes

R: But hhhh. (1.2) do we really want them?

I: [°Yes°

R: [We've got ten thousand Niueans living in New Zealand

I: °Mm mhm°

R: three thousand of them live in- three thousand Niueans left in Niue

I: Ye(h)ah

R: Is that right? Or should we turn around an' send'em all back again.

I: Yeah (0.4) °mm mhm° (1.0) What- Do you feel there should be restictions on other kinds of immigration say from Britain and Europe ↑too? (4.2)

R: Ye::s. (0.4) There sh- Yes there shou:ld be. I'm ve:ry ve:ry- (1.0) Like it's not free entry now from Britain to-

I: Mm [mhm

R: [from Britain anymore.

I: Yes

R: A::nd (2.0) the National government, when they were in office, their sort of criteria was if we need the people to work here [yes we'll have them.

I: [Mm mhm

I: Yes (1.2)

R: Which is a good idea=If we- if we need boiler-makers yeah let's get boiler-makers in. If the New Zealand boiler-makers don't wanna work that's the:ir problem

I: Yes

R: There's a job there if they want it, if they don't want it

I: Mm [mhm

R: [Fi:ne.

I: Yeah

R: >But then I don't think they should get the dole either<

I: Mm mhm (0.4) Right

R: Ya'know with- with the La- the Labour Party- the Labour <u>con</u>ference was talking about importing more Islanders

I: [Yeah

R: [What are we gonna do with them we've already got (0.2) sixty thousand unemployed?

I: Yes

R: They're not gonna <u>work</u> (0.4)

I: Mm [mhm

R: [Or if they <u>do</u> work they're gonna take someone else's <u>job</u>

I: Yes (0.4) [yeah

R: [So ya'know however many you bring in here (0.6) that's what the unemployment's gonna go up [by

I: [°up by°

I: °Mm mhm° (0.4)

R: An' it's gonna cost the state <u>more</u>

I: Yes (0.4) °mmm°

R: To pay for them. (2.2)

I: Yea:h it's a difficult problem isn't it? .hh ↑ehm (.) Finally (.) the last section of questions (1.0) is about'em (0.6) New Zealand as a multi-cultural society (.) Do you think there's still differences between Maori and Pakeha people in terms of temperament and interests (0.6) or are we really (.) o:ne- (0.4) one nation, one people (2.2)

R: There <u>is</u> a lot of <u>difference</u> (1.0) uhm New Zealand is basically a <u>whi:te</u> (1.0)

I: °Mm mhm°

R: a white society a::nd (1.0) <u>some</u> of the <u>Maoris</u> fit in

I: °Mm mhm° (1.6)

R: And the ones- some of the ones in the cities fit in the ones in the country (1.6) are quite happy where they ↑are

I: °Mm mhm°

R: U::hm (2.6) so probly- (they don't/it may not) really bother them I don't really know.

I: Yeah

R: But then you've got the misfits that <u>don't</u> fit in.

I: Yeah

R: A::nd (0.6) and you've got- (1.4) Like (0.4) with this u:hm (2.0) Treaty of Waitangi thing

I: Mm mhm

R: You've got a minority.

I: Yes

R: that expect the- expect more

I: Mm mhm (0.6)

R: A:::nd if you see that going to its full extent it will eventually go to an underground terrorist organisation.

I: Mm mhm

R: That- because they don't get <u>the:ir</u> way >although probly with the Labour Party they will get their ↑way<

I: Mm mhm

R: A::nd (1.4) they will eventually start striking back an' blowin' things up

I: Yeah (0.6)

R: We've got Joe- (   )- (we've/with) Joe Hawke at Bastion Point

I: °Mm mhm°

R: When le:aders of the tribe

I: °Mm mhm°

R: turned round an accepted the government's

I: Yeah (0.2)

R: thing. >They accepted the <u>land</u> the government gave them an' two hundred thousand dollars compensation.<

I: °Mm mhm°

R: Then Joe Hawke said "No we don't agree" He's not even recognized by the elders of the tribe.

I: Yeah

R: Yet he's meeting with the- (0.4) with the Labour Party's lan- Lands Minister

I: °Mm [mhm°

R: [And they're gonna work something out

I: Yeah (0.4)

R: Yeah sure they'll work something out it's just (his) pressure group

I: Yes (0.2) mm mhm

R: And <u>that's</u> (0.4) whe:re a lot of Labour Party votes come from

I: Mm mhm

R: is from the Maoris and the Islanders

I: Yeah (0.8)

R: Because that's probly what they're told to vote so they vote it

I: Yes

R: They probly don't under↑stand

I: Ye:s (1.4) °Mmm° (1.0) What- what do you think New Zealand's <u>gained</u> from (.) Maori culture if anything (I mean ya'know) (5.2)

R: That's difficult to say I don't really know (.) [u::hm

I: [(°mm°) (4.2)

R: Because their herit- (0.6) New Zealand is now a white society an' their heritage is <u>not</u> (.) our heritage

I: Yes (0.4) mm mhm

R: A::nd it's just sort of an interest sort a thing

I: Mm mhm (0.6)

R: An' then when- Ya'know an' I think a lot of people (0.4) tend to get turned <u>off</u> (1.0) when you have (1.0) I mean like basically what Maoris are going on for they want a group they want their own second parliament to [govern the Maoris

I: [Yes

I: Mm mhm

R: What they're after is what is in South Africa

I: Yeah
R: That's what they're after
I: Mm mhm (1.0)
R: <u>But</u> if you turn around an' told them that they'd say "No we don't"
     [But that's what they want
I: [Yeah
I: Yeah
R: They wanna <u>split</u> the society basically and send all the Maoris (0.4) to the
     south island and the whites on the north island
I: Yeah (0.4) mm mhm
R: They'll govern themselves an' we'll go[vern] ourselves
I: Mm mhm
R: But if that's what you <u>said</u> to them (0.2) they would disagree
I: Yes (1.0)
R: An' it strikes me as ever [so that's what they want
I: [°Mm mhm°
     (0.4)
R: They wanna govern them↑selves (1.0)
I: ↑So (1.0) mhm what do you think about something like having the four
     parliamentary seats (0.6) D'you think that's an anachron↑ism (0.4) or
     something that should be continued. (1.0) The four Maori seats,
R: Well if New Zealand is an equal- (0.4) is s'posed to be (0.2) equal rights for
     everybody (0.2) it's wrong!
I: Yeah
R: A:nd why: <u>shou:ld</u> (1.0) ya'know I mean a <u>Maori</u> can stand from- stand for
     [(0.4) any other seat
I: [°Mm mhm° (1.0)
R: It's just that the Pakehas can't stand for those four seats
I: Yes
R: And that is not fair
I: °Mm mhm° (1.0)
R: And [that's not right
I: [°Mm mhm°
I: °Mm mhm° (1.0) °Right° (1.6) Why do you think there's such a gap in
     educational achievement between Moari and Pakeha in schools particularly
     seventh form sixth form and higher ya'know (0.2) university education (2.0)
R: I think it goes back to the home life (1.4) A lot of it
I: °Mm mhm°
R: U::hm (2.0) if the fact that especially with (2.0) ( ) with the Islanders (1.4)
     They're just not really interested.
I: Mm mhm
R: All the Islanders in their own Islands, basically they're brought up to work
     on the plantation.
I: Yes (0.4) [°mm mhm°
R: [U::hm they come over he:re, we haven't got them he:re, (0.6)
     They're <u>not</u> really interested

I: Yes

R: U:hm (2.0) yeah y'know you just- You look at the sort of the parents an' you
     look at the kids the parents aren't interested.

I: Mm mhm

R: An' they're not prepared to sit down every night while their little child- her
     little child does the school chapter an' sit an' read'em a story

I: Yes

R: Or sit an' pla:y with it They'll jus ya'know (0.4) send it to bed

I: °Mm mhm° (0.6)

R: eventually. Ya'know or it'll jus- (.) falls down and goes to sleep when it's
     tired

I: Yes (0.4) yeah

R: A:nd (0.6) so they get- they get no: encouragement from their parents to do
     ↑well

I: Mm mhm (1.2)

R: And quite frankly if you don't push a kid he's not gonna do anything

I: Yes (0.4) yes

R: So there's no harm in pushing them (.) it's for their [own good

I: [(yes)

I: [Mm mhm

R: [But they don't (1.0)

I: Do you think having say the Maori language in schools might- might help
     (or you're uhm) (1.4) say the Mary- Maori language taught in primary
     schools to both Pakeha and Maori children

R: I don't really see the point in it (1.6)

R: U:hm (2.2) It's okay yeah they can have it if it's something that- if the kids
     wanna learn it they can learn it.

I: [Yes

R: [But if they don't wanna learn it they don't have to

I: Mm mhm

R: U::hm (2.2) it cou- I can see- could see it causing di↑vision

I: Mm mhm (1.0)

R: Because there's a lot of parents that would turn'roun ya'know (1.0) "You
     will not require the kids to learn it"

I: °Mm [mhm°

R: [(I mean) Uhm (1.4) if- ya'know like fer instance they're gonna have
     to sacrifice something else

I: Yes (0.6)

R: An' aw'right they'd probly sacrifice English, well I'm sorry I'd see why they
     should.

I: Yeahm [mm mhm

R: [Because English is important because it's the language of the
     country

I: Mm mhm

R: An' if you can't speak an' write properly

I: Yeah

R: You're not gonna get anywhere.
I: Yeah
R: You've got to be able to sit an' write letters and ↑talk
I: [°Mm mhm°
R: [and hold discussions with people
I: Mm mhm
R: An' if you can't do that you might as well forget it
I: Mm mhm (1.6)
I: Right so you- (1.0) °mmm° What do you think about the so-called positive
    discrimination measures. (0.6) U:hm say keeping a quota of places at
    Medical Schools fo:r a Maori student (0.6) and bursary- (0.2) special
    bursaries and financing=
R: =Why? It's an equal country. It's s'posed to be an equal country
    [Why should they have a right?
I: [°Yeah°
I: °Mm mhm°
R: to there being (0.4) ten places that would be just competed against?
I: Yes
R: Does it- (0.6) The only- Aw'right <the only thing would be then that'um>
    (0.6) does that mean that the other- out of a hundred places does that mean
    the other ninety places are just for whites?
I: [Yeah
R: [It won't be
I: Mm mhm
R: It'll be the:y will be able to apply: for a:ll one [hundred positions
I: [Mm
I: Yes
R: But ten will be guaranteed for Maoris If there's (0.4) only eighty good white
    one- white people
I: Ye:s
R: that means they'll have twenty there
I: Mm mhm (1.0)
R: But the whites will only be able to apply for ninety of the places
I: Yeah
R: So that's where you run into problems. They want- they want t- to be
    guaranteed something
I: Mm mhm
R: Plus they wanna have a free shot at everything else as well
I: Yeah (0.4) so it's undemocratic really
R: Yeah (0.4) [you're giving them two chances where everybody
I: [°Yeah°
R: else has got [one
I: [One mm mhm (0.6)
R: Or they haven't even got one because it's been cut down
I: Yes
R: They've got point eight of the chance where the Maoris have got (3.2)

I: Oh well [wh(h)at ev(h)er

R: [They've <u>double</u> They've [got <u>more</u>

I: [Yeah Yeah (1.0) So do you thi- do you think there's any racial prejudice in New Zealand? (0.6)

R: Yes a lot. (0.2) But [I think- (0.2) I think you- (0.2) they ask for it

I: [°Mm mhm°

I: °Yeah°

R: Now you've got (0.4) Billy T. James taking off the Maoris yeah that's what Maoris are like unforturnately

I: Yes (0.4) yeah

R: A:n ch- (1.0) There are some who can laugh at themselves

I: Mm mhm

R: and there are some- these two guys that <u>I</u> know, they- one's a Samoan an' one's a Maori, an' they're re::ally nice guys

I: Yeah (0.4) [mm mhm

R: [Ya'know he's- whenever they're out they're always clean they're tidy

I: Mm mhm

R: well-presented [well-dressed, they- ya'know they've got ↑<u>bra:ins</u>

I: [Mm mhm

I: Mm mhm (0.4)

R: If the:y can do ↑it (.) so can the others.

I: Yeah (0.6)

R: It's just that they want to

I: So there's a sort of a- it's a reacting to reality then (0.4) the racial prejudice

R: Mhm the:y either fit in or they don't fit in

I: Yeah (1.0)

R: An' the easy way is not to fit- Well (1.0) for some's not to fit in

I: Yeah

R: To go on the dole it's easy money They got all day to laze round an' do nothing

I: Yeah (0.6) Do you think there's sort of discrimination for getting jobs? That if you have a Maori candidate an' (0.8) ah a white candidate that (0.4) preference would be given to the white candidate by some people? (0.6)

R: Ye:s (0.2) There would- Yes there would be.

I: °Yeah°

R: But then quite often- (1.0) if you had a Maori candidate who was as <u>good</u> ([.) or <u>better</u> [I would say they would <u>get</u> the job

I: [Yeah   [°Mm mhm°

I: °Mm mhm° (0.6)

R: It's <u>normal</u>ly that- Okay <u>that</u> argument gets put in that Maoris never get the jobs okay but you look .hh when they turn up for an interview

I: Yes

R: <u>What's</u> he wearing <u>how's</u> he sitting

I: Yeah

R: How's he talking >ya'know what I mean< an' there's no point in having a receptionist that picks up a phone "Yeah g'day 'ow are ya" ((strong New Zealand accent))

I: Ye:s (0.4) [mm mhm

R: [I mean they want someone that is- (0.4) that is gonna put their clients at ea:se

I: Right (.) [Mm mhm

R: [You don't wanna shop a- a shop assistant who's smelly

I: [Yes

R: [who's got un-dirty unkept hair [an' tattoos all over your

I: [Mm mhm

R: arms [an' fingers all that sort of thing

I: [Yeah

I: Mm mhm

R: Because people are not gonna feel- (0.2) they're not gonna- (0.4) wanna buy things from people like that

I: Right (.) mm mhm (1.2) So sometimes the bias is justified really (0.4) yeah

R: Mhm. (1.2)

I: Do you feel positive about'a:: or optimistic about the future? (.) of race relations in this country or do think we're gonna see race riots and (0.4) difficulties (0.6) that affect- as in say America

R: Phhhh.

I: in the: (0.4) sixties? (8.0)

R: U:hm (1.0) I don't know. Sometimes yes an' sometimes no.

I: Mm mhm (1.2)

R: They're gonna ha- you're gonna ha- they're gonna have problems with gangs

I: °Mm mhm° (0.6)

R: But (0.4) that is jus because they've got nothing better to do.

I: Mm mhm (0.8)

R: And they're not gonna do anything. They're not gonna- they don't wanna do anything.

I: Mm mhm (1.0)

R: More than l(h)ike↑ly A lot of'em come he:re (0.4) because it's easy money, they can live off the ↑dole

I: °Mm mhm°

R: They can (0.4) rent a state house

I: °Mm [mhm°

R: [Whereas in the Islands they've gotta ↑work

I: [Yes

R: [Ya'know they can come here an' don't have to work.

I: °Mm mhm° (1.0)

R: U:hm (3.4) they can bring all their friends over an' charge them (some) rent for houses (or something like- like that)

I: °Mm mhm°

R: An' where does all the money go.

I: Yes

R: Back to the Islands

I: Yeah (1.2) °Mm mhm° (0.6)

R: U:hm (2.2) <u>Ye:s</u> I could <u>see</u> problems (0.6) if they did-=<u>if</u> (0.6) they do all get fired up it would be a frightening force

I: Yes (0.6)

R: There'd be no other choi- ya'know I don't know what you'd do with them.

I: Yeah (0.4) [mm mhm

R: [Cause there's so many mixed marriages an' it would be the ones in the mixed marriages that would suffer

I: Yes

R: A lot of the time because they'd be <u>trapped</u>

I: Yeah

R: They'd be <u>caught</u> into- between two cultures

I: Mm mhm (1.0)

R: So I don't know what they're gonna do. .

I: Yeah

R: (I mean) (2.6)

I: So you think they could- (.) it could come to violence?

R: It <u>could</u> come to violence [yes

I: [Yeah (0.6)

R: I mean well it's not safe at this- It's not safe in Otara (right/at night) now

I: Yeah

R: You- you have to- you've just got to drive through there an' look at the shops

I: Ye:s (0.4) °mm mhm°

R: U:hm hhh. why: <u>do:</u> the kids go through there an' break all the windows?

I: Mm mhm

R: They jus wanna <u>take</u> something that's not ↑<u>theirs</u>

I: Yes

R: basically

I: Mm mhm

R: They <u>don't</u> wanna save up for it [They <u>don't</u> wanna go an' get

I: [Mm mhm

R: a job an' <u>buy</u> it

I: Yes

R: They jus wanna <u>take</u> it

I: Mm mhm (0.4)

R: But then that comes down- (0.4) i:n the Ma:ori culture

I: °Mm mhm°

R: (People think that uh) "Well <u>every</u>thing belongs to <u>every</u>body"

I: [Yes

R: [They're jus <u>bor</u>rowing it

I: °Mm mhm°

R: So you can turn around an' ask ( ) when a Maori (.) <u>takes</u> something "Why did you <u>take</u> it" "I was jus <u>bor</u>rowin' it"

I: Ye:s (0.4) yeah (0.6)

R: "He wasn't <u>using</u> it so I <u>bor</u>rowed it" (0.6)

I: Yes so the problem is different- diff- different cultural definitions of theft
R: (°That[’s right/of theft°)
I: [°that Maoris have mm mhm°
R: <u>What</u> do you do about it? Well I mean you <u>can’t</u> let’em take this out on the
     <u>street</u> (0.4) cause they’d <u>do</u> it all the ↑<u>time</u>
I: Yeah (0.4) mm mhm
R: <u>But</u> (1.0) <u>that’s</u> how you got- you- you <u>can’t</u> really e:du:ca:te them <u>whi:le</u>
     there are <u>people</u> (1.2) while you’ve got <u>people</u> that are going on about
     (<u>Maoritanga</u>)
I: Yes (0.4) mm mhm
R: And i- it <u>should</u> be more into the <u>f:ront</u> Okay yes it probly <u>should</u> but you’ve
     still got to educate the people that they live in a <u>white</u> society now
I: Yes (0.4) mm mhm (2.0)
I: All right (1.0) Okay ↑uhm (1.4) do you think New Zealand’s a class society
     in the sense that (0.4) the kind of schools that you go to a:nd’em the suburb
     you’re bo:rn in (1.0) influence the kind of jobs you get or not (8.2)
R: tsk (.) There’s a lot of <u>stigma</u>
[. . .]

((Approximately 6 second gap in recording))
     (2.2)
R: It does- You <u>do</u>. Depending on where you <u>do</u> live does to a degree depend
     on how far you can <u>go</u>
I: Yeah
R: But <u>not</u> comple<u>tely</u>.
I: [Mm mhm
R: [Like there are kids from Re<u>muera</u> who’ve dropped out
I: Yes
R: That’ve- ya’know (1.4) °just don’t [(learn/read/earn) anymore°
I: [°Mm mhm°
I: Mm mhm
R: Just (learn/earn) e<u>nough</u>
I: Yeah
R: Whereas you’ve got kids in <u>O</u>tara
I: °Mm mhm° (0.6)
R: That’ll work their <u>butts</u> off an’ do really <u>well</u>
I: Ye:s (.) [So it’s fairly <u>mo</u>bile
R: [It’s very-
I: It depends on <u>what</u>? The sort of in<u>herent po</u>tential of the <u>child</u>
     [really   [yeah
R: [Yeah and it- [it goes back to the <u>parents</u>
I: Yeah (0.4) [°mm mhm°
R: [If the parents are prepared to sit down with their kids an’ (0.4)
     help the kids an’ be [interested
I: [Mm mhm
I: Ye:s

R: The kids would go on but- (0.6) wherever you are, if the parents don't
    wanna ↑know
I: Mm mhm
R: then sooner or later the kid's gonna take off "No I'm not gonna have it."
    (they're not asking you-) you're not asking- the parents aren't asking the kid
    "How's it going in school? What's happening."
I: Yeah
R: So the kid's not telling anyone

NEW ZEALAND INTERVIEW 44

I: U:hm (0.4) The first set of questions are actually very (0.6) general ones
     (0.4) and people find them quite d(h)ifficult as a result I think. (0.6) U:hm
     (1.2) now first of all you're- (.) one of those people that (.) sort of feels a
     bo:nd (.) still with Britain so that ah (0.4) if you went to Britain (0.6) you'd
     have a sense of coming ↑home Do you feel that New Zealand's still a very
     British (0.4) country or do you think that that's (0.4) over and done with
     now

R: No I think it ↑i:↓s (.) u:hm (2.0) uhm most- (1.6) yes I- I- I would we're
     fourth an' fifth generation New Zealander (0.6) uhm but (0.6) we know
     where our beginnings are >ya'know in Eng[land< so uhm (0.4) ye:s

I: [Mm mhm yes

R: [ya'know

I: [And so it's a meaning[ful

R: [I'd like to go- [yes I'd like to [go an'

I: [Yeah   [yeah

R: find (1.2) [where they are

I: [(   )

I: Yes

R: One day [((laughs))

I: [((laughs)) yeah yes (1.0) (Would you-/What do you-) (.) One
     thing that's been happening in the six years I've been away is a sort of
     closer union with Australia economically. (0.6) How far do you think
     that should go, Do you think perhaps that we should go (0.6) the whole
     way an' seek a political union (1.0) with Australia and become one
     big

R: No I don't think so [no

I: [No [yeah

R: [Right

I: That would be a sort of loss of identity,

R: I think so (.) [yes definitely

I: [(   )

I: Yeah

R: Right uhm (1.2) An' I think there's a- there's a rivalry always there between
     Australia and New Zealand

I: Y(h)es [.hhh yeah

R: [ya'know that uhm thad be ↑lost

I: Yes

R: An' I- I [wou- I think that's: good for competition

I: [Yeah

I: Yeah

R: Really

I: Right (1.2) ↑Uhm I mean because overseas people see: (0.2) Australia and
     New Zealand as very interchangeable but of course to a New Zealander it's
     like the Canadian American difference (1.2) for a New Zealander there's a
     great (1.0) you know we're quite separate from Australia (0.4)
     [I mean we like to think that we are

R: [Mm mhm
?: Yes
R: Yes
I: Yeah (1.0) ↑Uhm (0.8) what are the things that you: value about living in
   New Zealand (0.6) things that (0.8) really appeal to you about life here or
   (1.0) that you see as the most positive aspects
R: Well we're not poo:r, none of us are
I: Yes
R: A:[nd
I: [Mm mhm (0.6)
R: You might think "O:h that's okay for her she's on a farm" but we're not I
   mean we're only employed
I: Mm mhm
R: Ya'know (0.2) u:hm (0.4) but there's no nee:d for anyone in New Zealand
   (0.6) to be ↑poo:↓r
I: Mm mhm (0.8)
R: A::nd (0.4) there's still plenty of ro:om (0.4) in New Zealand ya'know (0.2)
   and (.) if you want to live in the country you ca:n (0.4) even if that means
   going and renting a [place you can do it
I: [°Mm mhm°
I: Yes (0.2) yeah
R: A:nd (4.0) [I don't think we're- we're at it- we're not-(0.2)
I: [( )
R: uhm spoilt (2.0) in the sense I- as I think American's are
I: Y(h)eah
R: U:hm (0.6)
I: What too much material
R: Ye:as
I: goods
I: Yeah
R: All right [then there's always- you- (1.0) ehm your extremes
I: [Yeah
R: [I suppose
I: [Yeah
R: There are a few but- but basically the- (0.6) the average New Zealander is
   (1.8) is [ya'know unspoiled
I: [Yeah
I: Yes ye[ah
R: [I like to think that
I: Yes
R: Perhaps I'm wrong
I: Oh no I(h) [th(h)ink that's quite right Yeah
R: [((laughs))
I: ↑.hh[h yeah
R: [Uhm (2.0) O::h (3.0) I think at the moment we're still a fairly happy
   country
I: Mm mhm

R: and there- there are undertones of- of racial (1.0) uhm disharmony which
   could come (1.0) to- out here you can see that they could possibly come to
   feeling (what way) (.) the [government and other (1.2) people act=
I: [Mm mhm
R: But at the moment I think really we're- we're a rea:sonably happy country
I: Yes (0.4) yes Mmm (1.0) Has anything- what are the things which ehm
   (0.6) you see as negative an' which irritate you (.) so that if you were (0.4) a
   benevolent dictator (0.2) things that you'd try and change (5.0)
I: If any I mean th[ere may be nothing
R: [Well that's it you see I mean I'm a- (0.8) uhm (2.2) °a::h
   let's see° What happens in the outside world doesn't always
   [really concern me I mean [I'm happy
I: [°Yes°   [°Mm mhm°
R: with- (0.6) with my lot [and what's around me [and (2.0) a::h
I: [Yes   [Right
R: you can see things are wrong I mean every now and then you get stirred up
   enough to feel that ya' [know well I'd like to go out an' shoot (Holmes)
I: [Yeah
I: ((laughs)) [yes
R: [He's uhm- [ya'know he- all he's [doing is just
I: [Yes   [Yeah
R: upsetting the country (0.2) And (1.0) But- (3.0)
I: Right
R: Obviously the economic situation is bad and unem[ployment's
I: [Mm mhm
R: bad but (0.6) I think relatively speaking everywhere in the world is
   (a:lso:/out of sight/so)
I: Yes (0.6)
R: we are (0.6) you know not too bad compared with everywhere else
I: Yes certainly with Britain (0.6) for sure [yeah
R: [Yes
R: But of [course everyone- A- a- people in New Zealand seem to
I: [Yeah
R: think "Oh that's dreadful I mean [it's New Zealand it
I: [Ye(h)ah
R: shouldn't be like that"
I: Yes (0.2) you think we've got too use[d to sort of periods of full
   employment and
R: Y[es
I: [prosperity [and we're sort of (.) learning a new way of
R: [Mmm
I: coping with a (0.2) modern life really
R: [Yes
I: [Yeah (0.4) yeah (1.4) ↑U:hm (1.6) do you think e:h (0.4) Well who are the
   people that you admire (0.2) most or respect most, (1.0) It's a d(h)ifficult
   qu(h)estion because you- it's difficult to think of people on the
   [spur of the moment

R: [Do you mean uhm (0.2) [family
I: [In public life [or
R: [Or public life?
I: Yes yeah Who- who are the people that (0.4) you'd like say your children to
    copy or emulate (1.2) that really you think a very positive (0.2) fo:rce in
    [New Zealand
R: [Well I thought Rob Muldoon was
I: Yes
R: Uhm [all right I don't want (0.2) a son growing up who has to
I: [°Yeah°
R: be a Rob Muldoon I think [uhm (0.8) it takes an extraordinary
I: [Mm mhm
R: person to be him (0.2) but u:hm (0.6) I am a Rob Muldoon fan
I: Yes yeah (0.2)
R: So [uhm
I: [Mmm (1.0) That his (0.2) qualities of courage you think or
R: Ye:s
I: Yeah
R: A::nd (2.0) (h)anyone blames him for everything (0.2) so he must have
    been a fantastic man
I: ((extended laugh))
R: to have been able to do [all these wicked things
I: [Yes
I: Y(h)ea [((laugh))
R: [((laugh))
I: O:h y(h)eah ((laugh))
R: Uhm on the face of such adversity
I: [Y(h)eah ↑.hhh yeah
R: [U::hm
R: A::hh. (0.4)
I: So you think there's too much of a backlash against him at the moment now
    that eve[rybody's sort of leaping on the bandwagon
R: [Mmmmm
I: [to sort of criticize him yeah
R: [Oh of course Oh definitely there is at the [moment [yes I mean
I: [((laugh))[Yes
R: every[thing the government (.) do at the moment they're sayin
I: [Right
R: ["Oh (.) [we're doing far better than (.) Rob Muldoon's government
I: [Yes   [((laughs))
I: Yes (0.2) [yes
R: [An'- and I think the media an- an' everyone say that- kept on
    promoting him as (.) Ros Mul- Rob Muldoon's government 'til everyone
    was convinced it only Rob Muldoon who was doing it
I: Who was to blame
R: [Mmmm
I: [Right (.) yeah

R: I think in years to come that- (0.6) ya'know if uhm (0.4) in history eh he
    will be (0.4) n- known as a great man
I: Yeah yeah
R: (take time from his- i'ts g(h)onna take) (.) [(Probably take years yeah)
I: [ten years or so yes yeah
[. . .]
I: What do you think about the- the- the new breed of women politicians
    which have been emerging in the last uh
R: Like Annie Hercus
I: Ye:s and [(0.4) further back Marilyn Waring
R: [((throat clear/little cough)) (1.0) U:hm all right (1.0) they-
    they've got their opinions a:nd (0.6) but I think they went too fa:r
I: Mm mhm
R: and (1.2) because I believe that (0.6) u:hm any woman is as liberated
    [if she wants to be
I: [Mm mhm
I: Yes [yeah
R: [There are a lot of women who don't want to be that-
    [they're quite happy being (.) [dominated
I: [Yeah   [(Right)
I: Yes (.) [yeah
R: [and (0.6) an' if a woman re:ally wants to get to the top in something
    (.) you can ↑do it
I: Yes (0.4) yeah
[. . .]
R: but No:: I think if you want to([.) the opportunities are [there
I: [You can   [Yes
I: [yeah
R: [it just needs to take them
I: Right (0.4) yeah
R: A:nd (1.0)
I: And so it's no use sort of really blaming ah other pe- men [for ah
R: [Not in New
    Zealand [no
I: [Yeah (0.8) Yeah (0.6)
R: Uhm (1.4)
I: Yes (0.4) I mean because ehm (2.2) what do- I mean there- One of the old
    images about New Zealand men used to be the sort of rugby racing and
    beer (0.2) image ya'know very m[uch
R: [Mhm
R: I think [there's probably still (0.4) yes [some like that
I: [(   )   [Yeah
I: Yeah
R: But u::h[m
I: [Things are changing now
R: I think [so
I: [(Right) [Mm mhm

R: [I mean (0.6) you find that men and women i- it's uhm (0.4) alo- a lot of partnerships

I: Yes

R: And the wue- women are [doing as much as the men and the men

I: [(Right)

R: uhm (0.6) ya'know appreciate ↑that

I: Yes (0.4) yeah

R: U:hm (1.2) No maybe it was once but then (.) there again the women (1.0) it was their fault because (1.0) really all they did was stay at home an- an' have children

I: Yes

R: They had the big families

I: Yeah

R: Now when you only just have two or three an' you've got more time to get out an' help the men

I: Yes

R: uhm they realize (0.4) [I mean ya'know they're not stupid

I: [Right

I: [((laughs)).hhh yes

R: [((laughs))

R: I think it's up to women in most cases

I: to [yeah

R: [(Ya'know)

I: Do you think New Zealand is sort of a class society in the sense that there's barriers (0.6) to kids uhm achieving depending on the suburbs they're born in an' the schools they go to an' (0.8) those sort of things or do you think we have got equal opportunity really (0.8) so that any kid can wou- (.) fulfill his potential. (5.0)

R: U:hm (2.4) we:ll a:hm (0.4) yes I thi:nk so: u:hm (2.0) I'm thinking really of kids that come from Flaxmere uhm

I: Yes (1.6)

R: You hear a lot about (1.0) well e:ve:n just reading sort of some things that happen in the newspaper you think "(Oh I hate all Flaxmere kids)" (0.4) [must be (.) shocking

I: [Hhh.
  Yes [.hh

R: [Uhm an' I sorta- (0.4) that's making me wo:nder (0.2) it's- if they have got the same opportunity (0.4) hearing that

I: °Mm mhm° (1.0)

R: if I consider that like that perhaps other people consider it as a bit of a stigma

I: Right [yeah

R: [A:nd (3.0) I don't know I- I [ho:pe we still (0.6) well

I: [Yeah

R: everyone has an opportunity

I: Yes

R: I mean (2.0) the parents have still got an opportunity to send those children to different schools

I: [Right (0.4) yeah
R: [I mean they're still able to do that in New Zealand
I: Yes (0.4) yes (0.6) yeah
R: U:hm (2.0)
I: It's not as bad as somewhere like Britain whe:re (1.2) it tends to be (0.2) a
     fai:rly rigid
R: Ye:s
I: class system so if you're born into one aspect of that class (0.2) then it's
     quite difficult to move out of [it
R: [Mhmm
I: U:hm (0.8)
R: No well ya'see I mean I know a lot of children that are sent to [school name]
     I think [fo:r that reason (.) [the parents are worried
I: [Yes!   [Yeah
I: [Yeah
R: [U:hm (1.4)
I: Mm mhm
R: >So that< the opportunities are there (3.0)
I: All ri:ght (0.6) U:hm (0.6) one of the things that I:- (.) I'm interested in is
     the: (0.6) Springbok tou:r of nineteen eighty one because that seemed (0.6)
     a very profou:nd (0.2) sort of event for New Zealand a very unprecedented
     event
R: Mm mhm.
I: A:nd (0.8) I know it's a long time ago n(h)ow .hh can (0.2) is it something
     that you felt strongly about at the time=can you remember back to what
     you thought (0.6) during that period=did you think that'a (0.4) the teams
     should have come (0.4) o:r
R: Yes I did (0.2) I felt the teams should've come (0.2) u:hm (4.0) I think
     u::hm (0.6) the news media (2.0) u:hm made the most of it (0.4) an'
     perhaps stirred up a lot
I: Mm mhm
R: U:hm because- (1.8) it was mainly the extre:me grou:ps which took over
I: Yes (0.4) yeah
R: Uhm and stirred people [up an'- and groups like that ca:n
I: [(Right) Mm mhm (0.8)
R: They can agitate normal people who- who really wouldn't (1.2) probably
     even think much about it
I: Right [yeah (.) yeah
R: [into doing things that they wouldn't normally do (0.2)
I: [Yes
R: [A:nd (.) ya'know the innocent people and they're usually the ones that get
     caught in the- ya'know ([1.2) up in it
I: [Mmmm
R: U:hm (3.0) ya'know sport is- (.) is something where we should be able to
     make contact with- (.) with everyone (1.2) A::nd (3.0)
I: So that really [it's sort of   ]building bridges
R: [I think they should-]
I: [in a way yeah

R: [Ye::s I- I still think they should have been able to come
I: Yes
R: because I mean (2.0) why do they pick on tha:t ya'know they ca- I mean
    South African people come for so many other [things
I: [Yeahhhh. .hhh well trade
    a[n' (   )
R: [And that's why I think it really was something that was (0.4) orchestrated
    between (1.2) uhm the extre:me groups
I: Yes [(yeah)
R: [And the media
I: Yeah (1.0) And makes- (0.4) sort of whip people up [into a
R: [Yes into a frenzy
    over it [I mean if you (0.4) you <u>can</u> do that [I mean ya'know
I: [Yeah   [Yahhh. Ye(h)s
R: the media's a- [a powerful thing
I: [People are very suggestible aren't [they
R: [Yes
    they [are I mean w(h)ell how el- else did- did Hitler
I: [Yeah
I: Yes
R: u:hm [(0.8) ever do what he did
I: [Yeah
I: Yes! (0.6) That's right yes (2.0) Yeah (0.8)
[. . .]
I: .hh What did you think of the police's handling of the whole thing (0.6) I
    mean they're in a bit of a (0.8) invidious position (an' as someone was
    telling) the analogy that people were (   ) for meat in a sandwich
    you know between [(0.6) yeah
R: [Well that- Yes u:hm (1.0) I think that they did the
    best that they could (1.0) a:nd with it being a first time (0.2) sort of
    [thing like [that
I: [Yes   [yeah (1.0)
R: A::nd (1.2) no doubt they've learnt a lot
I: Ye:s (1.0)
R: [And they made mistakes and (2.0) I guess that's natural on a
I: [Yeah
R: first- a first thing
I: Yes
R: like that
I: Yeah (1.2) It was very surprising in Britain to see ah (0.6) ya'know because
    for us it really came out of the blue because we hadn't any build up or
    anything and then we just saw New <u>Zealand</u> was suddenly on the television
    .hh [an' normally yo(h)u don't hear anything yeah
R: [with riots
R: Yes
I: Yeah and it all seemed very unexpected and it jus (0.6) was very sort of
    surprising
R: Ye[::s

I: [Did it seem that way to you or did you kind of see it coming (0.2) over
       the months (0.4) [beforehand
R: [It <u>did</u> >sort of< build up=I'll just shut th[at door
I: [Yes (1.0)
R: U:hm (1.0) I guess ((DOOR SLAM)) yes it did build up but then when you
       (.) saw it on T.V. (1.0) u:hm (0.4) ya'know what was really happening
I: Yes
R: U:hmm (0.4) yes you couldn't really believe that they were New Zealanders
I: (([laugh)) yes
R: [behaving like that
I: Yeah
R: °But° (0.6)
R: I [think I guess we've all got it in us haven't we (0.2)
I: [Mm
I: I suppose so yes (1.0) Mmm so u:hm yeah (1.4) So what do you feel for it
       (0.6) I mean some people I've talked to have said yes they- they think that
       Springbok should <u>co:me</u> (0.4) but because of the effect on the country was
       so <u>bad</u> that ehm (0.6) future tours shouldn't be considered. (0.6) Do you
       feel that or do you feel that the principle was- (0.2) [was more important
R: [I think they should still
       come. This- this- this is the thing uhm (1.4) <why: is it that the tour is
       singled out?>
I: Yes (0.4) Mm [mhm
R: [U:hmm and other things are- they're let come=the tennis
       teams Well there's jus' hundreds of things
I: Yes
R: that come.
I: Yeah
R: A::nd (1.2) I really think that ru- ya'know rugby is being <u>used</u>
I: Yeah (0.2) [yeah
R: [And why give way to a minority?
I: Right (0.4) [yeah
R: [U:hm (0.2) all right that- that's being (1.0) pretty one-eyed
       u::hm (1.0) because no doubt people'll get hurt u:hm (2.4) But- (2.0) I
       guess that that's the (price of everything/principle of the thing)
I: Right (.) ye:ah (.) It really became a sort of law and order issue didn't it?
R: Ye::s
I: [Yeah
R: [Yes u:hm (1.4) °well our [whole- whole law and order system
I: [°Mhm°
R: should be (0.4) done over anyway but°
I: Yeah? Like- (0.4) is that something (0.4) controvers- Well (.) what I wanted
       to ask about next was uhm (1.0) whether you saw New Zealand as a more
       violent society generally in terms of assault and crime
R: It is.
I: and so on [yeah
R: [at the moment ye:s
       [u:hm mainly because I think that (1.0) the- the laws are

I: [Yeah
R: just (1.0) they're not (1.0) being used to their fullest to [start with
I: [Yeah
I: Mm mhm
R: U::hm (4.0) it's- it's a breakdown isn't it? The police don't seem to able to
     do their jo:b
I: Yes
R: U:hm they can catch the criminal (0.4) but they bring him to court (0.2)
     the judges don't seem to (2.0) hhh. impo::se the- (1.0) hhh. the seve:re
     (0.2) penalties that they <u>shou:ld</u>
I: Yeah
R: U:hm (1.4) there's a breakdown some[where
I: [(yes)
I: Yeah
R: And it's definitely to do with our (0.4) la::w.
I: Yes! (0.6) yeah. (0.4) Do you think ehm (1.0) that bringing b- ya'know
     things like (0.2) capital punishment should be reconsidered (0.2)
     [as a deterrent [yeah
R: [I do   [Yeah I'm afraid I do
I: Yeah
[. . .]
I: Right (1.2) yes so you'd e::hm (0.4) there's a case then for bringing back
     (0.6)
R: I think [so u::hm
I: [Yeah (Yeah I'm sure) (1.2)
R: But loo:k at what ra:pists are do:ing I mean we didn't he:ar of ra:pists
     [even a fe:w years ago
I: [Yeah
I: That's right (0.2) yeah
R: And now every weekend- I'd cut their ([0.4) whats its off
I: [((laughs))
R: I mean I think that's <u>dre::ad↑ful</u>
I: Yea:s (0.6)
R: And to think that this bloke Pa:lmer has actually let two: rapists out of
     [prison
I: [O::h the chap- the: [I don't remember his name
R: [Is it Palmer?
I: That's right [yes
R: [yes (1.0)
R: That- (0.4) he is- is overri:ding (0.4) [the la:ws that the
I: [Yes
R: government has set do:wn.
I: Yes (0.4) yeah
R: There must be hundreds of people in prison who are- who are
     [dy:ing (0.2) of cancer or of some different disease
I: [Right (0.4) yeah
I: Heart disease [or whatever
R: [Eh yes

I: Yeah [yeah
R: [Anything
I: Yes
R: And to <u>let</u> two rapists- and one was a <u>third</u> time convicted
I: O::h that's right ([.) yeah
R: [That- that's shocking I mean that's just ah making it a
     real mockery
I: Yes (0.4) yeah
R: U:hm (0.4) ya'know I feel like going out an' shooting ↑hi:m
I: ((laughs)) yeah
R: I mean it makes you wonder <u>if</u> he's got any <u>daugh</u>ters
I: Yes (0.2) [what if that's [right
R: [or   [what- would he care if wife was raped?
I: Yeah (0.4) really
R: Or do they not- (.) believe that it- it I:s an eno:rmity to- to
I: Right
R: to- (.) to a woman to be raped?
I: Yes that's right I mean it- to me it must be one of the worst things that can
     ever happen to a- (0.4) to you I imagi[ne yeah   [yeah
R: [It <u>must</u> be [<u>surely</u> U:hm (0.2)
I: Mm mhm (0.4) Particularly uh ya'know if it's a sort of (0.4) some of these
     awful gang rapes [and that kind of thing which
R: [Ye::s
I: are just ehm (0.4) yeah (1.0)
[. . .]
R: A:nd (1.2) I'm not afraid but I take precautions.
I: Ye:s right [it's sensible isn't it [Mm mhm
R: [Ya'know   [I mean some people wouldn't bother-
     wouldn't go to work at night I know [that
I: [Yeah
R: And they wouldn't stay in the house on their own but
I: Yeah
R: I believe [you can't live like that
I: [Yeah
I: That's right I mean it's like giving in in a way
[. . .]
I: >One of the-< The other thing that (.) I'm interested is the (0.4)
     multiculturalism and (0.6) what people think about sort of race relations
     (0.4) scene. >Sort of< There's been quite a change in that over the six
     years I've been away, There's a much greater emphasis now on ehm Maori
     culture and the use of the Maori language (1.0) an' so on. (0.6) Do you
     think in general that's been (0.4) uh constructive or (1.4) what do you feel
     about the way things are going (0.2) on that front? (2.0)
R: I think they'll end up having Maori w:ars if they carry on
     the way [they have I mean no it'll be a Pakeha war
I: [((laugh))
I: Yes

R: U::hm (1.6) they're ma:king New Zealand a racist cu- country uhm but
    ya'know you usually feel (.) think that racism is uhm (1.4) putting th-
    putting ([.) the darker people down
I: [Yes
R: [but really they're doing it (.) the other way around
I: [( )
I: A sort of [reverse [racism
R: [I feel   [yes
I: Yeah
R: U:hm (1.4) everything (0.6) seems to be to help (0.2) the Maori
    people, (1.0) a::nd ya'know (0.4) I think (1.4) at the moment sort of
    (0.6) the Europeans are sort of (0.4) They're just sort of watching
    [and putting up with it
I: [Yeah
I: Yeah
R: But (.) they'll only go so fa:r
I: Right yeah
R: U:hm (1.0) tsk (1.0) ya'know we- we've got (.) Maori friends out he:re uhm
    who we have into the house so yu- ya'know they're friends (0.6) U:hm (2.0)
    but when things happen an' they- they suddenly say "Oh they're going to
    make (.) M- Maori language compulsory"
I: Yeah (.) yeah
R: U:hm (0.4) but that is an- antagonizing
I: Yeah
R: And- (1.4) the Maori friends that we::'ve got (1.0) they don't agree with it
I: Yes (.) yeah
R: U::hm (0.2) okay yu- you've got extremists th[ere too
I: [Mm mhm
R: the ones who feel that ya'know that everyone should learn it but u:hm (2.0)
    I think the average Maori sort of perhaps is worried ↑too
I: Yeah So there's a sort of split in the Maori com[munity
R: [Yes (0.6)
I: between the: yeah (.) yeah (2.0) Yes (1.0)
R: An' I- I know that uhm (2.0) you know there is a- a problem in the
    schools here (.) the- the blacks and whites sort of thing a::nd (1.0)
    there's a Maori lady down the corner down here (1.4) an' she's got two
    boys (1.0) well she was thrilled that her boy was going to a class with a lot
    Europeans
I: ((lau[gh)) yes
R: [Because she was worried [uhm that he would get into a class
I: [( )
R: with quite a few Maoris and therefore they'd form a gang
I: Yes ([.) and he'd stop worki[ng yeah
R: [And   [and once they're a gang [then
I: [Yeah
R: they- they (loll it not seem to apply) themselves
I: Yes

R: If they (.) ya'know are not interested- got more interested agitating in the classroom than
I: than working
R: Mmm
I: Yeah (.) Right (.) I know
R: But I- I don't- It makes you wonder sort of the people that make (2.4) these laws and rules Do they know what's really going on
I: ((l[augh))
R: [in the- in the
I: yeah
R: you know the average school and
I: Yeah
R: an' home and everything
I: Probably not
R: No::
I: Yeah (2.0) Yes so there's really (.) ehm (1.4) that there could be sort of racial strife in the future because eh (2.0) sort of tensions have been created [by this [sort of programme.
R: [YES   [Yeah
I: Yeah [yeah
R: [I'm sure there are
I: Yes yeah (1.0) What do you think- there's all this discussion going on at the moment about Waitangi Day and uhm (0.6) ya'know whether (0.4) we should (.) celebrate it at all or celebrate it- in what- what way should we celebrate it and all the rest of it. What do you feel about (.) that (.) that topic? (0.4) Do you feel that that we should ta keep on with Waitangi Day or that we should have some other day for a national holiday (3.2)
R: Well each year there seems to be (1.0) quite a fuss over it and really uhm (0.2) I mean (3.2) it's just another day I mean (.) [ya'know you don't
I: [Yes
R: sort of think "Oh! the Treaty of Wai[tangi Day's today ya'know
I: [((laugh))
I: Yeah
R: and think about how they all got together an' so on I mean you just think "Oh! [It's a holiday on Monday ya'know
I: [It's a holiday ye(h)ah.hhh
I: Yeah
R: I think it's- it's lost it's
I: Yeah (1.0)
R: ya' know to people
I: Yeah one of the big disputes seeems to be over the land and (0.6) that's something again- Maori Land Marches and so on that's happened in the years I've been away↑ Do think there's a case there or (0.4) that really this is just another (0.8) sort of divisive ehm (0.4)issue (2.2)
R: Aw'right at lot of them sold land for very little (0.4) and (0.4) for axes an' (1.4) and whatever (.) wasn't it

I: Yes
R: Blankets (2.2) <u>But</u> (0.4) when (1.0) my: (.) ancestors came here (1.2) and
     (0.4) (an' land) and made up (0.4) uhm (0.4) ya'know just pastoral land
     and then sold it it was sold for very low- little ↑too
I: Yes
R: But you can'[t go back and say "Well I want to be compensated for what-
I: [Ye(h)ah (0.4) yes (1.0)
R: A::nd (1.0) I think you've got to go o::n (0.4)
I: Mm mhm
R: And the Maori likes to forget that they came and (.) ate the Moriori
I: Y(h)eah
R: They- they [put that into the back of their minds.=They seem
I: [Yeah
R: to think that they were the fi:rst here
I: Yes
R: But really (1.2) I wonder if perhaps when we came here we should have
     done what any other (0.6) uhm invading country would do and that's WIPE
     OUT
I: Yes
R: the <u>lot</u>!
I: Yes (1.0)
R: Which is what they did
I: Yeah (0.4) yeah (0.4) So it's really (0.8) in a way it's-
R: It's pa::st hi:story
I: Yeah y[eah
R: [You can't- you can't go back
I: Yeah
R: And the more you go back the more you're antagonizing uhm ↑every↓one
I: Yes
R: You're not- you're not solving the situation
I: Yes
R: I think you ma- you're making (0.6) a worse- a different situ[ation
I: [Mm mhm So
     really we have to sort of work together
R: Yeah
I: [into the future
R: [Yeah
R: [Mmmm
I: [(   ) (1.0) One of the <u>big</u> problems seems to be with ehm sort of
     educational <u>difference</u> because it's very <u>noticeable</u> that at sixth and seventh
     form levels an' in universities that there was very few (.) Maori students
     ([.) left in the classrooms
R: [Yes (1.0)
I: Do you <u>think</u> that uhm (1.2) what do you think can be done about that Do
     you think we should change the school system (0.4) u:hm (0.4) as a result
     or (0.8) uhm is that something that really can't be ah (0.2) solved that way
R: The Maoris who wa::nt to get on and <u>do</u>:: things <u>do</u> it

I: Yeah (1.4)
R: They <u>a:re</u> a lazy ra:ce most of [them.
I: [( ) (1.2)
R: U:hm (1.0) how can you change a- a race that's uhm (0.4) what?
     inheritance uhm
I: Ye(h)ah
R: <u>Re:ally</u>
I: Yes (0.6)
R: But the ones who- who- who want to get on <u>do</u>! Tha- that's
I: Mm mhm
R: wh- (0.4) I mean there's some- some (0.4) terrific statesmen an' and (1.0)
     Maoris who've done ya'know great jo[bs
I: [jobs
I: Ye[ah
R: [U:hm (0.4) there's still a lot of the ones who come through
I: Ye[ah
R: [U:hm (.) so therefore they have got their (1.4) their ones to look up ↑to
I: Yeah
R: A::nd (2.2) I mean what else <u>could</u> be done for them
I: ((laugh))
R: ((laugh))
I: Yeah (1.0) So it's-
R: They have scholars- scholarships and- and things that (.) we European just
     <u>don't</u> have
I: Yeas (0.4) yeah
R: But they have just the same opportunity towards money and jobs an'
     everything that we have so that therefore (0.4) u:hm (1.2) ya'know I think
     they do have a lot of opportunities that- that- that we haven't got and if they
     [can't make the most of them
I: [( ) (0.6) It's really their problem [I spose
R: [Yes
I: Yeah (0.4) yeah (1.2)
R: And perhaps they should help themselves more
I: Yes
R: I mean one another
I: Yeah A lot of people that I've talked to have been eh (0.6) irritated about ah
     positive discrimination a:nd the fact that (there are/their) quota of places for
     Maori students at medical schools [and thing like that Is that something
R: [Mmm
I: that you (0.4) feel strongly a[bout at all
R: [Well I'm not no but tha- ech not as yet
[. . .]
R: therefore [I haven't come across that situation
I: [Yes
R: but yes I could quite easily be I guess
I: Yes

R: U:hm (.) because if they're going to just hold open so many places for
    Maori students they're not getting the best
I: Yes (.) yeah
R: U:hm they should take the best of whoever they are
I: Regardless of [race
R: [Yes
I: Yeah
R: U::hmm (0.4) surely that's the point in anything if you want (.)
    uhm (0.4) good teachers (1.2) you don't just take that bloke because he is a
    Maori uhm (0.4) you want your children educated by the best
I: Yes
R: teachers
I: Yeah
R: If he's a Maori so what (.) [but not because he is a Maori
I: [Yes
I: Yes (2.0) Yeah so- ((throat clear)) (1.2) One of the other things that em
    there's seems to be a lot of discussion now about the four Maori
    parliamentary seats and whether they should (.) continue or not. What-
    what do you feel [about that
R: [Well that there again that's another thing that's
    discrimination I mean .hh okay they've got their four seats now but to
    actually think about (.) uhm (0.4) raising it (0.4)
I: Yes
R: U:hm (1.2) that's wrong!
I: Yes
R: I mean (.) we're not only a Maori European country now, our Polynesian
    uhm intake is something terrific
I: Yeah
R: Uhm we don't see it down here of course but in Auckland well where's their
    representative in parliament?
I: Yes (.) ye[ah
R: [I mean you can get all carried awa:y
I: Y(h)es
R: But if you're going to try and keep to em (0.4) an integrated
I: Yeah
R: society (0.4) they shouldn't have Maori ↑seats
I: Right [yes
R: [When someone like Ben Couch can go ahead
    and become an MP [in his own right
I: [Yes (0.2)
I: Mm mh[m
R: [Those are the sort of Maoris that you want= it's the same with- (.)
    ah the sort of Europeans that you'd want [the ones who-
I: [Right mm mhm
R: who fight for it and- and want it
I: Mm mhm (0.4)

R: U::hm (0.4) I mean there's hundreds of Europeans that you wouldn't (1.2)
you wouldn't want to ehm (0.4) deny (.) well that you want to best

I: Yes (.) right yeahm (0.6) Yes I- I'm going to interview [name of person] t-
tomorrow morning and [I'm going to ask him ([ )

R: [Oh yes   [My dad taught him

I: Really?

R: Mmm

I: ↑O::h

R: He's [father's name]

I: Yeah

R: And he taught him at [school name]

I: O::h [yeah that's interesting

R: [yeah

[. . .]

I: What- what do you think are the em (1.2) the sort of positive aspects of
Maori culture that we should (0.4) take out and adopt an' e:hm

R: WELL I DON'T [THINK WE SHOULD- WE: SHO:ULD take

I: [if any

R: out and adopt any of them.

I: Yes

R: Their- their Maori culture is their OWN.

I: Yes

R: And it's unique to them u:hm: (1.2) I mean there's nothing I think more
sti:rring than- than to go along (0.6) uhm (0.8) to a Maori concert and hear
them singing it [and doing

I: [YEAH

R: An' that's THE::M.

I: Yes (.) [yeah

R: [I don't want to COPY them that- that's something that's unique
and it's- it's terrific

I: Yes (0.4) yeah

R: U::hm (1.0) I think they must keep their own identity

I: Yes (0.6) Right Mmm

R: I- I am against Maoris and whites (0.4) marrying and having ch[ildren

I: [Yes

R: because I- I- I feel it's awful for the children

I: Mm mhm

R: And they never become whites

I: Yes

R: They always become Maoris

I: Yes

R: A:nd (.) just the [colour

I: [(That's right) Yeah

R: So therefore they should stick to their own race

I: [Mm mhm

R: [uhm (.) they are uniquely ([.) Maoris

I: [Yeah

R: [They- they've got something that we can ne:ver have
I: [Yeah
I: Right! yeah then should eh (0.4) feel part [this- this [yeah
R: [Yes   [Yes
I: Yeah
R: Definitely
I: Yeah [sure
R: [An' I think a lot of them do:: [uhm
I: [Yeah
R: But you- you get an' (0.4) a lo::t with chips on their shoulders
I: Yeah
R: And I'm sure they're ones that- that have come from a- a Maori ah
    European (1.0) u:hm ma:rriage that perhaps has been a (2.0) a fighting or a
    split mar[riage that-[
I: [marriage [yes
R: and [that's where they've got their chip from
I: [Yeah
I: Right [yeah
R: [They don't really know who they belong to but because they're the
    colour they are they're [Maoris
I: [Yeah
I: Right (2.0) Yes (1.4) Yeah so- and so that- an' the Maori people that'em
    (0.4) you know they- they feel (0.4) similarly that really it's up to Maori
    people to foster their own culture [an' (   )
R: [Yes
I: Ye[ah
R: [Yes
I: Yeah and that so- (0.6) you get th- the impression that this business about
    land rights an'uhm (0.4) Maori language an' so on is really it's just a small
    part of the Maori community that ah
R: Well we've got our stirrers haven't we
I: Y(h)eah hh. Yeah [.hhh
R: [U:hm
I: Yeah
R: Ya'know so obviously ya'know th[ey have theirs
I: [they have too ((laugh)) [yes
R: [A:nd (0.4)
I: Yeah. (2.0)
R: I mean they- they've got their- their- their very good people who are uhm
    (0.2) the leaders (1.4)
R: But you don't see them agitating
I: Yes (1.2)
R: It's the sa[me with ah Europeans
I: [Mm mhm
I: Yes
R: Ya' know
I: Mm mhm

R: I mean I've got no time for the- (0.2) the leader of HART an'
I: Yeah
R: Uhm ((laugh)) aw'right (0.4) he's- he's probably doing what he thinks is-
(1.4) an' are just doing their- (our stirrers) to stir us along but (1.4)
I: Mmm (1.0)
R: I think sometimes they- (1.0) they stir (up) (.) people who haven't got
(those/their) sort of interests up
I: Yes (0.4) Right (1.4) Yeah (2.0) U:hm (1.4) but if- do think in general
that'a (1.0) Pakeha people in this country have eh b- been too tolerant
and that (.) from that point of view (0.6) there's not that much prejudice or
discrimination (0.4) or do you think that (0.4) ehm Pakeha people
have got to look to themselves a bit to eh (0.6) change their attitudes
now.
R: Well you see (.) I think that (has/is) built up too u:hm (2.0) When I went to
schoo:l (1.0)
[. . .]
we were all one ya'know
I: Yes
R: So (0.4) uhm (0.6) (before ever being/we were aware of there being) Maori
but (0.4) so ↑what Uhm it wasn't really made a thing of
I: Right.
[. . .]
I: The- the kids from an earlier age are becoming more
R: Ye[s
I: [super conscious of it do you think?
R: [Yes u:hm
I: [right
R: And that's not only (2.0) that seems to come from- from the Maoris as well
(.) uhm (0.8) ya'know uhm (0.6) They're making themselves apart
I: Right yeah [mm mhm
R: [Whereas they weren't before.
I: Mm mhm (1.0) Yeahm
R: So:: uhm (0.6)
I: Things are getting worse
[. . .]
I: What d- what do you think about ehm (0.4) some of the people I've talked
to have said that eh (0.4) that they sort of resent having race relations
conciliator and race relations office because the- the results been loss of
(0.6) freedom of expression, I think this is something I read actually in ah
one of Bob Jones' (0.4) books for the New Zealand Party. Ehm (1.0) do you
think that's the case that people are becoming sort of overly (1.0) sensitive
about what their saying an' think (0.4) that we're becoming more (0.4)
censored [(   )
R: [I think definitely
I: Yeah
R: Especially as far as race (.) relations
I: Yeah.
R: Yes. (0.2)
R: Mmm.

I: Right yeah (1.0) What about'em immigration a lot of people in Britain that
     I talk to are (0.4) not exactly resentful but wish they could come out to New
     Zealand and immigrate (here) but it's now a very difficult for people to:
     immigrate unless they've got a particular (0.4) kind of trade

R: Mm[m

I: [Do you feel that'a (0.6) New Zealand's population is about right or do
     you think that we should (1.2) could cope with some more (.) people (5.0)

R: U::hm hhh. Well I think- isn't it that we've just about got an open door
     policy with the Islands?

I: Yes (0.4) yeah

R: Which I think's bad

I: Yeah

R: U::hmm because really they seem to be causing more problems than
     anything

I: Right [yeah

R: [An' I would rather we had immigrants in from England

I: Right [yeah

R: [U::hm (0.2) than (0.4) leaving it just open to (.) just anyone coming
     in from the Is[lands

I: [( )

I: Ri[ght

R: [just because they happen to have a relation (0.2) or just com↑ing

I: Yes (0.4) yeah

R: I think that's wrong

I: Mhm [yeah

R: [Because they're not happy here. It's- it's no good for the:m.

I: Right [yeah

R: [as- as well as uhm they create problems (0.4) for ↑us (1.0)

I: Right (.)

R: yeah (0.4)

I: yeah

R: I certainly don't think they're happier [here

I: [Yeah (1.2)

R: Mmm

I: Yeah (0.4) What about'em (0.4) there's been (0.4) one area- parts of world
     that we haven't had very much immigration from (has been) Asian (0.4)
     countries and India Pakistan an' places like that (.) u:hm do you think that
     (0.2) that's one area of the world that we could look to more (1.0) to get
     more people from or do you think (0.2) really that our roots lie in Britain
     an' Europe an' that's where we should be (0.4) orienting ourselves.

R: Well look at the mess Britain's in (0.4) I mean they've let (1.0) the Arabs
     and the Indians an' (1.4) all sorts in haven't they

I: Yeah

R: And they're in a me:ss.

I: Ye(h)ah [(right)

R: [So: (0.4) shouldn't we lear:n from [that

I: [( )

I: Right (0.2) mm mhm

R: A:nd (5.0) As I say I can't see why we can't have uhm (1.2) immigrants
    from Britain in.
I: [Yes
R: [I really can't
I: Yes Well a lot of Brit(h)ish people wo(h)uld .hhh would agree with you an
    uhm they- certainly they want to come and so on [yeah
R: [Yes
I: Uhm there's just- You've got some visitors, just (0.4) a couple of
    back[ground
R: [It's a railway station here
I: things if you don't mind. i-if you don't [regard it as an
R: [(No it's okay)
I: invasion of privacy one (.) what's your age.
R: Thirty- Oh! I'm thirty seven next month.
    ((both laugh))

Index